Dogface Soldier

THE AMERICAN MILITARY EXPERIENCE SERIES
JOHN C. MCMANUS, SERIES EDITOR

The books in this series portray and analyze the experience of Americans in military service during war and peacetime from the onset of the twentieth century to the present. The series emphasizes the profound impact wars have had on nearly every aspect of recent American history and considers the significant effects of modern conflict on combatants and noncombatants alike. Titles in the series include accounts of battles, campaigns, and wars; unit histories; biographical and autobiographical narratives; investigations of technology and warfare; studies of the social and economic consequences of war; and in general, the best recent scholarship on Americans in the modern armed forces. The books in the series are written and designed for a diverse audience that encompasses nonspecialists as well as expert readers.

WILSON A. HEEFNER

Dogface Soldier

THE LIFE OF GENERAL
LUCIAN K. TRUSCOTT, JR.

UNIVERSITY OF MISSOURI PRESS   COLUMBIA AND LONDON

University of Missouri Press, Columbia, Missouri 65201
Printed and bound in the United States of America
All rights reserved
5 4 3 2   14 13 12 11 10

Library of Congress Cataloging-in-Publication Data

Heefner, Wilson Allen, 1931–
  Dogface soldier : the life of General Lucian K. Truscott, Jr. / Wilson A. Heefner.
    p. cm.
  Includes bibliographical references and index.
  ISBN 978-0-8262-1882-7 (cloth : alk. paper)
  1. Truscott, Lucian King, 1895-1965. 2. Generals—United States—Biography. 3.
United States. Army—Biography. 4. World War, 1939–1945—Biography. I. Title.
  E745.T78H44 2010
  355.0092—dc22
  [B]
                        2010001659

♾™ This paper meets the requirements of the
American National Standard for Permanence of Paper
for Printed Library Materials, Z39.48, 1984.

Design and composition: Jennifer Cropp
Printing and binding: Thomson-Shore, Inc.
Typefaces: Minon, Trajan Pro, and Cracked

DEDICATED TO THE MEMORY OF 1ST LT. JOHN D. BENEDICT

59th Armored Field Artillery Battalion, Task Force Butler.
Killed in action, August 25, 1944, near Condillac, France,
in the battle for the Montélimar Square.

1st Lt. John D. Benedict. John D. Benedict File, Alexander
Hamilton Memorial Free Library, Waynesboro, Pennsylvania.

Contents

LIST OF MAPS

PREFACE

Dogface Soldier is the first comprehensive biography of Gen. Lucian K. Truscott, Jr.[1] It will be of interest to military historians in general, but especially those with an interest in the interwar American Army and those with a particular interest in the North African, Mediterranean, and southern France theaters of operation in World War II. It will also be of interest to those historians and general readers who are attracted to biographical studies of the great captains of World War II. This book is particularly timely because of the favorable reception of Rick Atkinson's two recently published best-seller books devoted to the North African and Mediterranean theaters, *An Army at Dawn: The War in North Africa, 1942–1943* and *The Day of Battle: The War in Sicily and Italy, 1943–1944,* both of which have stimulated renewed interest in those virtually forgotten campaigns, especially among general-interest readers. John S. D. Eisenhower's *They Fought at Anzio* and Lloyd Clark's *Anzio: Italy and the Battle for Rome, 1944* have also excited new interest in the decisive but often overlooked Anzio campaign, in which Truscott played a vital role.

My interest in General Truscott dates to 1992, when I met Martin Blumenson in Paestum, Italy, while on a tour of World War II battlefields in southern Italy. During one of our discussions he said that he considered Lucian Truscott to be one of the greatest of the American World War II combat commanders, and his memoir, *Command Missions: A Personal Story,* the best memoir of any written by an American general of that generation. Blumenson went on to say that he was mystified that no historian had taken on the task of writing a biography of this outstanding soldier, and suggested that I consider doing so. However, I busied myself with other writing tasks until the spring of 2001, when I joined Mr. Blumenson for dinner in Paris. As we renewed our friendship Martin asked me if I had given any further thought to writing a biography of Truscott, and urged me to take on that task. Thus stimulated, I began my research, and soon became completely captivated by the life and career of this too-long-neglected "dogface soldier."

Lucian Truscott was arguably one of the best combat commanders in World War II, but today is little known outside of military and military history circles, where many continue to hold him in high regard and laud his memoirs of his interwar years and World War II.[2] In this biography I have examined in depth the influence of his forebears and the heritage of honor, honesty, and courage of conviction they passed on to him; of his family roots in rural Texas; of his growing-up years and his experiences as an elementary schoolteacher in Oklahoma; of his wife, a descendant of Thomas Jefferson, in molding his character; and of his thirty-year career in the Army, where he earned a reputation as an honest, forthright, outspoken, fearless, and aggressive senior commander, which led to Central Intelligence Agency director Gen. Walter Bedell Smith's choosing him in 1951 to be the senior CIA officer in postwar Germany, an era of his life about which little has been written.[3]

ACKNOWLEDGMENTS

I should first of all like to thank General Truscott's son Lt. Col. James J. Truscott, USAF (Ret.), San Antonio, Texas, and Lucian K. Truscott IV, Los Angeles, California, the general's grandson, for permitting me to conduct extensive interviews of them, and for responding so graciously to my numerous e-mail and telephone requests for information and assistance. Their recollections of General Truscott and the Truscott and Randolph families provided a rich mine of personal information available nowhere else.

I owe an immense debt of gratitude to the staff of the George C. Marshall Research Library, Lexington, Virginia, the repository of the Lucian K. Truscott Jr. Collection. I am particularly indebted to Joanne Hartog, director of Special Projects/Library, who patiently assisted me in countless ways during my numerous research trips to the library. Peggy L. Dillard, assistant, Library and Archives, provided the digital copies of the photographs from the library that appear in the book and secured the necessary permission to reproduce the photographs. Paul B. Barron, the director of the Marshall Library and archives, also provided valuable assistance.

The U.S. Army Military History Institute Archives and Library at Carlisle Barracks, Pennsylvania, is a treasure trove of resources consulted for decades by military historians from throughout the world. I have relied on their staff for research assistance on numerous projects for almost twenty years, and they once again responded in splendid fashion during my research into General Truscott's life and career. Richard J. Sommers possesses an encyclopedic knowledge of the institute's archival and library holdings and was always on hand to assist me. I should also like to acknowledge the aid of Richard L. Baker of the Army Heritage and Education Center, collocated with the institute.

It is always a pleasure to visit the National Archives at College Park, Maryland, and work with the thoroughly professional archivists there. I should like to extend special thanks to Mitchell A. Yockelson, archivist nonpareil, respected military historian in his own right, and colleague and friend. Lawrence H. McDonald was particularly helpful and patient as he introduced me to the CIA Research Tool during my research on General Truscott's CIA years. William B.

Mahoney, Timothy K. Nenninger, John E. Taylor, and Carolyn Gilliam were on hand to lend aid.

I should also like to acknowledge the assistance of individuals from numerous Army and other governmental agencies who promptly responded to my requests for assistance and for materials pertaining to Truscott's career: Michael L. Browne, Joanne Knight, and Virginia Navarro of the Combined Arms Research Library, U.S. Army Command and General Staff College, Fort Leavenworth, Kansas; Leo J. Daugherty, command historian, U.S. Army Accessions Command, Fort Monroe, Virginia; Kenneth Finlayson, deputy command historian, U.S. Special Operations Command, Fort Bragg, North Carolina; Shellie Glass, U.S. Army War College Library, Carlisle Barracks, Pennsylvania; Robyn Hall, director of licensing, Oklahoma Board of Medical Licensing and Supervision, Oklahoma City; Dorinda Harvey and Denise Mullins, County Clerk's Office, Cleveland County, Norman, Oklahoma; Linda W. Hee, Tropic Lightning Museum, Schofield Barracks, Hawaii; James B. Knight and James Tobias, U.S. Army Center of Military History, Fort Lesley J. McNair, Washington, D.C.; Scott Koch and Kathryn I. Dyer, information and privacy coordinators, Central Intelligence Agency, Washington, D.C.; Herbert L. Pankratz, archivist, Eisenhower Presidential Library, Abilene, Kansas; CW2 Jonathan D. Ward, commander, 3d Infantry Division Band, Fort Stewart, Georgia; Michael Warner, Center for the Study of Intelligence, Central Intelligence Agency, Washington, D.C.; and staff members of the National Personnel and Records Center, Military Personnel Records, St. Louis.

I would be remiss if I failed to acknowledge the contributions and assistance of individuals and of personnel affiliated with other governmental and nongovernmental agencies: the staff of the Albemarle-Charlottesville Historical Society, Charlottesville, Virginia; Paul G. Anderson, Bernard Becker Medical Library, Washington University School of Medicine, St. Louis; Verna Bonner and Willa Kral, Department of Genealogy, Corsicana Public Library, Corsicana, Texas; Jean Carefoot, Texas State Library and Archives Commission, Austin; David Chapman and Catherine Coker, Cushing Library, Texas A&M University, College Station; Joan Freie, Registrar's Office, St. Louis University School of Medicine, St. Louis; Mary Ann Heiss, Department of History, Kent State University, Kent, Ohio; Judge Robert N. Jones, Jr., Chatfield, Texas; Carol A. Leadenham, Hoover Institution Archives, Stanford, California; Brenda Lynn and Peter J. Rizzo, Museum of Polo and Hall of Fame, Lake Worth, Florida; Jean McCracken, Cleveland County Genealogical Society, Norman, Oklahoma; Patty McWilliams, Shawnee, Oklahoma; Jörg Muth, doctoral candidate, Department of History, University of Utah, Salt Lake City; Stephen T. Powers, Fort Collins, Colorado; Lori Robbins, Special Collections, McCracken County Public Library, Paducah, Kentucky; Nick Terry, Chinati Foundation, Marfa, Texas;

Tony Whisenhut, Kent County Historical Commission, Benjamin, Texas; and M. White, Montgomery County Genealogical Society, Litchfield, Illinois.

I owe a special debt of gratitude to editor in chief Clair Willcox of the University of Missouri Press, who never lost his enthusiasm for my manuscript and was a source of encouragement when my own spirits flagged. I am especially grateful for the assistance and advice of John Brenner, my project editor. I would also like to thank Annette Wenda for her insightful copyediting. Christopher Robinson of Laurel, Maryland, prepared sixteen of the maps for the book. Brig. Gen. John S. D. Eisenhower, AUS (Ret.), graciously granted me permission to reproduce seven maps from his book, *They Fought at Anzio,* which were also prepared by Mr. Robinson.

I should like to thank my son, Jay W. Heefner II, project engineer at the California Institute of Technology, who was always available to assist his marginally computer-literate dad in navigating the mysterious pathways to resolve the incompatibilities of the three Macintosh operating systems and the two versions of Microsoft Word for Macintosh I used during the writing of this book. I should also like to acknowledge the contributions of Paul J. Hauben, professor of history, emeritus, University of the Pacific, Stockton, California, who performed the initial editing of my manuscript.

However, I am solely responsible for any errors that might appear in this biography and pray that they are errors of omission rather than of commission.

Dogface Soldier

Introduction

To Think Like an Army

Lucian Truscott was one of the most highly rated combat commanders in World War II, but today his name does not enjoy the renown of a George Patton or an Omar Bradley.[1] Roger J. Spiller notes that, "in a miscarriage of history, he has disappeared from the view of all but the most serious students of the war."[2] This neglect seems all the more remarkable when we recall that he was the only American officer who commanded in combat a reinforced infantry regiment (regimental combat team), an infantry division (ID), a corps, and a field army.

Eric Larrabee has described the qualities of the superior combat leader:

A commander must be able to "think like" the unit he commands. All its weapons and their capabilities, the terrain on which it is disposed, the state of its supply and of its training and its morale—in short, what it can reasonably be expected to do—all must be an extension of his own mind. To think like a platoon over a few hundred yards is no great trick; to think like a division over a score of square miles is difficult, but the gene pool seems to cast up an adequate number of men who can manage it. To think like a corps is an unusual gift . . . and to think like an army is a rarity in itself.[3]

Truscott was intimately familiar with the capabilities of all of the weapons available to him, including tactical air support and naval gunfire support, and became one of the Army's most effective commanders of combined arms forces at corps and army level. As a cavalryman roaming the great American Southwest, he had developed a keen eye for terrain and how to utilize its features to maximum effectiveness. Many will remember him for his outstanding abilities as a trainer and teacher. His training standards were inevitably set high, and his methods were harsh, sometimes bordering on brutal. However, he always shared in the hardships and discomfort of his men, believing that one must lead from the front rather than from a map board or a desk.

That Truscott possessed the "unusual gift" of being able to "think like a corps" is readily confirmed by his service as commander of VI Corps.[4] When Lt. Gen. Mark W. Clark decided to replace VI Corps commander John Lucas, whom he deemed "tentative and 'worn out,'" he chose Truscott, who "ranked first on Eisenhower's list of division commanders best suited for corps-level command." Assessing the situation after assuming command of VI Corps, "Truscott was appalled to discover how close the [Anzio] beachhead had come to disaster." The very first day he was out visiting his major units on the front lines, and his appearance in the forward areas "quickly galvanized the beleaguered defenders of the beachhead." Within a week he had revitalized the forces there, enabling them in late February to halt a last-ditch German attack to destroy the beachhead, and to preserve its integrity for the spring breakout and the drive to Rome.[5]

After the fall of Rome and the withdrawal of VI Corps from combat, he immediately launched into planning and training for his corps' participation in the invasion of southern France, which proved to be one of the most successful operations of World War II, demonstrating Truscott's ability to lead a large amphibious and airborne assault on a defended shore. Subsequently, *Time* named him the "ablest sea-to-land commander in the United States Army."[6] Although his drive northward in the Rhône valley after the landings was hampered by a shortage of fuel and vehicles, preventing him from bringing optimum pressure against the withdrawing enemy troops, his corps reached Lyon nineteen days after the assault, and by the middle of September was driving toward the Belfort Gap and the upper Rhine beyond it.

At about that same time George C. Marshall and Dwight D. Eisenhower, convinced that he possessed the rare gift of being able to "think like an army," agreed that Truscott should be considered as the next officer to command an army in General Bradley's 12th Army Group. Instead, when General Clark assumed command of 15th Army Group Eisenhower recommended that Truscott, because of his knowledge of the Italian theater, replace Clark as Fifth Army commander. Truscott subsequently carried out his duties in such a capable manner that Eisenhower ranked him second only to Patton for his services as an army commander during the war in Europe, describing him as an "experienced, balanced fighter; energetic; inspires confidence."[7]

Ken Stringer and David L. Bongard assert that Truscott's "open, direct and forceful leadership earned him the respect of his men and his superiors alike," and Carlo D'Este writes that he "was admired as much as he was feared . . . [and] more than one officer refused a promotion in order to stay with him." When he took command of the 3d Infantry Division in North Africa he found poor disciplinary standards and an attitude toward training that lacked "the fire and intensity" he expected in a division that might be called into combat at any time. By insisting on strict discipline and achievement of a high degree of physical fitness for both officers and men and a comprehensive training program, he soon molded the division into a fighting force that "earned a reputation as the best trained and disciplined in Patton's Seventh Army." British military historians Dominick Graham and Shelford Bidwell consider him to be "a first-class professional soldier," and his 3d Infantry Division was "in the opinion of a discerning British observer [Maj. Gen. A. J. C. Block] the best in the Allied armies in Italy." Truscott exuded "an energising current [that] flowed from him down through the command hierarchy to the rank and file." When asked at the end of the war which division was the best he faced either in Italy or in Western Europe, Field Marshal Albert Kesselring unhesitatingly named Truscott's 3d ID, which he had faced on the Italian front.[8]

Truscott served his entire World War II career in two theaters that were in effect secondary fronts, the Mediterranean and southern France theaters. Even before the invasion of Normandy in the spring of 1944 the news from the Italian front in American newspapers was frequently overshadowed by the coverage of Nimitz's and MacArthur's marines and soldiers in the Pacific theater. Many Americans viewed the combat in the Italian theater as merely a holding action until the Americans and British could open the main war-ending offensive in northern France. Most observers during that time had little appreciation for the viciousness of the fighting and the abominable terrain and weather facing the GIs in Italy and shared the view of most senior American military officers that the decisive battles against the Germans would be fought not on the Italian boot but in Western Europe and on the steppes of Russia. As a result of his service in those "secondary" theaters of operations, Truscott "was denied the fanfare that accompanied the war in northwest Europe and emerged from the war as the most unacknowledged of America's top commanders." Truscott himself realized that the major and decisive actions would take place in eastern France and Germany. He expressed to General Marshall in late 1944, at the time Marshall asked him to assume command of Fifth Army, his preference to serve under Eisenhower in Europe rather than return to Italy.[9] But ever the loyal and obedient officer, Truscott placed his service to country ahead of personal preference and attention from the press.

However, the operations on these secondary fronts did play a vital role in hastening the defeat of the Axis powers by denying Hitler the use in northwestern and eastern Europe of the German forces engaged in the savage fighting in Italy and southern France. If he had been able to employ those divisions along the western front, Hitler could have resisted even more stubbornly the advance of Eisenhower's armies and the Soviet forces. As one of the most able of the Allied senior commanders in Italy and southern France, Truscott undoubtedly made a significant contribution to the Allied victory in Europe.

Despite his distinguished career and his many accomplishments, Truscott had his detractors, some of whom allege he drank too much.[10] Alcohol did play an important role in the social lives of Lucian and Sarah Truscott throughout Truscott's career, as it did in the lives of many of their contemporaries. Even during some of the heaviest combat in which his command was involved, Truscott kept to his daily ritual of cocktails before and during lunch and dinner, and hosted frequent parties and formal dinners during which he and his guests consumed large amounts of liquor and wine. Rick Atkinson notes that "cognac, scotch, gin, and two ounces of rye before supper remained staples in the Truscott mess." Those habits carried over into his Central Intelligence Agency and retirement years, indeed until his death. However, Atkinson; James Wilson, his wartime aide; Thomas Polgar, a CIA operative who served with Truscott; and James Truscott, his son, have stated without equivocation that his drinking never adversely affected his ability to carry out his official duties, an opinion shared by Maj. Gen. Robert T. Frederick, who commanded the 1st Special Service Force on the Anzio beachhead.[11]

One of the more outspoken of Truscott's detractors was Brig. Gen. Paul M. Robinett, who had served with the 1st Cavalry Regiment at the same time that Truscott served with the 17th Cavalry Regiment on the Mexican border during World War I. Robinett subsequently served in Tunisia, where he commanded Combat Command B, 1st Armored Division (AD), during Truscott's tenure as Eisenhower's deputy chief of staff (COS) at his advance command post (ACP) at Constantine.[12] In his paper "The Tender Threads of Fate," Robinett describes Truscott as "an ill-tempered Texan, who was steeped in self righteousness." He goes on to say that "shortly before World War II, Truscott had the good fortune to serve with Colonel Dwight D. Eisenhower" on the IX Corps staff at Fort Lewis, Washington. Although Robinett does concede, almost reluctantly, that Truscott conducted the Italian campaign and the German occupation in creditable fashion, he concludes that Truscott rose to high command not because of his qualities and abilities as a soldier but, in large part, because "he was carried along on the tail of Eisenhower's kite until he commanded the Fifth Army, with considerable credit to himself in the Italian Campaign, and then the Third Army, in succession to George S. Patton, Jr., during the occupation of Germany. The tender threads of fate had carried an unpromising lieutenant of cavalry to high command in battle and in the administration of conquered Germany."[13] Very few if any of the men who served with Truscott or under his command would share or agree with Robinett's conclusions, as attested by the glowing Efficiency Reports rendered on Truscott's performance during war and peace by such discerning military commanders as Dwight Eisenhower, George Patton, Mark Clark, Jacob Devers, and Alexander Patch, and the high opinions of him expressed by respected historians such as Martin Blumenson, Carlo D'Este, John S. D. Eisenhower, Cole C. Kingseed, Mark Perry, and Roger J. Spiller.[14]

Despite his toughness, Truscott possessed a softer side. Although he was often profane in his speech, he was always a gentleman in the presence of ladies.

He enjoyed the company of women, always including them on his guest lists for dinners and parties, and women were attracted to him. They appeared to discern that beneath that brusque and flinty exterior there was a man of compassion and sensitivity, one even capable of tears. Beatrice Patton recounted that when she traveled by train from Heidelberg to Luxembourg for her husband George's interment in the American cemetery there, Truscott accompanied her, but was afraid that because he had succeeded George as commander of Third Army Beatrice would not want to speak with him, even though they were old friends. However, when she extended her hands to him, Truscott immediately embraced her and "burst into tears." His son Lucian recorded that on one occasion when his father was talking about combat and his experiences at Anzio, "tears came to his eyes when he described the innumerable dead, on both sides, how he would never forget how young they all were. . . . And tears came to his eyes again when I left for Korea a few days later in July, 1950."[15]

The softer side of Truscott is evidenced particularly in his wartime letters to his wife, Sarah, whom he always addressed as "Beloved Wife." He often expressed his love for her and how much he missed being with her, writing at various times, "You are in my thoughts a thousand times a day. . . . I think of you when I am lonely at night. . . . I love you." On the eve of the North Africa landings he told her, "I can see your lovely eyes and sweet smile," and on the day after Christmas of 1943 he wrote, "I only wish that I was close enough . . . to kiss your sweet lips and hear you say you love me." Truscott saw their marriage as a partnership in which Sarah played a key role, stating in one letter that he attributed any success that he had achieved to her influence, a sentiment echoed by their son Lucian: "Her influence on him was immeasurable." She taught him "perfect manners, neatness, orderliness . . . [and] helped him become the gentleman who in later years would feel perfectly at ease with both infantry privates in foxholes and royalty in palaces."[16]

After the war, as he was enjoying his retirement years in Bluemont, Virginia, Truscott, recognizing that the Cold War threatened not only the United States but also Western Europe, including two of the countries that he had worked so energetically to defeat, Germany and Italy, heeded his country's call once again. When Lt. Gen. Walter B. Smith, director of the Central Intelligence Agency, asked him in 1951 to give up his well-earned retirement for a new career, Truscott, old warhorse that he was, responded without hesitation. His four-year term as senior adviser and chief of the CIA mission in Germany spanned some of the most critical years of the Cold War.

In late 1954–1955 he supervised the Berlin tunnel operation and the tapping of Soviet landlines of communication, which, during the eleven months and eleven days of the operation, yielded rich rewards for the agency, "information that was invaluable in the days before reconnaissance satellites and other, more sophisticated means of collection became available."[17] Another critical

Cold War role played by Truscott was as the CIA's senior war planner, Europe, when he established coordinated planning with the U.S. European Command to carry out joint covert operations in the European theater.[18]

Shortly after his return to Washington to serve as CIA director Allen Dulles's special assistant, Truscott found himself at the heart of the investigation of the October 1956 Hungarian uprising, when President Eisenhower directed him to determine the exact role that the CIA operation RED SOX/RED CAP had played in encouraging and assisting the uprising.[19] As a result of his investigation and similar investigations by the American military intelligence services, Truscott was able to determine exactly what the CIA's RED SOX/RED CAP operatives had promised the Hungarian freedom fighters about American intentions to support them. He concluded that there was "a failure on the CIA's part to recognize the differences between insurrectional violence, mass uprisings, and revolutionary action" and found that when, as in the case of the Hungarian uprising, a country's "indigenous military and security forces were slow in putting down an uprising or appeared to be having some difficulty, the Soviets were prepared to use all necessary force to preserve their interests." He was particularly appalled to find that despite their failure in Hungary the same CIA operatives were preparing to carry out a similar operation in Czechoslovakia. Firmly believing that such operations would increase "the prospect of a general war in Europe to an intolerable level," he recommended that President Eisenhower order all such operations to cease. After consulting with the Joint Chiefs of Staff the president directed Allen Dulles to terminate RED SOX/RED CAP immediately.[20]

Even after his retirement from the CIA, Truscott continued to receive recognition of his contributions to the U.S. Army and his country. In 1961 he was singularly honored when, on October 11, Lt. Gen. Edward J. O'Neill, commanding general of First Army and former assistant G4 of VI Corps from 1942 until the end of 1944, presented to Maj. Gen. William C. Westmoreland, superintendent of the United States Military Academy, a portrait of Lieutenant General Truscott, wearing his fabled leather jacket with attached Fifth Army shoulder insignia and his trademark scarf. In his presentation speech General O'Neill stated that Truscott was "one of the truly great American commanders of the war." The portrait was hung in Grant Hall, where it became one of only two portraits whose subjects were not West Point graduates, the other being Gen. George C. Marshall.[21]

On April 29, 1966, Truscott's contributions to victory in World War II received posthumous recognition when Sarah, Lucian III, and James attended a ceremony at Carlisle Barracks, Pennsylvania, the home of the U.S. Army War College, to dedicate Truscott Hall, a twenty-unit bachelor officers' quarters. Maj. Gen. Eugene A. Salet, commandant of the college and former commander of the 2d Battalion, 15th Infantry, 3d Infantry Division during Truscott's southern France campaign, presided at the dedication of the building that bore the name of "one of the U.S. Army's outstanding combat leaders during World War II."[22]

Truscott wrote two books, *Command Missions: A Personal Story,* published in 1954, and *The Twilight of the U.S. Cavalry: Life in the Old Army, 1917–1942,* published posthumously in 1989. He wrote *Command Missions* while serving with the CIA in Germany in the early 1950s, and completed the manuscript of *The Twilight in the U.S. Cavalry* during the final years of his life. His son Lucian took over the task of editing the latter manuscript for publication.

Reviews of both books have been generally laudatory. S. L. A. Marshall has stated that Truscott's *Command Missions* proved that "when it comes to skill in letters American high commanders need no longer bow to the superiority of the British and Germans," and that "what distinguishes his memoir above others is its utter lack of austerity and pretension. Truscott is something better than a skilled writer; he is a born reporter. . . . [He] describes in intimate detail what makes the wheels go around" at high levels of command. Charles Poore wrote that *Command Missions* "is one of the finest and deepest and liveliest of the memoirs of the war. . . . Nowhere will you get a better understanding of what went on in England, Africa, Italy, Southern France and the dark early occupation days in Germany." Hanson W. Baldwin, military editor of the *New York Times,* commented that Truscott's narrative "is simultaneously a study in leadership, a case book of strategy and tactics and a solid slice of history written from the records by a man who was there," but goes on to state that Truscott, "like most good commanders . . . is not a virtuoso with a pen." Furthermore, Truscott's "outspoken criticisms and estimations of personalities and general-ship" led Baldwin to conclude by the time he finished reading that there was "an over-weening self-assurance on General Truscott's part." However, he commended Truscott for being "one of the few high-ranking World War II commanders who has had the moral courage and honesty to include personalities in his memoirs of combat."[23]

The Twilight of the U.S. Cavalry has also received critical acclaim. Edward M. Coffman, in the foreword, states that the book "is an incomparable intro-duction not only to the cavalry but also to the Old Army by one of its most distinguished veterans, who also happens to be a very talented writer. . . . With carefully chosen words, he evokes the sights, sounds, and even the smells of those days." Col. Leonard L. Lewane wrote that Truscott's book "is a 'must' for all cavalrymen of yesteryear as well as their lineal descendants of current day armored cavalry squadrons and regiments," and Clarence E. Wunderlin, Jr., of Kent State University, stated that "*The Twilight of the U.S. Cavalry* merits being assigned in any course on the history of the United States Army."[24]

I believe that both of Truscott's memoirs are valuable contributions to the interwar and World War II literature, giving readers valuable insights into the

U.S. Army during those crucial years as recorded by one who was there, a true wordsmith who had never completed a formal course in English composition beyond the high school level. His eloquence approaches that of Ulysses S. Grant in his *Personal Memoirs,* with little of the self-serving prose and lack of objectivity that characterize the memoirs of such World War II notables as George S. Patton, Jr. *(War as I Knew It),* Douglas MacArthur *(Reminiscences),* and Bernard Law Montgomery *(The Memoirs of Field-Marshal Montgomery).*

In the almost half century since Lucian Truscott's death, little has been written about the accomplishments of this great battlefield commander who contributed so much to the defeat of Germany in World War II and was so intimately involved in the early days of the Cold War in Europe as a member of the Central Intelligence Agency. It is my hope that this volume will serve as an introduction of this great soldier and patriot to a new generation of military historians.

Chapter 1

The Early Years

Both the paternal and the maternal forebears of Lucian King Truscott, Jr., came to the United States from the British Isles. His paternal great-grandfather, Thomas Truscott, was born in Cornwall, England, in 1796, and immigrated to America in 1821, settling near Springfield, Illinois, where he began farming.[1] Thomas fathered two sons, James Joseph and George. James, born in 1832, became an attorney and married Margarit Jane Kirkland. Together they raised five children, the youngest of whom was Lucian King, who was born in Kane, Illinois, on October 5, 1864.[2] Some years later the family moved to Arkansas, and then to Texas, ultimately settling in China Lake, north of Abilene, where he was elected county judge. In 1886 the citizens of China Lake honored Judge Truscott by changing the name of the town to Truscott.

At about the age of thirteen or fourteen Lucian began working as a farm- and ranch hand, and then as a cowboy, participating in several cattle drives up the Chisholm Trail to Abilene, Kansas. He later enrolled in Missouri Medical College in St. Louis, graduating in 1891.[3] Following his graduation, Doctor Truscott returned to Texas, where he established a practice in Benjamin, the county seat of Knox County.[4]

On April 2, 1891, in Paducah, Kentucky, Doctor Truscott married Maria Temple Tully, who was born in Illinois in 1866 and was a descendant of Irish immigrants.[5] Tully's father, John Cavan Tully, a prominent businessman in Paducah and an ordained pastor, performed the ceremony.[6] The newlyweds moved to Chatfield, Texas, near Corsicana, where Doctor Truscott opened a practice and where they began raising their family.

Chatfield lies approximately fifty miles southeast of Dallas and in 1891 had a population of approximately five hundred. Lucian K. Truscott, Jr., was born there on January 9, 1895. Two sisters, Loretta and Patsy, were also born in Chatfield, in 1893 and 1896, respectively; a third sister, Dixie, was born in 1904, after the family had relocated to the Oklahoma Territory.[7] As the only physician in town, Truscott soon became a prominent and active member of the community, and his wife began teaching music at the Elizabeth Institute, a private preparatory school.[8] Much of Doctor Truscott's practice consisted of house calls, made in a horse-drawn buggy driven by Will Coleman, a young black man who lived with the Truscotts and worked as a handyman for them. He became a close friend of young Lucian, who would often accompany Will in the buggy as he ran errands for the family.[9]

In the winter of 1900–1901, the Truscott family moved to Remus, Oklahoma Territory, southeast of Oklahoma City, where Doctor Truscott set up his practice and purchased an eighty-acre farm.[10] Young Lucian began his formal education in a one-room school in Remus, where his mother taught grades one through four in the rear of the room, grades five through eight meeting in the front of the room. While in Remus, Doctor Truscott "dabbled in race horses, and farms, disastrously . . . so in the fall of 1903 the family moved to Maud," just a few miles east of Remus, then to Konawa, twelve miles to the south, then back to Maud, and finally back to Remus and the Orchard Farm. In 1908 the Truscott family moved once again, to Stella Township in the northeast corner of Cleveland County,[11] where Lucian completed grade school and one year of high school. In the summer of 1911, at the age of sixteen, Lucian dropped out of high school and enrolled with his mother in the Summer Normal School in Norman to earn certification as a schoolteacher.[12] At summer's end Lucian had in hand his certification as a teacher, and, "only 16 at the time, he stretched his age to 18, applied for and 'got' a country school, six miles from Stella, and during the eight month term walked to [and] from school daily."[13]

In the fall of 1912 Doctor Truscott relocated his practice to Edna, roughly sixty miles east of Oklahoma City, and the next year to Eufaula, about thirty-five miles south of Muskogee. Lucian and his mother dutifully followed Doctor Truscott to the two towns, where in successive summers they completed Summer Normals. When in the fall of 1914 his father decided to move once again, this time to Onapa, young Lucian decided to remain in Eufaula, where he accepted the position of principal at Mountain View School in nearby Mellette, a position he held until he enlisted in the Army in 1917.[14] While living in Eufaula young Lucian was instrumental in constructing the First Christian Church sanctuary and "introduced the idea of leaving the church doors open to the public through out [sic] the week, because the church belonged to the people, and he believed religion should be an all week practice rather than a Sunday gesture."

During his teaching years Lucian was "a normal healthy specimen of American youth . . . [who] did not drink, smoke, or swear." He "took part in the annual track meets, minstrel shows, and everything the teachers' organizations and schools participated in, or administered." He was an "omnivorous" reader, particularly enjoying history. The family home had a "fairly good library," and long before finishing grade school, he had read the "standard 'classics.'" However, he also enjoyed such books as Sherlock Holmes detective stories, which were forbidden in the house, forcing him to hide them in the woodpile. Lucian's one ambition was to become an Army officer, and he was soon to realize that ambition.[15]

In the classroom and as a principal young Truscott was honing his skills as a teacher, administrator, and leader, skills that he would later employ so effectively during his Army career as a troop leader and commander and as an instructor at the Cavalry School and at the U.S. Army Command and General Staff School. His early addiction to reading would become a lifelong obsession in an effort to compensate for his lack of the formal education that most of his Army peers possessed.

Growing up in rural Texas and Oklahoma in a tightly knit family with a proud pioneering history gave young Truscott the opportunity to develop other traits that would serve him in good stead during his military career: initiative, self-reliance, competitiveness, loyalty to family and friends, love of country, and an adventuresome spirit, inspired no doubt in part by his great-grandfather, who left his home and family in Cornwall to come to America, and by his father, who spent his early years as a ranch hand and as a cowboy on the Chisholm Trail. Under the tutelage of his father, Lucian also became an expert horseman, which played an important role in his developing into an outstanding cavalryman and one of the Army's best polo players and equestrians.

Particularly important was the emphasis his family placed on education. Truscott's father and his maternal grandfather were respected physicians, his mother a gifted schoolteacher. A paternal uncle, Thomas I. Truscott, was a college graduate who became a teacher and school principal. His paternal grandfather was a lawyer, county judge, and a cofounder of Texas A&M College. Following in their footsteps, Truscott would avail himself of every formal and informal educational opportunity that presented itself during his Army career.[16]

As Truscott was nearing the end of the school year in the spring of 1917, President Woodrow Wilson went before a joint session of Congress the evening of April 2 to deliver the most important speech of his political career. The speech lasted just thirty-two minutes, but set in motion events that would take the United States into the war then raging in Europe.[17] Wilson's call to arms spread rapidly throughout the nation, and soon a young elementary school principal in Eufaula, Oklahoma, heard it and prepared to answer the president's call.

On April 6, 1917, the United States was woefully unprepared to go to war. Despite the authorization by Congress in the National Defense Act of 1916 to double the strength of the Regular Army to approximately 11,450 officers and 223,500 enlisted men over the following five years, on April 1, 1917, the Regular Army had a strength of only 5,791 officers and 121,797 enlisted men. It also "lacked the arms, equipment, and the organization to train [the Army] and the ships to transport [that Army] to the European battlefields." The Selective Service Act, which Wilson signed into law on May 18, 1917, would provide the enlisted men necessary to bring the Army to a wartime footing.[18] However, those men would need a large number of officers to train them and lead them into combat. How was the Army to procure and train the vast number of officers needed for that mission?

In 1913 Grenville Clark, a New York attorney, convinced Maj. Gen. Leonard Wood, a physician and chief of staff of the Army, to establish a military training camp at Plattsburg, New York. "There, largely at their own expense, Clark and other professionals and businessmen . . . were trained to be reserve officers in a five-week course conducted by Regular Army personnel." The "Plattsburg Movement" soon expanded to other eastern cities, and by the time of America's entry into World War I some 16,000 men had received training at those camps and had formed the Military Training Camps Association.[19]

In April 1917 the MTCA first suggested the idea of officer training camps to the War Department and offered to assist the Army in recruiting for the officer corps. The secretary of war eagerly accepted the offer and on April 17 published general orders authorizing the camps. Sixteen Officers' Training Camps (OTC) were established, each accommodating approximately 2,500 candidates.[20] The first group of candidates began training in May, and consisted of 7,957 previously commissioned reserve officers and approximately 30,000 selected civilians.[21] One candidate, a veteran of the Plattsburg camps of 1915 and 1916, described the candidates as "the same core of patriotic elites who had organized the Business Men's Camp, plus an additional influx of equally enthusiastic rookies of humbler background."[22]

On April 29 Lucian K. Truscott, Jr., one of the "enthusiastic rookies of humbler background," presented himself to the Regular Army examining officer in Muskogee as an officer candidate. He carried with him a notarized affidavit stating that he was a 1911 graduate of Stella High School but that papers attesting that fact had been lost in a fire that destroyed his father's house in December 1916. He further certified that he had completed additional work in "Training classes" equivalent to the first year of college work. The examining officer found him to be five feet, nine and one-quarter inches in height and approximately 170 pounds in weight, and recommended that he be admitted to the Officers' Training Camp at Leon Springs, Texas, a short distance northwest of San Antonio and the site of present-day Camp Bullis. However, Truscott soon received other orders that directed him to report to Fort Logan H. Roots, three miles north of Little Rock, where he reported on May 17 to become a student in the first Officers' Training Camp conducted during World War I.[23]

He was assigned to Troop No. 1, 12th Infantry Regiment, one of approximately 2,500 men assigned to the regiment.[24] For the next three months the students received intensive instruction in basic military skills from Regular and reserve officers and some Allied instructors: "close order drill, School of the Soldier, weapons and marksmanship, route marches, scouting, patrolling, elementary tactics, and, in the artillery and cavalry units, horsemanship. Primarily, it hardened the men physically and inured them to regimentation."[25] During those months the students were under extreme pressure, constantly being evaluated by the instructors. Although some of the students failed to measure up and were discharged, Truscott performed well, garnering ratings of "Satisfactory" in military bearing and deportment and the following proficiency ratings: Field Service Regulations, 88 percent; Drill Regulations, 100 percent; marksmanship, 71 percent; signaling, 100 percent; sketching, 80 percent; and spelling, 100 percent.[26]

It was a requirement that a board of officers prepare an Efficiency Report for all students completing OTC to determine the fitness of those persons for appointment as officers. On August 1, Capt. Edwin A. Hickman of the 17th Cavalry, president of the board, completed the following Efficiency Report for Truscott: "He is a graduate of the Stella High School, Newalla, Oklahoma. This student, without any previous military training, has done excellent work in this camp. He possesses an excellent mind and seemingly is accurate and painstaking in all his work. He has taken examination in this camp for Provisional 2nd Lieutenant in U.S. Army, and is excellent material for an Army officer." The board ruled that he was eligible for a commission as second lieutenant of cavalry, Truscott's preferred branch, in the Officers' Reserve Corps (ORC) or as a provisional second lieutenant in the U.S. Army.[27]

On August 15 Truscott joined the other 1,531 "survivors" as they received their commissions, representing 61 percent of the approximately 2,500 who had begun the training. Truscott was appointed a provisional second lieutenant of cavalry and was ordered to report to the 17th Cavalry Regiment at Camp Harry J. Jones outside Douglas, Arizona. After taking his postgraduation leave, Truscott joined the regiment on August 29.[28]

Reflecting many years later on his experiences at OTC, Truscott stated that "even after our training, our military background was sparse, to say the least. Most of us were completely ignorant of things military. . . . Military education at the training camp had been austere and elementary. It had been conducted for the most part by instructors who seemed to know little more than the candidates. But most of us were eager and looked forward with anticipation to joining Regular Army units where we would learn from professionals."[29]

"FORWARD" WITH THE 17TH CAVALRY

On August 29 Second Lieutenant Truscott joined the 17th Cavalry at Camp Harry J. Jones, where the regiment had been deployed since May because of disturbances along the Mexican border, less than a mile to the south.[30] At that time the 17th Cavalry had a strength of 46 officers and 1,482 enlisted men.[31] Truscott later recalled that over the next few days the regimental adjutant, Lt. Daniel A. Connor, took him and his fellow second lieutenants on a series of horseback rides "to familiarize [them] with the area and to introduce [them] to the mounted service." After several "quiet, gentle rides" with Connor, the new officers met Lt. Edwin N. (Pink) Hardy, "one of the senior hard-bitten officers of the regiment," who began the officers' formal training in equitation, including many hours of riding at a slow trot without stirrups that "went a long way toward developing [their] cavalry seats!"[32]

They also participated in drills and other formations with the troops to which they were assigned and, under the watchful eye of an experienced noncommissioned officer (NCO), acquired those essentials of command that they would apply in putting their platoons through mounted and dismounted drill formations by "voice command, signal, and whistle." Close friendships often developed between the officers and those noncommissioned officers who guided them in their early years, friendships that would last throughout their long careers.[33]

The young officers also received instruction in their troop areas, where they were introduced to the complexities of morning reports, duty rosters, management of rations, property inventories, and inspections of the troop areas; practiced signaling using semaphore and "wig-wag" flags, the standard means of communication at that time; and were introduced to the organizing and management of a pack train, a skill that Truscott would use with great effectiveness a quarter of a century later in the mountains of Sicily and Italy. They also received extensive training in the use and employment of the traditional cavalry weapons, the pistol, saber, and rifle, as well as the newly introduced machine gun.[34]

In March 1918 the 17th Cavalry joined the 1st and 15th Cavalry Regiments to form the 3d Brigade of the 15th Cavalry Division, which had been organized for overseas service. All outlying units of the regiment were recalled to Camp Jones, where they prepared for early movement to France. The 15th Cavalry Regiment soon left for France, and the 1st Cavalry received orders to deploy. However, the 17th remained at Camp Jones for the next eight months, and with the signing of the Armistice all hopes for service in France vanished; "the heart sick [sic] troops had nothing to do, but bear it philosophically."[35] Truscott later wrote that the signing of the Armistice "deflated the hopes for service in France for many adventuresome souls," possibly expressing his personal disappointment at being denied an opportunity to serve in combat.[36]

Truscott received a temporary promotion to first lieutenant on March 22, 1918. On May 29 Col. George H. Morgan, then commanding the 17th Cavalry, requested that a board of officers be appointed for examination of Truscott and five other officers who had received temporary promotions to "make recommendations as to the suitability and fitness of such officers for permanent appointment and as to whether or not their temporary commissions should be terminated at once." In the case of Lieutenant Truscott, Colonel Morgan asserted the following: he exhibits "weak character, no initiative, is not a good platoon leader."[37]

On direct examination the prosecuting counsel asked Colonel Morgan to specify why he considered Truscott to have weak character. He replied, "He has no initiative.... [H]e never accomplished anything." To corroborate his opinion Morgan described a recent incident where Truscott had been placed in charge of transporting some property from the railroad station to the camp, during which "valuable property was lost." However, Morgan, when questioned by the board, admitted that a survey officer appointed to investigate responsibility for the loss of the property absolved Truscott of any responsibility for its loss. Several officers who had served or were serving with Truscott also testified before the board and affirmed that he was a very capable and intelligent officer. On June 13 the board unanimously recommended that "First Lieutenant Lucian K. Truscott, 17th Cavalry, be continued in his present status." The secretary of war approved the board's finding on August 2,[38] and on December 10 Truscott became a provisional first lieutenant.[39]

On June 21, just eight days after the board's favorable finding, Truscott was hospitalized, presumably because of pneumonia.[40] Maj. William Mann Randolph, chief of the surgical service and commander of the camp hospital at Camp Harry P. Jones, successfully treated the illness, and on July 2 Truscott was discharged from the hospital and returned to duty with Troop M.[41]

Doctor Randolph was a member of the distinguished Randolph family of Virginia and a descendant of Thomas Jefferson. He had established his practice in Charlottesville, Virginia, in the early 1890s, where he married Mary Walker Randolph, also a descendant of Thomas Jefferson. The couple had eight children, five daughters and three sons.[42] In 1913 Doctor Randolph, accompanied by his family, moved to Douglas, Arizona, where he became surgeon for the Phelps-Dodge Corporation, a mining company. On July 12, 1917, he received a commission as a U.S. Army medical officer at the Camp Jones hospital.[43]

For several months prior to his hospitalization Truscott had been dating one of Doctor Randolph's daughters, Sarah, and shortly before his discharge from the hospital, Doctor Randolph invited him to join the family for dinner. In the Randolph household twenty-one-year-old Sarah served as the principal housekeeper and was in charge of preparing and serving the dinner to which young Truscott had been invited. As Sarah hurried back and forth between the kitchen and the dining room, Lucian "never took his eyes off of her" during the entire evening, according to Sarah's mother. The couple drew even closer during the following months. "One thing led to another and they were married in 1919 [March 29]," in Bisbee, Arizona.[44]

Sarah Nicholas Randolph was born in Charlottesville on December 8, 1896, "a fourth-generation granddaughter of Thomas Jefferson," and graduated from Charlottesville High School in 1915.[45] Growing up in the Randolph home and thoroughly imbued from her earliest days with the traditions of her Randolph heritage, she learned all of the social amenities that were so important to the well-bred young ladies of the Virginia Randolphs. Her son Lucian described her as "a true southern gentlewoman . . . [and in] an earlier generation [she] could have *been* a Scarlett [O'Hara]."[46]

The day after the marriage of Lucian and Sarah the 17th Cavalry received orders to move to San Francisco, where it would sail aboard an Army transport for Hawaii on or about April 5. The regiment, with all of its organic weapons, equipment, and supplies, except horses, which had been shipped earlier, left Douglas in sections during the third and fourth of April. The main body of troops traveled by train, the enlisted men in tourist sleepers, and the officers in standard Pullman cars. Field ranges were set up in one baggage car, and kitchen police carried meals prepared there to the regimental personnel in the various cars. After arriving in San Francisco the morning of the fifth the unmarried enlisted men detrained and boarded the U.S. Army Transport (USAT) *Sherman,* while married officers and enlisted men reunited with their wives and families, who had preceded the regiment to San Francisco. A few hours later the *Sherman* cast off and sailed through the Golden Gate.[47]

The ship was filled to capacity with the personnel of the 17th Cavalry, other Army personnel en route to stations in the Philippine Islands, and U.S. Navy, Marine Corps, and State Department personnel en route to various stations in Hawaii and the Far East. Because of a lack of sufficient cabins, junior officers were assigned quarters separate from their wives, who were assigned to cabins with older women. Truscott recalled that after getting over their initial bouts of seasickness, the officers and their wives were able to participate fully in the "enjoyment of good meals, fine weather, and the pleasant associations and agreeable amusements of transport life. Every afternoon there was entertainment: boxing matches, song-and-dance acts, band concerts, wrestling matches, and dramatic skits." On the eighth day of the voyage the *Sherman* neared the island of Oahu, and the personnel on board soon experienced the "one thrill that can come only once in a lifetime. It is the view of Diamond Head against the blue Hawaiian sky, the entry of the ship into Honolulu Harbor." The ship docked early on the thirteenth, and debarking began immediately. Staff cars were there to transport families to Schofield Barracks, while the troops marched the few blocks to board a train also bound there, some twenty-five miles from Honolulu and one thousand feet above the coastal plain.[48]

On arrival the regiment moved into the cavalry area, Castner Barracks. The four three-story concrete buildings in the troop area were arranged in a quadrangle around an open grass-covered square that served as the parade ground, one building housing the headquarters, the other three housing the troops. The officers' quarters across the street from the headquarters building formed two horseshoes, with the Officers' Club situated between the "heels" of the horseshoes. Adjacent to the stable area was a large plateau that served as the drill field. Located near the drill field were gardens and a small village where Japanese workers employed on the post lived. They tended the gardens, the produce of which supplemented the basic ration of canned foods.[49]

One of the problems facing the regimental officers was that of morale among young enlisted soldiers isolated on an island far from friends and family. Numerous athletic activities, movies, and service clubs partially addressed those problems, but the nearest town, Wahiawa, was only a small village that offered very little in the way of recreation. Honolulu offered many attractions, among the most famous being Waikiki Beach, and was easily accessible by rail or auto, although few officers and even fewer of the noncommissioned officers had cars. About ten miles north of Schofield Barracks were the fine beaches of the North Shore.[50]

The Officers' Club was the center of social activities for the officers. There were frequent regimental dances, dinner dances, bridge parties, and pool and billiards. The club Sunday-night dinners were especially popular. A new sport for many of the younger officers, including Truscott, was polo, which had long been popular in the islands. Interested officers purchased the necessary mallets, balls, and helmets, selected their horses, and set about learning the game.[51]

In June transports began disembarking recruits from the mainland to bring the regiment up to strength. The regimental commander decided to assign the recruits to a separate detachment to undergo an intensive basic training course of eight to ten weeks. During the course of the year more than two thousand recruits completed the training program conducted by regimental officers and NCOs, an assignment that Truscott described as "an onerous but rewarding duty."[52]

From October 16 through October 27 the regiment participated in a field exercise conducted by the Hawaiian Department. The 17th Cavalry took up defensive positions to repel an assumed enemy naval force along the one hundred miles of the Oahu coastline, excluding the sector in and around Pearl Harbor and the city of Honolulu, the defense of which was the responsibility of the Coast Artillery. From October 23 through 27 a presumed state of hostilities was declared, and the troops established outposts in all sectors and carried out patrols and other tactical operations.[53] On his return from the exercise Truscott learned that he had received a permanent appointment as a first lieutenant in the Regular Army.[54]

Throughout 1920 all troops of the regiment "performed the regular routine garrison duties and participated in rifle and pistol practice." They also concentrated on the training activities that had occupied cavalry units "since time immemorial—mounted drill and stables in the morning, troop non-commissioned officers' schools and routine fatigue details and athletics in the afternoons." Athletics occupied a great deal of the troopers' off-duty hours, and baseball, tennis, basketball, football, soccer, and boxing were particularly popular. Polo continued to be popular among the officers, who participated in games against civilian teams from Oahu, Maui, and Kauai, where they made a "credible showing."[55]

A personal highlight for the Truscotts in 1920 was the birth of their daughter, Mary Randolph, on May 5. The family was doubly blessed when Sarah's mother was able to come to Hawaii to celebrate the birth of her granddaughter.[56]

On April 5, 1921, Truscott received notification that he had been promoted to captain, effective July 1, 1920. In less than three years Truscott had advanced from second lieutenant to captain, an unusually rapid advance for an officer of the Regular Army of that era, when many officers served as lieutenants for as much as fifteen years. However, he would not completely escape the promotion logjam—he would serve fifteen years as a captain.[57]

Meanwhile, congressional actions in the nation's capital were to have a major impact on the 17th Cavalry. The National Defense Act of 1920 authorized an army of 14,000 officers and 365,000 men but appropriated only enough funds to support an Army of 150,000, necessitating a reorganization that included the inactivation of the 15th, 16th, and 17th Cavalry Regiments; the 17th Cavalry soon received orders transferring it to the Presidio of Monterey, California, where it would be deactivated.[58] The regiment arrived in Monterey on September 25, and the following day the 17th Cavalry was deactivated and officers, enlisted men, and all records were transferred to the 11th Cavalry Regiment.[59]

However, the Truscott family did not accompany the regiment on its voyage to California. Sarah was in the ninth month of her second pregnancy, and because of this Lucian was placed on detached service with the 11th Field Artillery Regiment at Schofield Barracks on September 15. Two days later Sarah gave birth to Lucian K. Truscott III at Tripler Army Hospital. Again, Sarah's mother had journeyed to Hawaii to join her daughter and her family in celebrating the birth of her grandson. Captain Truscott, Sarah, Mary, and Lucian III sailed from Honolulu on October 6 aboard the USAT *Thomas,* arriving in San Francisco on October 13.[60] There Truscott received orders assigning him to the Presidio of San Francisco, where he remained until November 23, when he was reassigned to the 1st Cavalry Regiment at his former post, Camp Harry J. Jones in Douglas, Arizona, reporting there on January 4, 1922.[61]

During his second tour of duty at Camp Jones, polo would become a vital part of Lucian Truscott's life, and he would remain active in the sport during his subsequent prewar assignments. His older son wrote that his father became "one of the best players in the Army. . . . And he played to *win.*" He told his young Lucian one day,

Listen Son, goddamit. Let me tell you something and don't you ever forget it. You play games to *win*, not lose. And you fight wars to win! . . . And every good player in a game and every good commander in a war, . . . every damn one of them has to have some sonofabitch in him. If he doesn't, he isn't a good player or commander. And he never *will* be a good commander. . . . It's as simple as that. No sonofabitch, no commander.[62]

Chapter 2

ON THE ROAD TO HIGH COMMAND

During the fall of 1922, the Army decided to close Camp Harry J. Jones and move the 1st Cavalry Regiment to Camp Marfa, Texas, which was much closer to Fort Bliss, the home of its parent 1st Cavalry Division. Camp Marfa had larger training areas that would provide ample space for maneuvers scheduled for the fall of 1923, "the largest-scale mounted maneuvers heretofore attempted and the largest concentration of cavalry since the Pershing Expedition."[1]

During the field exercise the 1st Cavalry Brigade, consisting of the 1st and 4th Cavalry Regiments and supporting forces, maneuvered with the 2d Cavalry Brigade from Fort Bliss in an area north of Marfa. As Truscott described it, during the exercise's first phase the two brigades maneuvered against each other "in extremely realistic situations that provided training in all kinds of combat." In the second phase the two brigades formed as the 1st Cavalry Division and conducted a "field exercise designed to afford training in maneuvering as a unit and to show the power of the division artillery and other weapons in an exercise involving the use of live ammunition." The division remained encamped in the area for a week following the conclusion of the maneuver to enjoy a time of rest and relaxation. However, duty soon called, and the 1st Cavalry Regiment returned to Camp Marfa to resume its usual garrison duties and unit training, with squadron tactical exercises usually occurring weekly and regimental exercises taking place monthly.[2]

The passage of the National Defense Act of 1916 had "established a comprehensive, modern school system for the Army," and Army officers, including Truscott, recognized that attendance at their branch schools "was the next step on the military educational ladder and therefore in a successful military career." Accordingly, in August 1920, while stationed in Hawaii, he contacted Sarah's uncle Hollins N. Randolph, a prominent Atlanta attorney, requesting that he use any personal influence he might have to persuade the adjutant general, Maj.

Gen. P. C. Harris, to appoint him as a student in the Cavalry School at Fort Riley, Kansas. Randolph promptly wrote to General Harris, citing Truscott's qualities as a man and an officer, and asking Harris, "if it is at all possible, to interest yourself in him, with a view to obtaining this appointment." On August 13 Harris informed Randolph that he could not comply with the latter's request since "the list of officers detailed to the Cavalry school for this year has been closed," pointing out that only officers stationed within the continental United States could attend the school, and recommended that Truscott submit an application to the school after his return from Hawaii. On January 5, 1925, Captain Truscott submitted his formal application to attend the 1925–1926 Troop Officers' Course at the Cavalry School, which the adjutant general approved on April 22.[3]

Truscott received orders to attend the Troop Officers' Course that would begin in September 1925. At roughly the same time Maj. Harry D. Chamberlin, the captain of the Fort Bliss polo team, invited Truscott to join his team in the United States Polo Association's Inter-Circuit Championships in Philadelphia, the inaugural United States Polo Association national tournament. However, in order to play on the team, Truscott would have to be a member of the Fort Bliss garrison, and on June 9 Truscott's request for transfer to the 8th Cavalry as commander of Troop E at Fort Bliss was granted.[4] He spent the summer carrying out the normal duties of a troop commander during the morning training period, while polo practice consumed the afternoons.[5] In late summer Truscott requested authority to delay the date he was scheduled to report to the Cavalry School, September 14, pointing out that the polo tournament in Philadelphia did not begin until September 12. In a supporting endorsement Chamberlin stated that "the success of this expedition is largely dependent on Capt. Truscott's playing with the team." On September 5, just after arriving in Philadelphia, he received word of the change in his reporting date for the Cavalry School to September 30.[6]

The Philadelphia Country Club hosted the tournament, and prior to the beginning of the tournament the Fort Bliss team "appeared as a likely candidate for the honors." The team proceeded to meet all expectations, becoming national champions and taking home the Julius Fleischmann Trophy.[7] As Lucian Truscott reported to Fort Riley to begin his studies at the Cavalry School, he must have done so very satisfied with his contributions to the success of the Fort Bliss polo team.

When Truscott and his family arrived at Fort Riley they were assigned quarters at Godfrey Court in the post hospital, forty wards of which had been converted into apartments for student officers. Beaverboard partitions seven to eight feet in height formed the walls of the apartments, the dividing partitions extending about halfway to the ceilings of the apartments. The original ward washrooms, toilets, and showers were the bathrooms for the student officers and their families.[8]

At the time Truscott began his studies the Cavalry School conducted three year-length courses: the Troop Officers' Course, in which Truscott was enrolled, the Advanced Officers' Course, and the Advanced Equitation Course. Truscott's class was made up of fifty-six officers, mostly captains, divided into two platoons. The school week consisted of five 8-hour days, but students usually spent several additional hours in study each night.[9] Truscott's class received 304 hours of instruction during their yearlong course. Patrolling (17 hours), serving as an advance guard (17 hours), dismounted and mounted daylight and night combat (58 hours), reconnaissance and counterreconnaissance missions (18 hours), rearguard and delaying actions (13 hours), river crossings (14 hours), and staff duties and logistics (23 hours) received particular emphasis.[10]

There was an active social life at the school, beginning with the commandant's reception and dance at the beginning of the academic year. Similar functions occurred weekly throughout the year, and there were many impromptu gatherings of officers and their wives. Formal receptions marked the arrival of all visiting dignitaries, such as the chief of staff of the Army and the chief of cavalry. The holidays were occasions for particularly festive celebrations.[11]

At some of the less formal gatherings alcoholic beverages were available, despite the fact that Prohibition was still the law of the land. Moonshine was readily accessible in nearby Junction City, and Truscott recalled that a farmer who lived on the south side of the Kansas River had "converted a portion of his corn into a liquid form. This potent distillate he dispensed to a select clientele of customers, mostly officers on the post, for the very reasonable price of six dollars a gallon." Also popular among the officers was "home brew," prepared from sugar and malt syrup, readily available from the local grocer. The officers bottled the brew on Sunday evenings, so that it was "properly aged" by the time classes let out the following Friday afternoon.[12]

After successfully completing the course of instruction, which totaled 304 hours, Truscott joined his forty-seven classmates and two Cuban army officers at graduation ceremonies on June 10. The many activities of June Week, a class party and a round of individual cocktail parties, dinners, and buffet suppers, had strengthened the many new friendships formed during the class year.[13]

Truscott was directed to report as a student in the Advanced Equitation Course by September 5. Col. R. J. Fleming, the assistant commandant of the Cavalry School, who described Truscott as "self-reliant, energetic, hard worker, practical" in a Special Efficiency Report, had recommended him for that course. "The Advanced Equitation Class consisted of twelve officers, selected from the Troop Officers' Class of the preceding year, for special training to become instructors in the subject. The class received almost no academic instruction, devoting virtually the entire time to equitation, horsemanship, and related subjects."[14]

In March 1927, approximately two-thirds of the way through the demanding course of instruction, Truscott learned he would report "for duty with the staff and faculty" of the Cavalry School for a period of four years upon completing his current course of instruction. In a Special Efficiency Report on Truscott's performance in the Advanced Equitation Class, Colonel Fleming reported that the "Director, Department of Tactics states 'this officer's work in the Department of Tactics is considered of exceptional quality showing great application and study on his part. He is recommended as an instructor at this school.'" [15]

Truscott was undoubtedly pleased to assume once again the challenging role of teacher after a ten-year hiatus, although recognizing that as an instructor in the Cavalry School he would confront challenges he had not faced as a teacher in the public schools of Oklahoma. Beginning in 1927 the number of hours of instruction in the Troop Officers' Course had been dramatically increased, from 304 hours when Truscott was a student to 1,421 hours. One of the most significant increases was in dismounted combat, where cavalrymen would function as infantrymen, with particular emphasis on musketry, rifle marksmanship, and the employment of machine rifles (presumably automatic rifles) and machine guns. Despite the increased workload the course reorganization would require him to assume, Truscott realized that his new assignment would also afford him and his family greater opportunity to participate in the many professional, social, and recreational activities offered at Fort Riley, including riding classes, book clubs, bridge clubs, and ladies' clubs. [16]

On December 26, 1930, Sarah and Lucian became parents for the third time, when James Joseph Truscott was born at the Fort Riley hospital. The youngest Truscott was named in honor of his great-grandfather, Judge James Joseph Truscott. [17]

Truscott's six-year tour of duty at the Cavalry School came to an end in the spring of 1931, when he received orders transferring him to Fort Myer, Virginia, just across the Potomac River from Washington, D.C., to join the 2d Squadron, 3d Cavalry Regiment, the "Brave Rifles," as commander of Troop E. [18] The 3d Cavalry's motto, "Brave Rifles," came from an accolade that Gen. Winfield Scott gave to the regiment during the Mexican War after its action at Churubusco, south of Mexico City, on August 20, 1847. [19]

Truscott found his Troop E noncommissioned officers to be of unusually high caliber. Some had been commissioned officers in the late war, while others had refused commissions in order to remain with their fellow "noncoms" from Company E, who had shipped to France together in 1917. In 1931 those same noncommissioned officers continued to occupy key positions in the troop. Truscott found them to be "thoroughly competent in every respect, . . . [and] presented a challenge in leadership to any officer assigned to command the troop." [20]

The main duties of the 2d Squadron included "participation in parades, escorts of honor for the president and visiting dignitaries, ceremonial parades and reviews on the post, exhibitions, and the normal peacetime training" common to all troops. However, one of the most important duties of the cavalrymen at Fort Myer was to provide funeral escorts. Because of all of those special duties, carrying out a broad and effective training program was difficult and required the commanders to remain flexible in planning their training schedules. The small drill field had to be shared among four cavalry troops and three artillery batteries, which posed special problems, especially for the cavalry officers and men who were accustomed to the wide expanse of training areas in the southwestern United States.[21]

During the winter each troop and battery participated in the weekly "Friday Rides" in the Riding Hall, which were attended by the people of Washington and visiting distinguished national and foreign dignitaries. The Friday exhibitions became so popular that "there were often six thousand applications for the eighteen hundred seats available" in the upper and lower galleries at each end of the Riding Hall. Each troop and battery over the years had developed one or more drills or exhibitions, and Truscott's troop developed a musical ride that featured twenty-four riders and a jumping exhibition performed by a platoon hurdling a series of obstacles, one on each of the long sides and one midway at each end of the Riding Hall, with a square pen placed diagonally in the center. "The exhibition ended with trios of riders crossing through the square pen jump in the center of the hall from each of the four directions in a perfectly timed and coordinated movement."[22]

Truscott wrote that "during the winter of 1931/32, the gloom of the Great Depression was settling over the nation, despite presidential assurance that 'prosperity was just around the corner.'" Military personnel felt the sting of the effects of the sinking economy when Congress in 1932 imposed "on the services an unpaid furlough equal to 8 1/3 per cent of their active duty [days] and barred increases of pay for promotion and automatic in-grade raises." In March 1933 military pay was "further reduced in the general 15 per-cent salary slash of government employees. The new legislation was particularly hard on the lower enlisted and junior-officer grades."[23] It is a testimony to their love for and loyalty and devotion to the Army and their country that future World War II senior commanders such as Marshall, Eisenhower, Bradley, Ridgway, Gavin, Clark, and Truscott, and their families, persevered through such trying times, remaining faithful to the very institutions that at times treated them with such callous disregard.

During the winter of 1931–1932, as the Depression was worsening and as more and more people began to feel its effects, "hunger marches" began to take place around the nation.[24] One group of men among the millions of unemployed who believed they had a particularly strong grievance to present to Congress and the president were the world war veterans. Many of those veterans returned to civilian life and found their old jobs filled by men who had not served in the war. Although the veterans had received a small discharge bonus from the federal government and from some states, they harbored bitterness over the loss of their prewar jobs. Soon, some veteran organizations began agitating for "adjusted compensation" or a bonus from the federal government "to balance out the difference between their modest military pay and the high wages enjoyed by civilian war workers" during the war. In the spring of 1924 Congress enacted the Soldiers' Bonus Act into law over the veto of President Calvin Coolidge. The act provided compensation to be paid at the rate of $1.25 for every day of overseas service and $1.00 per day of service within the United States. However, the veterans would not receive the bonus money until 1945.[25]

Unsatisfied with that provision of the law, the veterans pressed for immediate cash settlements, but Coolidge, his successor, Herbert Hoover, and Republican congressmen resisted their appeals. With the onset of the Depression the intensity of those appeals dramatically increased, culminating in a march of unemployed veterans from throughout the country on the nation's capital. Alerted to the approach of the marchers, Gen. Douglas MacArthur, the Army chief of staff, directed on May 25 that his deputy chief of staff, Maj. Gen. George Van Horn Moseley, prepare to confront the marchers.[26]

Washington police chief Pelham Glassford's plan was to assemble the marchers in Anacostia Park on the east bank of the Anacostia River, where he would create a tent city to house them. Soon the population of veterans and their families swelled to approximately twenty to twenty-five thousand in Anacostia and in vacant government buildings throughout the Washington area. As the stay of the veterans lengthened, some residents of the Washington area began to view the gathering as "Communist-led and a threat to the city," leading an impatient President Hoover to order the District commissioners to have Chief Glassford evict those veterans occupying the government buildings in downtown Washington. Like Hoover, MacArthur was also growing impatient with the police department's handling of the veterans and ordered that a truck mounting a 75mm gun and an armored car mounting .30- and .50-caliber machine guns be moved to Fort Myer, where soldiers had begun riot training.[27]

As the evictions finally began on July 28, the police were assaulted with bricks and concrete. In the melee Glassford was thrown down a flight of stairs and stripped of his pistol, and two veterans were killed. The commissioners then appealed for federal troops to intervene, and Hoover ordered the troops into action.[28] At 2:55 p.m. Secretary of War Patrick J. Hurley telephoned MacArthur and ordered him to proceed with federal troops to the scene of disorder, surround the area, and clear it of the veterans. His troops were to accord "every consideration" to women and children in the area, and the troops were to "use all humanity consistent with due execution of this order." However, Hoover had already contacted the War Department, and at 1:30 p.m. MacArthur issued orders to assemble the troops at the Ellipse, south of the White House.[29]

Among the troops ordered into action was the 2d Squadron, 3d Cavalry, with Maj. Alexander D. Surles in command and Maj. George S. Patton, Jr., attached as executive officer. MacArthur decided that he would accompany the troops, "not with a view of commanding the troops but to be on hand as things progressed, so that he could issue necessary instructions on the ground." Maj. Dwight D. Eisenhower, who was on the War Department staff and was serving as an assistant to MacArthur, advised him that "it seemed 'highly inappropriate' for the military head of the Army to be present with the evicting force." MacArthur dismissed Eisenhower's advice, stating he was doing so because "it was a question of Federal authority in the District of Columbia and because of his belief that there was 'incipient revolution in the air.'" [30]

In midafternoon Major Patton informed the troop commanders that the squadron had been ordered into Washington to put down the riots. The commanders joined their troops, and, as described by Truscott, "the squadron then pounded down through Arlington National Cemetery, over the recently completed Memorial Bridge, and halted on the Ellipse south of the White House at about half past two o'clock," where an infantry battalion from Fort Washington joined it. Moving out in a column of platoons, with the cavalry in the lead and accompanied by a few world war tanks, the soldiers moved down Pennsylvania Avenue toward the Capitol. At Third Street and Pennsylvania Avenue N.W. the column stopped at a partially demolished building still occupied by veterans. Infantrymen entered the building, meeting some resistance that was quickly eliminated with a few tear-gas grenades, and forced hundreds of veterans into the streets. The cavalry quickly surrounded the men and drove them to the vicinity of Missouri Avenue. The cavalrymen then formed in a single rank facing the thousands of shouting veterans and, according to Truscott, "sat like statues and answered back not a word. Their only action was to apply the flat of a saber whenever individuals tried to slip through the thin lines. Theirs was a magnificent illustration of Regular Army discipline." Soon tensions increased and tempers flared. The veterans threw a few rocks and bricks at the troopers, knocking two unconscious. Receiving orders to disperse the mob, the troopers, with drawn sabers, moved forward into a hail of bricks and stones, driving the veterans across the Mall toward the Anacostia River, where they halted to allow the mob to disperse. [31]

Hurley, "fearful that the government was looking too oppressive and wanting to contain the public relations damage," sent Hoover's direct order to MacArthur that the Army not pursue the bonus marchers across the river into their encampment. When he received the order MacArthur flatly ignored it, stating he was "too busy . . . and could not be bothered by people coming down and pretending to bring orders." [32] Shortly after darkness fell MacArthur ordered the squadron to move across the bridge spanning the river. After entering the camp at about half past ten, the cavalrymen halted to allow the veterans time once again to clear the area. Then the infantry moved in to clear the camp, which soon was a "mass of flames." By the morning of the twenty-ninth the veterans were gone, the camp "a smoldering mess."[33] Truscott's Troop E spent that afternoon assisting in clearing bonus marchers from buildings and streets in Southeast, Northwest, and Southwest Washington. About five thirty the squadron received orders to return to Fort Myer.[34]

In his memoir Truscott recorded that "the emergency indeed was over. . . . The remnants of the BEF [Bonus Expeditionary Force] were streaming out of Washington, as one correspondent described it: 'The bonus army, bedraggled, hungry, shabby, moved out along the roads that led away from the Nation's Capital. . . . The BEF had died in the same confusion in which it was born.' . . . And never again would such a movement be repeated in Washington. Cavalry training and special training for riot duty had paid off."[35]

During his time with the 3d Cavalry, Truscott continued his polo career, culminating in his being selected to join the U.S. Army polo team that was invited in the spring of 1934 to compete in Mexico City against the Mexican All-Army Team in a three-match series. The first match took place at El Campo del Marte (Field of Mars) in Chapultepec Park on Sunday, April 8. Early in the first period a Mexican rider and his pony struck Truscott's pony, causing it to trip and then somersault, breaking the pony's neck. Truscott was knocked unconscious by the collision and the fall but resumed play about ten minutes later. However, during the second period it became apparent that Truscott had been more seriously injured than initially suspected, and he was replaced at the end of the period. The Americans went on to trounce the Mexican team 12–4. Truscott's injury prevented his playing in the second match, which the American team won in overtime. He managed to join the team for a third match, but "was less than fifty per cent efficient," as the Mexican team defeated the American team. Speaking during the closing ceremonies, the American ambassador to Mexico, the Honorable Josephus Daniels, stated that the "series had done much to further the understanding and friendly relations between the two countries."[36]

On April 13, 1934, Truscott was ordered to report to Fort Leavenworth, Kansas, in late summer to begin studies in the 1934–1936 course at the U.S. Army Command and General Staff School. Truscott could look back on his three years of service with the Brave Rifles with considerable satisfaction and pride, having received four official Efficiency Reports during that period, in all of which his rating officer and battalion commander, Major Surles, rated him as a "superior" officer, the highest rating achievable. Surles described Truscott variously as "an officer of superior ability in command duty"; "[he] possesses unusual force and self reliance"; "a forceful, highly proficient officer of unusual capabilities"; "one of the most efficient and capable officers I know"; "possessed of exceptional judgement, force, and resourcefulness"; "this officer is the most capable all-round troop commander I have encountered"; "a forceful and determined field soldier." Surles also repeatedly stated that in time of war, Truscott was qualified to serve as a lieutenant colonel, and in one report stated that he was capable of commanding a regiment.[37]

The mission of the Command and General Staff School (CGSS), formed in 1922 from the combining of the Army's School of the Line and the General Staff School, was "to provide a one-year course instructing in command and general staff duties from reinforced brigade through army corps level." In 1928 the course was lengthened to two years after the one-year course was found to be of "insufficient time to teach all that was necessary regarding the operation of the reinforced brigade, the division and the corps."[38] Captain Truscott reported for duty on August 27, 1934, where he joined 120 other students, all but three of whom were captains or majors.[39] Truscott, Sarah, Mary, Lucian, and James moved into their quarters at 322-G Doniphan Avenue.[40]

The instruction at the school was based on a succession of "building blocks," beginning with "basic tactical information on such topics as organization of the infantry division, field artillery weapons and technique and the operation of cavalry with other arms." As the course progressed, increasingly more complex studies and exercises were introduced, until by the end of the course the students were working with combined arms forces, including air forces, in such operations as defense and attack of a river line and amphibious landings on hostile shores. Approximately 70 to 80 percent of the instruction time dealt with tactics.[41]

Graduation ceremonies were held on June 19, 1936, for Truscott's class, in which Truscott ranked thirty-second in overall academic standing.[42] He was one of five in the class who would eventually command divisions in World War II combat, and was the only one who would rise to both corps and army command.[43] In Truscott's Efficiency Report dated June 30, 1935, Lt. Col. J. A. McAndrew, the director of the First-Year Class, rated Truscott's overall performance as "Excellent." McAndrew described him as "earnest, studious, reliable," and gave him a superior rating in "Attention to duty (the trait of working thoroughly and conscientiously)," and indicated that he would "especially desire" to have Truscott serve under his command in either peace or war. The following year, Col. W. B. Burtt, the director of the Second-Year Class, rated Truscott as "Superior" in all rated categories except "Military bearing and neatness," where he rated him as "Excellent," and pointed out that Truscott's skills in horsemanship and horsemastership were "outstanding specialties of value in military service." He also described Truscott as "hardworking, dependable, thorough," and his estimate was that Truscott was of "superior" value to the service. Maj. Gen. H. J. Brees, the commandant of the school, rendered a "Special School Report" on Truscott, dated June 20, 1936, in which he gave him an "Excellent" overall academic rating.[44]

Attesting Major Truscott's impressive performance as a student was a recommendation forwarded to the chief of cavalry in December 1935 that he be named an instructor at the Command and General Staff School. In February 1936 the War Department ordered Truscott and five of his fellow students to report for duty as instructors upon completion of their current studies.[45] Truscott was assigned to the academic Third Section, Defensive Operations, and was to remain a member of that section for his entire tenure on the faculty. His section was responsible for instruction in defensive operations, marches, reconnaissance, security, counteroffense, and lines of communication.[46]

While at Fort Leavenworth, Truscott continued his pursuit of higher education, spending many hours in home study of books and journals from the post and CGSS libraries. Sarah joined him in studying the French language, in which Lucian became sufficiently fluent to translate the *French Cavalry Journal* for the library of the Command and General Staff School.[47]

On April 2, 1940, after almost four years as an instructor at the CGSS, Truscott received orders to report not later than September 10 as a student in the 1940–1941 course at the U.S. Army War College, the capstone of the Army's formal school system, located at Washington Barracks (now Fort Lesley J. McNair), D.C. Truscott applied for and was granted two months of leave beginning July 11.[48]

Truscott was the subject of seven Efficiency Reports during his nearly four years as a CGSS instructor. In all of those he received an overall rating of "Superior" and was consistently rated as being of superior or highest value to the service and possessing "superior qualifications for higher command and staff training." One of his raters, Col. F. W. Honeycutt, described him as "loyal, conscientious, accurate, dependable," and another, Col. K. B. Edmunds, described him as "keen, energetic, of pleasing personality, dependable and efficient. A deliberate, calm, stable character and an original thinker."[49]

As Truscott and other officers awaiting reassignment met informally before leaving Fort Leavenworth, their discussions often turned to the future of the cavalry arm. Truscott recorded that "the cavalry was definitely on the defensive. Many officers of the General Staff in Washington and in other branches believed that aviation, mechanization, and motorization could perform all cavalry missions . . . [and] in the keen competition for the limited funds and manpower available in those depression days, the cavalry bore the brunt of budget cuts in both manpower and money." The 1st and 13th Cavalry Regiments had already been formed into the 7th Cavalry Brigade (Mechanized), and there was an ongoing effort to motorize divisions. As a result, in 1940 "most cavalry officers were seeking an opportunity for experience in the new field of armor."[50]

In June the Truscott family's plans to move to Washington were abruptly halted when the War Department suspended the U.S. Army War College classes indefinitely, "an action called for by the Protective Mobilization Plan," developed in 1939 at the order of Gen. Malin Craig, Marshall's predecessor as chief of staff, which provided a concept for mobilization of the U.S. Army and the

National Guard "as a covering force ('Initial Protective Force') for the defense of the United States."[51] Truscott's previous orders were revoked, he was relieved of assignment to the CGSS faculty on June 28, and he was directed to report to the 1st Cavalry Division at Fort Clark, Texas.[52]

The Truscotts decided to visit Sarah's parents in Charlottesville prior to moving to Fort Clark, after Lucian was placed on academic leave June 11–28 and was granted two months of ordinary leave beginning on June 29.[53] Only their son James accompanied them on the trip to Charlottesville, since Mary was to begin secretarial studies at the Katherine Gibbs School that summer and Lucian III began studies at Millard's Preparatory School in Washington, D.C., to prepare for the entrance examinations for the U.S. Military Academy. As he departed Fort Leavenworth for the drive to Virginia after his nearly six-year sojourn there, Truscott reflected that "no one who left the Command and General Staff School in 1940 had any idea when and where the war would come, but few doubted that the United States would become entangled in the European struggle in due course."[54]

As the Truscotts neared the end of their stay with Doctor and Mrs. Randolph at "Wild Acres" late that summer, Truscott received orders that revoked his assignment to the 1st Cavalry Division at Fort Clark and assigned him to the 1st Armored Division at Fort Knox, Kentucky, effective at the expiration of his current leave of absence.[55] He was one of many field-grade cavalry officers being transferred to Fort Knox, the home of the Armored Force that had been created by a War Department directive on July 10, 1940, where they were assigned to the 1st Armored Division for initial indoctrination and training.[56]

Chapter 3

PRELUDE TO WAR

In August 1940 Fort Knox, thirty-five miles south of Louisville, was the home of the Armored Force, organized on July 10, 1940, and commanded by Brig. Gen. Adna R. Chaffee. It "was built around the 7th Cavalry Brigade (Mechanized) and the 6th Infantry (Armored) at Fort Knox"; the seven infantry battalions of the Provisional Tank Brigade at Fort Benning, Georgia; the 70th Tank Battalion at Fort Meade, Maryland; the Armored Force Board; and the Armored Force School and Replacement Training Center. Chaffee also commanded I Armored Corps, activated on July 15, 1940, which consisted of the 1st Armored Division, successor to the 7th Cavalry Brigade at Fort Knox, and the 2d Armored Division, organized from the Provisional Tank Brigade at Fort Benning.[1] On his arrival at Fort Knox, Truscott learned of his promotion to lieutenant colonel, to date from August 18, and on September 24 he was assigned as the executive officer of the 2d Battalion, 13th Armored Regiment.[2]

Fort Knox in 1940 was a virtual beehive of activity as the Army and the nation began mobilizing for possible war. Roads, streets, buildings of all kinds, and bridges were under construction throughout the post. The streets and roads were filled with all types of vehicles: tanks, half-tracks, armored cars, motorcycles, and jeeps. Accommodations for the hundreds of incoming officers, many of whom were field grade, were particularly few. As a result, pyramidal tents on floored frames were erected adjacent to the Officers' Mess to accommodate those officers and their families who were awaiting assignment to units of the Armored Force. Lucian, Sarah, and James lived in one of the pyramidal tents, sharing central latrine facilities with other families and eating most meals at the Officers' Mess. James Truscott remembers that as the autumn chill arrived, the Truscotts and other families purchased electric heaters for their tents, but the resulting electrical overload soon caused the "main circuit breakers to pop," necessitating a ban on the use of the heaters.

At that juncture the Truscotts moved into rented civilian housing in Louisville.[3]

Prior to joining units, all officers underwent instruction in driving and performing first-echelon maintenance on every type of vehicle in the Armored Force and learning to use weapons organic to each vehicle.[4] After joining their units they continued seemingly unending drills and training exercises. Still, there was time for social activities for the officers and their families, although the constraints imposed by the intense training activities and the crowded living conditions, coupled with the uncertainty of the times, had their effects. Gone were the days of stable tours of duty, when officers and their families were almost always assured that they would remain in any one assignment or on any one post for three or four years. Orders to move now could come at any time.[5]

Truscott's tour as the 2d Battalion's executive officer was quite brief: on November 7 he was assigned as the 13th Armored Regiment's S3, an assignment for which he was admirably qualified after his six years of duty as a student and faculty member of the CGSS.[6]

As the regimental S3, Truscott served as the principal staff adviser to the regimental commander for all activities relating to plans, operations, and training. He and his assistants prepared regimental training schedules, delineated training objectives, drew up plans for command post and field training exercises, observed and evaluated all training and exercises, and presented their observations and recommendations for further training to the regimental commander. In combat the S3 would, based on the commander's guidance, prepare all regimental operation plans and orders, including overlays and maps. Superior performance by Truscott as regimental S3 could provide a significant boost to the advancement of his career, possibly opening the path to the position of regimental executive officer or even a senior command in the Armored Force. However, if such hope existed in Truscott's mind, it appeared to be dashed when he learned in early February 1941, after just a little more than three months' service as the S3, that he was to "be detailed as a member of the General Staff Corps . . . assigned to the General Staff with troops, effective upon his arrival at Fort Lewis, Washington," for duty with the IX Corps.[7]

Despite his abbreviated tenure as the 13th Armored Regiment's S3, Truscott appeared to impress his regimental commander, Col. Raymond E. McQuillin, who rated his overall performance in that position as "Superior," giving him the same rating in his performance as an instructor, in his handling of officers and men, and in his training and tactical handling of troops. He described Truscott as "a capable well informed and thoroughly dependable officer, especially well qualified as an instructor and for Staff and Command duty."[8]

As Truscott, accompanied by Sarah and James, prepared to leave Fort Knox, he did so with a feeling "akin to resignation." He had been "looking forward to increased opportunities as the Armored Force expanded," but believing that "an officer should accept assignments without question," he accepted the unexpected transfer, which had been made "without my consent and rather against my will."[9]

IX Corps, a tactical and administrative command headquartered at Fort Lewis, served under the Fourth Army headquarters in San Francisco. The 3d and 41st Infantry Divisions were the principal combat units of the corps, and the 115th Cavalry served as the corps cavalry regiment. Maj. Gen. Kenyon A. Joyce, who had commanded the 3d Cavalry Regiment during Truscott's tour of duty with the regiment in the early 1930s, commanded the corps. Serving as Joyce's chief of staff was the former chief of staff of the 3d Infantry Division, Col. Dwight D. Eisenhower.[10]

Truscott assumed his duties as assistant to Lt. Col. Leonard R. Boyd, the IX Corps G3, on February 24, and soon met Colonel Eisenhower, thus beginning a close friendship with a man who in the coming years would play a decisive role in his career. Planning began immediately for the implementation of a training program that Maj. Gen. Lesley J. McNair's General Headquarters (GHQ) had ordered all divisions in active service to complete, assigning responsibility for planning and conducting the exercises to the newly organized corps headquarters. The program included command post exercises "to afford training in command and staff procedures and communications," as well as field exercises, in which divisions conducted "such operations as a night march and organization of a position, advance and attack in a meeting engagement, organization of a position," followed by exercises controlled by umpires that would pit one division against another. For IX Corps the field exercises, using live ammunition, would take place on the Hunter Liggett Military Reservation in central California near the town of Jolon. Holding the exercise in California "would afford the elements of the corps training in a strategic movement of several hundred miles, as well as the advantage of operating on unfamiliar terrain."[11]

The corps staff had approximately four months to prepare for the exercises. A particularly heavy load fell upon the G3 personnel, who had to prepare the actual problems for the exercises and select and train the umpires for the controlled maneuver. In addition, the terrain over which the exercises would take place at both Fort Lewis and Hunter Liggett had to be reconnoitered. A complicating factor was that the two assigned divisions were operating under different Tables of Organization and Equipment (TO&Es).[12] The 3d Infantry Division was a "triangular division," while the 41st Infantry Division, recently mobilized from the Washington and Oregon National Guard, retained its "square" organization.[13]

After completing the command post exercises at Fort Lewis in early April, the two divisions moved by motorized road march to Hunter Liggett for the field exercises. At their conclusion Truscott stated that "many of the officers and men who participated in the exercises will never forget them. They were so realistic that only the shot and sound of battle were missing. Dense forest growth, utter darkness of moonless nights, frequent rain, and occasional fog—all contributed to the realistic nature of the exercises and increased the value of the training. The exercise also demonstrated the relatively high state of training of the officers and men and their readiness for whatever was to come their way." However, all did not share Truscott's sanguine view. During one of the field exercises a group of officers from GHQ, including General McNair's deputy, Brig. Gen. Mark W. Clark, was present to observe. Their final report on the exercise "criticized practically every one concerned with the exercise from General Joyce on down."[14]

Apparently taken aback by the negative comments, General Joyce forwarded the GHQ critique of the maneuver to Colonel Eisenhower, now serving as Maj. Gen. Walter Krueger's chief of staff at Third Army headquarters at Fort Sam Houston, Texas.[15] After reviewing the critique Eisenhower informed Joyce that "some of the criticisms were obvious and could and would be made about any troops in the service." He then went on to comment on the specific criticisms, but "noted with particular satisfaction that the division[sic] were away the best so far seen [by the observers], and that the Corps Headquarters functioned efficiently." He also told Joyce that he had met with "part of the GHQ crowd" at Fort Sam Houston the previous week, and they had "agreed that you had developed the IX Army Corps into a gang of first class fighting men."[16]

While participating in the corps exercises at Hunter Liggett, Truscott wrote to his wife regularly. On June 17 he told her of Eisenhower's appointment as the Third Army chief of staff and stated that his "regard for [Eisenhower] has grown steadily ever since I came to Lewis." He also told her that he would become the new G3 of IX Corps, and that Col. Charles H. Corlett had replaced Eisenhower as IX Corps chief of staff. Truscott confided his opinion of the new chief of staff to his wife: "He is not the man Eisenhower is, but then there are few like that."[17]

In August IX Corps once more took to the field to participate in Fourth Army maneuvers in southwestern Washington and the Olympic Peninsula, pitting III Corps, stationed at the Presidio of Monterey, and its two infantry divisions, the 7th and the 40th, against IX Corps.[18] The exercise apparently went well, except for a "colossal traffic jam" that resulted when the troops of the two corps collided as they attempted to move in opposite directions to their home stations along the same limited road net after the exercise had concluded. That experience drove home to all participating officers the vital necessity of carefully planning for and coordinating movements of large bodies of troops over limited road nets.[19]

In early September Truscott and several other IX Corps staff officers received orders to report to Camp Polk, Louisiana, "for temporary duty in connection with the Second vs. Third Army Maneuvers" that were to be held September

15–30.[20] Truscott was detailed to serve as part of the GHQ Director Group.[21] Some 472,000 men, including twenty-seven divisions, participated in the maneuvers, which took on added importance because of increasing Nazi aggression in Europe and the Middle East. Chief of Staff Marshall also hoped to "draw the nation's and Congress's attention to its army's deplorable state of preparedness." The many deficiencies uncovered by the Louisiana and the earlier Tennessee maneuvers resulted by year's end "in the forcible retirement of hundreds of senior officers," including "thirty-one of forty-two army corps and division commanders. . . . Those who survived scrutiny were considered the nucleus of the rejuvenated army."[22]

After the conclusion of the maneuvers General McNair cited the participating IX Corps officers for contributing "greatly to the successful direction of the maneuvers." In his endorsement of the copy of McNair's letter that he forwarded to Truscott, Lt. Gen. J. L. DeWitt, commanding general of Fourth Army, stated that he "noted with pleasure the commendation of the Chief of Staff, G.H.Q., for the services you rendered as part of the G.H.Q. Director Group, during the recent Second versus Third Army Maneuvers," and directed that a copy of the communication be filed with his next Efficiency Report.[23]

Less than two months after returning to Fort Lewis, Truscott received orders assigning him once again to the 1st Cavalry Division at Fort Bliss, where he would assume command of the 5th Cavalry Regiment, one of the Army's most distinguished regiments.[24] Truscott's tour of duty with IX Corps had been a significant one: he had met and worked with Dwight Eisenhower; participated in army-level maneuvers; worked in the headquarters directing the massive Second and Third Army maneuvers, where he earned favorable notice from the GHQ commanding general and chief of staff; and gained valuable high-level staff experience. In addition, his immediate superior, Col. Leonard R. Boyd, assistant chief of staff, G3, IX Corps, was particularly impressed with Truscott's ability, giving him an overall "Superior" rating in both Efficiency Reports he rendered and describing him as "an outstanding officer whose training and experience fit him for duty as a General Staff officer. He has unusual ability to prepare and direct field exercises and maneuvers. He is loyal, enthusiastic, ambitious, and thoroughly dependable." Boyd went on to rate Truscott's present and future value to the service as "Superior" and stated that Truscott was fit for duty not only as a General Staff officer but also as a commander.[25]

However, the most significant acknowledgment of Truscott's outstanding abilities came from General Joyce in a letter recommending him for promotion to colonel:

> As assistant to the Corps Operations Officer this officer has proven himself to be highly efficient. He is loyal, industrious, enthusiastic and extremely capable. He has at times been required to carry the load of the operations office by

himself, which he has done most successfully. His sound tactical sense has been fully demonstrated in the preparation of corps problems, the conduct of which he has supervised. His knowledge of training requirements is extensive. He should be a full colonel in either command or staff capacity. His promotion is recommended.[26]

Truscott, Sarah, and James motored from Fort Lewis to Fort Bliss, where the family moved into on-post quarters. On November 22 Truscott assumed command of the 5th Cavalry Regiment, 1st Cavalry Brigade, 1st Cavalry Division. The 1st Cavalry Division, reorganized in 1940–1941, was composed of more than seven thousand officers and men and nearly six thousand horses. As a harbinger of the mechanization that was soon to affect the entire division, the division reconnaissance squadron was composed of two scout-car troops, a motorcycle troop, and a light tank troop. Truscott believed the reorganized cavalry division to be "a powerful combat unit, capable of operations in any kind of terrain." Maj. Gen. Innis P. Swift, one of the preeminent cavalrymen of his time, commanded this formidable division.[27]

On a warm, sunny December Sunday, only sixteen days after Truscott had assumed command of the 5th Cavalry, most of the cavalrymen at Fort Bliss were enjoying a respite from their arduous training duties, spending time with their families or their buddies, attending church and Sunday school, or listening to their radios in the barracks or dayrooms. Suddenly, the music was interrupted by an excited voice announcing, "The Japanese are attacking Pearl Harbor." Disbelief quickly gave way to shock, which soon became bitter anger against the nation that had launched such a treacherous attack against a nation at peace. The anger intensified over the next weeks as the Japanese attacked and then invaded the Philippines, driving the American forces back into the Bataan Peninsula and finally to the island fortress of Corregidor. Fueling the anger was the realization by the men of the 1st Cavalry Division that many of the defenders of the Philippines were fellow cavalrymen.[28]

The Fort Bliss garrison reacted quickly, sending out patrols along the Mexican border and setting up combat outposts to guard tunnels, bridges, and other vital structures to thwart any attempts by enemy agents to infiltrate the border. Training activities intensified, emphasizing small-unit tactics and leadership training of officers. Also receiving emphasis were the principles of dismounted combat, since American cavalrymen were expected to be as proficient in that type of combat and in the use of infantry weapons as the infantrymen themselves.

General Krueger, as commander of Third Army and Southern Defense Command, also ordered that all cavalrymen in his command receive training in dismounted marching, since it might become necessary for the cavalry division to function as an infantry division in an emergency, which indeed was how the

1st Cavalry Division was ultimately employed in World War II in the Pacific theater of operations. During the winter of 1941–1942 the troops and squadrons undertook progressively longer marches of five, ten, and fifteen miles with full field equipment. This training culminated in a regimental march of twenty miles at a minimum rate of two and one-half miles per hour, a rate that Truscott's entire regiment, both officers and enlisted men, exceeded.[29]

Gradually, after the initial shock of the attack on Pearl Harbor and the entry of the nation into the war wore off, post social life returned, although somewhat restricted by the heightened security measures, the exodus of personnel transferred to other units, and the intensified training activities. Children, including young James Truscott, continued to attend the post elementary schools or the nearby city high schools, the weekly dinners and dances at the Officers' Club continued, the polo and football fields and the basketball courts bustled with activity, and the ladies busied themselves with their clubs and teas.[30]

A major event in the Truscott family's life occurred on December 31, 1941: Lucian Truscott received a temporary promotion to colonel, to date from December 24. It was undoubtedly with great pride that he exchanged the silver oak leaf of a lieutenant colonel for the spread-winged eagle of a colonel.[31]

During the early months of 1942 Truscott continued to prepare his regiment for the combat into which he hoped to lead it eventually. In April, however, his planning for the regiment's future was abruptly interrupted. As Truscott wrote, "On a Thursday morning in April, I had ridden out over the mesa to observe squad combat exercises below the rim. I had watched several exercises and was waiting for the range to clear and another to begin, when the regimental messenger dashed up and breathlessly informed me: 'Sir, Colonel, Washington's trying to get you on the phone. Sergeant Major says it's important and they want you to call right away.'"[32]

When Truscott galloped up to his headquarters, his adjutant informed him that Brig. Gen. Mark Clark, chief of staff of the Army Ground Forces (AGF), wanted him to return his call immediately. When he did so, Truscott learned that Clark wanted him to come to Washington within the next two or three days to leave for "an important assignment . . . a whale of an important job." He would be going overseas "for extended field service in a cold, not arctic, climate." Shortly thereafter, Truscott received a radiogram from Headquarters, Army Ground Forces (HQAGF), ordering him to report to the New York port of embarkation (POE) in Brooklyn for subsequent overseas shipment.[33]

When Truscott informed Sarah of his new assignment overseas, they decided that she and James would return to Charlottesville, where they would live with Sarah's parents at Wild Acres for the duration of his overseas tour. Mary had recently joined them at Fort Bliss, but she would not go with Sarah and James to Virginia. She had met a young cavalry officer, 1st Lt. Robert Wilbourn, and the two were united in "a whirlwind marriage" as James and his mother were packing to leave Fort Bliss. When Lieutenant Wilbourn left with the 1st Cavalry Division in 1943 for the Pacific theater of operations, Mary joined her mother and brother in Charlottesville, where she took a job as a secretary.[34]

Son Lucian had enlisted in the Army in 1941. After completing his studies at Millard's Preparatory School, he had passed the West Point entrance examinations in 1941 but was unable to secure a congressional appointment to the academy. He therefore decided to enlist in the Army, hoping to earn one of the academy appointments reserved for highly qualified Regular Army enlisted men. In 1942 he secured that appointment and entered West Point in the summer of 1942.[35]

Two days after he had talked with Clark, Truscott flew to Washington, thus beginning what he described laconically as "four eventful years." In his Official Military Personnel File now rested the latest Efficiency Report for the five-month period that he had served as commander of the 5th Cavalry Regiment. Brig. Gen. K. S. Bradford, commanding general of the 1st Cavalry Brigade, rated Truscott "Superior" in all categories and in the narrative portion of the report stated, "Colonel Truscott is one of the most efficient officers I have ever known. He is hard working, intelligent, forceful and has a real regard for the welfare of every man in his unit. During his command of the 5th Cavalry, he has improved the regiment in every way. He should be promoted to grade of brigadier general."[36]

Chapter 4

BIRTH OF THE RANGERS

Upon his arrival in Washington, Truscott reported for temporary duty with Army Ground Forces, commanded by Lt. Gen. Lesley J. McNair.[1] He immediately went to General Clark's office, where Clark explained to him that the Americans and British had agreed to an invasion of the European continent in the spring of 1943 and that Truscott and a number of other officers had been selected to join the staff of Vice Adm. Lord Louis Mountbatten, commander in chief of the Combined Operations Headquarters (COHQ), which was responsible for the British Commandos and for British amphibious training. Clark told Truscott that Maj. Gen. Dwight D. Eisenhower, head of the Operations Division of the War Department, would give him his specific instructions and that he was to report to Eisenhower's office in the Munitions Building for temporary duty with the ODWD.[2]

There, after inquiring of Truscott's recent activities and news of mutual friends, Eisenhower explained to Truscott why he had been called so suddenly to Washington. General Marshall had just returned from England, where he had conferred with the British about a planned cross-Channel invasion of the European continent in the spring of 1943, although if contingencies such as the imminent defeat of the Russian forces in the East required it the Allies could establish a limited front in France in the fall of 1942. He told Truscott that even as they spoke American forces were beginning to concentrate in the British Isles to undergo amphibious training and other training exercises to prepare for the invasion.

Although confident that American forces would be well trained for the operation, Marshall expressed concern that since none of the soldiers would have actual battle experience before invading Europe, he hoped that he could provide a small number of men in each assault unit with actual battle experience who could serve as instructors for their units and during the actual assault would serve as examples for their comrades. With that in mind he had arranged with Lord Mountbatten for a group of American officers, headed by Truscott, to serve in COHQ. The other officers of the team would join Truscott shortly, and while awaiting the arrival of those officers, Eisenhower suggested that Truscott avail himself of the opportunity to review all available information, talk to the officers who had accompanied Marshall to London, and gather the essential data to review with the other members of his team prior to meeting with Marshall in a few days. When Truscott pointed out to Eisenhower that his lack of any battle or amphibious operations experience and his limited contact with the U.S. Navy and the Army Air Corps in his career as a cavalryman might pose a problem as he met with the battle-seasoned British officers, Eisenhower replied, "I consider that your background as a cavalry officer, your experience with the Armored Force, your experience as an instructor at Leavenworth, your experience on a corps staff, and even your experience as a polo player especially fit you for this assignment. You know that Lord Louis wrote a book on polo. You can learn, can't you?"[3] Reassured by Eisenhower's comments, Truscott set about meeting with the officers who had accompanied Marshall to London, reviewing with them the plans for the invasion, the differences in British organizations and methods, and the potential problems Truscott's team might face.

Truscott and members of his team then embarked on a very busy and hectic schedule, attempting to learn in a very short time as much as possible about various British headquarters and British staff organization and procedures, relying on the British officers then posted to Washington for aid. Eisenhower assisted Truscott by discussing with him the problems he faced and by inviting him to sit in on discussions he had with other officers in the Operations Division, other divisions of the War Department, naval and air officers, congressmen, and the myriad of other visitors to his office.

In a few days General Marshall, whom Truscott had never met, sent for him. Marshall's first comment was that at age forty-seven, Truscott was an older man than he had wanted for the assignment, pointing out that Lord Mountbatten was forty-three and that most of his staff were younger and all had battle experience. He then went on to say, however, that "some of your friends assure me that you are younger than your years, and that your experience especially fits you for this assignment." After describing Mountbatten and his organization and its current activities and the part it would play in the upcoming cross-Channel operation, Marshall emphasized to Truscott the importance he attached to designing a training program that would give a small number of American soldiers sufficient battle experience that when they joined the American assault units they would "be able to counter the fears and uncertainties which imagination and rumor always multiply in combat . . . and would be able to disseminate practical information among their comrades."[4] Under Mountbatten's command British units would soon be carrying out raids on the German-occupied Continent, and it would be the team's responsibility to recruit volunteers from American units in the British Isles to participate in the training received by the British units and to join them in their upcoming raids.

Truscott then returned to Eisenhower's office and gave him a detailed report of his conversation with Marshall. At the conclusion of Truscott's report, Eisenhower called in a stenographer and dictated a letter of instructions to serve as a guide for the operations of Truscott and his team in England, as well as a letter of instruction to the commanding general, U.S. Army Forces in the British Isles, "on the subject of War Department representation at British headquarters."[5] The letter of instructions for Truscott directed the CG USAFBI to attach Truscott and his team to Lord Mountbatten's staff, where they would be working members, not merely observers. He outlined the following missions for the team:

> To study the planning, organization, preparation, and conduct of combined operations, especially those of Commando type . . . ; to initiate plans for participation by American troops in these operations to the fullest practicable extent with a view to affording actual battle experience to maximum personnel . . . ; to provide information and recommendations relative to the technique, training, and equipment involved in these and related operations . . . ; and to promote in every practicable way the spirit of cooperation and team play between the Allied forces.

In carrying out his mission Truscott was to retain as much as possible "the existing American command and administrative organization" and hold to a minimum the formation of new organizations and installations. Eisenhower emphasized that he should "keep in mind at all times that the principal objective of this program must be that of providing actual battle training for as many as practicable of our personnel."[6]

Truscott and his group had been originally scheduled to leave for London on or about May 4, but the date of departure was postponed to May 10, permitting Sarah and James to join Lucian in Washington for final good-byes before his departure. After a long flight, with stops in Montreal, Newfoundland, and Iceland, Truscott and the rest of his group reached Prestwick, Scotland, on May 16. During the overnight train ride to London, Truscott spent several hours in his compartment with a companion from the flight, Viscount Bowe-Lyon, who described the personalities of some of the men whom Truscott would soon meet and also described the psychological effects the German bombings had upon the British people, something Truscott had never before considered. In the morning, as the train approached London, Truscott saw for himself the destruction wrought by the enemy's bombs: partially and completely destroyed train stations, factories, warehouses, and homes.

Two representatives of Lord Mountbatten met Truscott and his party when the train arrived at St. Pancras Station the morning of May 17 and escorted them to the Grosvenor House, a luxury hotel near Hyde Park, where they were quartered until they were able to secure lodging in the home of Mrs. Gordon Leith at 1-A Manchester Square in early June. On May 18 Truscott was assigned to the plans section of HQ USAFBI,[7] and he and three others of his group were attached to Combined Operations Headquarters, British Army, to "carry out the instructions of the Commanding General [USAFBI]."[8]

After settling into his quarters, Truscott reported to HQ USAFBI, also located on Grosvenor Square, where Brig. Gen. Charles L. Bolté, the chief of staff, greeted him and promptly ushered him into the office of Maj. Gen. James E. Chaney, CG USAFBI, who had been in London since 1941, organizing the European theater of operations. Chaney examined Eisenhower's letter of instructions cursorily, but "gave no indication that he had any previous knowledge of [Truscott's] assignment or any interest whatever in the mission [he] was sent to perform."[9] After making a few short remarks, Chaney dismissed Truscott, who spent the remainder of the day visiting members of Chaney's staff and making a call at the American Embassy. As he met with members of the staff Truscott sensed a strong sense of disapproval of the idea that American officers were going to be working members of a British staff. Chaney and his deputy and G1, Brig. Gen. John E. Dahlquist, repeatedly expressed their disapproval of the idea, stating that liaison officers should carry out contact between Allied staffs. That attitude prevailed until General Eisenhower arrived in June to become the theater commander.

That same day Truscott and his fellow team members traveled to COHQ in the War Office Annex, where Mountbatten gracefully welcomed the Americans as working members of his staff and briefly explained the organization and functions of the headquarters: it was made up of ground, air, and naval officers, who would play a key role in "planning, training for, and carrying out the invasion agreed between the two countries." Mountbatten predicted that the combined Anglo-American staff of his headquarters would be the forerunner of the combined staff that the cross-Channel attack and the continuing operations would require. After his meeting with Mountbatten, Truscott wrote his wife, "I think that little of the newspaper enthusiasm about him is an exaggeration. . . . I see in him a hardness and perhaps a selfishness—or ambition that I have heard no one mention. I have mentioned it to no one but Eisenhower."[10]

Truscott was impressed with the emphasis his British compatriots placed on security. American officers, many of whom had had no access to classified information during their careers, were not nearly so security conscious. To illustrate the importance the British attached to security procedures, Truscott related a personal incident that almost ended his assignment to COHQ. After attending a meeting during which the cross-Channel invasion had been discussed, Truscott returned to his room and made a few notes about the discussion on a scrap of paper. As he prepared to go to dinner, he gathered up the materials on his desk, thinking he had included the notes, secured the material in his desk, and left, locking his room door. The next morning Mountbatten's senior intelligence officer, the marquis of Casa Maury, visited Truscott and handed him a piece of paper, asking him if he recognized it. Truscott admitted that it was the paper on which he had made some notes and asked the marquis how it had come into his possession. He said that it had been found in the courtyard in front of Truscott's quarters and had been turned over to him. He went on to point out that if he had informed Mountbatten of Truscott's breach of security, Mountbatten would have asked Marshall to relieve him immediately. Truscott offered no excuse and told the marquis that he "should let no consideration for an American officer stand in the way of what he would consider his duty if a British officer were involved." The marquis replied that since no harm had been done, "it would be better for future allied relations if no further action were taken." He also felt that Truscott "would never again be so remiss with regard to security measures," and his opinion proved to be correct.[11] In fact, Truscott related the incident on many subsequent occasions when he was trying to impress upon officers the importance of strictly adhering to all security measures.

At approximately the same time that Truscott was censured for his security lapse, he received great news: he had been promoted to the temporary grade of brigadier general, to date from May 24, and promptly informed his wife. The former elementary school teacher and principal, who lacked even a high school diploma, had come a long way indeed since he had pinned on the gold bar of a second lieutenant at Fort Logan H. Roots almost twenty-five years earlier. Truscott "was to find the promotion to general officer rank to be of no small assistance in [his] relations with others with whom [he] had to deal."[12]

Very early in his planning for American soldiers to gain battle experience, Truscott decided that such experience could best be gained by organizing a special unit along the lines of the British Commandos rather than by utilizing an existing American unit. To learn more about the organization and training of the Commandos, Truscott and his group traveled to locations within England and Scotland to observe various training exercises that COHQ was conducting. Among the most important of those trips was one where they observed two rehearsals for Operation RUTTER, a planned raid on the French port of Dieppe. On May 26 Truscott submitted to General Bolté his recommendations for the formation of American Commando units. He recommended that there be five or six companies, each numbering from four hundred to five hundred men. He also recommended that tentative Tables of Organization and Equipment similar to those of the

British Commandos be prepare and then forwarded those recommendations to the War Department for approval, which he received on May 28.[13]

Truscott then drafted a letter to Maj. Gen. Russell P. Hartle, commanding general of United States Army Northern Ireland Forces, "directing him to proceed with the organization of the unit with the least practicable delay." The unit, a battalion formed from troops in the USANIF, was to consist of a headquarters company of 8 officers and 69 men, and six lettered companies, each with 3 officers and 63 men, for an aggregate of 26 officers and 447 men.[14] Complying with Truscott's request, Hartle issued a June 7 directive to all forces under his command, assigning to each major unit quotas to be filled by volunteer officers, noncommissioned officers, and enlisted men who possessed "qualities of leadership of a high order, with particular emphasis on initiative, judgement, and common sense . . . natural athletic ability, physical stamina and [who] should be without physical defects." The selected personnel would move to Carrickfergus, Northern Ireland, where the battalion would organize.[15]

Before Truscott's departure from Washington, General Eisenhower had told him that if he found it necessary to organize new units he should choose a name for the units other than "Commandos," since that name would always be associated with the British units. From many names submitted to him for consideration, Truscott chose "Rangers," since "some of the oldest units in the Regular Army were originally organized as Rangers, and have carried the tradition into every war in which the nation has been engaged . . . and who exemplified such high standards of individual courage, initiative, determination, ruggedness, fighting ability, and achievement," qualities that he hoped to instill in the organizing battalion.[16]

General Hartle recommended that his aide, Maj. William O. Darby, an artillery officer who had graduated from West Point in 1933, command the Ranger battalion. "He had had experience in both pack and motorized artillery, as well as with cavalry and infantry . . . [and] had had amphibious training with one of our divisions in the United States." Truscott accepted Hartle's recommendation, and, as future events would demonstrate, it was a wise choice.[17] Darby selected a New York National Guard cavalry officer, Capt. Herman W. Dammer, as his executive officer (XO), and gave him responsibility for organization of the battalion staff, while simultaneously serving as the battalion S3.[18]

Darby and Colonel Hayford, a V Corps staff officer, personally interviewed and selected from the volunteer officers those who were to constitute the Ranger battalion. The selected officers, in groups of two, visited all units in Northern Ireland and interviewed at each unit headquarters the enlisted volunteers from that unit. All of the selected volunteers were then collected at Sunnyland Camp, Carrickfergus, where the battalion was activated on June 19.[19] Sixty percent of the volunteers came from the 34th Infantry Division, 30 percent from the 1st

Armored Division, and the remainder from other units of V Corps.[20] On that same day the battalion detailed seven officers and twelve enlisted men for temporary duty with the 2d Canadian Division at Coles, Isle of Wight, where it was training for a raid on Dieppe.

On June 25 Brigadier Leycock, commanding general of the Special Service Brigade, arrived at Sunnyland Camp to inspect the Rangers, whose basic training Leycock's officers and men were to conduct during the month of July at the Commando Depot at Achnacarry on the west coast of Scotland. The battalion, now comprising some six hundred officers and men, began training there on July 4.[21]

The training program for the Rangers was arduous and was supervised by the founder and commandant of the Commando Depot, Lt. Col. Charles E. Vaughn, known affectionately as "Laird of Achnacarry" or "Rommel of the North."[22] "Ranger officers carried out the same training as their men, and were expected to be the first to face its challenges." The training emphasized speed marches with full field gear, the Rangers on one occasion covering ten miles in eighty-seven minutes. Additional challenges included river and stream crossings, cliff climbing, weapons training, scouting and patrolling, small-unit tactics, hand-to-hand combat, map reading, first aid, amphibious training under live fire, and night operations. Safety was secondary to realism in training. The live-fire exercises were especially dangerous.[23]

The training particularly emphasized discipline and the need for cooperation among the unit members in facing the challenges of the training program and the actual combat that was to follow. Soldiers who did not measure up or were found to be unfit for physical or psychological reasons were returned to their units. When the training at Achnacarry concluded on July 31, Truscott visited the Commando Training Center and found that only five hundred of the more than six hundred who had begun the course had completed it. The others had been "weeded out," although one man had been killed and several had been wounded in live-fire exercises.[24]

On August 1 most of the battalion moved to the vicinity of Dorlin House, Argyll, Scotland, to undergo training in landing operations, while a detachment of four officers and forty enlisted men were placed on detached service with Nos. 3 and 4 Commandos to train for the Dieppe operation, scheduled to take place later that month. After completing the training at Dorlin House on August 31, the battalion moved to Dundee, Scotland, to work with No. 1 Commando, then training for Operation TORCH, the invasion of North Africa. On September 24 the battalion was assigned to the U.S. II Corps and attached to the 1st Infantry Division at Corkerhill Camp, near Glasgow. In mid-October the Rangers participated in a final assault exercise at Loch Linnhe, Argyll, and on October 26 boarded former ferryboats in the River Clyde, joining a convoy that soon set sail for North Africa.[25]

DIEPPE

The British had for some time been carrying out raids along the German-occupied coastline from Saint-Nazaire, France, to Norway, and although those raids had been successful in tying down German garrison troops and in raising the morale and fighting spirit of the British people and their armed forces, they had done little to halt the advances of the enemy in the East. In the summer of 1942 the British government found itself under considerable pressure from the Soviet Union and the United States to open a second front in Europe to draw off some of the forces driving into the Soviet Union homeland.

However, Great Britain lacked the forces and means to mount a full-scale amphibious operation and sustain a lodgment on the Continent. Its major ally, the United States, was still mobilizing, and the forces mobilized to date were not sufficiently trained to take part in such an operation. But the Allies believed that they could mount a raid that would cause the Germans to consider the possibility of a major attack in the West and compel them to strengthen that sector with forces withdrawn from other areas of operation, including the eastern front. Such a raid would also provide an opportunity to gain experience in large-scale amphibious operations and to test new equipment and operational techniques. Churchill referred the matter to his chiefs of staff and to Mountbatten's Combined Operations Headquarters. The chiefs and Mountbatten suggested a large-scale raid against a port along the Pas de Calais coastline and recommended Dieppe, where German coastal convoys and E-boats frequently harbored and lay only seventy miles from the British coastline, close enough to allow the raiding force to approach under cover of darkness and well within the range of British aircraft.[26]

Mountbatten's staff concluded that the operation should be a reconnaissance in force rather than a raid, since the former would provide an opportunity to demonstrate whether the Allies could mount a large-scale amphibious operation and then sustain the forces in the lodgment area. The plan that the chiefs ultimately accepted called for a heavy aerial bombardment of the objective, followed by a frontal assault by tanks and infantry directly on the town's beach, with supporting landings both east and west of the town. Airborne troops would seize and destroy the two heavy gun batteries at Varengeville and Berneval that commanded the approaches to Dieppe. The chiefs dubbed the operation RUTTER and scheduled the assault for early July, when the tides would be suitable. Mountbatten's planners soon discovered that the operation was too large for only the Commandos to carry out and recommended that regular ground troops be added. The 2d Canadian Division, commanded by Maj. Gen. John H. Roberts, which was already in that area, received the nod, bringing the force to a total strength of six thousand.

Intelligence indicated that Dieppe was not heavily defended and that the beaches were suitable for landing infantry and tanks. Although there was some concern expressed, particularly by Mountbatten, about a direct frontal assault of the enemy position, the plan was approved. One half hour before the main assault, two Canadian battalions would land, one to the east (Blue Beach) and the other to the west (Green Beach) of Dieppe, to seize the headlands overlooking the town. Another battalion would follow across Green Beach to seize the airfield behind the town. Two battalions from the 2d Canadian Division, supported by a tank battalion, engineers, and naval gunfire, would assault Red and White Beaches in front of the town, while a battalion of paratroopers would attack the coastal batteries at Varengeville and Berneval. One Canadian battalion would serve as a floating reserve and land on call on the main beaches. It would form a defensive perimeter toward the end of the operation when the assaulting divisions began their withdrawal. The operation was to begin between July 4 and July 8, weather permitting.

On May 20 the Canadians began intensive amphibious training on the Isle of Wight, where they were joined on June 19 by seven officers and twelve enlisted men from Truscott's newly formed Rangers. Early in July the troops boarded their assault craft, but adverse weather conditions and a German bombing raid convinced Mountbatten to cancel the operation.[27] However, Truscott believed that the aborted operation had been of considerable value for the commanders and staffs, who had gained valuable experience in planning and making preparations for a sizable amphibious operation, in the process uncovering many problems in "communications, security, coordination, planning, and administrative arrangements, all of which could be corrected before the operation was again mounted."[28]

Mountbatten and his staff immediately began lobbying Churchill and the chiefs to authorize another assault on Dieppe. Despite the concerns of many, including Gen. Bernard L. Montgomery, that the security of the operation might have been compromised by the failed attempt to launch RUTTER, Mountbatten received authorization to plan another operation, JUBILEE. The new operation, a raid rather than a reconnaissance in force, would utilize much of the plan for RUTTER, the only major change being that two Commando companies rather than airborne troops would neutralize the German coastal batteries at Berneval and Varengeville.[29]

About a week before the scheduled date of the operation, Mountbatten informed Truscott that in addition to the observers he chose to accompany him to Dieppe he could select about fifty Rangers who would actually participate in the landings. Consequently, Truscott ordered Major Darby to select six officers and forty-four enlisted men from his battalion who would be attached to either the Commandos or the Canadians.[30] For reasons not stated, Darby selected only four officers and thirty-six enlisted men to participate in JUBILEE.[31]

The troops attacking Dieppe would encounter significant difficulties. During the more than two years it had occupied the town the German 571st Infantry Regiment had created a strong set of defenses behind the beaches, including barbed-wire entanglements, booby traps, and concrete pillboxes, as well as artillery, machine guns, and antiaircraft guns on the headlands and flanks. The only significant potential weakness in the defenses was the relatively small number of defenders, approximately seventeen hundred, defending a roughly ten-mile front.[32]

The attacking forces came largely from the 2d Canadian Division and its supporting Canadian 14th Tank Battalion. Augmenting the infantrymen and tankers were Nos. 3 and 4 Commando and Royal Marine A Commando. Supporting the raiding force were the Royal Navy, the Royal Air Force (RAF), and four American B-17 squadrons.[33] The plan of attack called for the Canadians to land over two beaches fronting Dieppe, while other Canadian units landed to the east and west to seize the headlands and destroy enemy artillery positions, a radio station, and the airfield at St. Aubin. The tank battalion was to land behind the infantry on the beaches and assist in the capture of Dieppe. The mission of the Commandos was to capture and destroy the batteries at Varengeville and Berneval.

Truscott was alerted about noon on August 18 that he and the other American observers were to proceed to Portsmouth that evening. When Truscott asked General Clark, Eisenhower's deputy, for authorization to observe JUBILEE, Clark refused on the grounds of security, since Truscott had been intimately involved in the planning for Operation TORCH. Truscott immediately appealed to General Eisenhower, who granted the authorization. On his arrival at Portsmouth, Truscott boarded HMS *Fernie,* which immediately got under way to join the forming convoy.[34]

Preceded by minesweepers the convoy began its voyage to Dieppe. For several hours the journey was uneventful, but at about four in the morning the horizon was illuminated by a star flare and enemy gunfire—the craft carrying No. 3 Commando had encountered a small German convoy. The ensuing sea fight scattered the craft carrying the Commandos, and most of the men never reached shore. In addition, the fight had alerted the German defenders, who soon overwhelmed those few Commandos who came ashore at Berneval. One landing craft, carrying some Rangers, was unable to land and cruised westward to Dieppe, where the Americans went ashore and joined in taking under fire shore batteries and enemy aircraft. The Canadian units that landed at Puys to the east and Pourville to the west of Dieppe met similar resistance and were unable to carry out their assigned missions. Only No. 4 Commando to the west was able to complete its mission, capturing and destroying the guns of Hess Battery, after which it withdrew safely.

The main attack in front of Dieppe took place a half hour after the flank landings. The Canadians landing over the eastern beach met heavy machine-gun fire, were unable to breach the seawall, and were driven back, suffering heavy losses. To the west the Canadian infantrymen were able to seize the casino in their sector, and a small number of men were able to enter the town. Learning that Canadians were in Dieppe, Maj. Gen. John H. Roberts, the force commander, committed his reserve forces, but they met a similar fate on the bloody beaches in front of Dieppe. The tank battalion, landing behind the infantry, met "an inferno of fire" that brought its advance to a halt. Although immobilized, the gallant tankers continued to fight to the end.[35]

Truscott had been watching the action on the beaches from the deck of the *Fernie* as the ship moved shoreward. Suddenly, a crash threw him against the railing of the causeway next to which he had been standing. The whole ship shuddered, and he felt something strike his boot and clatter to the deck. He picked up the object, a metal nut that had torn loose when a shell struck aft of the superstructure, killing or wounding sixteen men. The captain immediately turned the ship seaward, laying a smoke screen as he did so.[36]

The performance of the RAF was disappointing. Although the units were at first able to provide air cover for the ships in the Channel, their initial ground attacks were unsuccessful in taking out any significant numbers of the emplaced artillery. At first they encountered no opposing German aircraft, but as the day wore on, increasing numbers of German fighters appeared. One of the aims of the RAF senior commanders had been to draw out the Luftwaffe, which they succeeded in doing. However, to the RAF's dismay, their aircraft losses exceeded those of the Germans.[37]

At about nine o'clock General Roberts made the decision to withdraw the force, and by late morning the withdrawal and evacuation were under way. The evacuation at all beaches was chaotic, as men rushed for the landing craft, sometimes causing them to capsize. Other craft were destroyed by German fire. Compounding the problem was a shortage of landing craft, some having been ordered to return to England after landing their troops. At approximately one o'clock further attempts at evacuation were abandoned, leaving large numbers of troops stranded on the beach to face death, wounding, or capture by the Germans. When the *Fernie* received news of the order to begin the withdrawal, "Brigadier Mann, Chief of Staff, 1st [*sic*] Canadian Division," turned to Truscott and remarked, "General, I am afraid that this operation will go down as one of the great failures of history."[38]

As the evacuation proceeded, the *Fernie* once again headed toward the shore. Nearing the beachhead, the ship encountered enemy machine-gun fire that struck it repeatedly. Truscott now had a close-up view of the beaches and was particularly impressed by the courage of the men manning the landing craft who, even though under "withering fire," continued steering their craft toward the shore to evacuate the waiting men. Some craft successfully reached the beach, took waiting men on board, and turned seaward. Others were struck by the withering incoming fire and sank.[39]

With the *Fernie* bringing up the rear, the convoy then began its sad return to Portsmouth, bearing those who had survived the landings unscathed and those who had been wounded during the vicious fighting. On board the *Fernie*, Truscott recalled that "every nook and cranny was filled with wounded for we had taken on board from the landing craft all that we could carry." German aircraft pursued the convoy almost to the English coast before turning away, bombing and strafing the withdrawing ships. Fortunately, the *Fernie* was not hit, although some bombs and shells came, in Truscott's words, "uncomfortably close."[40]

Truscott found himself drawn to a wardroom, the floor of which was carpeted by wounded men. As he watched them he pulled a bag of tobacco from his pocket and rolled a cigarette for himself. Seeing Truscott smoking, one of the wounded men asked him, "I say, you wouldna have another un about yuh?" Truscott gave the man his cigarette and then continued to roll cigarettes for the other wounded until the tobacco sack was empty. Soon the only sounds he heard "were the labored breaths of grievously wounded men and the cheerful words of thanks from those who smoked." Near midnight the *Fernie* reached Portsmouth, where the wounded were transferred to hospital trains. After bidding farewell to the ship's captain and other officers whom he had accompanied on the voyage, Truscott caught the train to London, "a sadder and wiser man."[41]

"Of the 4,963 Canadians who embarked for the operation, only 2,210 returned to England, and many of those were wounded. There were 3,367 casualties, including 1,946 prisoners of war; 907 Canadians lost their lives."[42] Of the forty American Rangers who had participated in the raid, two officers and five enlisted men were missing, and seven enlisted men had been wounded. Four of the missing enlisted men were later reported to be prisoners of war.[43] 2nd Lt. Edwin V. Loustalot, originally listed as missing, was later declared dead, the first American soldier to die in ground combat on the European continent.[44] Pvt. Frank Koons, who served with No. 4 Commando, became the first American soldier to kill a German in the European theater and received the Military Medal for bravery, the third-highest British decoration for enlisted men for military gallantry.[45]

The day after the raid Truscott wrote to his wife, "I have seen war—and have been in danger—and have seen men die, on land, in the sea, in the ship. . . . It was a thrilling experience. . . . It was not a success—and all told was a rather grim and gory business. But I have learned many things from having gone, and confirmation of many others. . . . I have seen gallantry and courage in the raw."

Although JUBILEE was a tactical failure, Truscott believed it "proved the practicability and feasibility of the amphibious invasions we were then planning . . . [and] was convinced that the force engaged at Dieppe could have captured the place and established a beachhead had the operation been undertaken with that in mind rather than as a raid with an immediate withdrawal." Gordon A. Harrison concluded that the Allies learned much from the raid, which impressed "planners [for OVERLORD] with the hardness of the enemy's fortified shell and the consequent need for concentrating the greatest possible weight in the initial assault in order to crack it." Whether it was a direct result of the Dieppe raid or not, "planning in the winter of 1942–43 [for the cross-Channel attack] took a new turn" and abandoned the plan for "many separate regimental and commando assaults . . . [for] one main landing in an area capable of development into a lodgment for the whole Allied invasion force." Leonard Mosley states, "The only people in any way satisfied by the raid were those advisors of Winston Churchill, like [Professor Frederick] Lindemann and [Gen.] Sir Alan Brooke [chief of the Imperial General Staff], who thought it would prove to the Americans once and for all that a second front across the Channel was unthinkable for at least another year."[46]

Truscott would put to good use the experience he gained from the Dieppe operation as he participated in the planning for and execution of Operation TORCH and the additional three major amphibious operations in which he would play key roles in the next two years. As he looked back on the operation, he concluded that "the Allies had gained experience on how to plan and conduct large scale assaults, and what weapons and equipment such assaults would require. It gave the German General Staff cause for alarm as to where the next blow would fall. . . . A little more than two months later, TORCH flamed in Africa," the first major Allied offensive operation in the European and Mediterranean theaters of operation, which would be commanded by his old friend Dwight D. Eisenhower and in which he was to play an important role.[47]

Chapter 5

OPERATION TORCH

THE INVASION OF NORTH AFRICA

In September 1941, Gen. Sir John Dill, chief of the Imperial General Staff, directed the British military planners to draw up plans for a return of the Allies to the European continent, taking into account the capabilities of the Americans to support that operation. The planners concluded that although "the greatest contribution to the Allied cause in 1942 would be to divert enemy forces from the Eastern Front," the German fortifications along the Channel coasts of the occupied countries precluded such an operation in 1942.[1]

American planners were also giving attention to an early attack on the German forces in Western Europe and, "committed to the policy of defeating Germany first," began in early 1942 to move troops to the British Isles. To command and control those troops, Headquarters, U.S. Army Forces in the British Isles (HQ USAFBI) was established in London, and V Corps was sent to Northern Ireland.[2]

On February 28 General Eisenhower, then chief of the War Plans Division of the War Department, issued a memorandum articulating the views of Gen. George C. Marshall, the Army's chief of staff, on implementing the policy of "Germany first." A key recommendation in the memorandum was that the United States should plan for and conduct early operations in Western Europe to draw sizable elements of German ground and air forces from the eastern front and defend the Middle East and Indian theaters.[3]

Eisenhower and his staff immediately set about developing a plan for employing American forces to implement the "Germany first" policy. It envisioned three operations: BOLERO, the buildup of men and matériel in the British Isles for a cross-Channel attack in 1943; ROUNDUP, the 1943 invasion of the Continent; and SLEDGEHAMMER, a limited attack to be launched in the fall of

1942, but only if the "German successes became 'so complete as to threaten the imminent collapse of Russian resistance unless pressure is relieved by an attack from the west by British and American troops.'"[4]

On April 1 President Roosevelt approved the plan and sent Harry Hopkins, one of his closest advisers, and Marshall to London to win agreement from the British to place it into action. On April 9 Marshall presented the plan to the British Chiefs of Staff, who, after lengthy discussion with the Americans, accepted it on April 14, with the reservation that any action in 1942 would have to be determined by developments on the eastern front. Later that evening Churchill told Marshall that he accepted the plan with "no hesitation."[5] However, scarcely had Marshall and Hopkins left England when Churchill began to have doubts about the feasibility of a cross-Channel attack in the near future. In June, when he and Gen. Sir Alan Brooke, who had replaced General Dill, visited Washington, they indicated that although the Allies should still be prepared to mount an attack in 1942, they should consider alternative operations "in case no sound and successful plan for the cross-Channel attack could be contrived," proposing as one of the alternatives an attack in North Africa.

That suggestion did not sit well with Marshall and the other American Joint Chiefs. Marshall believed that "if the Allies did not divert enemy forces from the Russian front in 1942 a full-scale attack might be ineffective in 1943." Further, Marshall believed that American participation in an attack in North Africa would make the continuation of BOLERO in 1942 impossible and would delay, if not make impossible, the carrying out of ROUNDUP in 1943.

On June 25 the American Chiefs of Staff established their headquarters for the European theater of operations in London to oversee the buildup of U.S. forces in Great Britain and named General Eisenhower theater commander. Three weeks later Roosevelt sent Adm. Ernest J. King, chief of naval operations, Marshall, and Hopkins to London to get from the British an agreement for operations in 1942, stressing to them the importance of getting American forces into action to aid the Soviets that year, a necessity that Soviet Foreign Minister Vyacheslav M. Molotov had pointed out in a May meeting with Roosevelt. The president still believed that SLEDGEHAMMER would serve that purpose, but if facts showed it to be impossible, then they were to consider other options to use American forces in 1942.[6]

On the day of his arrival in London, July 18, Marshall asked General Truscott to meet with him in his suite at Claridge's Hotel. Marshall greeted him warmly and immediately began inquiring about his assignment and his activities, his impression of Mountbatten, and his opinions of British organization and methods. He then asked Truscott to join him in a Scotch and soda and to stay for dinner. After dinner the questioning continued, with Marshall specifically asking how the people at Combined Operations felt about SLEDGEHAMMER. Truscott told him that the raid planners believed an operation to seize the Cherbourg peninsula "was not only practicable and within our means, but that it would be a desirable operation to undertake during the fall in preparation for ROUNDUP the following spring . . . [but] that the next higher level in COHQ—the Advisers—had disagreed with them." About ten o'clock Generals Eisenhower and Clark joined them, and Admiral King and a few others came in a little later. Marshall repeated to them what Truscott had told him and directed them to prepare an outline plan that he could present to the British Chiefs of Staff when he met with them to discuss the 1942 and 1943 operations.[7]

However, by the time of their meeting with Marshall, King, and Hopkins, the British had arrived at a firm conclusion that their commitments in other theaters of war would preclude their participation in a 1942 attack on the Continent and that carrying out SLEDGEHAMMER would "ruin prospects for ROUNDUP in 1943." Hearing the British objections, Marshall realized that an alternative plan for 1942 would have to be developed and so informed Roosevelt. Roosevelt and Churchill discussed the matter further, and on July 25 Roosevelt accepted the plan to invade North Africa that year, and told Churchill and Marshall, King, and Hopkins of his decision. In early August, Roosevelt chose Eisenhower as the commander of the operation, code-named Operation TORCH. However, just as Marshall had feared, the North African operation, by diverting resources and men to it, would interfere seriously with BOLERO in 1942, rendering ROUNDUP in 1943 impracticable.[8]

On July 25 Mountbatten told his planners that the Combined Chiefs had decided the previous day that TORCH would be the next operation, that President Roosevelt had accepted the plan, and that they were to initiate planning for the operation immediately. TORCH included the seizure of Casablanca, Oran, Algiers, and the whole of French North Africa and would require at least twelve divisions, landing at three or more sites. Although both British and American forces would be used, only American troops would be in the assault waves for "political reasons." Planning for ROUNDUP and SLEDGEHAMMER, now code-named WET BOB, would continue, although Mountbatten emphasized that if TORCH were carried out, it would postpone ROUNDUP until 1944, and specifically directed Truscott and three British officers to prepare "an appreciation visualizing SLEDGEHAMMER–WET BOB blossoming into ROUNDUP perhaps in 1944." The final decision for TORCH would be made on or before September 15.[9]

After Truscott returned from the Dieppe operation, Mountbatten informed him that General Eisenhower had assumed overall command of TORCH and that he would name an Allied staff to take over the planning for the operation in Norfolk House, London. Having promised Eisenhower that COHQ would cooperate with him in every way, Mountbatten appointed Truscott as head of a "syndicate" that would "coordinate and direct the work" of three additional syndicates, the four syndicates totaling some twenty men, all of whom Mountbatten would make available to Eisenhower to assist in planning the operation. The final plan for the operation called for assaults on the Atlantic coast of French Morocco and at Oran, Algiers, and Bône. However, the British, believing that naval resources were insufficient to support the proposed simultaneous landings in French Morocco and inside the Mediterranean, recommended that the French Morocco landings be abandoned, which the planners initially accepted.[10]

Maj. Gen. George S. Patton, Jr., whom Marshall had selected to command the Western Task Force that would be sailing from the United States to land in French Morocco, arrived in London on August 9. The following morning Patton visited Norfolk House, where Truscott briefed him on the plans as of that date, pointing out that the current plan did not include a landing on the Atlantic coast of French Morocco, instead calling for Patton's task force (TF) to land at Oran. In view of the change in plans for Patton's task force, Truscott made his syndicate available to Patton to assist him in preparing his initial plans and estimates.

After Truscott's briefing Patton, who had known Truscott since their polo-playing days and time together at Fort Myer in the early 1930s, offered him a command in his task force. Truscott replied that "if there was to be any fighting [he] certainly wanted to be in on it," and if Patton could convince Eisenhower to release him, he "would be happy to go with him." Patton later informed Truscott that Eisenhower had given his approval.[11]

Several days later Eisenhower named Maj. Gen. Mark W. Clark deputy commander in chief for TORCH, with responsibility for planning and gathering an Allied staff for the simultaneous assaults at Oran, Algiers, and Bône. The assault force for Oran was to come from the United States, would be commanded by Patton, and would consist of one infantry division, a regimental combat team, and a regiment-size armored force.[12] The British 78th Division, with an attached American RCT, was to make three landings to secure Algiers and two nearby airfields. Darby's 1st Ranger Battalion was to land and capture Bône and an airfield six miles inland. A follow-on British force of brigade strength would land at Bône when conditions permitted.

Since Patton would have to undertake the detailed planning for his force's mission after he returned to the United States, he directed Truscott and his group to obtain prior to his departure the information that he would need to direct his staff in the planning process. By the time he left England on August 19 Patton carried with him "the intelligence which we had assembled, a skeletonized assault plan which would provide a basis for further planning, and outline military, naval, and air plans for all of the assaults."[13]

Before he left for Dieppe, Truscott had discussed with Patton his future assignment for TORCH, and they had reached an understanding that Truscott would remain in London for only a week or so after his return from Dieppe and then would join Patton in Washington. However, on his return Truscott learned from

Clark that he would remain in London as Patton's deputy, there to represent Patton and "to insure complete coordination of the various assault plans and to keep General Patton informed of current decisions and developments."

On the twenty-fifth Truscott told Patton that the plan for TORCH had once again been changed—a landing on the Atlantic coast by Patton's Western Task Force was again being considered—and that he had put his team to work "on Casablanca, as well as investigating Spanish Morocco and Tangiers." Apparently, the American Chiefs of Staff felt that an operation solely inside the Straits of Gibraltar posed potential danger to the assault forces because of the possibility that Spain might permit the Germans to send a force through the country to seize Gibraltar and trap the Allies within the Mediterranean. Also, seizure of Casablanca would provide a large modern port, as well as good road and rail connections to Oran and Algiers.

As Truscott and his group continued their planning for the Casablanca operation, they had to consider the reaction of the Vichy French forces in Morocco to the American landings. Although they hoped that the French would put up only "token resistance," the plans had to be drawn up assuming that the Americans might meet stiff French defense, since intelligence revealed that there was considerable support in Morocco for the Vichy government of Marshal Henri Pétain.

Initially, the syndicate had considered a direct assault on the city of Casablanca itself, but rejected it because of the port's strong seaward defenses and the strong French naval forces based there. They next looked at beaches near the city but found them unacceptable. There were, however, a few ports farther from the city that would permit successful landings unless the weather conditions were extremely violent: Fedala, a few miles north of Casablanca; Port Lyautey, approximately 80 miles north; and Safi, about 130 miles south of the city.

The outline plan that the group developed called for the main landings to be made by one division and an attached armored RCT in the vicinity of Fedala to seize its port. The assault force, assisted by air and naval forces, would then capture Casablanca. A secondary landing would be made opposite Port Lyautey near the mouth of the Sebou River to open the river and seize an airfield that lay a short distance inland. When Patton left London he carried with him a draft of that plan, and now Truscott forwarded copies of the updated plan and current intelligence to Patton on September 6.

On the same date Patton sent his initial estimate and plan for the Casablanca operation to General Eisenhower. The plan called for the landing of a division less one RCT but with an attached armored RCT at Fedala. Two battalion combat teams and an armored battalion combat team would carry out a secondary landing at Rabat, roughly midway between Port Lyautey and Fedala, to capture an airfield there. One infantry BCT and one armored BCT were to make a "subsidiary" landing at Safi to capture the port and secure a beachhead. If

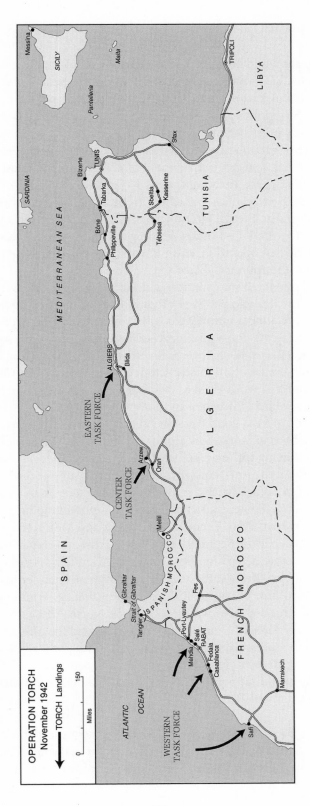

additional armor could be landed, it would drive inland some 60 miles to seize Marrakech. One RCT would be held as a floating reserve.

Eisenhower sent Patton's estimate and plan to Truscott for his review and comments. In his reply, copies of which were sent to Patton, Truscott pointed out that Patton's proposed attack on Marrakech would have little or no effect on the capture of Casablanca and that emphasis should be placed on securing at least one airfield and neutralizing its French aircraft. He and his group felt that the best chance for early capture of an airfield was at Port Lyautey. Otherwise, carrier-based aviation, parachute troops, and saboteurs would have to be used to neutralize French aircraft. The final plan for Patton's Western Task Force substituted the Port Lyautey landing for the proposed assault at Rabat and retained the Safi operation, since it would provide the necessary armor to assist in the assault upon Casablanca.

Two vital elements of information that Patton was missing were up-to-date intelligence estimates and aerial photographs of his area of operations. Such intelligence came almost entirely from British sources, and Truscott found it necessary to delay his departure for Washington in order to acquire that vital information. Fortuitously, two Frenchmen were smuggled into London at just that time. One was Carl Victor Clopet, who had lived in Casablanca for twelve years and had worked there in salvage operations, giving him "an intimate knowledge of ports, beaches, and coast defenses along the entire Moroccan coast as well as internal conditions in French Morocco." The other was Jules Malavergne, who had worked as a pilot on the Sebou River at Port Lyautey. In addition to having intimate knowledge of the river, he was able to provide information about the pro-Nazi sentiment in Port Lyautey, which was stronger than elsewhere in French Morocco. Both men were sent on to General Patton.

Having obtained the necessary intelligence and photographic coverage of the assault areas, Truscott, Maj. Theodore J. Conway, and Maj. Pierpont M. Hamilton prepared to depart on September 19. While Truscott was paying his respects to Eisenhower before departing, Gen. Charles de Gaulle's chief of staff was ushered into Eisenhower's office. He told the supreme commander that General de Gaulle had asked him to convey his expectation that he would be named the commander in chief of any invasion of French North Africa, to which Eisenhower laconically replied, "Thank you," and dismissed the officer.[14]

Unable to bid a personal farewell to Lord Mountbatten, who was in an operations meeting, Truscott left a letter for him. On September 18 Mountbatten replied, stating how disappointed he was that he had been unable to meet with him. He went on to tell Truscott:

> It has been the greatest privilege for a British officer to have so distinguished an American officer on his staff and I suppose it must be the first time in history that a British naval officer has had an American general on his staff.

We British are not awfully good at expressing our feelings, as you probably know, and you may not therefore have guessed what a very warm feeling all of us had for you, but it has increased our confidence in the ultimate victory of the United Nations to feel that there are men of your calibre in high positions in the American army.[15]

Truscott looked back on his time at Mountbatten's headquarters very fondly, stating that he had "learned much from my British associates, especially in the preparation of staff papers and the technique of planning." What he had learned was "invaluable to [him] throughout the war."[16]

OPERATION GOALPOST

Upon his arrival in Washington, Truscott reported to the Munitions Building, the home of the War Department. There he learned that he would command Sub–Task Force GOALPOST, which would carry out the assault on Port Lyautey. The sub–task force totaled 9,079 officers and men and included the 60th RCT, an armored BCT, elements of a tank battalion, and seven self-propelled coast artillery antiaircraft batteries.[17] Truscott's mission was to capture the airfield at Port Lyautey, where the American aircraft brought to North Africa aboard carriers would land and take off to carry out their missions.

On September 26 Truscott attended a meeting of commanders of the Western Task Force, at the conclusion of which he traveled to Fort Bragg, where the infantry and armored units of his sub–task force were located. When he arrived there he found to his consternation that he had no assigned staff and immediately began a search for staff officers. To serve as chief of staff he turned to an old friend, Col. Don C. Carleton, who had served as his S3 in the 5th Cavalry. The other principal staff officers whom Truscott selected were Lt. Col. Oliver T. Sanborn, Jr., G1; Maj. Pierpont M. Hamilton, G2; Lt. Col. Van H. Bond, G3; and Lt. Col. Donald M. Libby, G4. Until Carleton and the others arrived, Maj. Theodore J. Conway, who had joined Truscott at Fort Bragg on September 28, would serve as his "staff."[18]

As Truscott turned to the planning he realized that "there was much to be done and all too little time for doing it." His advance parties were due to report to the port of embarkation on October 7, and the loaded transports were to clear their berths on October 16, just a little more than two weeks hence. In the interval a multitude of tasks lay before him and his staff, including the preparation of detailed intelligence plans; communications, administrative, air, and naval gunfire plans; loading and embarkation plans; orders for movement of troops to the POE; and rehearsal plans, as well as the gathering of all available intelligence. On October 9 Truscott met with the commanders of his assault units, Col. Frederic J. de Rohan, commander of the 60th Infantry RCT, and Lt. Col. Harry Semmes, commander of the 1st BCT, 66th Armored Regiment. He found both of them to be very capable officers, with well-organized staffs. Their units were well trained and at almost 100 percent strength and had received some amphibious training.

One major handicap was the fact that Rear Adm. Monroe Kelly, commander of the Northern Attack Group that would transport Truscott's sub–task force to Africa, had not yet assembled his command, and none of his staff was available, forcing Truscott to turn to Kelly's superior, Rear Adm. Henry K. Hewitt, commander of the Western Naval Task Force, for assistance in planning the operation. However, Hewitt was in Norfolk, and there were no locally available naval representatives at Truscott's level of command with whom he could work during the planning phase.

Colonel Carleton's arrival on October 5 considerably lightened the load that Truscott and Conway had been carrying, and by October 10 they had met most of their planning deadlines, including dispatching the advance parties to the POE and issuing orders for the movement of the remainder of the sub–task force to the port over the next five days by road and rail. On October 10 he forwarded the finished tactical plan for GOALPOST to Patton.[19]

Just two days later Truscott learned that many supplies, including ammunition, had not arrived as scheduled and that there were significant ship-loading problems. Truscott, Carleton, and Hamilton went to Norfolk to consult with Admiral Hewitt, where they learned the major difficulty appeared to be the inexperience of the port personnel, stevedores, transport quartermasters, and the troops themselves in loading the vessels for amphibious operations. The problems were ultimately resolved, and by nightfall of the fifteenth all of the troops had been embarked and by the following morning all of the supplies had been loaded. At 1:40 p.m. on the sixteenth the task force set sail from Norfolk for Solomons Island in Chesapeake Bay just off the mouth of the Patuxent River.[20] General Patton had traveled to Norfolk to observe the loading and confided to his journal, "While things were not going perfect, they were satisfactory. . . . I am just a little worried about [the] ability of Truscott. It may be [my] nerves."[21] Truscott's later performance at Port Lyautey would convincingly prove to Patton that his concern about Truscott's ability was without basis.

As the task force got under way, Truscott looked back on the past twenty days with considerable satisfaction. In that time he and his staff had organized a "Sub–Task Force Headquarters of sorts. We had planned and issued orders for an operation and a rehearsal. We had assembled and loaded a diverse command of more than forty units totaling nearly 9,000 men, 800 vehicles and tanks, nearly 100 towed weapons of various kinds, and 15,000 tons of cargo. . . . It is not surprising that there had been confusion, for one learns that it is a customary adjunct of war."[22] However, all things considered, it was a tour de force by Truscott and his staff.

Truscott's sub–task force arrived off Solomons Island on the seventeenth, and immediately the troops began the rehearsal for the landings at Port Lyautey, practicing loading into the assault craft from cargo nets dangling over the sides of the ships, which also provided an opportunity for the ships' crews to gain proficiency in lowering and handling the landing craft. The rehearsal plan envisioned that one day would be spent in that exercise, followed by a daylight landing rehearsal the next day that would adhere to the operation plan "as closely as possible." Since the actual landing would take place at night, a night landing rehearsal would take place the following day. After each of the rehearsals Truscott had allotted time for identifying and correcting deficiencies and for additional training for both troop and naval commanders.

Aboard the USS *Allen,* Truscott once more studied the operation plan for Sub–Task Force GOALPOST. Truscott's forces had been given four missions, which in order of priority were the capture and securing of Mehdia and the airfield three kilometers northwest of Port Lyautey, capturing and holding Port Lyautey, capturing and securing the airfield at Rabat-Salé, and reconnoitering to the north and northeast to gain contact with hostile forces in the area while protecting the north flank of the beachhead.

To carry out the assigned missions one battalion landing team of the RCT was to land north of the mouth of the Sebou River above Mehdia, advance inland to a point opposite the airfield, cross the river in boats, and assist in capturing the airfield. A second BLT was to land on the beach in front of Mehdia and capture the coast artillery battery in Mehdia's Casbah, the old native quarter of the town. A third BLT would land south of Mehdia, move inland, secure the south flank of the beachhead, and advance rapidly to the northeast to the western outskirts of Port Lyautey to block its western exits and assist in capturing the airfield. The armored battalion would follow either of the latter two BLTs, advance rapidly to the south, secure the southern flank, and be prepared either to assist in the capture the airfield at Port Lyautey or to capture the airfield to the south at Rabat-Salé. As soon as the coastal batteries in the Casbah had been silenced, a destroyer carrying a special raiding detachment was to proceed up the Sebou River to the vicinity of the airfield, where the raiding party would go ashore to attack the rear of enemy forces and assist in the capture of the airfield. After the capture of the airfield and on Truscott's order, the pilots aboard the carriers were to take off, destroy hostile aircraft on the ground or in the air, provide close ground support for the ground forces, and carry out other support missions as ordered by the sub–task force commander.[23]

On October 18 the first of the rehearsals, a daylight landing, took place. The first problem confronting Truscott was that Hewitt's headquarters had restricted Truscott's force to the use of only one beach rather than the use of all of the available beaches as Hewitt had originally promised, because of fear of damaging the landing craft's propellers in shallow waters. That restriction would

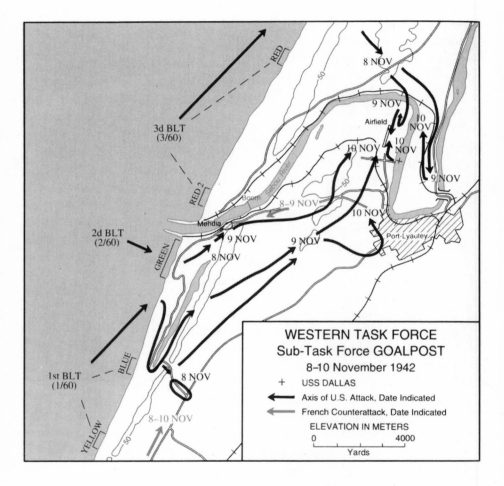

WESTERN TASK FORCE
Sub-Task Force GOALPOST
8–10 November 1942

+ USS DALLAS

◄━━━ Axis of U.S. Attack, Date Indicated

◄━━━ French Counterattack, Date Indicated

ELEVATION IN METERS

0   4000

Yards

3d BLT
(3/60)

2d BLT
(2/60)

1st BLT
(1/60)

RED

RED 2

GREEN

BLUE

YELLOW

8 NOV

9 NOV

10
NOV

10
NOV

10
NOV

10 NOV

9 NOV

9 NOV

8–9 NOV

8 NOV

9 NOV

9 NOV

8 NOV

8 NOV

8–10 NOV

Airfield

Mehdia

Port-Lyautey

Sebou River

Boom

necessitate landing one battalion after another on the single beach, immediately reembarking the landed battalion so that another could follow. In addition, they could land no vehicles. Truscott protested, but to no avail.

The exercise did not go well and clearly showed that both the troops and the boat crews needed additional training. After watching the landings for a time from the ship, Truscott, accompanied by Carleton, went ashore, located a telephone, and, ignoring the chain of command, immediately called Patton in Washington. Truscott explained to him the predicament he was facing, pointing out that the planned night-landing rehearsal would be a disaster if he were restricted to the use of only one beach and asked Patton to intercede with Hewitt. Patton refused to do so, explaining that he had "already had enough trouble getting the Navy to agree to undertake this operation. . . . Don't you do a damn thing that will upset them in any way," and hung up.[24]

Recognizing that he bore sole responsibility for the success or failure of GOALPOST, Truscott ignored Patton's order, called Hewitt in Norfolk, and explained the importance of the scheduled night-landing exercise and the necessity for having multiple landing beaches. As Truscott had suspected, Hewitt's staff had not consulted him prior to ordering that only one beach be used. Hewitt immediately authorized Truscott to use all of the beaches and to carry out the night rehearsal as planned.

However, that was not the last of the problems that Truscott encountered. The evening of the eighteenth Truscott received orders to send a number of ships, some of which were carrying assault battalions, back to Norfolk the next day for loading additional fuel, provisions, and supplies. Truscott believed that obeying the order would "preclude any night rehearsal, disrupt all plans for issuing final orders, and prevent a final conference with commanders," and immediately went to Admiral Kelly aboard his command ship to explain the situation. Kelly agreed to send a message to Hewitt requesting that the ships remain in the area another day for the night rehearsal before returning to Norfolk.[25]

But Truscott, believing once again that Hewitt's staff had ordered the ships' return without consulting Hewitt, called Hewitt, and found that he indeed knew nothing of the change in plans. Hewitt immediately told Truscott to ignore the order and go on with the planned night rehearsal. That night the rehearsal went ahead as scheduled, revealing numerous problems among both Army and Navy participants, which they immediately addressed and corrected. By two o'clock the next afternoon the exercise had been completed and all troops were back aboard their ships.[26] At seven o'clock Truscott called a conference aboard the *Allen* for all Army and Navy commanders involved in the operation, during which he discussed in detail the problems and shortcomings the rehearsal had disclosed. After the conference the convoy returned to Norfolk for the "topping off."[27]

On the twenty-second the *Allen* left its dock and moved out into the anchorage, while the other ships were at the piers completing the loading of the additional matériel and fuel. Here Truscott reviewed Patton's final messages to him and went over in detail with the assault commanders and their naval counterparts Operations Order 1 for Sub–Task Force GOALPOST. After the conference Truscott confided to his wife that "the planning of this whole operation has been a 'tragedy of errors.' . . . We had the rehearsal—and it was bad—even more so than I had expected. But we got something done, and I am not too pessimistic."[28]

The following day Truscott's ship left the anchorage. As a security measure each ship was to leave the Norfolk area separately, as if embarking for a training exercise or sailing to another port. On October 27 all ships of the Northern Attack Group would rendezvous several hundred miles east with other vessels of the Western Naval Task Force for the voyage to Africa. Truscott realized as his ship got under way that there were "many details to be checked and plans to be completed as to our course of action after we land," but that, "for better or worse, the die had been cast. As our plans were drawn up, so would we fight weeks later, two thousand miles away on the shores of Africa. My own mistakes and the mistakes of others in preparing this command for battle would be paid for in the lives of the Americans for whom I was responsible."[29]

On October 24 Truscott addressed all personnel aboard the *Allen* over the public address system. He explained their mission, what they were facing, and what he expected of them. Most of those aboard the *Allen* learned for the first time the mission on which they had embarked and the reason for the intense training they had just completed.[30]

Initially, the convoy sailed south, as if heading for the tip of Africa and the Indian Ocean beyond. After some days on that course the convoy turned northward "in irregular trace to confuse scouting submarines or aircraft." Truscott busied himself with completing final details of the operation and wrote the final draft of a message to be delivered to the French commander at Port Lyautey by Major Hamilton, his G2, and Col. Demas T. Craw, the commander of the air contingent of GOALPOST. The message emphasized that the American force "would take no offensive action unless the French first took hostile action" and appealed to the commander to follow the contained instructions to avoid bloodshed on both sides.[31]

On the morning of November 7 the convoy separated into its three task forces, Truscott's force moving north. During the voyage to the transport area he wrote to his wife,

> I want to tell you again how much I love you and how much you mean to me. I feel that whatever success has come to me so far has been entirely due to your influence. Your confidence in me and your certainty that I would succeed in whatever I did has been the spark that has kept my engine going.
>
> . . . I have even prayed and will continue to do so. With so much of the future of the world at stake, I have complete faith that God will not allow us to fail.[32]

The ships, guided by an American submarine lying off the mouth of the Sebou River, arrived in the transport area some eight miles off Port Lyautey at thirty minutes past midnight. However, because of a navigational error the ships entered the transport area in haphazard order, with the result that Truscott had no idea where his various assault transports were located. Leaving Carleton on board the *Allen*, Truscott and his aide boarded a landing craft and moved out into the confusing array of ships. Eventually, he was able to locate and board each of the assault ships and meet with the assault commanders and the naval officers. Although they were behind schedule, Truscott was hopeful that the assault forces would be able to land before daylight.

Truscott arrived back on board the *Allen* at three thirty, where he went immediately to the communications room. There he listened to a radio rebroadcast of General Eisenhower's message to the French people from his command bunker at Gibraltar. Through Eisenhower's message Truscott learned that the Allied assault forces had already landed along the North African coast, and he surmised that the landings and the broadcast by Eisenhower had most likely placed the French forces in the Port Lyautey area on alert. Shortly after, his fears were confirmed when five French vessels left the Sebou River's mouth and sailed slowly through the invasion fleet, one of the vessels warning them by a signal lamp that the forces ashore were on the alert for an expected five o'clock landing.[33]

As the assault teams were debarking and loading aboard the landing craft, Truscott reviewed his plan once again. He would land his task force on five beaches along ten miles of shoreline. BLT 2 was to land south of the Sebou River on Green Beach and destroy the coast artillery pieces in the Mehdia Casbah. BLT 1 was to land on Blue and Yellow Beaches, secure the southern flank, and advance to the airfield located on the west bank of the river north-northeast of Port Lyautey. BLT 3 was to land north of the river on Red 1 and Red 2 Beaches and advance on Port Lyautey from the northwest. If all went as planned, Truscott hoped to have the city and the airfield in American hands by nightfall of D-day.[34]

However, Truscott soon learned that all was not going according to plan. Heavy seas hindered the debarkation of the troops, further delaying the assault. As a result, only the first three waves of BLT 2 landed in darkness on Green Beach; all subsequent waves there and at the other beaches came in after dawn. In addition BLTs 1 and 3 missed their assigned beaches by twenty-eight hundred yards and five miles, respectively. Also, the GOALPOST forces encountered strong French opposition. French aircraft strafed the beaches at dawn, and the coast artillery guns in the Casbah targeted the transports with heavy fire, necessitating the ships' moving out of range, thereby lengthening the run-in to the shore by the assault craft. The fire from those guns also delayed the landing of the tanks.

BLT 1, having landed north of its planned landing area, faced a lagoon. The landing team struggled for five hours to round the south shore of the lagoon and begin its drive on Port Lyautey and the airfield but soon encountered heavy French machine-gun fire that pinned it down for the rest of the day. The BLT 2 landed on its designated beach, but a heavy French counterattack drove it almost back to the shoreline, inflicting heavy losses on the Americans.

About three o'clock Truscott, accompanied by half of his staff and twelve enlisted men, landed on Blue Beach. There he found much confusion, as some troops scheduled for Green Beach had landed on Blue Beach. Some of the landing craft had broached to the heavy surf, forcing their crews to abandon them, with a consequent loss of weapons and other equipment in the surf. He immediately boarded a half-track, followed the path of the BLT 1, and located its commander on a ridge east of the lagoon. Learning that he had not yet made contact with BLT 2, Truscott directed him to do so the next day and then returned to his command post on the beach, where Carleton soon joined him. Finding that the beach was still in chaos, and fearing that French aircraft might attack the beach the next morning, Truscott directed that order be established before daybreak. He also learned that BLT 2 had been stopped before it reached the Casbah and ordered that it renew its assault on the Casbah at daylight.

The next morning Truscott was encouraged to see additional armor landing and set off once again to visit BLT 1. He found that it had not advanced since the previous night and had not yet made contact with BLT 2. Truscott ordered the commander to press his attack toward the airfield, insisting that he capture it by nightfall. As he was retracing his route Truscott received a report that BLT 3 had arrived at the Sebou River north of the airfield and learned that BLT 2 was attempting to reorganize for the attack on the Casbah but had suffered heavy losses. Truscott doubted that the losses were as heavy as reported, since only a small number of wounded were on the beach and roughly two hundred stragglers were wandering aimlessly about the area.

Since the surf had grown very heavy overnight and during the day, necessitating the cessation of all landing operations that afternoon, Truscott realized that he would have to rely solely on the troops already ashore to destroy the coastal guns in the Casbah and open the Sebou River. Truscott therefore told Colonel de Rohan, the 60th RCT's commander, to round up all of the stragglers and send them to BLT 2. When he returned to Blue Beach, Truscott learned that more tanks had come ashore and directed one of the tank companies to join BLT 1, with orders to renew the attack against the airfield and capture it by dark. He then headed for Mehdia and BLT 2.

Shortly after he arrived there, two Frenchmen were brought to him, bearing the first news of Colonel Craw and Major Hamilton, the two officers Truscott had dispatched ashore with the early assault waves to contact the French commander to attempt to arrange a cease-fire before active fighting began. The

Frenchmen told Truscott that Craw had been killed and that Hamilton had been taken prisoner before they could make contact with the French commander and advised Truscott to send a force to free Hamilton. Since he had no such force to spare, Truscott told the Frenchmen to go back through the lines to obtain additional information.

There was, however, one piece of good news: the naval demolition party that Truscott had requested to remove a cable blocking access of the destroyer to the Sebou River had succeeded. The next morning Truscott heard heavy firing from the Casbah area, and as he looked seaward he saw the destroyer-transport USS *Dallas,* which carried the raiding detachment, enter the river. Standing proudly at the helm was Jules Malavergne, the former Sebou River pilot who had been smuggled into London and arrived in Norfolk just before Patton's task force set sail. As the ship disappeared from view below the fort in the Casbah, Truscott could hear the ship's guns open fire. He also received definite word that BLT 3 was on the river opposite the airfield.

Word soon arrived that BLT 2 had reached the walls of the Casbah but that heavy enemy machine-gun and mortar fire were holding up the attack and that air support was needed. The request went through, and soon aircraft were bombing the target. A few minutes later Truscott arrived at the Casbah to find that the battle was almost over. In a few minutes the surviving members of the French garrison surrendered, and Truscott directed the BLT 2 commander to continue his attack to seize the airfield.

Throughout the morning there had been heavy fighting in the sector between the Casbah and the airfield, but shortly after noon most of the fighting had ended and French troops were surrendering in large numbers. By the time Truscott arrived at the airfield he found it occupied by the tankers, elements of BLTs 1 and 3, and the raiding detachment that had debarked from the *Dallas* east of the airfield. Leaving orders for BLT 3 to secure the airfield, Truscott returned to Mehdia.

Late in the afternoon of the tenth Truscott received word from Carleton that the French commander and most of his men had been captured and the commander wished to arrange an armistice. Truscott told Carleton to inform the commander that he would not consider such a discussion until he released Hamilton. That night the French released the major, and arrangements were made for Truscott and the French commander to meet the following morning. Shortly after midnight a group of French officers arrived at Truscott's command post and informed him that Admiral Darlan had ordered all French forces to cease opposition.

During the night Truscott had hoped that Patton would send him instructions for his meeting with the French commander, but he received none. The next morning Truscott, accompanied by a company of tanks and his staff, met with Gen. Maurice Mathenet, commander of the French forces, in front of the main gate of the Casbah. Mathenet reiterated Darlan's order and told Truscott that he desired to make arrangements for the cease-fire. Truscott replied that he was not looking for a French surrender but only for their cooperation. He further explained that, subject to any future instructions from Patton, French soldiers who were not prisoners of war could retain their weapons and continue to occupy the barracks where they were currently housed, providing they pledged that they would not again take up arms against the Americans. The French were to hand over all American prisoners at once, following which the Americans would release the French prisoners they held. French civil officials could continue their usual duties but could not take any prejudicial actions against the Americans. The Americans would, however, occupy the port area in Port Lyautey. Mathenet agreed to the terms, and a cease-fire became effective on November 11.[35] Seventy-nine GOALPOST troops had been killed, and 250 were wounded. The French estimated that 250 to 300 men had been killed.[36]

THE LANDINGS AT SAFI AND FEDALA

General Patton had selected Maj. Gen. Ernest Harmon, commanding general of the 2d Armored Division, to command Sub–Task Force BLACKTONE in its assault and seizure of Safi, two hundred miles south of Mehdia. By daybreak of D-day Harmon's men had seized control of the port facilities and most of Safi. Eleven hours after landing the Americans controlled all of Safi and had accepted the surrender of the French forces.[37]

Seventy miles south of Mehdia Sub–Task Force BRUSHWOOD, commanded by Maj. Gen. Jonathan W. Anderson, was to seize the village of Fedala and then move south to capture Casablanca. The landings were complicated by high surf and navigational errors that carried many landing craft far from their assigned beaches and destroyed almost half of the landing craft, delaying the debarkation of the follow-on assault waves. Once ashore, however, the troops moved quickly against light resistance and by six o'clock they had captured Fedala. Later in the morning Col. William H. Wilbur came ashore at Fedala, carrying a message from Patton for the French commander in Casablanca. Miraculously, he was able to drive the sixteen miles to the city and deliver Patton's request for a cease-fire to the commander.

The following day the Americans began moving south toward Casablanca. The advance met only light resistance, but, slowed by shortages of personnel, vehicles, and supplies due to unloading problems caused by the loss of so many landing craft during the assault, the troops were forced to halt six miles short of the city's defensive perimeter. However, Patton, seeing the confusion on the beaches, quickly went into action and soon had supplies and equipment moving forward from the beaches. At midnight of November 9–10, the advance resumed, meeting heavy resistance. However, by five that afternoon the troops occupied positions opposite the French defenses east and south of the city, and the arrival of Harmon's tanks from Safi would complete the surrounding of the city. Having received no answer to his first cease-fire proposal, Patton dispatched his chief of staff to deliver another request. After learning of Darlan's orders for a cease-fire at Algiers, the commander in Casablanca ordered a cease-fire at 7:10 p.m.[38]

THE LANDINGS AT ORAN AND ALGIERS

The landings along the Mediterranean coast were made at two locations, Oran and Algiers. The Center Task Force, made up entirely of American units and commanded by Maj. Gen. Lloyd R. Fredendall, had the mission of capturing Oran. Approximately two hundred miles to the east of Oran, the Eastern Task Force, commanded by British Lt. Gen. Kenneth A. N. Anderson, made up of both British and American units, was to make the assault on Algiers, the headquarters of all French forces in North Africa. In deference to French feelings about the British, Maj. Gen. Charles W. Ryder, commander of the U.S. 34th Infantry Division, led the assault troops at Algiers. The Center Task Force was able to secure Oran within three days and accept the surrender of the French forces, suffering 126 killed out of a total force of 16,700. Only one of the landings at Algiers was opposed, and the troops quickly overcame that resistance and moved inland to capture a critical airfield just a few hours later.

Meanwhile, cease-fire negotiations between Ryder and a deputy of Admiral Darlan were taking place. When Darlan realized that further resistance was futile, he authorized his deputy to meet with General Ryder and negotiate a cease-fire. Agreement was soon reached, and the cease-fire for the Algiers area became effective at 8:00 p.m. on November 8.[39]

THE IMPACT OF ULTRA

In 1940 cryptanalysts working at Bletchley Park, Buckinghamshire, England, were able to break the Enigma cipher of the German Wehrmacht, and it soon became apparent that this capability would give "Britain and her Allies an immense advantage in the conduct of the war." Allied military operations in the Mediterranean theater became "the training ground" for the later use of ULTRA, the code name given to the intelligence derived from Enigma decrypts in the European theater, and TORCH was the first operation about which Bletchley Park received advance knowledge and for which it had been asked to provide intelligence assistance during its planning.[40]

In the fall of 1942 ULTRA "pointed reassuringly to the conclusion that neither of the Axis partners foresaw a landing in French North Africa." The Allies had sent out for the Germans' interception several notional or false invasion sites as a cover plan for Operation TORCH. After the war investigation of German records revealed that the German high command

fell for almost all of the "notional" objectives at one time or another. . . . [Generaloberst Alfred] Jodl, [head of the Operations Staff, Oberkommando der Wehrmacht, the Armed Forces High Command] was even rash enough on 7 November . . . to declare his belief that French North Africa was the *least* likely place for an Allied landing, because it might drive the French into the Germans' arms. . . . Complete strategic surprise—seldom achieved because it is so difficult to attain—was in fact gained on this occasion.[41]

TORCH was the first large-scale amphibious operation under hostile fire in which the American Army had ever participated. Although the operation ended in victory, one cannot discount the importance of the part played by the "inept resistance offered by French and colonial forces" in the Allied victory. The many landing problems experienced by all three task forces would undoubtedly have proved considerably more problematic if the Allies had faced a more determined, better-trained, and better-equipped enemy force. The operation had exposed the relative combat inexperience of the American troops vis-à-vis their British counterparts, but the Americans had performed generally quite well in their first combat outing, confirming their commanders' belief that they "would soon close the experience gap with their British comrades and enable the Allies to field well-coordinated forces of overwhelming power."[42]

With the cessation of hostilities Truscott moved into a comfortable villa in the Port Lyautey area, there to await further orders from Patton. On the day before Thanksgiving, he wrote his wife that he had known that the recently concluded operation would be a "hazardous mission and as it turned out, it was even more so." He also told her that Patton had visited the week before and had been "tremendously pleased with everything. He was loud in his praise of our accomplishments. Said he had recommended me for Major General and the DSM [Distinguished Service Medal]." He went on to tell her that the previous Sunday they had held a memorial service for his fallen men and dedicated the cemetery in which their bodies rested.[43]

On November 26, Thanksgiving Day, Truscott hosted a traditional Thanksgiving dinner at his villa. Capt. Alvin T. Netterblad, his aide, commented, "Boy, was that some dinner. Had a heck of a time finding enough tools, table cloth, proper Thanksgiving food and wine, but it turned out O.K. Lee did a wonderful job."[44]

Truscott had been suffering the pain of a "bad tooth" since December 15, but the pain was ameliorated by the news he received from Patton four days later that he had been promoted to major general, effective November 21, only six months after he had become a brigadier general. That evening the staff hosted a champagne party for the newly promoted Truscott at his villa.[45]

At Patton's invitation Truscott traveled by air to Casablanca on December 22. After lunch at his villa, Patton awarded Truscott the Distinguished Service Medal "for his outstanding contributions of planning and leadership prior to and during the action" at Port Lyautey. Patton went on to inform Truscott that although he had no vacancies in the Western Task Force for an officer of his grade, he had no objection to Truscott's contacting General Eisenhower to inquire about any plans that he might have for him. The following day Truscott and Conway left for Eisenhower's headquarters in Algiers aboard an A-20 "Havoc" light bomber.[46]

Since Truscott was leaving his command, Patton prepared the mandatory Efficiency Report for his service with the Western Task Force. Patton described Truscott as "a superior organizer and trainer, and a superb, fighting leader of men," recommending him for division or corps command. Of the 183 officers of Truscott's grade whom Patton knew, he rated him as number 4. He concluded by stating that "in addition to his outstanding leadership ability, General Truscott has superior ability as a planner." Undoubtedly, Truscott's performance as the commander of Sub–Task Force GOALPOST had removed from Patton's mind any doubts about the "ability of Truscott."[47]

As he looked back on the actions of his sub–task force, Truscott identified several shortcomings of the American forces: First, he was "astounded by the relatively large number of American soldiers who surrendered to our French opponents when they still possessed means of continuing the fight or who could have withdrawn to continue the fight elsewhere." Second, he was surprised to discover how small a proportion of individual weapons were actually employed in combat actions. He believed that future training should place greater emphasis on a unit's employing actively all weapons available to it. Third, he found that most officers and men "lacked confidence in themselves and were hesitant and uncertain in battle," waiting for "a superior to tell them just what to do." Fourth, he concluded that "few reports in battle could be accepted as true without verification" and that "the best means for evaluation [of a situation] was on-the-spot inspection since there was no substitute for personal reconnaissance in battle command." And finally, Truscott also found that the operation plans "were far too optimistic with respect to the time required to accomplish the operation" and did not adequately take into account the many unexpected and unanticipated difficulties and problems that units face once committed to combat.[48]

Chapter 6

DUTY WITH IKE

After French resistance in Northwest Africa ended, Lt. Gen. Sir Kenneth A. N. Anderson's forces began an advance on the night of November 24–25 from Algiers toward Tunis, some five hundred miles to the east. ULTRA had already revealed to Eisenhower that enemy reinforcements, arms, and supplies had begun arriving in Tunisia on November 10, and by "the time Anderson moved forward, both he and Eisenhower knew that an embryonic German occupation force had been improvised" and that the attack toward Tunis and Bizerte would not be as easy "as it would have been even a few days earlier."[1]

At first Anderson's forces encountered rather light resistance, but by the twenty-eighth German opposition had increased considerably. Soon the advance bogged down completely, as heavy rains made the roads almost impassable, compelling Eisenhower to call off the attack on December 24. One factor that undoubtedly influenced Eisenhower's decision to halt the advance was ULTRA intelligence indicating that Field Marshal Albert Kesselring, commander in chief, South, was pouring reinforcements and supplies, including a large number of tanks, into the Tunis area at a rapid rate. At the end of the year the Allied front in Tunisia extended some 250 miles from the coast west of Bizerte southward to just west of Gafsa.[2]

Truscott and Conway arrived in Algiers late Christmas Eve, where they learned that Admiral Darlan had been assassinated in the city earlier that day. They made their way to Eisenhower's headquarters, only to find that the general was visiting the front in Tunisia and would not return until the next day. After spending the night in the Alletti Hotel, the two returned to Allied Force Headquarters early the following morning, anxious to learn if Eisenhower intended to give Truscott a combat command in North Africa or send him to the United States. At AFHQ Conway and he met with General Clark, Eisenhower's deputy, and Maj. Gen. Walter B. "Beetle" Smith, Eisenhower's chief of staff, with whom they shared their observations of the situation in French Morocco and along the Mediterranean front. Eisenhower did not return until late Christmas Day and postponed his meeting with Truscott until the following day.

Eisenhower greeted Truscott warmly the next morning and told him that he would like him to remain in Algiers for a few days, explaining that he "was considering an operation, and if it materialized, he would have a job for [him]." Eisenhower explained that for the next few days he would be completely occupied in dealing with the aftermath of the Darlan assassination.

When Truscott returned on the twenty-ninth, Eisenhower told him that he had been "terribly disappointed" that the Allied drive on Tunis had been stopped, and he had decided to postpone that attack indefinitely. However, during his visit to the front he had discussed with his subordinates the feasibility of mounting an operation farther south by the 1st Armored Division (AD) and an attached RCT from the 1st Infantry Division (ID) to cut Field Marshal Erwin Rommel's line of communications between Libya and Tunis.

His staff had found such an operation to be practicable and believed that the forces could be assembled at Tébessa by January 22. To reduce his span of control Eisenhower planned to create an advance command post in Constantine adjacent to First Army Headquarters and proposed that Truscott become his deputy chief of staff there, to which Truscott agreed. He telephoned Patton in Casablanca to tell him of his new assignment, asked that he arrange for Carleton and the rest of his party to join him in Algiers the following day, and left for Constantine on January 1.[3]

As Truscott was establishing his command post at Constantine, Maj. Gen. Lloyd R. Fredendall's II Corps headquarters opened there the first week of January. Fredendall's staff immediately began planning to implement Operation SATIN, the seizure of Gabès or Sfax to cut the line of communications between Tunis and Rommel's forces and, it was hoped, draw the German forces in the north southward, thus allowing General Anderson to resume his attack to capture Tunis when weather conditions improved. Eisenhower would exercise overall command of SATIN through Truscott in the advance command post, which formally opened on January 17 in the nearly empty American Orphanage.[4]

Fredendall's plan was to attack eastward from the Friana-Gafsa area with the 1st AD and the attached RCT and "seize the bottleneck on Rommel's line of communications" at Gabès. After protecting their southern flank with land mines the Americans would then turn north and capture Sfax. Supply was the critical factor for the operation, but in a January 13 memorandum to Beetle Smith, Truscott stated that although the AFHQ S4 considered the operation to be a "knife edge proposition . . . [it will be] logistically sound if everything is one hundred percent."[5]

On January 17 Gen. Jürgen von Arnim's forces launched an attack on the juncture of the French and British sectors near Pont du Fahs to the north, pushing the French line back ten miles, causing heavy casualties, and destroying large numbers of tanks, other vehicles, and artillery pieces. Anderson, concerned about his right flank, requested the attachment of a combat command from II Corps to be employed to assist the French, an action that would have adverse implications for Operation SATIN.[6]

Eisenhower arrived at the Advance CP on a scheduled visit the next day, where Truscott briefed him on the situation. Eisenhower told the assembled officers that he had recently learned that General Montgomery's "Eighth Army expected to capture Tripoli within ten days and to be assaulting Rommel on the Mareth Line near the southern border of Tunisia by the first of March." If SATIN was carried out, Rommel's accelerated rate of withdrawal northward would threaten the southern flank of Fredendall's forces while at the same time Arnim's forces would endanger his northern flank. Based on the information from Gen. Harold R. L. G. Alexander and his evaluation of the situation, Eisenhower canceled SATIN on the spot and directed that II Corps serve as a mobile reserve on the southern flank, "prepared to attack when the Eighth Army should be assaulting Rommel on the Mareth Line."[7]

As the German advance continued against his right flank, Anderson requested once more the attachment of a combat command to the French forces. On January 19 Truscott decided to employ Combat Command B, commanded by Brig. Gen. Paul McD. Robinett, as Anderson had requested. Despite the commitment of CCB, the German advance continued, leading Anderson to express his opinion that he could place no reliance on the French troops and that "it would not be practicable for [CCB] to restore the situation on the French front." Truscott decided to present the situation to Eisenhower, who made plans to visit the Advance CP the following day, January 21. At that conference Eisenhower directed CCB to continue its attack and told Fredendall to continue protecting the right flank of the Allied forces and to assemble a force to attack Fondouk on January 23. On the twenty-third Fredendall telephoned Truscott to report that he could not attack Fondouk because the French once again refused to participate in the attack, forcing Truscott to call off the attack. Meanwhile, Robinett's CCB, aided by strong and effective air cover, continued its attack, driving the Germans back toward Kairouan.[8]

That same day, after meeting with Anderson and Gen. Alphonse Juin, commander of the French forces in Tunisia, Truscott recommended to Eisenhower that all French troops be withdrawn to training areas where they could defend lines of communication while rearming and reequipping. He also relayed a request from Anderson to meet once more with the commander in chief. Eisenhower agreed to meet Anderson and Truscott at Télergma the next morning, where Anderson and Truscott expressed their belief that they could place no reliance on the French forces and asked for at least four more American RCTs. After getting additional input from Brig. Gen. Lowell W. Rooks, his chief of staff, Eisenhower directed the attachment of II Corps to the British First Army. He also directed that every effort be made to convince Juin to withdraw the bulk of his forces for rest and refitting and said that eventually the 34th Infantry Division, less one combat team, would take over the French sector.[9]

After Eisenhower's departure, Anderson suggested that Truscott join him in presenting Eisenhower's proposals to Juin, since he might be more receptive if an American backed his presentation. At their meeting that afternoon Juin insisted that he retain a French sector, "preferably the least active," to which Anderson and Truscott agreed, assigning him a small sector in the northern part of the center of the Allied line, which would include the Pichon-Fondouq area, and a small part of the American line, both sectors to be commanded by a French corps commander. Truscott also placed some French forces with 5 Corps to the north and with II Corps to the south.[10] Truscott then cabled Eisenhower that Juin seemed "anxious to cooperate in every way" and recommended that Eisenhower convince Gen. Henri Giraud, the commander of French forces in North Africa, to approve Juin's actions.[11]

At about the same time the Germans halted their advance, and during the ensuing weeklong lull in the action Maj. Gen. Terry Allen's 1st Infantry Division arrived to relieve French and British troops in the central sector and CCB in the vicinity of Ousseltia. Also, the 168th RCT was assembling at Tébessa, and parts of the 1st AD were at Sbeïtla and Gafsa, the units at Gafsa preparing for an attack toward Maknassy on February 1. At Faïd a detachment of the French Constantine Division was holding the passes leading toward Sfax, and some weak French battalions were farther north around Fondouq and Pichon. Unfortunately, nowhere along the front was there a reserve. Such was the disposition of Allied forces on January 30 when the Germans launched a major attack, once more targeting an area defended by a French force.[12]

One of the main roads leading from Tébessa to Sfax passed through the Faïd pass, and Allied control of the pass was essential for any advance toward the German line of communications at Sfax. A detachment of about one thousand men from the French Constantine Division had been given that responsibility. On January 30 the 21st Panzer Division attacked the pass, quickly captured Faïd, and surrounded the French force, most of whom fled rearward to Sbeïtla. Receiving orders to retake the pass, Fredendall assigned the mission to Combat Command A (CCA), 1st AD.

Truscott had spent the night of the twenty-ninth with the II Corps at Tébessa. When he learned of the rout of the French at Faïd pass and the planned attack by CCA to regain the pass on January 31, he drove the next morning to the 1st AD CP near Tébessa, where he discussed the situation with Maj. Gen. Orlando Ward and his staff. He then drove on to Sbeïtla to meet with CCA's commander, Brig. Gen. Raymond E. McQuillin, an old friend from Fort Riley and Fort Knox days. When he arrived at McQuillin's CP he found him conferring with the

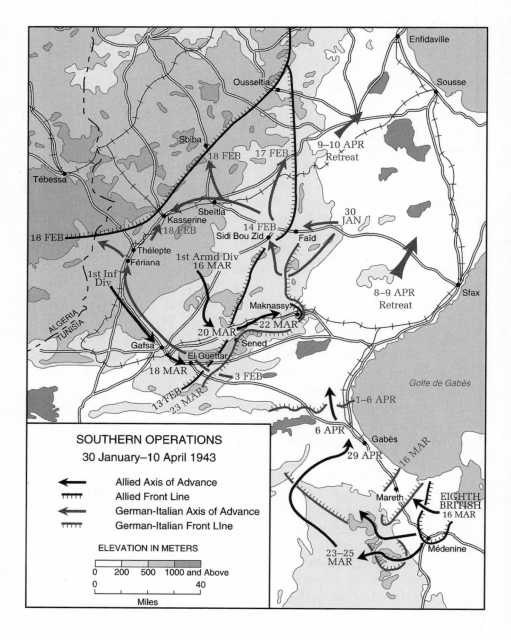

Enfidaville

Sousse

Ousseltia

9–10 APR
Retreat

Sbiba

18 FEB   17 FEB

Tébessa

30
JAN

Sbeïtla

Kasserine   14 FEB

18 FEB   18 FEB   Sidi Bou Zid   Faïd

18 FEB

Thélepte
Fériana

Sfax

1st Armd Div
16 MAR

1st Inf
Div

8–9 APR
Retreat

Maknassy

ALGERIA
TUNISIA

20 MAR   22 MAR

Gafsa   Sened

El Guettar

18 MAR

13 FEB   3 FEB

23 MAR

Golfe de Gabès

1–6 APR

SOUTHERN OPERATIONS
30 January–10 April 1943

6 APR

Gabès

29 APR

16 MAR

Allied Axis of Advance

Allied Front Line

German-Italian Axis of Advance

German-Italian Front LIne

Mareth

EIGHTH
BRITISH
16 MAR

ELEVATION IN METERS

23–25
MAR

Médenine

| 0 | 200 | 500 | 1000 and Above |

0   40

Miles

commander of the routed French forces, who explained that his troops had been so thoroughly hammered that even if CCA was successful in retaking the pass he would be unable to provide a force to hold it. McQuillin told Truscott that he planned to move CCA that night to Sidi Bou Zid to attack at daybreak with two columns from the west and from the southwest to capture Faïd and relieve the French forces remaining within the pass.

Early the next morning Truscott observed the northern attack from atop a butte, Djebel Lessouda. As the tanks and infantry moved toward the village, German aircraft appeared from the south and began bombing and strafing the Americans. As the action moved eastward Truscott and his aide jumped into their jeep and chased after the tanks. They soon came upon the rear of the now-stalled tank column and later learned that the southern attack force had met a similar fate. McQuillin's attack had failed, and the Germans had captured the pass.

Meanwhile, to the south, Fredendall was faced with a difficult decision: should he continue with the planned attack on Maknassy by Combat Command C and Combat Command D, or should he send one combat command to assist in the planned counterattack by CCA to retake Faïd and the pass on February 1 and attack Maknassy with the other? He chose the latter course of action, and on January 30 ordered CCC to move north and attack the left flank of the German force driving toward Sidi Bou Zid, approximately ten miles west of Faïd pass, and any force moving from Maknassy northward to assist in the German drive westward from the pass, while CCD moved eastward toward Maknassy. However, the next day Fredendall changed his mind and ordered CCC to turn south and join CCD's attack on Maknassy, effectively dooming CCA's attack on Faïd.[13]

CCC turned south late in the afternoon of January 31 and had reached and blocked the northern mouth of Maïzilla pass that night, prepared to continue the attack on Maknassy the next day. However, the Germans brought up reinforcements that night and counterattacked the next morning. The Americas repulsed the German attack, but received orders to delay movement through the pass until that afternoon. Although soft ground and antitank fire delayed their advance, the troops by nightfall were in position on the southwest and part of the northeast sides of Maïzilla pass. As CCC prepared to continue its advance the morning of the second they received orders to call off the attack and move north to counter an enemy threat against the Allied line near Hadjeb el Aioun.[14] The southern force also attacked toward Maknassy the afternoon of February 1 and by nightfall had seized Station de Sened. The attack continued on the second and third, and by noon of the third elements of CCD were about six miles west of Maknassy, when they received orders from Fredendall to call off the attack and withdraw to Gafsa.[15] "By February 3 von Arnim and Rommel had the results they wanted: the Allied counterattack on Faïd had failed, the

II Corps attack on Maknassy had been stopped and recalled, and Allied units were withdrawing." On that same day Eisenhower cabled the Combined Chiefs of Staff (CCS) and the British Chiefs of Staff (COS) that he had postponed operations against Gafsa and Sfax and that his "policy in Tunisia would be *offensively defensive* until Eighth Army were able to advance from Tripolitania."[16]

Early in the evening of January 31, Truscott was back at the Advance CP, there to find Anderson waiting. He told Truscott he believed conditions on the American front were preventing him from assembling the forces he needed to carry out the attacks in the North and requested discussing the matter again with Eisenhower. Accordingly, Truscott arranged for Eisenhower to meet them the next morning at the Télergma airfield, where Anderson explained to Eisenhower that the French forces had been reduced to such a level that he could no longer rely on them. He went on to say that the failed attacks at Faïd and Maknassy were an indication that the Allies were spreading their forces too thinly and that they were not accomplishing Eisenhower's directive that they build up strength in the North for the drive on Tunis. He proposed that the Allies shorten their lines by withdrawing from "exposed places like Gafsa, Maknassy, and Faïd." Truscott objected to such a withdrawal, pointing out that it might jeopardize the Allies' forward airfields. Eisenhower, however, authorized Anderson to withdraw from Maknassy, Gafsa, and other exposed points if it "would permit the desired concentration of force on the south flank" and stressed the importance of retaining Fredendall's corps as a mobile strike force on that flank. Eisenhower also informed them that General Alexander was coming from the Middle East Command to be his deputy and would command the First and Eighth Armies when they were close enough for one headquarters to exercise command of the two armies.

Eisenhower later questioned Truscott about the relationship between Fredendall and Anderson, and about British and American relations overall, learning that in Truscott's opinion Fredendall had "no liking for the British in general and for General Anderson in particular." Hearing this, Eisenhower directed Truscott to impress upon Fredendall the necessity of cooperating with Anderson. He also asked Truscott to come to Algiers to discuss the future of the Advance CP once General Alexander had arrived and set up his Army Group headquarters.

Truscott visited Fredendall on February 2, carried out Eisenhower's orders, and then flew to Algiers the next day, where Eisenhower told him that he would become commander of the 3d Infantry Division as soon as Alexander arrived. He would join the division in Morocco to prepare it for Operation HUSKY, the invasion of Sicily, scheduled to take place as soon as the Allies had defeated the Germans in North Africa. Eisenhower had decided to retain the Advance CP in Constantine, and Brig. Gen. Ray E. Porter would replace Truscott as deputy chief of staff.[17]

A general lull in combat actions characterized the ten days that followed Truscott's return to Constantine. In the center of the Allied line the 34th Infantry Division, less its 168th RCT, was joining the 1st Infantry Division in relieving the French troops. To the south the 168th RCT had arrived to reinforce CCA at Sidi Bou Zid, where McQuillin was readying plans to recapture Faïd. II Corps held Gafsa, Fériana, and Sbeïtla and was in contact with CCA at Sidi Bou Zid. Supplies, equipment, and troops continued to stream into the American sector.[18]

During the lull Eisenhower and his staff were attempting desperately to learn where and when the Germans would next strike the Allied line. Initial intelligence intercepts had led Brig. Eric E. Mockler-Ferryman, AFHQ G2, to announce that the "Germans would attack through Fondouk, go northwestward, rip through the defenses of the French in the center, and plow into the flank of the British forces in the north." Truscott had examined the same intelligence, and he believed that "there was nothing to substantiate this alarm over the possibility of a German attack from the Fondouk area toward Maktar," basing his conclusion on the absence of any "other factors in the situation as we knew it to support this conclusion of the intelligence sections," such as a change in enemy troop dispositions along the front or increased aerial surveillance in the Fondouq area. Instead, he reasoned, "the most damaging blow that the Axis could strike us would be to take from us forward airfields in the southern area."[19]

Fredendall agreed with Truscott that the greatest German threat was in the area where II Corps was deployed, pointing out that his G2 had gathered information supporting that conclusion: Arab workers had disappeared from the corps area, patrols were meeting increased resistance, and noise of moving vehicles had increased. Fredendall accordingly ordered Ward to hold Djebels Lessouda and Ksaira, flanking the road leading from Faïd to Sbeïtla, and to place mobile reserves at Sidi Bou Zid. However, Fredendall's plan for defense was defective. The troops on the hills would be vulnerable to encirclement by the enemy, and the two positions were not capable of supporting each other. Furthermore, Fredendall, lacking confidence in Ward, had forbidden him to maneuver his units without first receiving Fredendall's permission to do so, effectively freezing his division in place.[20]

A considerable amount of information about German intentions was conveyed in a directive from Comando Supremo (Italian High Command) received on February 11 at Bletchley Park but not decrypted until three days later. The Fifth Panzer Army was to begin an offensive in the Sidi Bou Zid area on the twelfth if possible, and Rommel, if able to do so, was to follow this offensive by the fifteenth, attacking Gafsa and exploiting toward Tozeur, about forty miles to the southwest. Unfortunately for the Americans, the attacks on Faïd and Sidi

Bou Zid had already begun the morning of the fourteenth, approximately twelve hours before the orders from Comando Supremo had been decrypted.[21]

On February 12 Eisenhower began an extended inspection tour of the southern front. The first stop was his Advance CP, where that evening Truscott hosted a party to celebrate Eisenhower's promotion to four-star general on February 11.[22] The next morning they traveled to the II Corps CP at Speedy Valley, where Eisenhower met with Fredendall and Anderson. That night the party visited Ward at his CP, and then, accompanied by Ward, went on to McQuillin's CP at Sidi Bou Zid. After conferring with McQuillin, Eisenhower and his party returned to Speedy Valley, where Eisenhower learned that approximately four hours after they had departed McQuillin's CP, the Germans had mounted an armored attack against CCA. Because McQuillin's tanks were so thinly spread, the Germans quickly punched through, but McQuillin was preparing to counterattack the next day. Learning of no attacks elsewhere along the front, Eisenhower concluded that the attack at Sidi Bou Zid was a local affair and left for Constantine that afternoon. When he arrived at his Advance CP the following day, Eisenhower learned that McQuillin's counterattack had failed and that CCA was withdrawing toward Sbeïtla, leaving behind on the Djebels two infantry battalions.

Anderson and his staff also believed that the action at Sidi Bou Zid was a diversion and that the main enemy attack would strike through the passes around Fondouk toward Maktar. Accordingly, he refused Fredendall's request for the return of CCB, then in First Army reserve at Maktar, to II Corps. He did, however, finally release a medium tank battalion, which joined CCC in a failed attempt to rescue the trapped infantry battalions on the Djebels. He also ordered Fredendall to evacuate Gafsa during the night. On the morning of the sixteenth Anderson finally released CCB to join the 1st AD at Sbeïtla, where Ward was "to hold defensively east of Sbeïtla." That same day Eisenhower learned that in the space of two days more than one hundred American tanks had been destroyed, two battalions of artillery had been overrun, and two infantry battalions had been lost in the fighting.[23]

Shortly after beginning his return trip to AFHQ, Eisenhower sent two handwritten messages to Truscott. The first directed him to tell Anderson's chief of staff to contact Anderson and have him dispatch infantry and antitank weapons to II Corps that same day and inform Fredendall that "every position to be held must be organized to the max. extent—at once—mines, etc. *Emphasize reconnaissance.*" The second message directed Truscott to contact AFHQ and arrange for certain of Eisenhower's key staff officers to meet with him after his arrival in Algiers that night; Truscott immediately complied with Eisenhower's orders and then dispatched Carleton to join the 1st AD at Sbeïtla and Conway to join the forces at Fériana.[24]

As the busy day drew to a close, Truscott reported the current situation to AFHQ. Fredendall was warning of an imminent enemy armor attack east of Sbeïtla, pointing out that if Sbeïtla fell the Maktar Valley would be exposed, Robinett's CCB was settling in behind Sbeïtla to thwart any enemy attack that reached the town, and Fredendall reported that he had received word that most of the infantry battalion trapped on Djebel Lessouda had been able to escape and had ordered the troops on Djebel Ksira south-southwest of Faïd to withdraw.

About one o'clock on the morning of February 17 Fredendall telephoned Truscott to report that eighty Mark IV and nine Mark VI (Tiger) tanks were fighting on the edge of Sbeïtla and that he considered the situation "extremely grave." Just after he finished talking with Fredendall, Truscott received a message from Carleton reporting that enemy tanks were "all around Ward's command post." At one thirty Fredendall reported he had received authorization from Anderson for II Corps to withdraw and had ordered CCC to do so to join French forces in establishing positions on the heights north of Thélepte, where a forward airfield was located, leaving a small covering force to defend Fériana until six in the evening. He also ordered another force consisting of an infantry and an engineer battalion to establish a defensive line east of the village of Kasserine, hold it until Ward's division had withdrawn through the position, and then withdraw and garrison Kasserine Pass for defense.

Later that morning Truscott received word from Carleton that Ward's forces had apparently beaten back the German attackers. Conway reported that "everyone had pulled out of Fériana," and people were destroying the aircraft and burning gasoline and other supplies at the Thélepte airfield but that forces from Fériana were establishing themselves on the heights above the airfield. "By now it was obvious even to General Anderson that this was the German offensive which intelligence officers had been so certain was to come through the passes around Fondouk farther to the north" and that some of Rommel's Panzers were involved.

At 10:45 a.m. Fredendall reported that American forces were on the heights above Fériana, that some forces were already withdrawing through Kasserine Pass, and that the 1st AD would start west at 11:00 a.m. After clearing the pass the division would take position south of Tébessa. CCA would start west at the same time but "delay en route and reach Sbiba at nightfall in order to insure protection of [Maj. Gen. Charles W.] Ryder's (34th Infantry Division) south flank." He also reported that the troops on Djebel Ksira were completely surrounded and that he was going to direct them to surrender. "That was bitter news."[25] However, the succession of German victories just completed did not satisfy Erwin Rommel. He intended to keep the enemy "reeling" by striking for Kasserine Pass, "gateway to Algeria."[26]

Meanwhile, Truscott was in "almost continuous communication with AFHQ concerning the situation and the reinforcements and replacement matériel which General Eisenhower was straining every resource to send to the front." Tanks were desperately needed, and Eisenhower had arranged for fifty tanks to be shipped from Casablanca and Oran and was working with the British First Army to obtain some fifty-four M-4 diesel-powered tanks that they had just received, recognizing that since the M-4 tanks used by the American forces were gasoline powered, the British M-4s would present some maintenance problems. On the eighteenth the British agreed to send the requested tanks to II Corps. Eisenhower was also attempting to find replacements, particularly infantrymen and artillerists. He had Rooks, his G3, tell Truscott that he was sending the artillery and regimental cannon companies of the 9th Infantry Division forward, with the rest of the division to follow as soon as transportation became available. One medium tank battalion equipped with obsolete M-3s and a tank destroyer battalion was also on the way.[27]

Fredendall had another serious problem that he discussed with Truscott on the nineteenth. His relations with Ward had continued to deteriorate, growing worse since the fighting began at Sbeïtla, and had reached a point where neither had confidence in the other. In his opinion Ward must be relieved and asked that Truscott place the matter before Eisenhower. Eisenhower and Truscott had previously discussed bringing General Harmon from Morocco to Tunisia, and now Eisenhower decided to do just that, telling Truscott he "was to inform General Fredendall that Harmon would be sent to him to use in any way that he desired." When Harmon arrived at II Corps on February 22 Fredendall placed him in command of the battle then taking place rather than giving him command of the 1st AD.[28]

KASSERINE PASS

Rommel had hoped that with the 10th and 21st Panzer Divisions assigned to him he could make a thrust on Tébessa from the Kasserine Pass and the area north of it and then continue on to Bône, eventually forcing the Allied troops to pull out of Tunisia, and so informed Kesselring and Comando Supremo on the eighteenth. About midnight Rommel received from Comando Supremo authorization to attack, but with the proviso that Le Kef rather than Tébessa was to be his initial objective. Although disagreeing with that plan of operation, Rommel made plans to kick off his attack the next morning as directed.[29]

He decided to attack Le Kef through both Sbiba Gap and Kasserine Pass and then concentrate his forces against the more lightly defended of the two.[30] By the morning of the nineteenth, when Rommel began to probe at Sbiba and Kasserine, the Allies had already assembled forces at both areas. At Sbiba Gap, which was in the French XIX Corps zone, the major elements were a British armored and an American infantry division, a British infantry brigade, and an American RCT. The force defending Kasserine Pass, approximately ten miles to the southwest, was much smaller. The major element was Task Force Stark, led by Col. Alexander N. Stark, Jr., commander of the 26th Infantry Regiment, and consisting of an infantry and an artillery battalion, elements of an engineer battalion, a tank destroyer battalion, and a battery of French artillery; Stark assumed overall command at Kasserine Pass. The 1st AD was assembled southwest of Kasserine Pass, and large belts of mines augmented the defenses at both Sbiba and Kasserine.[31]

Rommel launched attacks against the Allied forces at Sbiba the morning of the nineteenth and at Kasserine Pass in midafternoon. Finding enemy resistance less at Kasserine Pass, Rommel decided to make his major effort there. The German forces initially encountered stout resistance in front of the pass, but by effectively utilizing the tactics of infiltration and encirclement they progressively reduced the defensive positions, and soon large numbers of Americans were streaming to the rear. By midnight of the nineteenth "the situation was a perfect example of fluidity. Some troops were holding out, others were fleeing in panic, many were missing, and no one knew exactly what was going on. . . . The defense of the Kasserine Pass seemed about to disintegrate." The timely arrival of a small force of tanks, artillery, and infantrymen enabled the spent defenders to hold the pass until the next morning.

At half past eight on the twentieth the Germans renewed their attack through the pass, supported by artillery and joined by the Centauro Division. By the afternoon, as the American withdrawal through the pass was accelerating, Rommel decided to commit the 10th Panzer Division to galvanize the attack, and soon the enemy held the eastern end of the pass. By nightfall Stark had withdrawn his headquarters to the rear and at midnight learned that Rommel's troops were in firm possession of the pass.[32]

Within the pass the road from Kasserine forks, the northern fork leading to Thala, the southern to Haidra. The morning of February 21 was a time of decision for Rommel: should he thrust directly through Hamra to Tébessa, or should he drive to his assigned objective, Le Kef? He decided on the latter and sent his main force along the road toward Thala and Le Kef. About three miles south of Thala the Germans encountered stiff resistance, and, dismayed by the leadership of his attacking force, Rommel personally assumed command. The battle lasted for three hours, when, "with both sides finally exhausted and seeking brief respite, the fighters parted and stood back." Rommel had by that time returned to Kasserine, expecting his forces to drive through into Thala. However, the commander of the troops attacking toward Thala had decided to postpone the continuance of the attack until the next day.

During the night the four artillery battalions and two regimental cannon companies from the 9th Infantry Division arrived in Thala and early the next

morning opened up a devastating artillery bombardment of the German positions. When Rommel arrived at the position later that morning he concluded
that the Allied reinforcements precluded any hope of success.[33] That afternoon
he met with Kesselring, who had flown there after conferring with Arnim's staff
in Tunis. Kesselring found Rommel "in a very dispirited mood. His heart was
not in his task and he approached it with little confidence," and he detected an
"ill-concealed impatience to get back as quickly and with as much unimpaired
strength as possible to the southern defence line," believing that "further effort
[at Kasserine] was useless." After returning to his headquarters at Frascati, Kesselring ordered Rommel to call off his attack.[34]

On the afternoon of the twenty-third Truscott and his aide joined Eisenhower and Brig. Jock Whiteley on a visit to Tébessa. There they met with Fredendall and Allen and found much improved conditions all along the front and
"a distinct note of optimism." Eisenhower told the two that they should exert
every effort to destroy the German forces before they could make good their
escape.[35]

Thus ended the battle for Kasserine Pass. The Allies reoccupied Fériana and
Sbeïtla as the Germans withdrew. Within a few days the enemy forces were
back to where they had begun their operations on February 14. "Rommel had
accomplished little in the way of gaining elbow room in Tunisia and he had
sustained losses which could not be replaced."[36] There is some controversy
about the number of American casualties incurred during the battle: Anderson
records 2,546 missing but provides no figure for killed and wounded; Atkinson
states that "American losses exceeded 6,000 of the 30,000 men engaged in the
battle," of whom "half were missing"; and Howe lists a total of 1,866 as killed,
wounded, or missing, of whom 1,401 were in the 1st AD.[37]

Almost simultaneously with the end of the Kasserine battle came the end of
Truscott's tour of duty at Eisenhower's Advance CP. Truscott spent the remaining days of February visiting the sites of the recent fighting and meeting and
talking with the troops who had been involved in the battles. He found that the
evidence regarding the American troops' performance during the battle "was
often contrary to the [negative] reports that were then being given credence."
He elaborated on that conclusion in a letter to his wife, telling her, "We did not
do so well—chiefly because we fed our troops in piecemeal so that the Boche
really chewed them up properly. As you might expect though our American
lads have suffered no loss of morale. To them its [sic]much like losing a ball
game to a team they know they should beat—next time they 'will beat the hell
out of the SOBs'—and I think they will—they have become battle wise."[38]

On March 3 and 4 Truscott met with Eisenhower and Smith to discuss the
reorganization of II Corps and its upcoming operations under British command. When asked for his opinion about Fredendall, Truscott replied that Fredendall "had lost the confidence of his subordinates" and said that he himself

"did not believe the Corps would ever fight well under his command." He also expressed his belief that because of Fredendall's dislike for and distrust of the British he "would never get along well under British command." He went on to recommend that Eisenhower appoint Patton to command II Corps and assign Brig. Gen. Hugh J. Gaffey, then with the 2d AD, as Patton's chief of staff, recommendations that Eisenhower promptly accepted. The following morning Truscott and his party departed by plane for his new assignment as commander of the 3d Infantry Division.[39]

As he prepared to depart Tunisia for French Morocco, Truscott shared his feelings with Sarah: "You just cannot imagine how happy I am to be going to a command. . . . I guess Im [sic] to [sic] practical to ever be content as a staff officer. DE was most complimentary about the value of my recent works. Hesitated for quite a spell at letting me go at present time but finally did, although he said he might call me back in 24 hours."[40]

Years later Truscott recorded his observations and conclusions about the conduct of the Tunisian campaign. First, neither British nor American officers understood the "organization, tactical methods, and command and staff procedures" of the other's armed forces. British commanders, adhering to their tactical doctrine and organization, employed "American battalions and small units under their command with little regard for the integrity of units to which Americans were accustomed." Another contributing factor to American reverses "was the command method of most of the American commanders, who conducted their battles from a command post which they seldom left." Finally, Truscott greatly admired the attitude of the American soldier after he experienced defeat: instead of adopting the British inclination to consider "battle as something of a game . . . even in defeat," the Americans fought to win.[41]

1925 Fort Bliss National Champion Polo Team. Captain Truscott third from left. Courtesy of the National Museum of Polo and Hall of Fame, Lake Worth, Florida.

Captain Truscott, 1931. Courtesy of the National Archives.

(*Above*) Major General Truscott, July 2, 1943, North Africa. Courtesy of the U.S. Army.

(*Top right*) Major General Truscott, General Eisenhower, Lieutenant General Clark, and Major General Lucas in 3d Infantry Division Command Post, October 22, 1943. Courtesy of the U.S. Army.

(*Bottom right*) Major General Truscott (*in bathrobe*), Lieutenant General Courtney Hodges, Lieutenant General Clark, and Colonel Carleton in 3d Infantry Division Command Post, night of November 6, 1943, Cassino sector, Italy. Courtesy of the U.S. Army.

(Above) Newly promoted Lieutenant General Truscott. Courtesy of the George C. Marshall Research Library, Lexington, Virginia.

(Top left) Major General Truscott in VI Corps Command Post, Anzio beachhead. Courtesy of the George C. Marshall Research Library, Lexington, Virginia.

(Bottom left) Truscott and his staff celebrating his promotion to lieutenant general, September 19, 1944, Seventh Army headquarters, southern France. Courtesy of the U.S. Army.

(Above) Major General Crittenberger and Lieutenant General Truscott conferring at an airstrip in Italy, April 19, 1945. Courtesy of the U.S. Army.

(Top right) Lieutenant General Truscott, Brigadier General Carleton, Major Bartash, and Major Wilson, July 1945, Lucerne, Switzerland. Courtesy of the George C. Marshall Research Library, Lexington, Virginia.

(Bottom right) Truscott party in Egypt, August 9, 1945. General Truscott third from left. Courtesy of the George C. Research Marshall Library, Lexington, Virginia.

Oil portrait of Lieutenant General Truscott, 1945. Courtesy of the West Point Museum Art Collection, United States Military Academy, West Point, New York.

Retirement portrait of General Truscott. Courtesy of the George C. Marshall Research Library, Lexington, Virginia.

General Truscott's funeral procession, September 14, 1965. Courtesy of the George C. Marshall Research Library, Lexington, Virginia.

Chapter 7

OPERATION HUSKY

THE BATTLE FOR SICILY

On March 4 General Truscott assumed command of the 3d Infantry Division and arrived at division headquarters in Rabat three days later, accompanied by Carleton and Conway.[1] The next morning he met with the division principal staff and selected special staff officers, with all of whom he was "favorably impressed." That afternoon he conferred with the subordinate commanders and their staffs. Only two regimental commanders, Col. Thomas H. Monroe, 15th Infantry, and the recently appointed commander of the 7th Infantry, Lt. Col. Harry B. Sherman, were present; Col. Arthur H. Rogers and his 30th Infantry had been transferred to eastern French Morocco in December 1942. Although Monroe appeared to be satisfactory, Sherman did not favorably impress Truscott.[2]

After those meetings Truscott gained the impression that the division had developed a "'rear area' feeling" because of the "relative inactivity of duty in Morocco." As a result, "disciplinary standards had suffered and the attitude toward training lacked the fire and intensity" that Truscott believed a combat-ready division should possess. Addressing that problem would be Truscott's first priority. Two days later Carleton and he began a series of conferences that would eventually include most of the officers of the division, providing an opportunity for Truscott to meet his officers and to give them his "views on training for combat, on fighting, and on the responsibilities of leadership." During those meetings Carleton and he discussed their experiences in Tunisia, describing "what happened to American troops in their first battle with the Germans, and we pulled no punches" in telling them of "the weaknesses in our equipment, training, leadership, and will to fight."[3]

One change that Truscott instituted shortly after his arrival was his personal messing arrangements. Instead of dining in the division headquarters mess, which would necessitate his adjusting his schedule to that of the mess, Truscott set up a separate mess for himself and his chief of staff and aides. Carleton soon discovered another Chinese cook, who bore the same surname as his predecessor, Lee, who became the head chef of Truscott's mess, soon dubbed the "Canton Restaurant" by visiting officers.[4] Truscott eventually acquired three other Chinese enlisted men on his personal staff: Hong, his batman; Wong, who assisted Lee in the kitchen; and Woo, assistant cook and batman for Carleton.[5]

On the fifteenth of March Truscott took some time out to host Archbishop Spellman of New York when he visited the division. Later Spellman spoke at a dinner, praising the "splendid work our industrialists and our people were doing by turning out such splendid equipment we were getting in such great quantity." Truscott responded to the archbishop's comments by telling him what his recent personal observations in Tunisia had revealed: "We do not excel and all too frequently do not equal the equipment the Germans provide for their forces. . . . Of course I do not mean that our equipment is not good for it is, but the Boche [a disparaging World War I appellation for German soldiers] has been at this game—concentrating on it—longer than we have and has learned to 'keep ahead' if he can. We are having trouble catching up. But the boys do well—and will do better if we can give them the leadership they deserve."[6]

On March 15 the first elements of the division began their move to the Fifth Army Invasion Training Center on the shore of the Gulf of Arzew, approximately twenty miles northeast of Oran, and by April 28 the entire division had closed there to begin training for Operation HUSKY, the invasion of Sicily.[7] Truscott visited the center for the first time on the fifteenth and met with Brig. Gen. John W. O'Daniel, whom he had known in England. They looked over the regimental training beaches and the combat ranges, which led Truscott to comment that he was "well satisfied" with what he had seen. The center was ideal for training Truscott's men: there was a great variety of beaches available for practicing landings, and there was adequate space inland for all types of training, including the use of all the division's organic weapons. The major deficiency was the absence of "suitable impact areas for adequate training with naval gunfire."[8]

Truscott's division training program at Arzew stressed "coordination of all arms from airborne infantry to naval units" but also placed heavy emphasis on physical conditioning. Truscott had early on noted the poor physical condition of many men in the division and developed a program, speed marching, to address that problem. Speed marches had been "the backbone of the [Ranger] training at Achnacarry," and Truscott had undoubtedly been impressed by the positive effects that the speed marches had in improving the physical condition of the Ranger candidates and noted that the marches also pushed the men "to their physical limits so that their instructors and officers could see who might not be able to stand the stress of combat."[9] He was confident that "an average infantry battalion could approximate Ranger and Commando standards for marching" if he approached those standards gradually.[10] Ignoring the objections of his G3, he insisted that each battalion eventually reach a state of physical fitness that would allow it to march "five miles an hour for one hour, four miles an hour for the next two hours, and three and one-half miles an hour for the remainder of a 30-mile march." The men soon dubbed the speed marches the "Truscott Trot."[11] All units trained to achieve that standard, and within two weeks of arrival at Arzew almost every battalion had done so. The 4 percent of the men who were unable to reach that goal were given other assignments "so as not to jeopardize the combat efficiency of the units or the lives of fellow comrades."[12]

In the combined arms training involving infantry and artillery units, infantrymen learned to follow rolling artillery barrages closely, sometimes within one hundred yards of the falling projectiles, thereby gaining confidence in the accuracy of American artillery fire.[13] The "dogfaces" used mortars and machine guns firing live ammunition in simulated combat conditions, which resulted in some casualties but prepared them for the dangers they would soon face in Sicily.[14] They became familiar with all types of German and Italian antipersonnel and antitank mines and booby traps used in Tunisia and learned how to avoid, detect, and disarm them. The men also received training in attacking pillboxes and in the use of antitank and antiaircraft weapons.

The soldiers and naval personnel were introduced to and used every type of landing craft, "from LSTs [landing ship, tank] and LCMs [landing craft, mechanized] to rubber boats," and made many practice landings, under both daylight and nighttime conditions.[15] Selected division officers and enlisted men worked with naval personnel to form Shore Fire Control Parties, which would operate under control of the division artillery in directing the fire of naval guns. The two-week period at Arzew ended with a two-day landing exercise in the Pont du Cheliff area, where the beach and inland terrain closely resembled that which the division would encounter in Sicily. "Each RCT in training, except the 30th RCT, landed under cover of darkness and moved inland eight miles to its objective," defended by a reinforced infantry battalion from one of the other regiments.[16]

Truscott availed himself of every opportunity to address officers and noncommissioned officers he encountered during his visits to the training areas. He stressed the importance of being familiar with their weapons and tools, of being in the best physical condition, of developing a determination to achieve, and of learning to live and work together in the field. He also emphasized that "leaders must assume responsibility—must 'stick their necks out.'" They were to correct the mistakes of their subordinates, but they were not "to punish for honest errors of judgment," nor were they to hesitate to punish "any leader who failed to assume responsibility." He was pleased that under his command the division was developing "an obvious pride in attaining standards which had theretofore been considered practicable only for selected individuals. . . . Development of this individual and mutual confidence resulted in an *elan* and *esprit* which was to distinguish the 3rd Infantry Division throughout the war."[17]

On April 5 Maj. Gen. Geoffrey Keyes, acting commander of the I Armored Corps,[18] and some of his staff visited Truscott and discussed with him the HUSKY plan that applied to Truscott's task force, designated ENSA, which consisted of the 3d Infantry Division, one armored combat command, two airborne regiments, one Ranger battalion, and auxiliary and supporting units. ENSA was initially scheduled to land in the Mazana del Vacco–Sciacca area in the western end of Sicily and capture and secure the airfield at Castelvetrano and a landing field northwest of Sciacca by the evening of D+3 so that fighter and bomber aircraft could support the landing of the remainder of the command and the assault on Palermo by D+5. Patton would be in overall command of the invasion force, designated Force 343, which consisted of ENSA; Headquarters, I Armored Corps; Headquarters, VI Corps; and the 36th, 45th, and either the 1st or the 9th Infantry Divisions.[19]

Since most of his division staff was heavily involved in the training, Truscott decided to form a Planning Board similar to the syndicates with which he had worked in Mountbatten's headquarters. The board was headed by Lt. Col. Albert O. Connor, Truscott's deputy chief of staff, and consisted initially of principal assistants from each of the general staff sections, with representatives from division artillery and all attached units, as well as the engineer beach group and the naval support forces. The board would gather all pertinent intelligence and carry out all initial planning, keeping their respective commanders informed of the board's progress. When the time for preparing loading and landing plans arrived, regimental and subordinate staff officers would be added to the board. Such a board was an innovation that would relieve the principal staff officers of much of the planning responsibility and would ensure "the utmost in cooperation among all of the branches and services involved and the careful and coordinated planning of an infinite number of details."[20]

Shortly after Truscott assumed command of the 3d Infantry Division, Keyes told Truscott that AFHQ had informed him of the Navy's desire to have responsibility for conducting all amphibious training and asked for his opinion. Based on his experience with the Navy during the amphibious training for GOALPOST, Truscott recommended strongly that AFHQ limit naval responsibility for amphibious training strictly to naval matters and that responsibility for the amphibious training of the landing forces be vested in the commander who would assume command of those forces once they were ashore. AFHQ apparently accepted Truscott's recommendation, since it became standard operating procedure for all subsequent amphibious operations in the Mediterranean theater.[21]

Recognizing that his division would soon be encountering the mountainous terrain of Sicily, Truscott selected an area for mountain warfare training near Pont du Cheliff, where his troops would receive training for operating in mountainous terrain, using mules as pack animals.[22] However, only the 15th Infantry had completed the mountain training when the division received a new mission.[23]

Tunisian Interlude

On April 30 Truscott received a telephone call from General Rooks, AFHQ G3, who told him that General Alexander, commander of 18th Army Group, had requested an additional infantry division as reinforcement for the final Allied assault then under way in Tunisia. Rooks inquired if Truscott's division was in condition to go to Tunisia and quickly received an affirmative reply. Truscott immediately went to the I Armored Corps command post at Mostaganem and made arrangements for his Planning Board, which had just completed the outline plan for ENSA, to join the planners there. At ten o'clock that night the division received its movement orders from AFHQ, and "five hours later the 15th Infantry was on the road."[24]

Maj. Gen. Omar N. Bradley, commanding II Corps, had originally planned to have Truscott's 3d Division relieve the battle-weary 1st ID. However, as Truscott was moving his division forward to effect that relief, Bradley contacted him on the night of the fifth and told him that General Harmon had requested additional infantry to support his division's attack on a strongly defended German position on the peninsula east of Bizerte, and directed that Truscott send an infantry regiment to the Ferryville area for attachment to the 1st AD. Bradley had also ordered that an infantry regiment from the 9th ID and additional field artillery and antiaircraft artillery join Harmon's division for the attack. Truscott's regiment was to attack the following morning.

Truscott joined Harmon at his command post southeast of Ferryville early the next morning, and after breakfast the two set out on a reconnaissance mission to ascertain how far forward Truscott's force could assemble for the attack. As they traveled they found that Harmon's troopers and their tanks were already in possession of the entire peninsula excepting the high ridge overlooking the Mediterranean, from which there came no sounds of enemy fire. It was obvious to Harmon and Truscott that "the battle in Tunisia was all but done and that no large force would be required to clear the ridge."

When they returned to Harmon's CP, Truscott phoned Bradley and told him that in his and Harmon's opinion only the 15th Infantry would be needed for the attack on the ridge. Bradley agreed, and Truscott returned to his advance CP near Ferryville, where he dismissed all of the other units except the antiaircraft battalion. However, the 15th Infantry saw no combat on that day, for by noon Harmon was receiving the surrender of the German commanders.[25]

By May 10 the division, minus the 30th Infantry and some service elements, had concentrated in the Ferryville area, where it received the assignment of guarding prisoners of war and conducting salvage operations on the battlefield. The division had expected ten thousand prisoners, but they soon had forty thousand under guard. On the battlefield they found no serviceable wheeled or tracked vehicles, and salvage operations were mostly limited to gathering ammunition and rations, the latter for the use of the prisoners. On the eleventh Bradley ordered Truscott to move his division to Jemmapes in the Bône-Philippeville area to continue its training for HUSKY.

The following day Truscott attended a conference at II Corps for all commanders down to regiment and separate battalion level, where Bradley's staff summarized the "lessons learned." Truscott wrote that the conference "was not impressive," that none of the commanders were "'telling the truth' even though it hurts," and that there was "too much satisfaction with a mediocre performance," even though only the day before Bradley himself had admitted to Truscott that the campaign had shown that the "American soldiers [were] unwilling to close with [the] enemy—and that was his greatest worry." He ended his written comments with the plea, "Why not at least be honest with ourselves?"[26]

The victory in Tunisia ended the North African campaign, during which the American forces had made a major contribution to the victory, but at a high cost. The U.S. Army lost 2,715 dead, 8,978 wounded, and 6,528 missing. "At the same time, however, the Army gained thousands of seasoned officers, noncommissioned officers, and troops, whose experience would prove decisive in subsequent campaigns."[27]

The deployment of the 3d Division to the Tunisian front had interrupted its invasion training, "unnecessarily as it had turned out," and Truscott soon determined that the Jemmapes area was very unsuitable for resumption of invasion training. It was some miles from the coastline, along which there were no suitable beaches for practicing landings. Farther inland, a cork forest with very dense undergrowth covered the ground, with few clear areas for training. In short, the area would have been ideal for troops training for jungle operations, but it "was entirely unsuited for training in landing operations or for the kind of warfare which we might expect to encounter in Sicily." Truscott immediately began lodging a series of protests with AFHQ, asking for permission to assemble his division in the Bizerte area. In that effort he enlisted the assistance of Rear Adm. Richard L. Conolly, commander of Task Force 86, which would transport Truscott's division shore-to-shore for the invasion. "Persistent protests, like drops of water falling upon hard stones, eventually wore down the [AFHQ] staff resistance. On June 1st, we were ordered back [to the Bizerte area]."[28]

Meanwhile, the Force 343 assault sector had been changed from the western end of Sicily to the southeastern area of the island west of the British sector. Truscott would command the Licata-sector assault force, known as JOSS Force.[29] It would be the only component of Patton's Force 343 that would have all the types of naval vessels "entirely suitable for a shore-to-shore operation . . . [and] would become the first real test of shore-to-shore operations under actual conditions of war with adequate equipment." However, the number of vessels available would permit the landing of less than half of JOSS Force on D-day.[30]

There were four beaches in the Licata area, but beach intelligence could not provide assurance that all were suitable for landing. About five miles inland from the beaches was a range of hills, the rapid capture of which would be a priority, since control of the ridge would permit the rapid disembarkment of the remainder of JOSS Force. "The keynote of the operation was therefore speed and momentum, and the key to speed was simplicity." Truscott's plan was to land all of the division's infantry and tank support on all four beaches, if practicable, within sixty or seventy minutes, holding the armored combat command in reserve to land as an exploiting force when it was apparent the initial assaults had been successful. He planned to use one battalion from each regiment and the Ranger battalion as his initial assault forces on the four beaches.[31]

Although Truscott continued to visit the training areas on a regular basis and to drop in on his regimental commanders while in their areas, planning occupied the bulk of his time at Jemmapes. One of his major roles was in resolving problems that arose between his headquarters and higher headquarters. In one instance, the AFHQ G2 had refused Truscott's request for aerial photographs of his assault area on the grounds that such missions would jeopardize security and alert the enemy to the Allies' intentions. Making no headway against the adamant G2, Truscott ignored command channels and went to see his old friend Maj. Gen. James H. Doolittle, head of the Eighth Bomber Command, and explained his problem to him, his chief of staff, and his G2. The G2, a bomber pilot himself, accompanied Truscott back to Jemmapes, confirmed that aerial photographs were essential for the planning to continue, and made arrangements with the Royal Air Force aerial photography unit on Malta to fly the mission. Within a matter of hours of the completion of the mission Truscott received the photographs and an aerial photographic interpreter, who would remain with Truscott until he left for Sicily. Truscott telephoned all subsequent requests for aerial photography directly to Malta, receiving the photographs within twenty-four hours. Lucian Truscott was never one to let obstacles thrown in his path by higher headquarters prevent him from completing his missions. With the aerial intelligence in hand, Truscott, his staff, and the Planning Board "were soon able to complete the outline plan, prepare the order of battle, and get on with the preparation of landing and loading."[32]

During the first week of June the division concentrated south and east of Lake Bizerte to coordinate their training with that of the naval forces that would carry the division to Sicily and support its landing. The training particularly stressed fire-control operations prior to and during the landing operations and the disembarkation of the troops on the assault beaches. Still stressing physical conditioning, Truscott insisted that speed marches be the rule as the troops moved from their bivouacs to the training areas and back.[33] When Truscott learned that his loading-plan requirements for men and equipment exceeded the rated capacity of the LSTs, he embarked 18 officers, 450 fully equipped enlisted men, and 94 vehicles on an LST for a forty-eight-hour sojourn on Lake Bizerte, and found to his delight that the ship, its messing and latrine facilities, and its crew were in fact able to accommodate the overload with no problems.[34]

Previous operations had indicated that one of the serious problems encountered in amphibious assaults was the relaying of information about the forward progress of the assault forces on shore to the commanders still aboard the ships. Carleton suggested the possibility of using division artillery spotter planes, L-4 Grasshoppers, to fly over the beaches and report the situation to Truscott and his staff and to direct naval gunfire. Since Sicily was far beyond the range of L-4s based on airfields in North Africa, he consulted with the division artillery air officer, who suggested building a runway on the deck of an LST, from which the Grasshoppers could take off. Truscott accepted the idea, and work on the LST began on July 1, only nine days prior to the scheduled date for the invasion. A timber trestle overlain by a runway, measuring 216 feet long and 10 feet wide, with 1-foot sideboards to help keep the plane on the runway, was constructed down the center of the ship's deck.

On July 4 the LST moved to Lake Bizerte for the first-ever takeoff from an LST. The L-4 was hoisted onto the runway, and the ship turned into the wind. The pilot climbed into the cockpit, advanced the throttle, headed down the runway, and soared into the air with "room to spare." Impressed with the success of the takeoff, Truscott approved Carleton's idea, but suggested that two planes instead of one take off on D-day, providing a backup if one happened to crash or be shot down.[35]

Another issue facing Truscott arose from an unusual request from the 30th Infantry Regiment: permission to obtain about forty Arab donkeys or burros to carry ammunition above the basic infantrymen's load for each of the follow-on battalions that were to pass through the assault battalion and seize the inland objectives. Freed of carrying the additional ammunition, the infantrymen could move more quickly to their objectives. Truscott gave his approval, and the regiment carried eight or ten burros aboard each of its LCIs (landing craft, infantry) during one of its night practice landings.

When Admiral Conolly learned of this, he telephoned Truscott, saying, "General, . . . You have loaded a bunch of damn mules on my ships. And you have done it without saying a word to me!" Truscott replied that he was sure the admiral's planners were cognizant of the plan, but apologized for not having personally told him. He also stated that he would remove the animals if ordered to do so, but indicated that he did not agree with such a decision, pointing out that he considered them to be part of his arsenal of "weapons" with which he would engage the enemy. He finally won Conolly over to his side, with the admiral commenting, "Dammit, General, you are right. We will carry the goddam mules and anything else you want."[36]

A major problem confronting Truscott and his staff was that of logistics. JOSS Force was more than three times larger than the division, which was to be responsible for all of the force's supply and maintenance for the first twenty-one to thirty days of the operation. The increased logistical responsibilities could not be handled by the division staff as organized under the TO&E, and the additional command and staff elements and organizations to cope with that responsibility would have to be in place before the invasion. Truscott gave Lt. Col. Charles E. Johnson, his G4, the responsibility for developing that organization.

Johnson's solution, approved by Truscott, envisioned three echelons of support. First was the Force Depot, initially located at Bizerte, which would "furnish to the JOSS forces all those services and evacuation normally supplied to a division in the field by . . . [a Field] Army headquarters." The depot would move to Sicily on Truscott's order. Second, Near Shore Control "was a provisional headquarters set up to plan, control, and supervise the embarkation of all organizations and to load all supply ships" bound for the invasion beaches. The difficulties Truscott and his staff faced during the loading and embarkation of the Sub–Task Force GOALPOST were undoubtedly powerful motivating factors for the formation of this organization. Finally, the Beach Group, composed of engineers and medical and supply troops, "was to organize three of the four landing beaches so as to facilitate the force, to unload supplies and establish dumps, and, upon capture of a port, to repair and operate the port."[37]

One problem that Truscott and his staff never satisfactorily resolved was the "complete lack of participation [in planning] by the Air Forces on our level and almost complete lack of participation at any level below that of the high command," despite numerous requests from Truscott for an air planner to augment his staff, the exception being aerial intelligence officers General Doolittle had provided from Eighth Bomber Command. The result was that when JOSS Force sailed for Sicily Truscott had no information about what if any air support the force would have, including fighter protection for the convoy and the assault forces once ashore. Truscott believed that the lack of air force participation in planning contributed to the subsequent disaster that befell the transport aircraft carrying paratroopers of Maj. Gen. Matthew B. Ridgway's 82d Airborne Division off Gela and Sampieri.[38]

Early in June the 3d Division was still in need of about one thousand replacements, and AFHQ decided to obtain those men from the 34th ID, which was not scheduled to participate in the Sicily operation. Most of those men had no desire to join the 3d for HUSKY, and all wished to go home. Shortly after their arrival the division surgeon reported a case of self-maiming to Truscott, and the next day two or three new cases were reported, all of the men claiming to have "accidentally" wounded themselves. Although Truscott did not feel that those men were cowards, having already proved themselves in battle, he did recognize that they were suffering from "emotional strain caused by their recent disappointment . . . [that] had brought them to a point of mental imbalance."

Fearing that the few cases of self-maiming could spread like a "contagious disease" to other members of the division, Truscott convened a meeting of his subordinate commanders, at which he announced that the "surest measure of control would be to convict one case and publish a long sentence to the entire command with appropriate ceremony." That same night another case of self-maiming occurred, charges were prepared, a general court-martial was quickly convened, the accused was tried immediately, and he received a sentence of fifty years in prison, which Truscott approved, recognizing that higher headquarters might on review reduce the sentence. The sentence "was read with due formality to every member of his command. . . . There were no more cases of self-maiming in the command."[39]

The division's three weeks of intensive and vigorous training in the Lake Bizerte area culminated in Operation COPYBOOK, June 20–26, an exercise so realistic that most of the soldiers actually believed the invasion was under way "until the morning for the landing found the landing craft still off the African beaches." To Truscott's and his staff's relief the loading and landing plans were sound. Although the rehearsal did reveal some faults, they were promptly corrected. Importantly, the men of the Third ID gained "increased confidence in the ability of the Navy to land all troops on the proper beaches."[40]

On June 29 General Eisenhower visited Truscott and his division and attached units and subsequently shared his observations with General Marshall: "From every indication it is the best unit we have brought over here. The men are tough; for example, they frequently—that is several times a week—march five miles in an hour as part of their routine training. . . . The presence of skilled and round-the-clock leadership is apparent on every hand. Truscott is the quiet, forceful, enthusiastic type that subordinates instinctively follow. If his command does not give a splendid account of itself, then all signs by which I know how to judge an organization are completely false."[41]

On June 30 General Patton submitted an Efficiency Report evaluating Truscott's performance as commanding general of the 3d Infantry Division. He rated him "Superior" in all categories and stated that he would "especially recommend him [for command of] an infantry or armored division or corps." Patton rated Truscott number 5 on a list of 153 major generals whom he knew. In his endorsement of Patton's report, Eisenhower stated, "I know of no Major General who has more efficiently performed as a Division commander than General Truscott."[42]

On the evening of July 3 Truscott assembled all of the officers of the division and addressed them:

> Gentlemen, we are on the eve of a great adventure. We are about to set forth upon the greatest amphibious expedition the world has ever known. We are going forth to engage the enemy and defeat him. . . .
>
> You have learned what it is to follow closely your supporting artillery, and your men have learned not to be afraid of it. . . . You have learned how to land on your assigned beaches, quickly disembark, and move inward rapidly to seize your objectives.
>
> On the eve of this great adventure, we find ourselves anticipating success—or failure? No, instead we anticipate success . . . . We do not know the word "failure."[43]

THE BATTLE FOR SICILY

The island of Sicily is made up of ten thousand square miles of rugged terrain that lends itself well to defensive operations. The low hills in the South and West give way to more mountainous terrain in the North and East, the latter area dominated by Mount Etna, a huge active volcano. The roads, except along the coast, are narrow and poorly surfaced, with many steep grades and sharp curves. Messina, in the northeast corner of the island, was the key strategic objective for the campaign, but the beaches in that area were very narrow and beyond the range of Allied land-based aircraft support. Although the best areas for amphibious landings are in the northwestern and southeastern corners of the island, simultaneous landings in those two areas were rejected because the landing forces would be unable to provide mutual support. Therefore, the planners decided to land the invading forces, the British Eighth Army and the American Seventh Army, along the island's southeastern shore.[44]

General Alexander, commander of the 15th Army Group,[45] would direct the actions of the two Allied armies, Montgomery's Eighth Army and Patton's Seventh Army, composed of Bradley's II Corps, which consisted of four infantry divisions, one armored division, and one airborne division. Field Marshal Kesselring was in control of all German forces in Italy, including Sicily, while the Italian forces were subordinate to Comando Supremo (Italian High Command), headed by Generale d'Armata Vittorio Ambrosia, who had a thorough dislike of the Germans.[46]

Defending Sicily were some two to three hundred thousand Italian troops and approximately thirty thousand German ground troops. The Italians were organized into six coastal divisions, four infantry divisions, and local defense forces. The Germans had deployed two divisions in Sicily, the "essentially combat ready" 15th Panzer Grenadier Division, located mostly in the eastern part of the island, and the significantly understrength Hermann Göring Division, which was still in the process of arriving from the Italian mainland.[47] The overall commander of the Axis forces on Sicily was Generale d'Armata Alfredo Guzzoni, who had concluded that the defenses were entirely inadequate to defend the long coastline of the island. When he attempted to convince Mussolini that the situation in Sicily was very serious, Il Duce ignored the warnings.[48] Late in June Generalleutnant Fridolin von Senger und Etterlin arrived to serve as German liaison officer with Guzzoni's headquarters and to assume responsibility for coordinating Guzzoni's employment of German troops for the defense of the island.[49]

On June 26 Guzzoni, convinced that Sicily was to be the next Mediterranean target of the Allies and equally sure that the landings would take place in the southeastern corner of the island, met with Kesselring and Senger und Etterlin. In the eastern half of the island he planned to form a powerful counterattack force composed of the two German divisions to strike the Allied lines at the most vulnerable point. The Italian divisions would fight only delaying actions.

Although Kesselring also believed that the Allies would most likely land in the Southeast, he inexplicably planned to place most of his "essentially combat ready" 15th Panzer Grenadier Division in the northwestern corner of the island, since he could not rule out a primary or secondary landing there, while placing the "significantly understrength" Hermann Göring Division in the east, both to be employed as mobile reserve forces. Convinced that his assumptions were correct, Kesselring overruled Guzzoni.[50]

The Allies planned to land more than seven divisions simultaneously at multiple points along a one hundred–mile front in the southeastern corner of Sicily, supported by airborne assaults by elements of two airborne divisions. Eighth Army would come ashore on beaches "fronting the Gulf of Noto, just south of Syracuse, and on both sides of the southeastern point of Sicily." Seventh Army was to land along a seventy-mile stretch of beaches along the Gulf of Gela. The British forces were to make the main effort, and Alexander expected them "to drive quickly through Catania to the Strait of Messina." Seventh Army would have a secondary role, "supporting the British and protecting their flank as they moved up the east coast toward Messina," reflecting "British skepticism about American capabilities, a skepticism borne [sic] of the debacle at Kasserine Pass a few months before."[51] Patton's assault forces were to seize the airfields at Licata, Point Olivo, Biscari, and Comiso and capture the ports of Licata and Gela. A parachute assault by the 505th Parachute Infantry RCT and a battalion of the

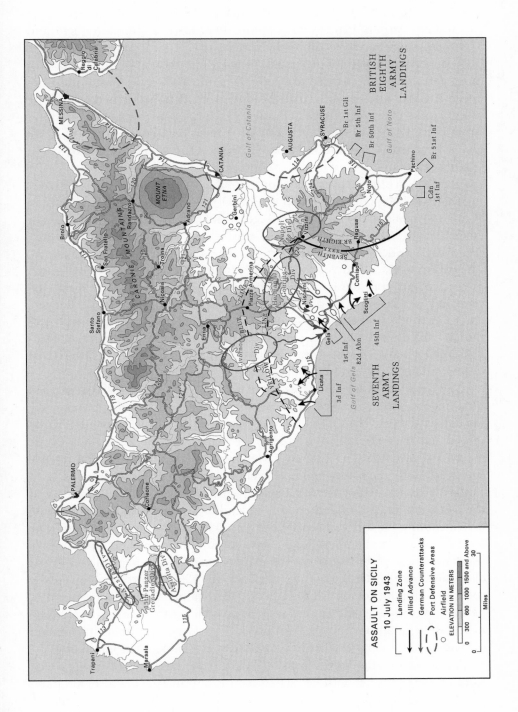

ASSAULT ON SICILY
10 July 1943

Landing Zone
Allied Advance
German Counterattacks
Port Defensive Areas
Airfield
ELEVATION IN METERS
0   300   600   1000   1500 and Above

Miles
0   30

504th Parachute Infantry, neither of which had yet seen combat, was to precede the landings. Most of Patton's other assault divisions, or elements of them, and his headquarters had seen combat in North Africa.

Because of the length of the assault frontage and the compartmentalization of the terrain, Patton decided to divide the command of the assault units between II Corps and Seventh Army headquarters. Patton assigned fifty of the seventy miles of army frontage to Bradley's II Corps, consisting of the 45th and 1st Infantry Divisions and the 1st and 4th Ranger Battalions. Truscott's 3d ID and its attached CCA of the 2d Armored Division and the 3rd Ranger Battalion would operate under Patton's direct control.

Patton's plan of maneuver called for simultaneous landings by all of his landing forces at 2:45 a.m., July 10. The 45th ID would land near Scoglitti in the South, move inland to Comiso and Ragusa, and link up with the 1st Canadian Division. The 1st ID and the 1st and 4th Rangers would land in the center, secure Gela and its neighboring airfields, and then move north to Niscemi. The paratroopers, scheduled to land a few hours earlier, were to seize the high ground inland from the 1st ID's beaches and block the road south from Niscemi and the road junction at Piano Lupo. Truscott's 3d ID and the 3d Rangers and CCA would land at Licata, capture the port and airfield there, and protect the left flank of the beachhead. Once the assault forces seized their initial objectives, the 1st and 45th Divisions were to drive north to Highway 124, the initial beachhead line, roughly twenty miles inland.[52]

JOSS Force was assigned the mission of landing on four beaches, code-named Blue, Yellow, Green, and Red from east to west, over a front of approximately ten to twelve miles. "The 30th RCT was to land on Blue Beach, advance rapidly inland and seize the hills overlooking the plain from the Salso River to the sea on the east side. The 15th RCT (less one battalion) was to land on Yellow Beach, seize the bridge and hills overlooking the Salso River," and assist in capturing Licata, its port, and the nearby airfield. "The Ranger Battalion and the 2nd Battalion, 15th Infantry, were to land on Green Beach, capture Monte Sole including the fort and coastal battery, and seize the port and town." The 7th RCT would land on Red Beach, "advance rapidly inland and seize the hills overlooking the plain that covered the approaches to Campobello and Palma di Montechiaro." After the capture of Licata "the 15th Infantry was to take the route to Campobello, the 7th RCT that toward Palma. Combat Command A, in floating reserve, would land as soon as possible on the first available beach in readiness to advance to the northwest." The success of Truscott's mission depended on the early capture of Campobello and Palma di Montechiaro.[53]

The evening of the fourth Truscott boarded the LST USS *Biscayne,* which would serve as his CP until he established his headquarters ashore. Although the usual practice in an amphibious operation is for the naval force commander to exercise command of the operation until the ground force commander has established his command post ashore, Admiral Conolly informed Truscott that he would consider Truscott to be in command of the entire operation even though the orders dictated otherwise. Truscott was particularly impressed with Conolly's offer since it meshed with his opinion that "landing operations which are a step in a land campaign should be the responsibility of the commander who must fight on shore."[54]

Since the three types of vessels carrying the division, LSTs, LCTs (landing craft, tank), and LCIs, had different sailing speeds, the division embarked from Bizerte in three echelons. On the second day the weather worsened considerably, a strong wind battering and slowing the progress of the convoys. However, "Admiral Conolly was equal to the occasion," and his superior navigational skills brought the convoys to the assault area on schedule.[55] As the airborne units began landing at 11:30 p.m. on July 9, Guzzoni learned of the locations where they had landed, correctly concluded that the Allies intended to land on the beaches in the southeastern corner of the island, and issued appropriate orders to the defending forces at 1:45 a.m. on the tenth, nearly an hour before the first Allied assault troops landed.[56]

At 3:40 a.m. Truscott received word that the landing craft were heading in and soon learned that the troops had landed on Blue, Yellow, and Red Beaches. However, there was no communication from the Rangers and the 2d Battalion, 15th Infantry, at Green Beach. Truscott flashed the report to Patton and then ordered that an L-4 aboard the modified LST stand by for takeoff. On order of Truscott, Lt. Julian W. Cummings took off from the ship and headed for Green Beach to assess the situation. He flew about three miles inland and soon saw the Rangers advancing up a hill and radioed the information back to Truscott's command ship.[57]

With the coming of daylight the *Biscayne* moved closer to shore, where Truscott observed that Blue and Yellow Beaches were quiet, with unloading of cargoes proceeding smoothly. At Red Beach, however, where resistance had been stiffer, Truscott and Conolly observed that the flotilla of LCTs had not yet landed, held back by the beach master because the beach was still receiving artillery fire. Recognizing the need to get the tanks ashore, Conolly ordered his commanders to land the LCTs immediately. Assuring himself that the tanks had begun landing, Truscott headed back to Yellow Beach, where he went ashore with his command group. There he learned that the JOSS Force assault had gone almost exactly as planned. Seven hours after setting foot ashore the Americans had seized Licata and its port and the nearby airfield and had quickly organized the beaches and the port for receiving supplies and reinforcements. American casualties were fewer than 100, and the division had taken more than 2,000 prisoners.[58]

Elsewhere, the attacks by the Allies had generally gone well. The Eighth Army met little resistance, and by the end of the first day was established ashore and "well on their way to Augusta." Some elements of the 45th ID had been dis-organized by the storm, with the result that its assault forces had been scat-tered along a ten-mile stretch of beaches. However, two of its regiments were seven miles inland by the end of the first day. The most serious resistance was encountered at Gela, but the Rangers and 1st ID infantrymen were able to capture and hold the town. By the end of the first day Patton's army had firmly secured a beachhead that extended over a fifty-mile front. His army had captured more than 4,000 prisoners at a cost of 58 killed, 199 wounded, and 700 missing.[59]

By noon of D+1 the 3d ID fully occupied its D+3 objective, the initial beach-head line (Yellow Line), and had captured Campobello and Palma di Monte-chiaro. An armored column from the 30th Infantry was advancing along the coastal road to establish contact with II Corps at Gela, which it did by mid-afternoon. By the close of D+1, contact had been established all along the Sev-enth Army front.[60]

At that point Truscott reviewed his mission orders. They did not specify a mission after advancing to the Yellow Line, other than that of protecting the left flank of Seventh Army. He recognized that the communications centers of Enna and Caltanissetta, which dominated the center of the island and controlled the approaches to the Catania plain, would likely be objectives for Patton and that his division might be ordered to attack in that direction. Therefore, he ordered Brig. Gen. Maurice Rose, the commander of the attached CCA, to carry out a reconnaissance and make preparations to attack and seize the town of Cani-catti, roughly seven miles northeast of Campobello. The next morning, July 12, General Keyes visited Truscott and, when informed of the plan, told Truscott that he was sure that Patton would have no objections to his taking Canicatti. Truscott then ordered Rose to carry out the operation, and by midafternoon CCA had captured the town. After relieving CCA with the 15th Infantry, Trus-cott ordered Rose to assemble in reserve at Campobello and be prepared to advance in the direction of Caltanissetta. On the thirteenth Rose began sending out reconnaissance patrols toward Caltanissetta, while the 7th Infantry recon-noitered toward Serra de Falco to the north, and the 30th Infantry moved from its position on the east flank to the Naro area, all in preparation for an attack toward Caltanissetta if ordered.[61]

On the third day within the beachhead Truscott met Michael Chinigo, a war correspondent from the INS (International News Service), who had landed with elements of Sherman's 7th Infantry without Truscott's knowledge. He learned that Chinigo had distinguished himself in the action that followed by answering a ringing telephone in the railroad station and informing, in "per-fect Italian," the inquiring railway agents farther inland that rumors they had heard about Allied landings were incorrect and that the Licata area was quite peaceful. Sherman subsequently recommended Chinigo for the Silver Star, and several months later Truscott had "the pleasure of pinning the decoration on him." Chinigo went on to accompany the 3d ID throughout the Sicily campaign, and later in Italy "his intimate knowledge of Italians and of Italy" proved to be "invaluable" to Truscott. Indeed, the two became close friends.[62]

By the thirteenth, although Patton's forces were making good progress, increasing German resistance and the rugged terrain were slowing Eighth Army's advance toward Catania, leading Alexander to shift the Seventh Army–Eighth Army boundary westward to permit Montgomery "to advance on a broader front into central Sicily and sidestep the main centers of Axis resistance."[63] The shift would strip from Seventh Army's sector Highway 124, which Patton had planned to use as the route along which II Corps would advance inland, swinging around the western slope of Mount Etna toward Messina, while the Eighth Army drove around the volcano's east side.

When Patton learned of the boundary shift early on the morning of July 13 he was furious and immediately began searching for an alternative plan that would give his army an opportunity to play a more decisive role in the capture of Messina. His mind fixed on Palermo, the capital of Sicily and the location of the island's largest port, capture of which would give Patton a port to support a drive by Seventh Army along the north coast of the island to Messina. As he moved his western forces toward Palermo, Patton planned to order Bradley's II Corps to drive north to the coast, cutting the island in two. To help convince Alexander to agree to his new plan Patton decided that he would first have Truscott's 3d Division capture the harbor at Porto Empedocle to support his westward drive.[64]

On the afternoon of the fourteenth Patton visited Truscott's command post for the first time and reviewed the progress of the campaign to date. Patton told Truscott that he planned to shift the axis of the Seventh Army advance to the west toward Palermo, but the capture of Porto Empedocle would be a necessary first step to provide him with a port through which to funnel supplies to support that drive. However, the port lay approximately three miles southwest of Agrigento, which Patton had orders not to attack in strength for fear of his getting involved in a battle that might endanger Eighth Army's left flank. As Patton had undoubtedly hoped, Truscott volunteered his opinion that based on a small reconnaissance mission he had sent toward Agrigento on July 13, he was confident his division could capture Agrigento "without too much trouble," and suggested that Alexander "would probably have no objection to [his] making a reconnaissance in force toward Agrigento on [his] own responsibility." Patton agreed and left the CP, after which Truscott ordered Sherman's 7th Infantry, with the 3d Rangers and a field artillery battalion attached, to attack the town.[65] Sherman's force moved out on the sixteenth, and by two thirty in the afternoon, the 3d Battalion had entered Porto Empedocle, where the Rangers joined them that evening. The next day the 1st Battalion fought its way into

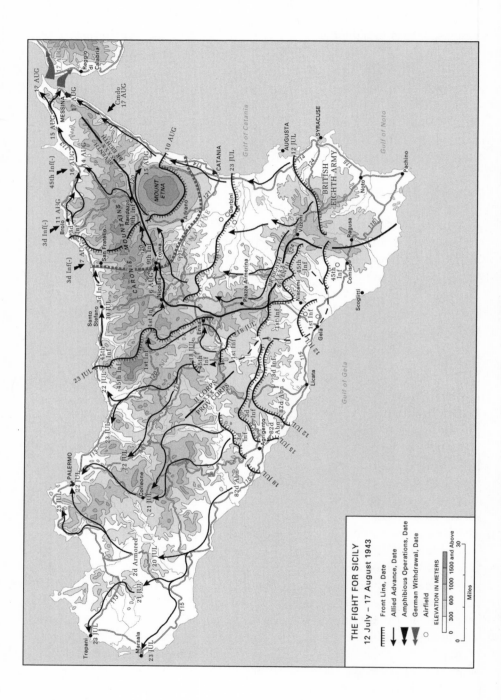

THE FIGHT FOR SICILY
12 July – 17 August 1943

Front Line, Date

Allied Advance, Date

Amphibious Operations, Date

German Withdrawal, Date

Airfield

ELEVATION IN METERS

300 600 1000 1500 and Above

Miles

0   30

114

Agrigento "from the east, overcoming scattered strongpoints and engaging in some street fighting," and by three in the morning the city had fallen.[66]

With Porto Empedocle firmly in his hands, Patton, accompanied by Brig. Gen. Albert C. Wedemeyer, who was visiting Sicily as General Marshall's personal representative, flew to Tunis on the seventeenth and informed Alexander of his plan to attack toward Palermo. Alexander gave his immediate approval, with the proviso that Patton's forces hold the road net near Caltanissetta. Patton promised to do so, later confiding to his diary, "If I do what I am going to do, there is no need of holding anything, but 'it's a mean man who won't promise.'" Wedemeyer, Truscott's classmate at the Command and General Staff School, subsequently visited the 3d Infantry Division and observed it in combat. In his judgment "it was the best-trained, the most aggressive, and the best-led outfit in Sicily. Truscott was one of the best combat leaders that I observed during the entire war."[67]

The afternoon of the eighteenth Truscott received Field Order (FO) no. 1 from Keyes, now commanding the Provisional Corps, consisting of the 3d Infantry, the 82d Airborne, and the 2d Armored Divisions, which Patton had formed to direct the advance toward Palermo.[68] The 3d and 82d were to advance to the northwest and be prepared to attack Palermo from the south and southwest. After those two divisions had broken through the mountains immediately to the north of the present positions of the corps, Keyes then planned to commit Maj. Gen. Hugh J. Gaffey's 2d AD "in a spectacular sweep to capture Palermo." Truscott knew from intelligence reports that the defending forces in his division's zone of advance were mostly Italian troops, since Guzzoni had ordered the 15th Panzer Grenadier Division to the eastern sector of the island.

The first forty miles of the advance to Palermo, some one hundred miles to the northwest, would take his forces through rugged mountains traversed by three twisting roads with "steep grades, hairpin turns, and many bridges," followed by an additional forty-mile course across a plateau that would bring it to the hills surrounding Palermo. Recognizing that the Germans could easily block the roads by the use of demolitions, Truscott planned to have his troops travel as quickly as possible to avoid giving the enemy time to employ their demolitions. He expected that his division would arrive in Palermo in five days and planned to be the first to enter the city. At five o'clock on the morning of July 19, "the drive for Palermo was on."[69]

Truscott deployed his forces as follows: Col. Charles R. Johnson, Jr.'s 15th Infantry took the eastern road, with the attached 4th Moroccan Tabor of *goumiers* paralleling the advance of the regiment on its right. Advancing on the center road was Rogers's 30th Infantry, while the 3d Ranger Battalion was assigned the western road, maintaining contact on its left flank with the 82d Airborne Division and the attached 9th Infantry Division's 39th Infantry Regiment, which were traveling on the coastal road. Sherman's 7th Infantry remained in reserve at Raffadali.

The first objective for Rogers's RCT was heavily defended San Stefano di Quisquina, some twenty air miles north-northeast of Agrigento. However, the twisting road, coupled with the frequent need to resort to cross-country travel, more than doubled that distance. In a remarkable feat of endurance, the 3d Battalion, traveling cross-country without rations or water resupply, marched fifty-four miles in thirty-three hours to reach the objective. The other two battalions, after fighting through demolitions and enemy delaying positions, arrived before the town on the twentieth. The attack was launched that afternoon, and just before nightfall the town fell.

While the battle at San Stefano was still under way, Truscott decided to deploy his reserve 7th Infantry by motor march in a wide envelopment to Castronova east of San Stefano the night of July 20, with orders to attack westward the next morning to capture Prizzi in conjunction with the 30th Infantry's attack on San Stefano. Sherman kicked off his attack early the next morning and soon was in Prizzi. Truscott then directed him to continue his attack northward to Corleone, while the 30th "turned west and north on a parallel road." Johnson's 15th was to remain in the area of Castronova and be prepared to follow the 7th Infantry's route on order.

The evening of the twenty-first the 7th Infantry occupied Corleone and at 9:00 p.m. began its advance northward, with the 15th Infantry following in its wake. After moving his CP to Corleone, Truscott convened a conference with his staff and his regimental commanders at 2:00 a.m. on the twenty-second to outline his plans. The 7th was to advance "at top speed shuttling its rear battalions forward to block the eastern exits from Palermo north of Misilmeri." The 15th was to advance on a secondary road to the west of the 7th's route of advance "and occupy the heights overlooking Palermo on the south." The 30th was to assemble south of Corleone and serve as the division reserve. The 7th and the 15th moved out later that morning, and by noon the 7th was near Misilmeri and the 15th was at Piano del Greci. Both had encountered only sporadic resistance, and the Italians had surrendered in "such large numbers as to be embarrassing."

Truscott moved forward to an observation post near Piano del Greci, from which he could hear explosions within Palermo. Despite repeated requests for permission to enter the city to prevent further destruction by the Germans, he was ordered to hold on the present line. Finally, after civilians from the city met with Brig. Gen. William W. Eagles, who was with Sherman at Villabete, and offered to surrender the city, Keyes gave permission for Truscott to send reconnaissance patrols into Palermo to protect the port, which he did. When Patton and Keyes entered Palermo at the head of an armored column at about ten thirty that night, they were greeted by dogfaces of the 3d ID. Palermo had fallen just seventy-two hours after the division began its advance toward the city, two days earlier than Truscott had estimated.[70] To celebrate his division's rapid advance to and capture of Palermo, Truscott ordered his aide Lt. Jack Bartash "to make [the] rounds of Regimental COs with a case of Champagne for each with the compliments of General T for their splendid work" over the past few days.[71]

By the twenty-fourth Keyes's Provisional Corps was in complete control of the western half of Sicily and had captured 53,000 of the enemy, mostly Italians, at a cost of 272 American casualties (57 killed, 170 wounded, and 45 missing). In addition, Seventh Army had seized 189 guns of 75mm caliber or larger, 359 vehicles, and 41 tanks. To the east, in the II Corps sector, the 180th Infantry Regiment of Troy H. Middleton's 45th ID reached the northern coast of Sicily thirty-one miles east of Palermo on the twenty-third, cutting the island in two.[72] By July 23 the Eighth Army occupied a line extending from the Gulf of Catania westward through Gerbini and then northwestward to the area at the junction of Highways 117 and 121 southwest of Nicosia.[73]

On July 20 Alexander directed Patton to send strong reconnaissance patrols to the east along two main routes, Highway 113 along the coast and Highway 120 running eastward from Petralia, the location of the 1st ID, through Sperlinga, Nicosia, and Troina. In part Alexander's decision to turn Seventh Army to the east was his recognition that with the British drive bogged down south of Catania, Montgomery would need Patton's assistance to capture Messina. The vital port would now be the target of Patton's drive from the west and of Montgomery's attack from the south.[74]

Three days later Alexander told Patton that instead of sending reconnaissance patrols to probe eastward he was to "employ his maximum strength along the two roads." To implement Alexander's order, Patton decided to augment II Corps, to which he had assigned responsibility for the entire Seventh Army front, by reassigning units from the Provisional Corps to Bradley's corps. He also requested the remainder of the 9th Infantry Division be brought over to Sicily for the push through the mountainous terrain, realizing that he would soon be losing the 82d Airborne and the 45th Infantry Divisions, which were to be withdrawn to prepare for the invasion of the Italian mainland.[75]

Alexander also directed Patton to leave sufficient forces in western Sicily to mop up any remaining enemy forces, and for that duty he chose Keyes's Provisional Corps less the units he had ordered to join the Messina drive. Truscott had been anxious to participate in the drive to Messina, but Patton assigned the attack on the coastal road to the 45th ID. Therefore, the 3d ID busied itself for the first few days after the fall of Palermo collecting and evacuating enemy prisoners and carrying out police duties within Palermo. When relieved of those duties by other Army troops, the division went into bivouac for refitting and refurbishing to prepare for any additional combat for which they might be called.

Truscott established his headquarters in a villa owned by Princess di Gang, a lady-in-waiting to the queen of Italy. He had hardly settled into the plush quarters when he received word on the twenty-sixth to report to Patton in his headquarters in the Royal Palace in Palermo. "Over a highball" Patton told Truscott that he would like to beat Montgomery in the race for Messina. Truscott answered, "with some brashness, and doubtless a measure of conceit—I was never modest where the 3rd Infantry Division was concerned," that adding the 3d ID to the advance was one way for him to win that race. Patton told Truscott there was a possibility that the 3d might get into the fray by relieving Terry Allen's 1st ID, which had been in action longer than any other American division. The next day Truscott dispatched staff officers to Bradley's headquarters and Allen's headquarters to assess the situation. However, when he visited Truscott three days later, on July 30, Keyes told him to begin relieving the 45th ID the next day near San Stefano di Camastra on Highway 113, some sixty to seventy road miles east of Palermo. On the thirty-first the 30th Infantry relieved elements of the 157th and 179th Infantry Regiments west of San Stefano, and by midnight of August 1, "the 3rd Infantry Division was concentrated in the area, and the race for Messina was on."[76]

As Truscott studied the maps of the road net over which his division was to advance to Messina, he noted that he would be confronted with problems he had not previously faced. In earlier operations he could fix an enemy force with his lead elements and then employ other forces to envelop the enemy and strike him in the flank or rear. There had also been several roads over which to move replacements and supplies, so that if one road were blocked, alternate routes could be utilized. On this advance his vehicles and any supporting armor would be confined to a coastal plain "no more than a few hundred yards in width. The only road, Highway 113, was a first-class concrete strip which followed the shore line closely," but to the south of the highway there were few parallel roads, and most of those were mostly dead-end roads. Off-road, the terrain was trafficable only by mules and men on foot. The weather was insufferably hot, with little cooling wind. Complicating the terrain and weather problems was the fact that most of the enemy his soldiers would now face would be Germans, not Italians. Recognizing the problems of off-road movement, Truscott organized his roughly four hundred mules and the one hundred horses the division had acquired into a provisional pack train and a provisional mounted troop. The animals were to prove very helpful in the advance to Messina, where Truscott would utilize the mules as pack animals and call on the mounted troop to outflank enemy positions in terrain that motorized or tracked vehicles could not navigate.[77]

During the advance the division would face a series of heavily defended delaying positions, sited to take advantage of the many natural defensive features the terrain provided, which would make frontal attacks very costly. However, bypassing of the positions would be difficult because of heavy enemy minefields covered by enemy artillery, machine-gun, and rifle fire. Further, vehicular movement would be extremely difficult, since the enemy had destroyed many bridges. Therefore, he planned to move forward by thrusting one element along the axis of advance, clearing terrain overlooking the highway. Simultaneously, other elements and their mule pack trains would be moving through the difficult terrain south of the road to hit the enemy's flanks and rear, aiming to encircle the enemy position and trap the Germans occupying the defenses. However, the enemy had the advantage of being able to hold to the last minute and then disengage and withdraw to the rear in their vehicles, while the American dogfaces followed on foot.

On August 3 Keyes informed Truscott that Patton had arranged with the U.S. Navy for landing craft and naval personnel to lift one battalion combat team in an amphibious operation behind German lines and offered the craft and crews to him. Truscott chose Lt. Col. Lyle W. Bernard's 2d Battalion, 30th Infantry, with attached artillery, armor, and engineer elements, for the mission. The first landing site would be at Sant' Agata di Militello, a few miles east of Monte Fratello, where Truscott expected to encounter the first enemy strong point.

Earlier, on the first, two battalions of the 30th Infantry had begun advancing eastward and, after a fierce firefight at Caronia, were in position east of the town on the second. The 15th Infantry passed through the 30th and continued the attack toward Monte Fratello, reaching the German lines in front of the twenty-two hundred–foot well-defended mountain on August 3. The next day the 15th mounted an attack on the German position but made little progress. The excellent observation afforded the Germans occupying the flat top of the mountain made any movement on the road almost impossible, and efforts to advance south of the road were unsuccessful. At that point Truscott decided to turn to Bernard's BCT and have it land behind the German position on the seventh. However, the attack was delayed for a day after a German air attack sank an LST while loading was in progress.

By August 7 the 15th and 30th Infantry Regiments had been able to establish a position on the ridge south of Monte Fratello. The next morning the 7th Infantry attacked through the 15th along the coastal road, while the 30th attacked from the ridge south of the mountain and Bernard's BCT landed at Sant' Agata, attacking Monte Fratello from the east. The battle was soon over. Although 3d Division losses had been heavy, the men of the division had captured more than sixteen hundred prisoners and several batteries of artillery while destroying numerous tanks and other matériel. "It had been the toughest fight we had had so far."[78]

While Bernard readied his BCT for another landing, the 7th Infantry resumed the advance eastward from Sant' Agata, and despite increasing enemy resistance the dogfaces were able to advance to a position east of the Di Zappulla River.[79] On the night of the ninth, Johnson's 15th Infantry and its mule train moved south through San Marco di Lunzo to seize a ridge south of Naso, from which they would attack the town the morning of August 11, when Bernard's BCT was to land at Brolo. However, Truscott decided to postpone the attack and Bernard's landing for a day because he was unable to get artillery in place to support the 15th's attack and because the regiment had not yet secured the ridge.

When Truscott informed Keyes of his decision, the latter replied that General Patton would want the landing to go ahead, since "arrangements had been made for a large number of correspondents to accompany it, and there would be criticism if the operation were postponed." Keyes then placed a call to Bradley, who agreed with Truscott. Next, Keyes phoned Patton and told him that Truscott "did not want to carry out the landing operation." When Truscott took the phone and attempted to explain his reasons for the decision, Patton would not listen and said, "Dammit, that operation will go on," and slammed down the receiver.

An hour later Patton stormed into Truscott's CP, shouting at all whom he encountered. When he found Truscott, he screamed, "Goddammit, Lucian, what's the matter with you? Are you afraid to fight?" Truscott "bristled right back: 'General, you know that's ridiculous and insulting. You have ordered the operation and it is now loading. If you don't think I can carry out your orders, you can give the Division to anyone you please. But I tell you one thing, you will not find anyone who can carry out orders which they do not approve as well as I can.'" Immediately, Patton's anger disappeared, and he threw his arm about Truscott's shoulder, saying, "Dammit, Lucian, I know that. Come on, let's have a drink—of your liquor." This they did, and Patton departed shortly after, "in his usual good spirits." Truscott then turned to the problems at hand.[80]

The problems Bernard's BCT would face at Brolo were multiple: the force was understrength; no other battalion would be within ten miles; it would find itself hard-pressed to sustain itself for the many hours before linkup; the landing beach was not good, and the exits inland were poor; it would land close behind the German lines, extending from Cape Orlando south through Naso; and the German reaction to the landing would be quick and violent, more so than the BCT encountered at Sant' Agata. Therefore, Truscott decided "to commit every element in the Division, including a Ranger Battalion just recently attached." His plan was for the 15th Infantry to attack across the Naso ridge to the high ground overlooking Brolo, while the 7th Infantry would attack south of the highway and capture Naso. The Rangers would then infiltrate between them and through the German position and link up with Bernard's BCT.[81]

On the morning of the eleventh the 7th Infantry initiated its attack south of the highway, and despite heavy enemy machine-gun and mortar fire occupied Malo by 10:30 a.m., and then moved on to Pernicchia, which it occupied at 11:45 a.m. It then turned toward Brolo to the northeast, where the enemy was preparing a counterattack against Bernard's BCT, which had landed at 3:00

a.m. Initially, Bernard's landing force had encountered only light resistance, but the resistance steadily increased throughout the day. By 10:10 the Germans were massing on the east and west flanks of Bernard's troops, and Truscott was desperately urging all three of his regimental commanders to speed up their attacks and break through to Bernard's beleaguered men. At noon Bernard called for "ALL POSSIBLE ARTILLERY SUPPORT ON BROLO EAST 1000 yards," and Truscott initiated new requests for naval and air support. Throughout the afternoon the counterattack continued, as Bernard continued to plead for the reinforcing regiments to break through to his BCT. Despite having no artillery support the 15th Infantry had captured Naso by late afternoon and moved into the area around Castel Umberto. By early evening "the leading battalions of the 7th [were] making their way down the spurs to the rescue. . . . The 15th was on the spurs just above Mount Cipollo . . . [and] the leading battalion of the 30th was doing a speed march down the road from Cape Orlando." Bernard's BCT was finally rescued early in the evening of the eleventh, but it had been a close thing, and the enemy forces had escaped.

As Truscott later learned, Bernard had been unable to get his artillery and tanks up the steep exit from the beach onto the hill his infantrymen occupied. Seven of the eight guns and three of the four tanks that came ashore were lost, although two of the tanks were later recovered. At a cost of 167 casualties, Bernard's force had held, littering the area with German dead. As Truscott mused, "Had we delayed [the landing] a day, we might have captured most of the German force. Nevertheless, we had gained important time." By August 12 the division was occupying a line running from Brolo to Castel Umberto, but the cost to get there had been high. The 7th Infantry alone had 15 officers and 400 enlisted men killed, wounded, and missing, and the other elements of the division had suffered proportionate losses.[82]

On August 12 the 30th Infantry, less Bernard's battered battalion, continued the advance but was stopped almost immediately at Piriano by artillery and machine-gun fire from Cape Calavá. After bypasses had been constructed, Truscott moved the 15th Infantry and the 3d Ranger Battalion by motor march south to San Angelo di Brolo, from which they moved northeast across the mountains to Patti, capturing the town on the thirteenth.

It became imperative to move artillery and tanks forward to those infantrymen and Rangers, but just east of a tunnel at Cape Calavá the Germans had blown a 150-foot segment of the highway into the sea 100 feet below. The division engineer battalion moved forward, and on the twelfth began erecting a trestle bridge across the gap, with orders from Truscott to complete the bridge by noon the next day.

Truscott spent that day and night at the bridge site, occasionally grabbing a catnap as the work went on. Ernie Pyle, one of America's best-known war correspondents, happened to be visiting the 3d Division at that time and recorded that after nightfall one of the engineers dragging an air hose passed by the general during one of his naps, entangling Truscott's feet in the coils of the hose. Annoyed, the fatigued soldier glanced down at the "anonymous figure on the ground," and said, "'If you're not working, get the hell out of the way.' The general got up and moved farther back without saying a word."

By noon of the thirteenth the engineers had completed the bridge, a truly remarkable feat of field engineering that included a 60-foot trestle span, and jeeps began crossing, the first one carrying Truscott. Two-and-a-half-ton trucks were crossing by midafternoon, followed by twenty-five-ton loads by midnight. Although the 15th Infantry continued to pursue the withdrawing Germans, the latter withdrew in motor vehicles, making their capture by the foot-weary infantrymen difficult.[83]

The 15th continued its advance on the fourteenth and contacted the enemy at Fernari, where they drove "the Boche across the last cross road leading to the south by dark." From that point to Messina the terrain was not as difficult, and on August 15 the 7th continued the attack. By leapfrogging the battalions of the 7th Infantry, Truscott was able to have the regiment on the heights overlooking Messina by midnight. He immediately ordered a 155mm "Long Tom" to the crest, where it fired the first hundred rounds of American artillery onto the Italian mainland. That night patrols from the 3d Battalion, 7th Infantry, became the first Allied troops to enter Messina, just as the last Germans were withdrawing across the Straits of Messina.[84]

The following morning, the seventeenth, Truscott arrived atop the heights, where he accepted the surrender of the city from both Italian civil and military representatives. However, he did not enter Messina, since Keyes had told him to await Patton's arrival so that they could enter the city together. When Patton arrived at about ten in the morning, all the party got into the waiting vehicles and moved down the winding road into Messina. Just after the Americans arrived in the city, a British armored patrol entered from the west. The race to Messina had ended, and Patton was victorious.[85]

The following evening General Truscott invited all of the regimental commanders, his aides, and other selected officers to his CP at Rometta to join him in "victory cocktails and buffet supper. A very merry time was had by all. Scotch hightball [sic], cognac, and champagne keenly enjoyed after the mad dash to Messina."[86]

Hanson W. Baldwin has called the battle for Sicily "an Allied physical victory, a German moral victory." Some 60,000 to 75,000 Germans had managed to wage a defensive campaign against an Allied force of just under 500,000 that prolonged a projected two-week campaign to thirty-eight days, allowing, despite overwhelming Allied air and naval superiority, the evacuation of more than 100,000 German and Italian troops and more than 10,000 vehicles to the mainland of Italy. The battle had clearly "demonstrated the many limitations of interservice and inter-Allied cooperation," problems that would recur during the fighting on the Italian boot.[87]

However, "Sicily became the proving ground where the US Army came of age [and where] Lucian Truscott whipped the 3d Division into one of the finest infantry divisions in the Army."[88] His beloved dogfaces had played a vital role in the capture of both Palermo and Messina, applying well the lessons learned under Truscott's strict tutelage. Superbly conditioned by the strenuous physical training program he had initiated, including the now famous "Truscott Trot," his soldiers had moved vast distances over extremely rugged terrain at a speed unmatched by any other infantry unit on the island. When the terrain became impassable for vehicles, weapons and supplies continued to move to the front on the backs of the hardened infantrymen or on the backs of some 650 sure-footed mules they had brought with them from North Africa or had "requisitioned" from Sicilian farmers. So impressed with the effectiveness of the mule pack trains, General Bradley recommended that "in contemplated operations in mountainous terrain, plans should include facilities for supply by pack train."[89]

One other tactical innovation introduced by Truscott was the bypassing of well-prepared enemy coastal positions by short amphibious assaults by a BCT, supported by naval gunfire, into the enemy rear. The two such landings along the north coast of the island during the advance to Messina contributed materially to the speed with which the division reached its objective. However, the division's successes were bought at a cost: 381 killed, 1,398 wounded, 146 missing, and 2,983 nonbattle casualties. The count of the enemy dead and wounded was unknown, but 50,104 enemy soldiers became prisoners of war.[90]

On the twenty-fifth Truscott wrote Sarah about the capture of Messina and of his pride in the division. He asked her to pass on to her father, Doctor Randolph, his message that "Stonewall Jackson's Foot Cavalry are practically recruits beside my lads." He also wrote that "Georgie [Patton] sent me a barrel of cognac today—On the barrel is the division insignia about a foot square—and under it a painted streamer—'First in Messina.'" Three days later he once again expressed to Sarah the pride he felt for his dogfaces: "The world has never seen their equal since the days of Stonewall Jackson—and has never seen their superiors. All of my friends and most of the orthodox doughs thought I was a bit cracked of course—and that we would be no better or worse than any other when the bullets were flying. I reminded the lads today that in this operation we had been first in every objective." He then went on to quote jokingly *Newsweek*'s recent description of him: "One of the Army's best polo players and least joyful characters because of his stern face, strong large nose, and austerity."[91]

On August 25 Truscott sent a letter to Eisenhower in which he reviewed the 3d Division's campaign in Sicily. He particularly stressed how well his battalion commanders and two of his regimental commanders, Colonels Rogers and

Sherman, had performed. He was dissatisfied with Colonel Charles R. Johnson, Jr., and wanted to relieve him but indicated he would not do so "until [he] can be assured that someone worse will not be foisted off on me." He went on to say that he "was firmly of the opinion that any man fifty years old is much too old to command a modern infantry regiment in modern war." On September 1 Truscott did relieve Johnson of command of the 15th Infantry, stating that he lacked "clear, calm judgment and mental stability under stress of battle," that he failed "to exert personal leadership to attain the objectives he was ordered to attain," and that he did not possess "a sound, fundamental knowledge of the capabilities of a modern infantry regiment nor of the methods necessary to fight an infantry regiment successfully in modern battle." Truscott believed, however, that Johnson's combat experience "would fit him eminently for command of a replacement training depot."[92]

Chapter 8

FIGHTING ON THE "BOOT"

Truscott was aware even before the cessation of fighting in Sicily that planning was under way to invade the Italian mainland and eliminate Italy from the war. Although he was not privy to all of the details of the plan, he knew that the overall concept was to have Montgomery's "Eighth Army cross over the Straits of Messina, seize the Italian naval base at Taranto, and advance northward up the Italian boot in conjunction with a later assault somewhere in the vicinity of Naples by a combined British-American Force under the newly organized Fifth Army," commanded by Maj. Gen. Mark W. Clark.

He also knew that some American divisions were to be withdrawn from the Mediterranean theater and sent to England to begin training for the cross-Channel invasion scheduled to take place in the spring of 1944. Truscott had assumed that his division would be one of those because of its amphibious assault training and experience, and because of his earlier experience in Mountbatten's Combined Operations Headquarters. When he learned that the 3d ID was not one of those chosen to go to England, he was in fact relieved, since he knew that those selected to participate in the invasion would be involved in a long period of training, while his division was now almost certain to see early action in the coming Italian campaign.[1]

On September 3 Truscott learned that Montgomery's army had crossed the straits and landed on the mainland against only light resistance. The next day he received orders to report to Algiers with key members of his staff to confer with Clark and his staff about plans for future employment of the 3d ID in Italy. The morning of the fifth Truscott and Carleton, accompanied by the G2, G4, and division artillery commander, flew to Algiers, where they boarded the USS *Ancon* to meet with Clark and Admiral Hewitt and their staffs. Clark's G3, Brig. Gen. Don Brann, briefed them on the plans for AVALANCHE, the code name for the invasion of Italy at Salerno, following which Truscott's staff met with their Fifth Army counterparts, while Truscott and Carleton conferred with Clark and Brann about the landing and Fifth Army plans for the employment of the 3d Infantry Division.

AVALANCHE plans called for the 36th Infantry Division, coming directly from the United States, to land at Paestum, while two British divisions of the British 10 Corps would land farther north, opposite the city of Salerno. Salerno had been selected as the invasion site "because of its favorable sea approach, its proximity to Naples, and its being in range of fighter air cover from Allied-controlled Sicily." The capture of Naples and its port, fifty miles to the north, was the primary objective of the operation.[2]

Clark informed Truscott that the Italians had surrendered on the third and had agreed that they would not oppose the landings.[3] However, the surrender would not be announced publicly until after the landings. Since he expected no opposition to the landings, Clark believed that there would be no need to employ Truscott's division at Salerno, but he ordered Truscott to be prepared to land his division farther north, possibly as far north as Rome, an objective Clark was already eyeing. Truscott accepted Clark's optimism with some degree of skepticism, since his experience with the Germans led him to believe that even if the landings were unopposed, the Germans would soon react violently once the troops were ashore and advancing inland.[4]

Truscott and his party returned to his headquarters, bearing not only the information presented by Clark and his staff but also "considerable African booty in the form of leather briefcases, [a] new Packard sedan, and three cases of whiskey."[5] One of the first tasks that Truscott attended to after his return was to have his division signal officer establish a radio intercept net on the wavelengths of Fifth Army and the naval task force so that he could keep himself informed of the progress of AVALANCHE during and after the landings on the morning of the ninth. As he reviewed the status of his division he concluded that, despite a shortfall of two thousand officers and men, "it was fit and ready." Col. William H. Ritter had arrived and assumed command of the 15th Infantry on September 7, and Lt. Col. Ben Harrell, the acting commander, became Ritter's executive officer. The division now awaited orders defining its mission on the Italian boot.[6]

Expecting the Allies to land at Salerno, Kesselring ordered the 16th Panzer Division to assume responsibility for the defense of the presumed landing area until some of the German divisions to the south, now engaged with Montgomery's Eighth Army, could extricate themselves and move north and divisions in the Rome area could be dispatched south.

At 3:30 a.m. on September 9, Clark launched his attack, Lt. Gen. Sir Richard McCreery's 10 Corps landing north of the Sele River and the 36th Infantry Division of Maj. Gen. Ernest J. Dawley's VI Corps landing south of the river, with the 45th Infantry Division in floating reserve. On the far left flank of the British sector a

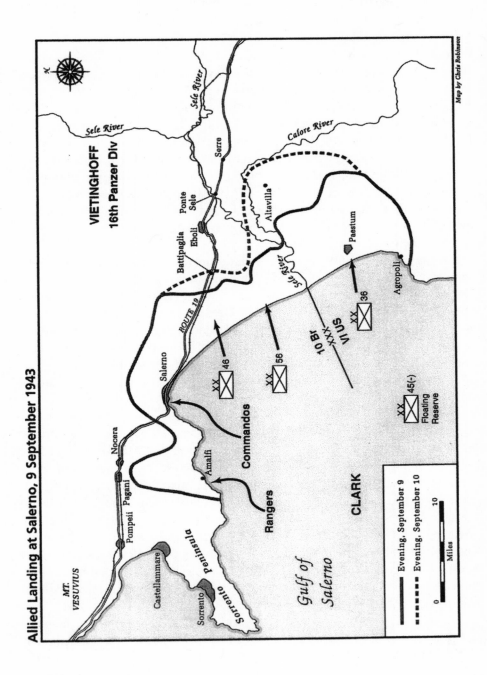

Allied Landing at Salerno, 9 September 1943

MT. VESUVIUS

Castellammare

Sorrento Peninsula

Sorrento

Gulf of Salerno

Nocera

Pompeii

Pagani

Salerno

Amalfi

Rangers

Commandos

XX 46

XX 56

10 Br
XXX
VI US

XX 36

XX 45(-)
Floating Reserve

CLARK

Paestum

Agropoli

Altavilla

ROUTE 19

Battipaglia

Eboli

Ponte Sele

Serre

Sele River

Sele River

Calore River

Sele River

VIETINGHOFF
16th Panzer Div

Evening, September 9
Evening, September 10

0   10
Miles

Map by Chris Robinson

force of the 1st, 3d, and 4th Ranger Battalions and Commandos "quickly ascended the dorsal mountain ridge of the Sorrento Peninsula, wresting control of a section of the ridge from the Germans and seizing the heights overlooking the Naples-Salerno road."

Southeast of Salerno, the British 46th and 56th Infantry Divisions landed on three beaches, and, despite a heavy Allied naval and air bombardment preceding the landings, encountered stout resistance. In the south, hoping to achieve tactical surprise, the 36th Infantry Division assaulted four beaches without naval or air support. However, the Americans failed to achieve the hoped-for surprise, and the fire from the intact enemy batteries produced heavy casualties within the early assault waves. Unfazed by the casualties, the Americans drove inland, and by nightfall had extended their beachhead to the foothills five miles distant. To the north, no part of the British 10 Corps beachhead was deeper than two miles. Importantly, neither 10 Corps nor VI Corps had been able to extend its flanks to the Sele River, resulting in a gap of some six or seven miles between the two corps.

On the tenth the 45th ID began to land north of the 36th Division. That same day the 16th Panzer Division shifted most of its strength northward, better to protect its communications with Naples. However, the gap between the two Allied corps persisted, inviting a German counterattack along the Sele River, completely splitting the British and American beachheads and endangering the entire operation. Compounding Clark's problems was the arrival of the first German reinforcements from the south, and two additional divisions were on the way from the Naples area. Hoping to exercise tighter command of his army, Clark moved his headquarters ashore near the Sele River.

Gen. Heinrich von Vietinghoff, commanding the Tenth Army, decided to contain the British by using the two divisions that had deployed from northern Italy and the 16th Panzer Division and to have the 26th Panzer and 29th Panzer Grenadier Divisions, which had just arrived from the south, strike through the Sele River gap and smash the north flank of VI Corps on the afternoon of the thirteenth. The attack kicked off on schedule, and "as dusk approached, nothing stood between the Germans and the sea but two American artillery battalions and Mark Clark's headquarters." Fearing that he might lose the beachhead since he had no other forces to reinforce the Sele River sector, Clark contacted Admiral Hewitt in his flagship and alerted him to prepare a plan to evacuate the VI Corps beachhead, possibly shifting the American forces to the British sector.

However, Clark had one other arrow in his quiver to save the beachhead: a drop of Maj. Gen. Matthew B. Ridgway's 82d Airborne Division paratroopers within the VI Corps lines. Clark sent an urgent message to Ridgway in Sicily the afternoon of September 13, requesting that he drop paratroopers within the beachhead that night. Within seven and one-half hours of receiving Clark's

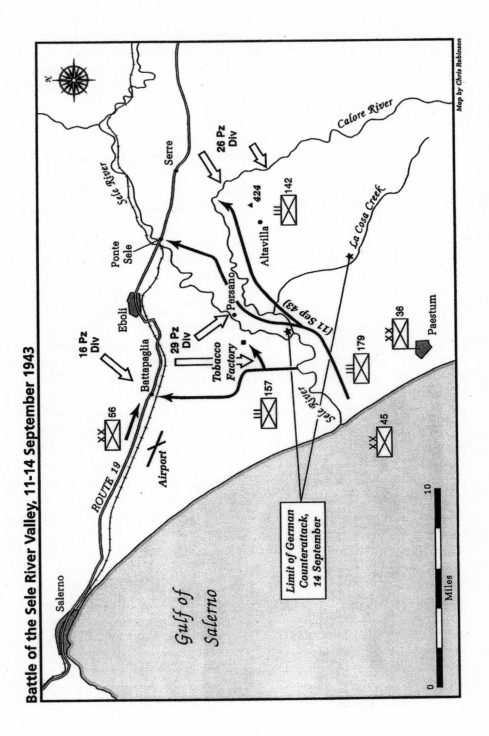

Battle of the Sele River Valley, 11-14 September 1943

Map by Chris Robinson

desperate message, Ridgway had the 504th Parachute Infantry RCT airborne and on the way to Salerno. That drop and another the following night by the 2d Battalion of the 509th Parachute Infantry Regiment at Avellino were both successful. The presence of the paratroopers, the heroic stand of the field artillery battalions and units associated with them, and effective naval gunfire support played major roles in saving AVALANCHE. After numerous German counterattacks on the succeeding two days failed, Vietinghoff asked Kesselring for permission to withdraw, and on the seventeenth the Tenth Army was on the road north.[7]

On September 15 Alexander visited Clark in the beachhead, where Clark told him that he believed Dawley's performance as VI Corps commander had been unsatisfactory and that he should be relieved, with which Alexander agreed. After gaining Eisenhower's concurrence, Clark decided to relieve Dawley of command on the twentieth.[8]

Although Truscott and his staff received some fragmentary news about the progress of the landings at Salerno, they learned little about the actual action that was taking place in the beachhead. On the afternoon of the eleventh Keyes visited Truscott's headquarters at Trapani to inform him that the situation at Salerno was "desperate." About nine o'clock on the night of September 13, Patton telephoned Truscott and told him that he was to come to Palermo the next day to meet with Clark. However, just before midnight a message from 15th Army Group ordered him to move his division to Salerno "as soon as possible." Truscott immediately called Brig. Gen. William W. Eagles, assistant division commander, Brig. Gen. William A. Campbell, division artillery commander, and his staff together and told them that beginning early the next morning they were to supervise the movement of the division to the staging area near Palermo, where the division would receive replacements from the 1st and 9th Infantry Divisions.

Early on the fourteenth Truscott and Carleton went to Palermo, conferred briefly with Patton, and left by a PT (patrol torpedo) boat for Salerno. There they boarded the *Biscayne,* Hewitt's flagship, only to find that he had departed on the *Ancon* after command of the operation had passed to Clark. After supper Truscott and Carleton went ashore and went to Clark's CP, where they learned from Maj. Gen. Alfred M. Gruenther, Clark's chief of staff, that Clark was visiting the British 10 Corps sector. Gruenther brought them up to date on the situation, pointing out that the operation had been "a near thing." He went on to state that Clark had expected Eighth Army to advance northward more rapidly. As they were talking, two war correspondents that had been with Montgomery's army arrived at the CP and told them that Eighth Army was only some forty miles to the south and that they had encountered no enemy forces on their northward journey, indicating that possibly the worst was over for the beachhead forces.

The next morning Truscott met with Clark, who told him that he would like to have the 3d ID in Italy as soon as possible, since he expected a renewal of the German attacks, and that it would be assigned to the VI Corps on arrival. He further suggested that Truscott and Carleton visit the front to acquaint themselves with the situation the division would encounter. They first visited the west flank of the 36th Division, where they found Brig. Gen. John O'Daniel, whom Clark had sent to the threatened area in the gap with an engineer battalion and some tank destroyers to organize a defense. He briefed them on the situation in his sector, emphasizing the ferocity of the German attacks the previous day, "a dramatic underscoring of how desperate had been the need for [additional] men" in the beachhead.

The two went on to visit Dawley and Maj. Gen. Fred L. Walker, commanding the 36th Infantry Division. Dawley explained that he had not expected to assume command of the beachhead until it had been secured, and when ordered to do so on D-day did not as yet have his staff assembled or communications in place ashore. Truscott and Carleton then returned to the Fifth Army CP, where they "found increasing optimism" about the ultimate success of the operation. After arriving in Palermo later that day they learned that their division had arrived in the staging area and had been brought up to nearly full strength by the replacements.

Early on the morning of the seventeenth as the first convoy of LSTs sailed for the Salerno area, the next convoy began loading, to be followed by a third convoy. That same afternoon a BBC broadcast announced that Eighth Army patrols had linked up with Fifth Army patrols, effectively ending the Salerno campaign. The first convoy began unloading in the beachhead the morning of the eighteenth, and by the end of September 20 the entire division, except for an administration center that had been left in Sicily, was assembled north of the Sele River. On the nineteenth the division began reconnoitering positions in the vicinity of Battipaglia.[9]

As early as September 10 Kesselring had "already drawn on the map . . . successive defence positions in the event of a retirement [of his forces] from southern Italy." Despite the failure of Vietinghoff's Tenth Army to throw the Allies back into the sea at Salerno and Rommel's urging Hitler to withdraw all German forces into northern Italy, Kesselring still believed that he could defend on a line below Rome. Hitler ultimately sided with Kesselring, who ordered Tenth Army to fall back to the Volturno River and hold that line until October 15. Vietinghoff was then to fight a series of delaying actions while withdrawing to a line running through Monte Mignano, the Reinhard or Bernhard line, which Kesselring ordered him to defend stubbornly. If forced to retire farther north, Vietinghoff was to withdraw to the Garigliano River–Rapido River–Monte Cassino line, the Gustav line, which he was to hold.[10]

The Fall of Naples, 1 October 1943

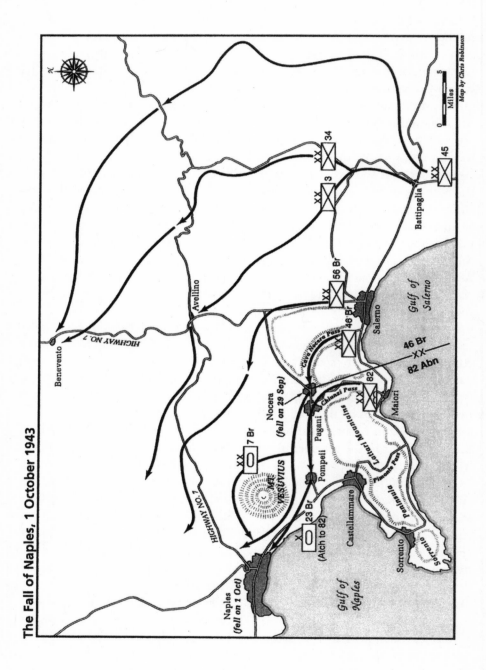

Map by Chris Robinson

On September 18 Clark called a conference of major commanders and key staff officers to discuss future plans for the employment of Fifth Army. He decided to have 10 Corps on the army left make the main thrust to Naples by advancing through the two major mountain passes held by the Rangers, and then continue to the Naples plain. VI Corps, consisting of the 3d and 45th IDs, would make a flanking movement through the mountains on the right, cut Highway 7 running eastward from Teora through Avellino to Naples, and maintain contact with the right flank of 10 Corps. Clark held the 82d Airborne and the 36th Infantry Divisions in army reserve. The appropriate orders went out to subordinate units on September 19, directing that the attack begin the next day.[11]

As the attacks toward Naples began, Clark relieved Dawley of command of VI Corps and replaced him with Maj. Gen. John P. Lucas, who had succeeded Omar Bradley as commander of II Corps in early September. Eisenhower, with Marshall's approval, reduced Dawley to his permanent grade of colonel and returned him to the United States; Marshall later promoted Dawley to brigadier general and gave him a training command.[12]

That morning the 30th Infantry pushed north from Battipaglia toward Acerno, encountering enemy patrols south of the town before nightfall. After developing and attacking the enemy defenses within and around Acerno during the next two days the regiment captured the town the afternoon of the twenty-second. That same day a battalion of the 7th Infantry, with an attached 75mm pack howitzer battery, moved to a ridge northwest of Curticelle to begin patrolling the Sabato Valley and to cut the road leading north from Acerno.

The next day the division continued its advance north to Montella and west to Avellino, encountering numerous blown bridges along the way, which brought the division engineers forward to construct bypasses or to replace the destroyed bridges with trestle or Bailey bridges, the latter "a knock-down steel bridge which is put together like a boy's Erector Set." Heavy rain that began on the twenty-sixth washed out roads and made off-road vehicular travel almost impossible, further slowing the advance. Fighting its way through enemy patrols and an occasional enemy outpost, the 7th Infantry entered Montella on September 30, the same day that the 15th Infantry, which had encountered practically no enemy resistance during its advance, arrived on the heights south of Avellino. While in the Avellino area, elements of the division made contact with the battalion of the 509th Parachute Infantry Regiment that had dropped there during the night of September 14. The paratroopers informed Truscott's men that the Germans were withdrawing to a line north of the Volturno River.[13]

On October 1 the 3d ID, in conformance with Fifth Army orders, began advancing in two directions: the 15th Infantry westward through Avello to assist 10 Corps in taking Naples and the 30th Infantry northward toward Montesarchio. After learning that the British had entered Naples without opposition,

Clark ordered VI Corps to turn northward toward Benevento and then move on to the Volturno River.

The next day Truscott joined Middleton, the 45th ID commander, and Maj. Gen. Charles W. Ryder, commanding the newly arrived 34th ID, at Lucas's CP, where they learned that Alexander's 15th Army Group had established two phase lines to control the advance of the British Eighth Army on the Adriatic side of the peninsula and the Fifth Army to the west of the British: one line ran from Termoli in the East through Isernia and Venafro to Sezza in the West, while the other lay well above Rome. Clark had as a result ordered 10 Corps to advance to the Volturno, force crossings of the river, and continue the advance to the first phase line. VI Corps was to capture Benevento and secure crossing sites on the Calore River west of the town with one division, which was then to move north of Benevento and join the British on the first phase line. The remainder of the corps was to move as quickly as possible northwest between Benevento and the corps boundary.

Lucas ordered Truscott to continue his advance to the Volturno along the roads they were then using. Accordingly, Truscott directed Ritter to move his 15th Infantry northward from Avello through Cancello to the mountains above Caserta. Rogers's 30th Infantry was to move along the mountain roads through Montesarchio and Airola to the junction of the Calore and Volturno Rivers. However, incessant rains and fierce German resistance slowed the advance of the two regiments. Compounding the difficulties were the muddy conditions of the roads, the obstacles created by the Germans to block the roads, and the many minefields and booby traps emplaced around the obstacles. But by the sixth most of the division had reached the banks of the Volturno, where it occupied a front of roughly fifteen miles extending west from the junction of the Calore and Volturno Rivers to Monte Tifata, opposite the Triflisco Gap. To the division's west was 10 Corps, and to its east was the 34th Infantry Division. For the next six days Truscott's men "patrolled extensively to and across the river, located infantry fords, reconnoitered for bridge sites, assembled bridging material and crossing aids and prepared plans for crossing" the river.[14]

On the evening of the seventh Lucas informed Truscott that Clark had ordered one division from VI Corps to cross the Volturno in the vicinity of Triflisco during the night of October 9–10, followed by the British 10 Corps the following night. However, Lucas had proposed a two-division crossing, the 3d ID at Triflisco and the 34th ID on the 3d's right, which Clark approved. Both divisions were slated to attack simultaneously at 2:00 a.m. on the tenth, but incessant rains created impossible road conditions along the entire Volturno front, forcing Clark to delay the crossings until the night of October 12–13.[15] When he received word of the postponement of the crossings, Truscott returned to his command post in the gardens of the Royal Palace at Caserta, where he was treated to a fine dinner of trout that his Canton Restaurant crew, headed by cook Lee, had caught in their "backyard fish pool," the royal fishpond within the gardens.[16]

Clark's final plan called for the British 46th Division to make the main crossing for 10 Corps between Cancello ed Arnone and the Tyrrhenian coast, while the 56th Division to the east would make a demonstration at Capua and attempt a battalion-size crossing in that area. In the VI Corps sector Truscott's 3d ID would make the main effort between Triflisco and Caiazzo, a front of sixteen miles, and after the crossing assist the 56th Division advancing along Highway 6 from Capua to Teano. On his right the 34th ID was to cross on an eight-mile front, assist the 45th ID in entering the upper Volturno valley, and then prepare to attack toward Teano.[17]

A formidable task lay before Truscott's men. The Volturno was swollen by the heavy rains to a width of roughly 150 feet and a depth of between 3.5 and 6 feet, and its rain-softened riverbanks ranged from 2 to 14 feet in height. Lacking enough assault boats for the operation, the troops constructed improvised rafts using empty gasoline and water cans, Navy life rafts, rubber pontoons from treadway bridges, life jackets, and rope guide lines. To achieve surprise Truscott ordered only half of his artillery to fire in the days preceding the crossing and concentrated his regiments in concealed bivouac areas.

He identified two hill complexes as key terrain on the enemy shore, the Triflisco ridge and Monte Caruso. Seizure of those heights was essential for his division to carry out their missions after the crossing. Believing that the Germans expected an attack against Triflisco, Truscott planned to have a battalion of the 15th Infantry and the three heavy weapons companies of the 30th Infantry feint at the Triflisco ridge by concentrating their fire there. The 7th Infantry would then make the main attack against Monte Caruso by crossing the river and driving directly toward its western tip. The 15th Infantry was to cross two of its battalions to the 7th's right, capture Monticello and Monte Mesarinolo, and occupy the eastern tip of the mountain. He told his regimental commanders that once they began the operation they were to continue forward without pause.[18] At 1:00 a.m. on the thirteenth the diversionary fire on the Triflisco ridge began, and one hour later the 7th Infantry and the other two battalions of the 15th began crossing the river to the east, all the while exposed to "long-range German machine gun fire [that] whipped the crossing sites." Despite the heavy enemy fire, the division "Report of Operations" records that both regiments made the crossing with only "light casualties." By noon the regiments were digging in on their initial objective, Monte Caruso, and were prepared to continue on to their next objectives. Truscott described the crossing to his wife, stating, "My lads waded a wide river 230 ft. yet under fire from the opposite bank. We killed a lot of Boche and captured a lot more. They went through the elite Herman [sic]Goering's like a dose of salts! My lads are OK—the best there are!"[19]

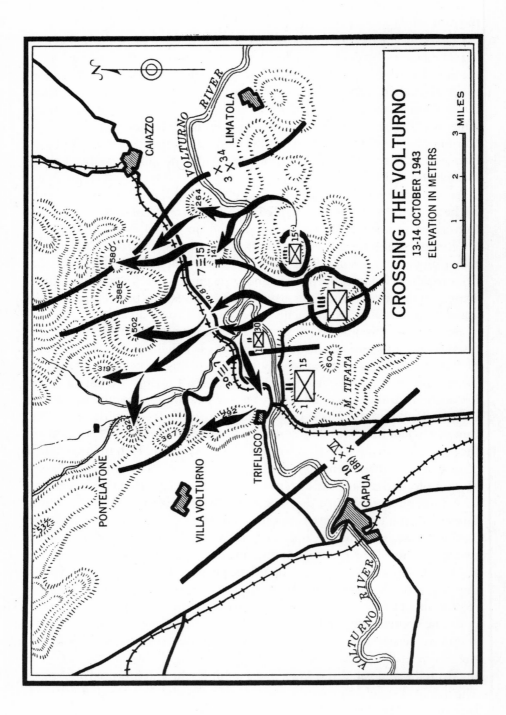

CROSSING THE VOLTURNO
13-14 OCTOBER 1943
ELEVATION IN METERS

0 1 2 3 MILES

VOLTURNO RIVER

CAIAZZO

LIMATOLA

3 × 34

264

580

580

502

319

192

367

533

PONTELATONE

VILLA VOLTURNO

TRIFLISCO

M. TIFATA

604

15

CAPUA

VOLTURNO RIVER

VOLTURNO RIVER

7 ≡ 15
141

No 81

30

192

30

1 30

15

10 (R)

In the afternoon Truscott ordered the 30th Infantry to cross the Volturno, but two attempts were unsuccessful because of stubborn German resistance and the failure of the 56th Division to cross the river on the left at Capua. That night Truscott sent one battalion of the 30th across the river in the 7th Infantry's sector. It soon occupied the eastern side of the Triflisco ridge, allowing the rest of the regiment to cross and occupy the entire ridge. The crossing of the Volturno that day had cost the division 314 casualties, as compared to a combined 230 for the other two divisions in VI Corps.[20]

The division engineers began construction of the division eight-ton truck bridge across the Volturno early on the thirteenth, and despite enemy artillery and machine-gun fire completed the bridge by eleven that night. A smaller bridge for quarter-ton trucks (jeeps) was completed downstream that same day, and the corps' thirty-ton truck and tank bridge crossing at Triflisco was begun and completed on October 14.[21]

To the west in the 56th Division sector there was only one route that crossed the river at Capua. When the division attempted an assault crossing near a destroyed railroad bridge there, the heavy fire from Germans on the Triflisco ridge convinced the division commander that a crossing of the Volturno in his zone was impractical. Therefore, Clark shifted the corps boundary to the east, giving the 56th Division access to the 3d ID bridges at Triflisco.[22] The shift in boundary had also placed the Triflisco ridge entirely within the 10 Corps zone, including Teano at the northwest end of the ridge, which had originally been Truscott's objective. As a result, Lucas shifted Truscott's axis of advance to the northeast toward Dragoni. Ryder's 34th, which had crossed successfully in its zone west of the abrupt northward bend of the Volturno, was to advance up the Volturno valley, cross the river again upstream east of Dragoni, and continue on to Raviscanina. Middleton's 45th ID would revert to corps reserve after it reached Piedmonte d'Alife.[23]

Truscott continued his attack, the 7th Infantry advancing northward through Liberi and Majorano to Dragoni, the 30th Infantry clearing the ridge along the west side of the valley as far north as Formicola, and the 15th Infantry advancing over a mountain trail northwest of Liberi to seize the high ground east of Roccaromana. "By Oct. 19 the division had consolidated its bridgehead across the VOLTURNO, seized all the high ground which afforded observation of the crossing and gained control of both exits from the valley to the NORTH."[24]

During the five-day advance from the Volturno the division had sustained 500 casualties. At that point Lucas, over Truscott's objections, ordered the 3d Division to halt its advance until the 34th ID had come abreast on the right. Lucas wrote in his diary that Truscott told him after receiving the order that "if I [Lucas] will just let him alone, he will take Berlin for me. A rash statement."[25] The twenty-sixth found the 3d Division "consolidating its position in the high ground immediately west of Dragoni." When the 34th ID to its right reached the head of

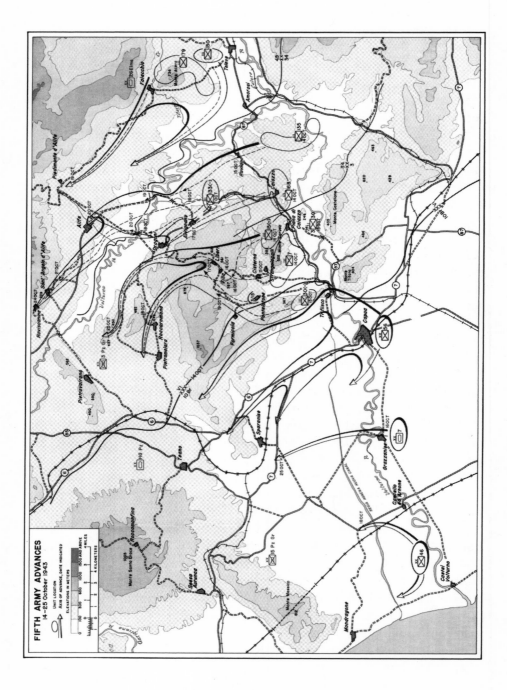

FIFTH ARMY ADVANCES
14–25 October 1943

UNIT LOCATION
AXIS OF ADVANCE, DATE INDICATED
ELEVATIONS IN METERS
0   300   600   1000   1500 AND ABOVE

0   1   2   3   4 MILES
0   1   2   3   4 KILOMETERS

the Volturno valley, Lucas planned to shift the axis of advance of the 3d to the northwest to seize the high ground that dominated the Mignano Gap.[26]

In the far West the 46th Division had launched its crossing under heavy artillery and naval gunfire early on the thirteenth. Despite the fire support, the first units across the river in the eastern sector of the division zone were forced to withdraw because of the strength of the enemy. Downstream, two battalions succeeded in crossing the river and began advancing the next day, while reinforcements landed behind them. By October 15 the division forward elements were four miles north of the river on the bank of the Regia Agnena Nuova Canal. 10 Corps, now including the 7th AD, continued its attack north, and by November 2 the 56th Division had advanced through Teano and held Roccamonfina, and the 46th and 7th Divisions had reached and were sending out reconnaissance patrols along the south bank of the Garigliano River.[27]

Four weeks after the launching of AVALANCHE, ULTRA revealed to the Allies the German strategy for the next few months: Hitler had ordered Kesselring to hold a line south of Rome through the winter, the "Winter line," and prepare a strong defensive line north of Rome, later dubbed the "Gothic line," to which the Tenth Army could withdraw later if necessary. To assist in holding a line south of Rome, Hitler had ordered the transfer of divisions from the Russian front to Italy. As a result of ULTRA's revelations the Allies realized by October 6 that all hopes of reaching Rome quickly were effectively dashed and that progress northward would entail costly assaults on well-defended German positions.[28]

Truscott recorded that in accordance with Fifth Army orders, "Lucas planned to have the 45th Infantry Division . . . cross the Volturno just east of Presenzano and advance northward west of the river to seize the heights above Venafro." Lucas directed Truscott to have his division seize Presenzano on the high ground overlooking the Mignano Gap from the east and occupy the gap. The 34th ID and the 504th Parachute Infantry, which had been attached to VI Corps, were to cross the Volturno above Venafro. All attacks were to begin on October 31.[29]

The Mignano Gap is a narrow valley passing between Monte Cesima on the east and Monte la Difensa, Monte Maggiore, and Monte Camino on the west. At the northern end of the valley are two mountains, Monte Rotondo and Monte Lungo, between which Highway 6 passes and continues on to the Rapido River and Cassino.[30] On the thirty-first the 3d Division attacked northwest from the Roccaromana area. On the left the 7th Infantry demonstrated toward Terro Corpo to assist the 56th Division's attack toward Roccamonfina and then continued northward along the west side of the gap, clearing the enemy from ridges east of Monte Camino. The 15th attacked northward along the east side of the gap, capturing Presenzano and Monte Cesima to assist the 45th ID's crossing of the Volturno. By November 5 one battalion of the regiment had

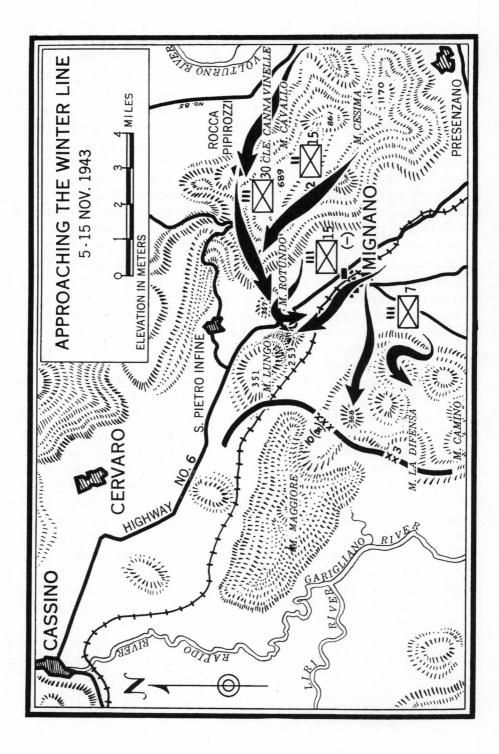

APPROACHING THE WINTER LINE
5-15 NOV. 1943

ELEVATION IN METERS

0 1 2 3 4 MILES

VOLTURNO RIVER

NO. 85

ROCCA PIPIROZZI

30 CLE. CANNAVINELLE

M. CAVALLO

861

M. CESIMA

1170

PRESENZANO

689

30 CLE.

15

2

15 (-)

MIGNANO

M. ROTUNDO

357

7

CASSINO

CERVARO

S. PIETRO INFINE

HIGHWAY NO. 6

M. LUNGO

351

253

368

10 (B)

XX

3

M. LA DIFENSA

M. CAMINO

M. MAGGIORE

GARIGLIANO RIVER

LIRI RIVER

RAPIDO RIVER

N

140

captured Mignano and was approaching the southern end of Monte Lungo, while the rest of the regiment was advancing from Monte Cesima toward the southern end of Monte Rotondo. In the 10 Corps area the British had, against practically no opposition, advanced to the lower Garigliano River and had captured Monte Massico and Teano. The rapid advance of 10 Corps and Truscott's division had undoubtedly been made possible by an intentional German withdrawal. However, the men of the Rock of the Marne division were soon to encounter far more difficult going.[31]

On November 5 General Gruenther, Clark's chief of staff, visited Truscott's command post to spend the night and visit the front. That evening during dinner Truscott received a call from Lucas informing him that Clark had decided to have Truscott move his 30th Infantry, then in division reserve, through the 45th ID's zone to Rocca Pipirozzi that night and attack Monte Lungo the next day. Truscott was "astounded" that Clark would order him to move a regiment twenty miles, with no prior reconnaissance of assembly areas, and to attack over difficult terrain without reconnaissance and with inadequate artillery support. He protested strongly to Lucas, even requesting permission to speak with Clark personally. According to Truscott, Lucas replied, "No, Lucian. Dammit, you know the position I'm in with him. That would only make it worse, and put me in a helluva hole. You have just got to do it." Truscott, always the obedient soldier, told Lucas that although he still disagreed with the order, he would do the best he could to carry it out. He immediately issued the necessary orders, and the men of the 30th responded magnificently. The regiment successfully moved to Rocca Pipirozzi by truck that night, and the attack kicked off the next morning. Four days later Lucas confided to his diary, "Truscott is one of the greatest soldiers in the Army. He never complains."[32]

At 5:30 a.m. on the sixth the 30th Infantry advanced westward from Rocca Pipirozzi and joined the 15th Infantry in the attack on Monte Rotondo. In the process the regiment encountered some of the most difficult and appalling weather conditions since the division's arrival on the Italian boot. The soldiers, already exhausted by five weeks of grueling combat in the Apennines, now faced steep slopes covered with slippery mud produced by the incessant rains and the traffic of men and pack animals. The weather was brutally cold, and fog severely hampered visibility. The trails were so narrow, steep, and slippery that many of the usually sure-footed mules and burros carrying food, ammunition, and other supplies fell to their deaths.

Despite those seemingly insurmountable difficulties the 2d Battalion was able to reach the foot of Monte Rotondo by midafternoon of November 7. As they attempted to scale the mountain the infantrymen met very heavy enemy small arms, machine-gun, mortar, and artillery fire that drove the attackers back to their line of departure. The next day the attack by the 15th and 30th Regiments resumed, the 15th attacking up the mountain's southern slope and the 30th moving in from the east. By that afternoon Monte Rotondo was in American hands. Over the next five or six days, as Truscott's dogfaces improved their positions, they repulsed repeated vicious enemy counterattacks.

However, the attacks against Monte Lungo and Monte la Difensa were less successful. The two regiments were able to gain only a lodgment on the southern nose of Monte Lungo, never gaining its crest, while to the west the 7th Infantry was engaged in a fierce struggle for Monte la Difensa. Attacking on the eighth the 7th was able to gain positions on the northeast slope of the mountain, but the Germans retained control of the crest. Despite repeated attempts to wrest control of the mountain from the Germans, the summit remained in enemy hands.

As Truscott's men came to the realization that they would not be able to capture Monte Lungo and Monte la Difensa, all of the other divisions, both American and British, faced a similar reality. The British to the left had been unable to secure Monte Camino, and the 34th and 45th Divisions had been able to gain only footholds on the heights west and northwest of Venafro; on November 15 Alexander halted operations in the Mignano Gap area. The next day the 36th ID relieved elements of the 7th and 30th Regiments on Monte Rotondo, and on the seventeenth relieved the remainder of the infantrymen on the peak. The 3d Division then moved into bivouac in the Riardo-Pietramelara–Baja Latina–Vairano area, ending the "fifty-nine days of Mountains and Mud."[33]

During the heavy fighting to gain control of the Mignano Gap, Truscott visited his frontline units on a daily basis, observing firsthand the appalling conditions they were facing: all supplies were carried in by men or pack animals; casualties were evacuated over the muddy and slippery trails by litter, the evacuations to the aid stations sometimes requiring hours; the bitterly cold and damp foggy weather and the continual rainfall precluded any hot meals for the exhausted troops; the fog also halted any air support for the infantrymen; company strength fell as casualties due to wounds and sickness mounted; and trench foot began to make its appearance. Those observations and his compassion for his men led Truscott on November 2 to write to General Gruenther. The theater commander had recently instituted a system for a limited number of men, chosen on a quota basis, to be rotated home. In his letter Truscott asked if any of the Fifth Army quota slots would be available for the list of officers and men of his command that he had forwarded to Clark. However, believing that such a rotation system to the United States would not work for ground forces on any large scale, Clark had established a rest and recreation program that provided for troops to be withdrawn from combat and sent back to Naples for five full days, where there were living accommodations, recreation rooms, movies, stage shows, and sightseeing trips to nearby spots such as Pompeii. Most important, there would be hot showers and hot "chow."

On November 5 the first eight hundred men left the division for Naples. Truscott saw the group off and described them: "Haggard, dirty, bedraggled, long-haired, unshaven, clothing in tatters, worn out boots, their appearance was appalling." When they returned from Naples they were "rested, clean, shaven and trimmed, and clad in new uniforms. . . . The effect of this rest camp program on the morale of the battle-weary men of the command was of inestimable value, and saved many men who would otherwise have broken under the strain."[34]

As the division moved into the Baja Latina area for rest and refitting, Truscott reflected on the past fifty-nine days of combat in southern Italy. The division had suffered 683 killed in action, 2,412 wounded in action, and 170 missing in action, totaling 3,265 battle casualties. There were also 12,959 non-battle casualties, many undoubtedly the result of prolonged exposure to the cold weather, virtually continuous rain, and mud. The known enemy casualties, that is, those dead actually buried in 3d Division cemeteries, those enemy wounded processed through division treatment facilities, and those captured enemy soldiers processed through division cages, were 265 killed, 86 wounded, and 547 captured.[35]

On November 22 Truscott convened an Officers' Call of all the division officers, at which he reviewed the campaign thus far in southern Italy, discussed "lessons learned," and put forth his suggestions and recommendations for future campaigns. He pointed out that the division had taken in stride the many obstacles encountered, such as the mountains and the rivers, and that of all divisions in VI Corps the 3d had always been first to seize its objectives. In his opinion those accomplishments were due to "Thorough basic training—High standard of discipline—Superior physical condition—Superior teamwork, and most important Gallant leadership." Truscott then went on to say that all the officers must analyze the lessons learned and make the results known to every enlisted man. He stressed that all officers, but particularly the junior officers, must "actually command," show "initiative—common sense," set the example in "courage, cheerfulness, devotion to duty," and enforce high standards of discipline. He particularly stressed that a commander cannot "command with a grease pencil" at the map board but must be up forward with his men as frequently as possible. Truscott concluded by thanking them for their past efforts and wishing them a happy Thanksgiving.[36]

On the twenty-fourth Truscott penned a report to General Eisenhower on the recently concluded operation. He pointed out that the incessant rain and the cold weather had produced great hardships for the troops in moving through the rugged mountains and had caused great physical discomfort, particularly since there had been a shortage of blankets and overcoats. Since the maneuver battalions usually had to operate off-road and in mountains, transportation and evacuation proved to be serious problems. Jeeps were able to get supplies fairly far forward, but men and pack animals had to provide the final carry. The divisional pack train, pack artillery battery, and mounted troop had been "worth their weight in gold," and he recommended that every division in the theater have such organizations. Supply of hot food was almost always impossible, forcing the men to consume K rations or cold C rations for days on end. He recommended to Eisenhower that he look into the possibility of providing pocket-size stoves for the men, similar to those used by the Germans, one of which Truscott had sent to Lt. Gen. Brehon B. Somervell, chief of Army Service Forces. He concluded by stating that "the unsolved problem in maintaining the combat efficiency of a Division" was that of replacements, and included a tabulation of the division casualties and replacements during the period of combat. Eisenhower replied to Truscott's letter on December 16, complimenting him on his organization and employment of a pack train and a pack artillery battery, and said that he had referred the letter to his staff for study of all of the information that Truscott had included in the letter.[37]

On the first of December Truscott addressed a similar letter to his old friend "Beetle" Smith. However, he discussed the problem of casualties and replacements in somewhat greater detail, pointing out that 75 percent of all division battle casualties were in the infantry battalions, 42 percent of all battle casualties and 36 percent of nonbattle casualties were riflemen and automatic riflemen, and 8 percent of all casualties were squad leaders. When the division did receive replacements they were often in large groups, making it difficult for companies to absorb them and weld them into "the team while engaged in battle," resulting in disproportionately higher casualties among the newly arrived replacements. In closing he commented on the quality of the American soldier: "Given adequate training, proper physical condition, and competent leadership, particularly in lower echelons, and he has no equal. These lads of mine have really done the impossible."[38]

Chapter 9

ANZIO AND THE ROAD TO ROME

On November 13 Truscott, along with Generals Lucas, Middleton, and Ryder, attended a commanders' conference with General Clark at the VI Corps command post to discuss future plans. At that time the Allied advance up the boot had spent its force, leaving Montgomery's Eighth Army on the Adriatic side of the peninsula deployed along the Sangro River from the coast inland to the crest of the Apennines near Isernia and the Fifth Army on the Winter line. Roughly twelve miles to the north were the Garigliano and Rapido Rivers, along which the Germans were busily constructing a formidable defensive position, the Gustav line.

Clark informed the assembled generals that General Eisenhower had agreed to delay until December 15 the departure of the LSTs that were scheduled to leave for England to prepare for the cross-Channel attack the following spring. That delay would allow Alexander to bring from Africa another division for Eighth Army and Gen. Alphonse Juin's French corps for Fifth Army. In addition, the 36th ID would replace the 3d Division in the line.

Alexander's plan for continuing the offensive was to take place in three phases: Beginning about November 20 Eighth Army was to cross the Sangro River near the coast and drive northward across Highway 5 to "threaten communications with German forces opposing the Fifth Army." About the end of November Fifth Army was to drive to and cross the Rapido River, and then continue northward up the Liri and Sacco valleys toward Frosinone and Rome. The third phase, designated SHINGLE and assigned to the 3d Division, possibly supported by an airborne RCT, was to make an amphibious landing south of Rome when the advancing Fifth Army forces had reached a point within supporting distance of the landing beaches. Alexander had chosen Anzio, a resort town on the Tyrrhenian Sea about thirty-five miles south of Rome and roughly sixty miles behind the Gustav line, as the landing site. The plan was to land Truscott's division with a seven-day load of supplies and ammunition, with the hope that a linkup between the beachhead force and the Fifth Army advancing from the south would occur within a week. Alexander hoped to launch the operation shortly after the middle of December and was hopeful that he could convince Eisenhower to delay the departure of the landing craft long enough to use them to carry Truscott's forces to Anzio.[1]

Clark had disposed his forces along the Winter line with 10 Corps on the west, II Corps immediately to its east, and VI Corps extending the front line westward from the right flank of II Corps to the Eighth Army boundary.[2] Clark's plan, issued on November 24, directed the 10th and II Corps to capture Monte Camino, Monte la Difensa, and Monte Maggiore west of Highway 6 and south of the Rapido and Garigliano Rivers, while VI Corps held the enemy to its front with harassing attacks. Following the capture of the peaks, 10 Corps would relieve II Corps in that sector, freeing up II Corps to join VI Corps in Clark's second phase, the capture of Monte Lungo and Monte Sammucro west and east of Highway 6, respectively, and the clearing of the Mignano Gap. In the third phase II Corps was to attack toward Cassino along Highway 6 and develop the town's defenses, after which the corps was to force a crossing of the Rapido River below Cassino. The 1st AD would then attack through the corps and begin its advance up the Liri valley, while II and VI Corps captured the mountains north and northwest of Cassino. If landing craft were available, the 3d Division would "in due course" land at Anzio; "if not, the Division would receive some other mission."[3]

The operation began the afternoon of December 2 with a massive artillery barrage. That night the 56th Division attacked toward Monte Camino, while on its right Col. Robert T. Frederick's 1st Special Service Force (SSF) assaulted the base of Monte la Difensa, reaching the summit by dawn. Their attack continued on toward Monte la Remetanea, which they captured on the sixth, the same day that the 56th Division occupied Monte Camino. To the east the rested and refitted 36th ID had attacked in driving rain on December 3 along a ridge leading to Monte Maggiore. With supporting artillery fire blasting the Germans out of their cavelike emplacements, the Americans advanced steadily and occupied the objective. "By December 9 the entire area south of Route No. 6 was in our hands, except for Mount Lungo," Clark proudly reported.[4]

On December 13 Clark summoned Truscott to Caserta and informed him that Alexander had changed the plan for SHINGLE, and now planned to land the 3d ID earlier, after the main forces had crossed the Rapido and Garigliano Rivers. Despite the fact that Truscott's forces would still land with only seven days of ammunition and supplies, and "there would be no craft available for resupply or reinforcement," Clark optimistically believed that just the presence of Truscott's division on the beaches at Anzio "would cause the Germans so much concern that they would withdraw from the southern front. [Truscott's] reaction was rather pessimistic." He did not believe "that there was even a remote possibility that the main force could cross the Rapido and drive up the Liri valley to join us within *a month*," let alone a week. He told Clark, "We are perfectly willing to undertake the operation if we are ordered to do so and we will maintain ourselves to the last round of ammunition. But if we do undertake it, you are going to destroy the best damned division in the United States Army for there will be no survivors." Clark reflected for a moment, and then replied that he would make a final decision after completion of the second phase of the current operation. On the twentieth Clark, apparently because of Truscott's objection, abandoned the plan.[5]

On the fifteenth the attempt to clear the Mignano Gap resumed, and by late the next day, after intense fighting that produced many casualties, the 36th Division and attached paratroopers and Rangers were in possession of San Pietro Infine, Monte Sammucro, and Monte Lungo, the peaks that overlooked the gap from either side of Highway 6. That same day Clark issued instructions for the commencement of the third phase of the operation, the attack on Cassino and the crossing of the Rapido River, to begin after December 20.

On Christmas Day Clark, who was unaware that Alexander was discussing with Churchill and Eisenhower that same day the possibility of retaining the landing craft in the Mediterranean theater until February, met with Keyes and Truscott at the II Corps command post and informed them that since the Anzio landing would apparently not take place, he planned to release the 3d Division to II Corps to force the crossing of the Rapido River below Cassino. After the division gained a lodgment on the north bank of the river the 1st AD would pass through and drive up the Liri valley. After leaving the CP Truscott put his staff to work on the plans, while he, Carleton, and Lt. Col. Ben Harrell, his G3, set off for the 15th Infantry's command post on Monte Lungo, from which Truscott could observe the river and the approaches to it. Although the river was almost overflowing its banks as a result of the heavy rains, Truscott believed that his assault battalions could cross without too much difficulty. However, laying in the bridges to support the assault forces on the far shore would be very difficult. The Germans and their artillery were firmly emplaced on the heights overlooking the crossing sites, and the artillery fire would devastate the engineers attempting to put the bridges in place and destroy the bridges as fast as they were constructed, stranding his infantrymen on the far shore. He concluded that the plan as laid out to him was unsound, and so informed Clark, who agreed, and called off the planned operation.

On the twenty-eighth Clark told Truscott that Alexander had informed him that the departure of the landing craft for England had been delayed until February 5 and that there would be sufficient craft available to carry two divisions.

Having obtained Alexander's authorization to land two divisions at Anzio, Clark had chosen the 3d ID and the British 1st Division, which would land under command of Lucas's VI Corps, and went on to point out that after the landings there would be only six craft available for resupply of the invasion force in the beachhead. He then directed Truscott to move his division to the Naples area to train for the landing.[6]

On December 13 Truscott had hosted a dinner at his headquarters, during which an ensemble from the 7th Infantry Regiment band played a variety of musical selections, one of which, "Dogface Soldier," played in march tempo, caught Truscott's ear. A few days later Truscott met with the leaders of each of his regimental bands and had the 7th Infantry ensemble play the tune, after which the bandleaders quickly wrote out a score that would become the official 3d Division march.[7]

The planning for SHINGLE began the first week of January, only three weeks before the scheduled date for the landing, January 22. Lucas and Truscott soon realized that the two divisions would need continued resupply of matériel and replacements "for an indefinite period of time" after the initial convoy had landed the divisions and supporting units, pointing out that "no one below Army level believed that the landing of two divisions at Anzio would cause a German withdrawal on the Southern front, or that there was more than a remote chance that the remainder of Fifth Army would be able to cross the Rapido River and fight its way up the Liri and Sacco valleys to join us within a month," a conclusion with which Clark agreed.[8]

The first week of January Gen. Sir Henry Maitland Wilson, who had replaced Eisenhower as Supreme Allied Commander in Chief of the Mediterranean theater of operations, convened a high-level meeting with Churchill in Marrakech, Morocco, to discuss SHINGLE. Representing Fifth Army were Col. E. J. O'Neill, G4, and Col. William H. Hill, G3.[9] At an afternoon meeting on January 7, when asked by General Alexander about maintenance of the beachhead, O'Neill replied that "it was impossible to go into the operation with only seven days maintenance," that the daily maintenance requirement was a minimum of fifteen hundred tons per day, and that twenty-four LSTs would be necessary for the maintenance of the beachhead force. After some discussion Alexander accepted the daily maintenance requirement put forth by O'Neill. That evening the group met with Churchill, who also accepted O'Neill's conclusions. Churchill next turned to the subject of the projected date for the operation. O'Neill and Hill explained that the date could be no earlier than the twenty-fifth because a rehearsal was absolutely necessary. Churchill insisted that a rehearsal was not necessary because "all troops were trained troops" and that "one experienced officer or noncommissioned officer in a platoon was sufficient."

O'Neill then presented his plan for supplying the force by loading trucks carrying overcapacity loads onto the LSTs, driving them onto the beach directly to the supply dumps for unloading, and then loading waiting empty trucks onto the LSTs for return to Naples for reloading. Churchill, Adm. Sir John Cunningham, and Smith, Eisenhower's chief of staff, summarily disapproved the plan. The following morning the final decision for the resupply operation was presented to Churchill: until February 3 there would be eighty to eighty-eight LSTs available, twenty-five until the thirteenth, and fourteen thereafter; Lucas would be authorized two thousand supply trucks; and the date for the invasion would remain January 22. Churchill believed this to be a good solution to the problem and ordered the planning to continue.

When informed of the results of the conference Truscott pointed out that the conferees had disapproved the one proposal, O'Neill's resupply plan, which would make "the maintenance of the beachhead possible." Despite being denied permission to adopt that plan, VI Corps nevertheless incorporated it into the corps' operation plan. "Without it, the maintenance of the forces eventually assembled at Anzio would have been impossible." Truscott also commented on Churchill's belief that no rehearsal was needed: "Landing operations depend upon complete mutual understanding and whole-hearted cooperation between the Military and Naval forces . . . [and] full scale rehearsal is the only way in which this understanding and cooperation can be tested. . . . Both General Lucas and I insisted that a rehearsal was an absolute essential and our views eventually prevailed."[10]

As the Allied commanders were preparing for SHINGLE, ULTRA served them well. In mid-November ULTRA revealed that Kesselring was concentrating reinforcements in the vicinity of Rome, which would be able to strike within a few hours after the Anzio landings. With that information in hand, Clark began an offensive across the lower Garigliano on January 17 to draw those two divisions southward, and ULTRA soon revealed that the action by Clark had achieved its purpose, when General Senger und Etterlin, commanding XIV Panzer Corps, asked Kesselring on the morning of the eighteenth for reinforcements. Kesselring, "still confident that there was no likelihood of a seaborne assault on his flank," quickly complied with Senger und Etterlin's request.[11]

On December 27 Clark issued the following order on which Lucas was to base his planning for SHINGLE: "1. Seize and secure a beachhead in the vicinity of Anzio. 2. Advance and secure Colli Laziali [Alban Hills]. 3. Be prepared to advance on Rome." However, as D-day grew closer, Clark and his G3, Brig. Gen. Don Brann, began to have doubts if Lucas would be able to hold the Alban Hills and defend the twenty-five-mile line of communications between the beaches and the hills with the allocated forces. Haunted by his experience at Salerno, Clark modified his order on January 12, instructing Lucas to *advance on* the Alban Hills, rather than to *advance and secure* the hills. "No longer obliged to seize the Alban Hills, Lucas was given the discretion to conduct the battle on his own terms."[12]

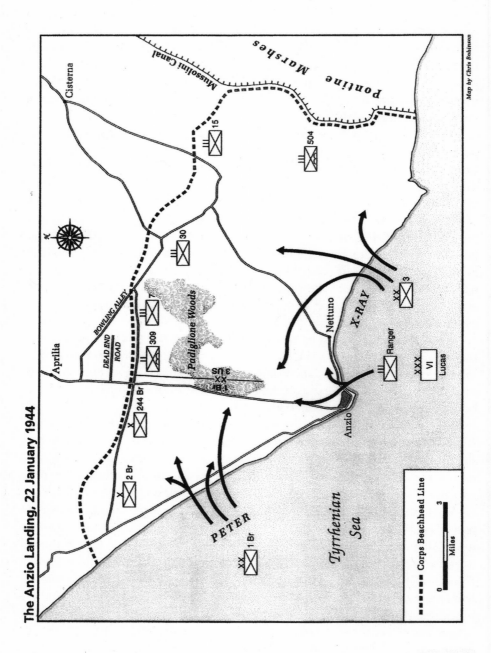

The Anzio Landing, 22 January 1944

Map by Chris Robinson

Lucas's final plans, completed and approved on January 12, set January 22 as D-day. At 2:00 a.m., "VI corps was to land over the beaches near Anzio and Nettuno in three simultaneous assaults." Truscott's 3d Division was to land assault battalions of each of his three regiments on the right of the beachhead south of Nettuno, with the mission of destroying enemy beach defenses and driving inland in the direction of Cisterna across the northwest branch of the Mussolini Canal to its initial beachhead line, some six miles from the beaches, its right flank protected by the Mussolini Canal and the Pontine Marshes. In the center, adjacent to the Anzio harbor, three battalions of Rangers, a chemical battalion, and the 509th Parachute Infantry Battalion would land. The 2d Brigade Group of the British 1st Division and Commando units would land six miles northwest of Anzio and link up with the Americans to consolidate the beachhead, centered on the port of Anzio. As rapidly as landing craft and ships became available, the 1st AD, less one combat command, would be landed in the beachhead.[13]

Lucas kept a close eye on the preinvasion training in which the units of his corps were engaged but remained deeply skeptical about the success of the operation, confiding to his diary that soon he would be ordering those men "into a desperate attack on a beach under conditions for which their training has not prepared them. No time for it. The political or other situation of which I know nothing will not give us time for training. Three months instead of three weeks would make all the difference in the world. Another week might save dozens of lives. But the order comes from a civilian minister of another nation who is impatient of such details and brushes them aside."[14] General Truscott would soon share Lucas's pessimism.

On January 17 the 3d ID mounted out of Pozzuoli and Naples, bound for the Salerno beaches to participate in the SHINGLE rehearsal beginning at two o'clock the next morning. When Truscott went ashore at about eight o'clock he found that the assault battalions had landed and moved inland, although not without some confusion. Because of a navigational error the landing craft carrying the troops were disembarked so far from shore that many landed on the wrong beaches, and all had landed late. Further, no tanks or tank destroyers had as yet landed, although all were to have been ashore by daylight. To make matters worse, the LSTs had opened their bow doors and lowered their ramps many miles farther out from the shore than planned and had discharged the DUKWs ("ducks," two-and-a-half-ton amphibious trucks) carrying the artillery into rough seas, resulting in the swamping and sinking of twenty or more of the DUKWs, carrying to the bottom artillery pieces and communications equipment. The situation on the beach was chaotic: "Only the infantry battalions were on their initial objectives. . . . Against opposition, the landing would have been a disaster." Truscott called off the exercise at nine thirty and returned to Pozzuoli. There he immediately began drafting a report on all that had gone wrong, laying most of the blame on the Navy, which had displayed an "obvious lack of control and lack of training." He concluded by stating that "to land [his] Division at Anzio as it was landed during the rehearsal would invite disaster if the Germans counterattacked with tanks soon after daylight," and urgently recommended another rehearsal for further training.[15] After reading Truscott's report Lucas agreed completely with Truscott's conclusions and recommendation for another rehearsal, stating, "The rehearsal for the 3d Division was terrible. . . . More training is certainly necessary but there is no time for it." However, Lucas confided to Truscott that he "felt himself to be in a difficult position with regard to General Clark, and he was unwilling to protest further although he had no objection to [Truscott's] doing so."[16]

Truscott went to see Clark and found him reading the rehearsal report. Clark agreed that the rehearsal had gone poorly but told Truscott that the date for the landing had been set "at the highest level. There is no possibility of delaying it even for a day. You have got to do it." Clark assured Truscott that he would replace the lost artillery pieces and other equipment, even taking it from the divisions currently "in the line if necessary," and requested a list of all that had been lost. After leaving Clark and returning to Pozzuoli, Truscott discussed the matter with Rear Adm. Frank W. Lowry, who was "deeply chagrined" and "in very low spirits" as a result of the poor performance of his personnel, but assured Truscott "that the Navy would do its utmost to set matters straight, and to put [Truscott's division] ashore exactly as [he] wished." Three days later the 3d sailed from Naples, destination Anzio.[17]

Rear Adm. Wilhelm Canaris, head of the Abwehr, had alerted Kesselring that the Allies had assembled a large number of vessels in the Naples harbor, "ample tonnage there for an invasion fleet," but Kesselring persisted in his belief that the "possibility of a landing was merely a hunch; there was no indication of the when or where." Perhaps relying too much on Canaris's intelligence report, but recognizing the threat posed by a new Allied offensive on the Garigliano front launched on January 17–18, Kesselring dispatched the 29th and 90th Panzer Grenadier Divisions, which formed his Army Group C reserve, southward to Generaloberst Heinrich von Vietinghoff's Tenth Army.[18] The move of those two Army Group reserve divisions south would prove to be advantageous to the Allies during the landings at Anzio.

Before boarding the LCI that would serve as his command post afloat, Truscott donned his two "sartorial lucky pieces . . . an old pair of faded pink cavalry breeches and a well-worn pair of high brown cavalry boots, both so shaky from past repairs that they are now saved for occasions when the going is really tough," as he expected the Anzio landing to be. Because of the cold, damp weather he put on his old leather jacket and wrapped around his neck the white silk scarf that he had fashioned some six months earlier from a parachutist's discarded silk map of Sicily, and which had become his personal trademark.[19]

The assault force, consisting of roughly forty thousand men and fifty-two hundred vehicles, was divided into two task forces, the Americans bound for the beaches south of Anzio and the British headed for their beaches northwest of Anzio. When the convoy arrived in the transport area off Anzio, the seas were calm, the weather was clear with little wind, and there were no signs from shore suggesting that the Germans had discovered the assault force. At about two on the morning of the twenty-second the assault craft were lowered into the water, where patrol craft formed them up to begin the run-in to the beaches.[20] All commanders had expected the initial assault waves to meet heavy opposition, but there was practically none. As Lucas recorded in his diary, "We achieved one of the most complete surprises in history. The Germans were caught off base and there was practically no opposition to the landing."[21]

The 3d ID landed on its beaches south of Anzio at roughly twenty minutes past two, encountering only a few mines and an understrength enemy battalion, and by daylight "main elements of the infantry regiments, artillery, and some armored units were ashore." By noon the infantry units were in possession of all initial objectives and were sending out reconnaissance patrols to the front and flanks. The 3d Reconnaissance Troop and the Provisional Mounted Troop "had reached and prepared for demolition all bridges on the Mussolini Canal from the sea to Bridge 7."[22]

To the division's left the three Ranger battalions had seized the port of Anzio, and the 509th Parachute Infantry Battalion, followed by the 504th Parachute Infantry Regiment, had occupied Nettuno two miles away. The British 1st Division had landed north of Anzio and by midday had advanced more than two miles inland. The Commandos had cut the road to Albano and had established a roadblock just north of Anzio. By midnight of D-day, VI Corps had approximately thirty-six thousand men, thirty-two hundred vehicles, and large quantities of supplies within the beachhead, "about 90 percent of the personnel and equipment of the assault convoys."[23] Just after six Truscott went ashore and found the operation proceeding smoothly. Contact had been established with the paratroopers in Nettuno, and by nine his division was "firmly established on the initial beachhead line." He returned to his command post in a woods just inland from the beach, where Private Hong had prepared a breakfast of ham and fresh eggs.[24]

On the afternoon of the twenty-second Kesselring surveyed the Allied beachhead and concluded that "the Allies had missed a uniquely favourable chance of capturing Rome and of opening the door on the Garigliano front" by failing to advance immediately on the Alban Hills, and believed that time was now his ally. He immediately ordered the XI Parachute Corps headquarters and the staffs of the LXXVI Panzer Corps from the Adriatic and the XIV Army Corps in northern Italy into the beachhead sector "in order to create a solid operational frame." He also contacted Vietinghoff on the twenty-second and ordered him to release from Tenth Army a corps headquarters and all combat units he could spare.[25]

By the night of the twenty-fourth the entire corps beachhead line had been secured. The 3d Division, with the attached 504th Parachute Infantry and three Ranger battalions, occupied a front that extended for twenty miles from the mouth of the Mussolini Canal on the right to the first overpass on the Albano Road. Rather than advancing immediately to the Alban Hills, both Lucas and Truscott believed that occupation of the beachhead line was essential to prevent enemy flank attacks from cutting off the advancing forces from the beach and preventing the unloading of supplies and reinforcements.[26]

At about five on the afternoon of the twenty-fourth a German air raid was launched against the beachhead, and immediately the antiaircraft batteries opened fire. One of the antiaircraft rounds dropped from the sky and exploded when it struck the ground about six inches from Truscott's foot. Some of the fragments perforated his riding boot, inflicting a superficial wound. He was taken to the 33d Field Hospital, where a surgeon removed the fragments and applied an adhesive cast to the foot and lower leg. Truscott refused the Purple Heart, but when he returned to his command post he found General Lucas, Col. Lawrence B. Keiser, Lucas's chief of staff, and Major Renne there, preparing the paperwork for his Purple Heart.[27]

Lucas had determined that if the corps were to advance beyond the beachhead, it would be necessary to hold the road centers at Campoleone in the British sector and Cisterna in the 3d ID sector. On the twenty-seventh Lucas called a conference to discuss his plan with Gens. W. R. C. Penney, Truscott, and Harmon, whose 1st AD, minus Combat Command C, had just arrived. It called for Penney's 1st Division, to which CCA of Harmon's division was attached, to make the main effort by attacking along the Albano Road to seize Campoleone. CCA would then pass through the division, turn to the left, and attack the Alban Hills from the west. Truscott's division, with the three Ranger battalions and 504th Parachute Infantry attached, would make the secondary effort by seizing Cisterna and cutting Highway 7, in preparation for continuing the attack to Velletri. The attacks were to begin during the night of January 28–29.[28]

Intelligence available to Truscott indicated that only the Hermann Göring Division, occupying strongpoints spread over a front of roughly twenty miles, would oppose his division. Truscott believed that the Rangers could easily infiltrate between the enemy strongpoints under cover of darkness and be in Cisterna "before the Germans realized what was happening." He discussed this with Colonel Darby, the commander of the Ranger force, who "agreed that this infiltration mission was exactly what the Rangers had been designed for," and assigned the mission to the 1st and 3d Ranger Battalions.[29]

The 15th Infantry and the 4th Ranger Battalion were to follow the 1st and 3d Rangers one hour later, break through the German defense line, and support

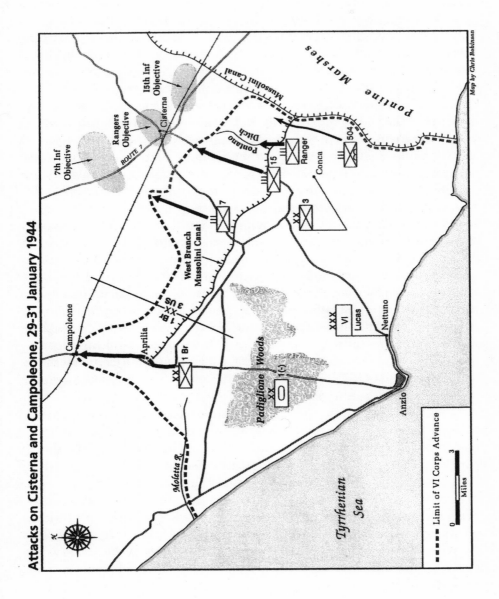

Attacks on Cisterna and Campoleone, 29-31 January 1944

Map by Chris Robinson

Limit of VI Corps Advance

the Rangers in Cisterna. The 504th Parachute Infantry was to make a diversionary attack to the right of the 15th Infantry by attacking along the east branch of the Mussolini Canal, while on the division left the 7th Infantry was to launch an attack to the northeast, pass west of Cisterna, and cut Highway 7, the Appian Way. However, Penney and Harmon later contacted Lucas and requested that Truscott's attacks be postponed for twenty-four hours, a delay that enabled Kesselring, who undoubtedly realized that Cisterna would be one of the prime Allied objectives, to reinforce the Hermann Göring Division.[30]

Unaware of the German reinforcements now facing him, Truscott ordered the 1st and 3d Rangers to begin their advance at 1:30 a.m. along the Pantano ditch that snaked northward from the west branch of the Mussolini Canal, and by dawn the Rangers were within eight hundred yards of Cisterna. However, as dawn broke the Germans detected the column of advancing Rangers and launched an attack by three self-propelled guns. The Rangers were able to take out the three guns, but a hail of enemy machine-gun, mortar, and sniper fire soon struck them. Caught in the open, the Rangers scattered to find any cover available. The battle raged all morning, and although a few of the Rangers were able to reach the edge of Cisterna, most remained pinned down in the open fields. The 15th Infantry and the 4th Ranger Battalion, which had left the line of departure (LOD) one hour later, attempted to reach the desperate Ranger force but were stopped below Isola Bella by heavy machine-gun fire. About noon the Germans sent tanks into the 1st and 3d Ranger positions. Although the Rangers fought back with rocket launchers (bazookas) and grenades, their weapons were no match for the tanks, and they soon found themselves surrounded. The few remaining officers ordered their men to attempt to escape by infiltration, but of the 767 Rangers who had begun the attack, only 6 were able to do so. Most of the rest were captured.

By nightfall the 15th Infantry and the 4th Rangers were holding a line just below Isola Bella. To the right the 504th Parachute Infantry had met stiff resistance during its advance along the canal but had reached both assigned bridges. However, the Germans destroyed the bridges before the paratroopers could secure them. On the division left the 7th Infantry kicked off its attack at 2:00 a.m. to cut Highway 7 west of Cisterna. The advance was soon slowed, however, when the dogfaces learned that the "evenly-spaced hedgerows" in the aerial photographs were in reality a series of twenty-foot-wide drainage ditches overgrown with briars, which the tanks, following closely behind the infantrymen, were unable to traverse. With the coming of daylight the advance battalion was hit by a fusillade of German automatic fire, resulting in heavy casualties. Sherman ordered his two other battalions forward, but those also ran into heavy resistance, but aided by tanks, tank destroyers, and intensive artillery and mortar fire, one battalion was able to clear the road junction south of Ponte Rotto, and by daylight of the thirty-first had advanced to its objective, a knoll above Ponte

Rotto. Because of the unexpectedly stiff German resistance Truscott ordered his division to organize along the line Ponte Rotto–Isola Bella–Cisterna Creek before resuming the attack. In the interval the Germans, expecting the Americans to resume the attack to cut Highway 7, moved in additional fresh troops to reinforce the weary and depleted Hermann Göring Division. To Truscott's left the British had also encountered heavy German resistance in their advance toward Campoleone. Although they reached Campoleone and penetrated the German main line of resistance west of Albano, they could go no farther. The attack by Harmon's 6th Armored Infantry Regiment to the west stalled in the impassable gullies the unit encountered.[31]

On the thirtieth Clark noted in his diary his disappointment with the "lack of aggressiveness on the part of VI Corps," and stated that a "reconnaissance in force with tanks should have been more aggressive to capture Cisterna and Campoleone." He was also "distressed to find that the 3d Division had led with the Ranger force in its attack on Cisterna. This was a definite error in judgment, for the Rangers do not have the support weapons to overcome the resistance indicated."[32] He visited Truscott the next day and "implied that they [the Rangers] were unsuitable for such missions." Truscott immediately reminded Clark that he "had been responsible for organizing the original Ranger battalion and that Colonel Darby and [he] perhaps understood their capabilities better than other American officers. [Clark] said no more. . . . That ended the matter. The remnants of the Ranger Force was [*sic*] returned to the United States a few weeks later." Black states that not all of the remaining 4th Rangers returned to the United States, as Truscott alleges. After being relieved from combat on October 25 the unit went into bivouac, where the men were divided into two groups, those veteran personnel, 19 officers and 134 enlisted men who would return home, and the others, who had not accrued enough overseas service and combat time to return to the United States. The latter Rangers were assigned to the 1st SSF.[33]

Early on February 2 Lucas called Truscott and informed him that Fifth Army had "*secret intelligence* that the Germans were in far greater strength than we had thought and were preparing to launch a counteroffensive to drive the beachhead into the sea." He told Truscott to halt all attacks and "dig in for defense and hold the Corps Beachhead Line at all costs." An ULTRA message intercepted on February 3 had indeed revealed Kesselring's detailed plan for a large-scale offensive against the bridgehead, "timed to start on 1 February if certain reinforcements had arrived by then," to drive to the sea down the Anzio-Albano road. That vital intercept reached Alexander and Clark in adequate time to warn them of Kesselring's plans, since the German reinforcements were late in arriving, delaying the attack.[34]

The German February offensive had three principal phases: first, preliminary attacks designed to pinch off the Campoleone salient and capture Aprilia

(February 3–10); second, a major drive down the axis of the Albano Road to the sea, splitting the beachhead in two (February 16–20); and, third, an attack in the Cisterna sector to break the main Allied beachhead defense line along the Mussolini Canal (February 28–March 2). As it turned out, the first attack would succeed, but the second and third attacks would be repulsed by a stubborn Allied defense of the beachhead.[35]

The first attack began on February 7 with converging thrusts against the British 1st Division in the Carroceto area. Over the next four days the British suffered heavy losses and were forced to give up Aprilia, a cluster of brick buildings known to the troops as the "Factory."[36] On the eleventh Lucas ordered the American 45th ID to retake the Factory, but repeated efforts over the next few days failed. "After the failure to retake the Factory, an uneasy lull settled over the forward area, although the Germans increased their attacks by air and heavy artillery on the beach and port areas." Both Lucas and Penney had become very concerned about the combat worthiness of Penney's exhausted division. On February 6 Lucas wrote in his diary that we "need replacements badly but am told there are none to be had. Where are all the troops we had in the United States?" Shortly thereafter, the arrival of major elements of the British 56th Division partially addressed Lucas's concerns, allowing him to strengthen the central sector of the beachhead. He divided the 1st Division sector, placing the 45th on the right and the 56th on the left of the sector, and ordering the battle-weary 1st Division into corps reserve.[37]

On February 7 Truscott met Clark at the Nettuno airport to receive the Distinguished Service Cross,

> for extraordinary heroism on 11 July 1943 near Agrigento, Sicily. Completely disregarding his own safety he personally directed the successful operation which extended the 3rd Division's Licata beachhead, and by his continuous presence with the forward elements, as well as his exemplary judgment and leadership, inspired his command to the early capture of Agrigento and the continuous attack northward. . . . By his intrepid direction, heroic leadership and superior professional ability he set an inspiring example for his command, reflecting the highest traditions of the Armed Forces.[38]

Kesselring felt that it was imperative to launch another offensive before the Allies could "make good their losses in the late fighting and before the intermediate positions in the bridgehead were too greatly strengthened." He discussed the matter with Gen. Eberhard von Mackensen, commander of Fourteenth Army, and decided to "launch the main attack on either side of Apulia [Aprilia] and to support it by two secondary attacks." Hitler reviewed the plan but, "to guarantee a pulverising effect on the part of our artillery bombardment," ordered the assault to be made on a narrow front by the Infantry Demonstration Regiment, "a home defence unit with no fighting experience."[39]

ULTRA revealed Kesselring's plans for the attack, dubbed Operation FISCH-FANG ("Fishing"), to the Allies just two hours before the attacks began on February 16.[40] Although bad weather had hampered Allied aerial reconnaissance, there was evidence of a buildup of German armor behind Cisterna, and there was an increase of German artillery emplacements to the west of Cisterna and around Campoleone. The Allies also knew with considerable certainty that the enemy had six to eight divisions available for the operation.

As the enemy attack began, the Allied forces were deployed as follows: In the east the 1st SSF held a six-mile front along the Mussolini Canal, and the 3d Division, with the 504th Parachute Infantry Regiment and 509th Parachute Infantry Battalion attached, held a front extending more than ten miles from just west of the canal bridge at Sessano through Isola Bella and Ponte Rotto to Carano. The 45th ID, the 56th Division, and the 36th Engineers manned the front extending westward from there to the coast. In corps reserve were the battered 1st Division and the American 1st AD, less CCB, which was still with II Corps in the South.[41]

Kesselring's attack began with an artillery bombardment along the entire VI Corps front, heaviest in the western sector. One half hour later the German artillery began counterbattery fire against the Allied artillery positions, followed soon after by advancing enemy infantry and tanks. In Truscott's sector the Germans launched only probing attacks of battalion or company size, all of which were easily beaten back. To the west the heaviest attacks fell upon the 45th ID in the Aprilia-Carroceto area, but even there the Germans made only slight gains. Although Lucas and some of his staff appeared to be somewhat anxious, Truscott felt that "the situation appeared to be well in hand as night came on" and, expecting the Germans to renew their attacks the next day, "turned in early that evening."[42]

On February 15 Lucas wrote that he "was afraid that the top side is not completely satisfied with my work, I can't help it." He also mentioned that Lt. Gen. Jacob L. Devers, commander of North African Theater of Operations, U.S. Army (NATOUSA), had visited him that afternoon and told him that after landing at Anzio he should have "gone on as fast as [he] could to disrupt enemy communications," intimating that "higher levels" also thought he should have done so. Lucas replied to his diary that if he had done so, he "would have lost [his] Corps," and "besides, my orders didn't read that way."[43]

That night Truscott received a telephone call from VI Corps informing him that Clark was relieving him as commanding general of the 3d ID and assigning him as deputy commander, VI Corps. He summoned Carleton and O'Daniel, his assistant division commander, to the CP, where they discussed his new assignment and its impact on the division.[44] Truscott's immediate re-action to Clark's decision was "one of resentment," since he had no knowledge that Clark had been considering the assignment. Although he believed that "General Lucas lacked some of the qualities of positive leadership that engen-dered confidence, and that he leaned heavily on his staff and trusted subordi-nates in difficult decisions," he had a feeling that perhaps he was being used to "pull someone else's chestnuts from the fire" because of the problems at Anzio.[45] The following morning Truscott received the formal orders appoint-ing him as VI Corps deputy commander and O'Daniel as commander of the 3d ID. Colonel Sherman was appointed acting assistant division commander, and Colonel Darby succeeded Sherman as commander of the 7th Infantry. After receiving the orders, Truscott spent some time conferring with O'Daniel, the regimental commanders, and his staff.[46]

Shortly after noon Truscott, accompanied by his aide Capt. James Wilson, went to the corps command post, which was located in the honeycomb of wine cellars beneath the Osteria dell'Artigliere (Tavern of the Artilleryman) in Net-tuno.[47] After graciously welcoming Truscott to the corps headquarters, Lucas reviewed the situation in the beachhead with him. There had been heavy fight-ing in the sectors of the 45th and 1st Divisions to the east and west of the Alba-no Road, respectively; the Allied air forces had bombed Carroceto, Aprilia, and Campoleone heavily that morning; the 179th Infantry had been driven back nearly to the Corps Beachhead line between Padiglione and the Flyover (over-pass) that crossed the Albano Road; and the 180th Infantry had been driven back to a north-south line along Spaccasassi Creek north of Padiglione. West of the Albano Road, in the "wadi country," the 56th Division had apparently checked the German advance. Lucas had ordered Harmon to counterattack north from the Flyover with one battalion to assist the 179th Infantry, and he had also ordered Eagles to counterattack with his division reserve to restore the line in the 179th's sector. However, in the command post Truscott detected "a feeling of desperation, of hopelessness," since no communications had come from either Penney or Harmon. Also, although "information was indefinite and confused, . . . the situation was far graver than we had realized in the 3rd Infantry Division."

Truscott's time as a combat commander had convinced him that "nothing ever looked as bad on the ground as it did on a map at Headquarters," and that the only place to assess a situation was at the point of contact with the enemy and decided to do just that. He and Wilson left the corps CP at midafternoon and, in a cold, driving rain, went first to Harmon's command post, where they found him to be in "good spirits." His tank attack had kicked off about noon, and although it had been halted by antitank fire and failed to recover the lost ground, his tankers had stopped the German attack, and the battalion was now lending its support to Penney's division. They then went on to the 45th ID CP, where he found Eagles to be similarly optimistic. Eagles believed that his division would hold and had issued orders for his 157th Infantry to counterattack the next morning to assist the 179th. After arranging for some of Harmon's tanks to support the 157th's attack, Truscott returned to the corps CP, reported his observations to Lucas, and retired to his command trailer.[48]

When Truscott reviewed the corps situation the following morning, he found that the Germans had driven a four-mile-deep salient into the center of the corps line and that there were six German divisions within the salient. However, Truscott viewed the glass as half-full: Eagles had one battalion in division reserve, Harmon had an armored infantry regiment and tanks that were not yet deployed, the 30th Infantry was in reserve near Campomorto, one brigade of the 1st Division was in corps reserve, and the 169th Brigade of the 56th Division was scheduled to arrive from Naples that morning, providing the corps with sufficient assets to launch a counterattack. As Truscott was discussing the proposed counterattack with Lucas, Clark arrived at the CP and, after hearing Truscott's plan to launch the counterattack the morning of the nineteenth, gave his approval. Lucas, who had initially opposed the counterattack, "reluctantly agreed."

Lucas and Truscott called Harmon and Maj. Gen. G. W. R. Templer, commander of the 56th Division, to a conference at the CP, and soon the commanders had agreed upon a plan. It featured a converging attack: Force H, under Harmon and composed of his 6th Armored Infantry, tanks, and the 30th Infantry, would attack "with regiments abreast northwest along the Diagonal Road [Bowling Alley] to seize ground just north of the Dead End Road"; Templer's Force T, consisting of the newly arrived 169th Brigade, would "strike north from the Flyover to seize the western end of the Dead End Road and establish contact with the 2nd Battalion, 157th Infantry, on the western shoulder of the salient." The attacks were to be supported by "all the artillery we could muster," and Clark was to arrange for "a maximum air effort."[49]

Leaving the corps staff and the division commanders and their staffs to complete the preparations for the offensive, Truscott accompanied Clark to Eagles's command post. During the trip Clark told Truscott that he would most likely order him to "replace Lucas within the next four or five days." Truscott replied that he had "no desire whatever to replace Lucas, a personal friend," and had agreed to his reassignment only because he realized that "some of the command, especially on the British side, had lost confidence in Lucas," and went on to say that he was perfectly willing to continue as Lucas's deputy as long as necessary. Clark said that he was glad to hear Truscott's opinion because he did not wish to hurt Lucas either and that there would be no change for the present.[50]

During supper that evening Carleton and he discussed why the recent German thrusts against the 45th and 56th Divisions had been so successful, attacks that they believed the 3d ID should have been able to repel. Feeling that the problem might be related to the manner in which the divisions employed their organic artillery, they checked artillery ammunition expenditures for the previous day. To their surprise they discovered that "one battalion of the 3d Infantry Division artillery had fired more rounds than had the [entire division] artillery of the 45th." The reason was that the German fire had destroyed communications and inflicted casualties among forward observers, artillery liaison officers, and company officers, and the 45th Division had no plans for ensuring continued artillery support under such conditions. The problem then became one of how to have the corps and division artillery battalions develop and implement plans to address such an eventuality that very night.

Truscott proposed sending an experienced field artillery officer and the newly assigned corps artillery commander, Brig. Gen. Carl A. Baehr, to visit the corps and each division, check the artillery plans, and issue necessary instructions to ensure coordination of fires if the usual means of communication became inoperable. Truscott chose Maj. Walter T. Kerwin, 3d Division artillery S3, for the job. Later that night Baehr and Kerwin reported to Truscott and received their mission: visit the units and present to them a system for "laying down prearranged final protective lines based on previous registration of various targets." Truscott told General Baehr that his sole duty was to accompany Kerwin and explain to any who might question the authority of a junior officer to order such changes that he was carrying out the orders of the corps commander. The next morning, the nineteenth, Baehr called Truscott and told him that Kerwin and he had completed their mission, adding that he had received "the best lesson in artillery that I have had in thirty-five years service in the artillery."[51]

At six thirty that morning Force H attacked after a half-hour artillery bombardment that included antiaircraft and naval guns. The advancing forces made fair progress against heavy enemy resistance, but then encountered mud and flooded creeks that restricted tank support until bridges had been laid. Despite those hindrances, by early afternoon Harmon's force had succeeded in advancing to the eastern end of Dead End Road. At the same time tanks of Force T were advancing from the Flyover up the Albano Road toward the western end of Dead End Road. However, the Germans knocked out several of the tanks and forced the remainder to withdraw, thus leaving Harmon's infantrymen in an exposed position. Truscott discussed the situation with Harmon, and the two agreed that despite the failure of Force T to reach its objective, the attack "had broken the back of the German offensive." To avoid unnecessary losses they also decided to withdraw Harmon's infantry to an area west of Padiglione, there to remain in reserve while they reorganized their defenses. Truscott and Harmon had evaluated the situation accurately, since ULTRA revealed that as early as the eighteenth Kesselring and Mackensen had concluded that "they had no choice but to call FISCHFANG off. . . . The tide had turned against them, and their troops never recovered the élan they had showed on the Anzio road during the last few days. . . . ULTRA had been a prime instrument of victory. . . . The successful defense of the Anzio perimeter in February 1944 was a turning point in the Italian campaign."[52]

The evening of February 22 Truscott received a call from Clark, who had just returned to the beachhead from Caserta. He asked Truscott to report to the Fifth Army advance CP in the cellar of the Villa Borghese, where Clark informed him that he was to assume command of VI Corps the next day. Truscott reminded Clark that he had no personal desire to succeed Lucas, that relieving him now when the situation in the beachhead was more stable "might have an unfortunate reaction on morale and undermine confidence among other officers," among whom Lucas was popular, and that some American officers might interpret his relief as a concession to the British, fearing that if they ran into difficulty a similar fate might befall them.

Clark listened politely to Truscott's comments but told him that he had already made his decision. He promised to see to it that "Lucas was not hurt," that he was being relieved without prejudice, that he intended to name him deputy commander of Fifth Army, and that he had already sent for Lucas to inform him personally of his relief. Realizing that General Marshall had already approved Clark's decision, Truscott returned to his trailer. After a late dinner and a treatment at a nearby Army hospital for an ailing throat, Truscott went to visit Lucas at his CP "to express his regrets." Lucas was obviously deeply hurt but said that he had no ill feeling toward Truscott and hoped their bonds of friendship would remain intact, which they did until Lucas's death in 1949. He was, however, "bitter toward General Clark and blamed his relief upon British influence."[53]

One of Lucas's last official acts as commander of VI Corps was to complete Truscott's Efficiency Report, in which he described Truscott as "a strong, self-reliant, taciturn officer of dominating personality. One of the most capable commanders of combat troops with whom I am acquainted. Inclined to be stubborn and at times boastful but not so as to interfere with his military efficiency. His tactical judgment is of an exceptionally high standard." He further stated that of all thirty-eight infantry division commanders with whom he had been associated, he would place Truscott "number one on the list."[54]

After visiting Lucas, Truscott returned to his trailer, where he opened a bottle of Scotch Clark had sent and began discussing with Carleton the problems that he would be facing as he took over VI Corps.[55] Although the beachhead had come "close to disaster," Truscott believed that the corps' assets were sufficient to have halted the German offensive much earlier if they had been utilized in a more effective and better-coordinated fashion. The "narrow escape" had resulted in "a general lack of confidence" throughout the corps, particularly within the rear-echelon units. Although the corps staff officers were competent, Truscott believed that plans had often been made without adequate staff analysis and that operation orders were often written after rather superficial review of intelligence estimates, cursory map studies, and inadequate reconnaissance before and during tactical operations.

There was also "a lack of understanding between British and American commanders and staffs, particularly between Corps Headquarters and the British divisions. General Lucas had put little trust in the British commanders and their troops, and the British commanders returned the compliment." The corps staff had made little or no attempt to become familiar with British staff organization and functioning or with British tactics, and few of the American officers came to appreciate or understand the "effect that Britain's ordeal and British manpower shortages had upon their tactical methods," an appreciation that Truscott had early on developed during his service in Mountbatten's headquarters.

Another problem was that in the rear areas of the beachhead most of the service troops and units were not under corps command. Truscott was a firm believer in unity of command and believed that all resources forward of the shoreline should be under corps command and control. As he discussed the problems in the corps' rear areas, Truscott pointed out that most enemy air attacks and long-range artillery attacks were directed to those rear areas and that there was a need for more antiaircraft artillery units, as well as means to suppress the enemy artillery fires from guns beyond the range of the corps' artillery pieces.

Finally, he expressed his dissatisfaction that both the corps and the army advance CPs were located underground, the former in the honeycomb of wine cellars beneath the Osteria dell'Artigliere and the latter in the cellar of Villa Borghese. None of the division command posts were below ground, and all of the hospitals and other installations in the rear operated above ground. The underground location of the corps and army CPs undoubtedly gave the impression that the corps and army commanders and their staffs were "unduly concerned for their own safety."[56]

Before leaving the beachhead Clark stopped by for a final discussion of the situation with Truscott. He told Truscott that he had ordered Lt. Gen. Sir Bernard Freyberg's New Zealand Corps "to press its attack on the southern front to capture the heights above Cassino and establish a bridgehead over the Rapido River." Truscott was to continue operations within the beachhead to restore the corps' forward positions and to prepare to resume offensive operations "with maximum strength" toward either Velletri or Albano in coordination with the advance of the southern force.

Accompanying Clark was Maj. Gen. Evelyn Eveleigh, whom Alexander had sent to investigate British conditions within the beachhead. Alexander had also offered to make Eveleigh's services available to VI Corps, an offer Truscott immediately accepted, appointing him as his British deputy commander, with specific duties to assist in coordinating British operations to remove the frictions that had developed between the commanders and troops of the two

Allies. Shortly after Clark's departure General Templer came in, and Harmon arrived soon after, and they joined Truscott and Eveleigh in discussing the current disposition of the British and American divisions along the front. The 45th ID had been hit particularly hard, and as a result Truscott reassigned division boundaries, extending the frontage of the 3d Division, reducing that of the 45th Division by half, and strengthening the 1st and 56th Divisions.[57]

One of the first and most important tasks facing a new commander is the forming of his staff. Truscott was familiar with Lucas's staff and considered them to be very capable, but at his first meeting with the VI Corps staff Truscott found that only a few of the general and special staff officers were able to present a comprehensive report on the command activities for which their sections were responsible. Truscott "gently and *firmly*" explained that beginning the next morning and thereafter every day at 8:00 a.m. he expected "full and accurate reports" from each staff section.[58] As a result of that meeting Truscott felt it necessary to bring from the 3d Division certain staff officers who were familiar with his customs and procedures. Therefore, he tapped his old friend and trusted confidant Don Carleton to continue as his chief of staff,[59] and selected Lt. Col. Ben Harrell as corps G3, Lt. Col. William B. Rosson as assistant corps G3, and Col. Kermit L. Davis as corps artillery executive officer. A little later he brought Col. Richard J. Myers from the corps' signal battalion to be his corps signal officer. Truscott retained all of Lucas's other staff officers.[60]

Although he kept the corps' staff offices in the wine cellar beneath the tavern, Truscott moved his and Carleton's offices into the tavern above. Behind his desk he hung an enlargement of one of Bill Mauldin's wartime cartoons featuring his beloved dogfaces, Willie and Joe.[61] He also established a small war room, where his staff could post maps and other data on the walls and where current and pending operations could be discussed. Carleton and he decided to procure separate quarters for the two of them, as well as Truscott's aides, Captains Bartash and Wilson, and the Canton Restaurant crew, and moved into a two-story house roughly a hundred yards from the CP.[62]

One of the most serious problems that Truscott faced was countering the threat posed by the German air force. Although the Luftwaffe had been active in Tunisia and Sicily, attacks on ground troops had been relatively rare. However, with the congestion of troops, vehicles, artillery units, and supplies on shore and the large number of vessels lying offshore, Anzio had become a remunerative target. Since the Allied air bases were more than one hundred miles distant, the beachhead had no air cover during the first and last daylight hours, a fact that the enemy quickly recognized and of which it took full advantage. To complicate matters further, the Germans had installed a ground station north of the beachhead to jam the Allied radar.

Not being knowledgeable about the employment of antiaircraft artillery, Truscott turned to the corps antiaircraft officer, Brig. Gen. Aaron A. Bradshaw.

To counter the radar jamming Bradshaw submitted a request for the newly developed SCR 584 radar equipment that was almost impervious to jamming. With the new radar directing and controlling the roughly sixty-four 90mm antiaircraft guns, supplemented by hundreds of guns of other caliber, including .50-caliber machine guns, the beachhead was able to mount a stout defense against the Luftwaffe, and by early March "the Germans almost abandoned high level bombing." With their high-level bombing runs blocked, the Germans concentrated more heavily on low-level attacks, against which the 90mm guns were relatively ineffective. Bradshaw, at Truscott's suggestion, divided the beachhead into five sectors, each guarded by smaller-caliber guns that would initiate a standard fire pattern when aircraft entered that sector. By the end of March the Germans had almost completely abandoned air attacks against the beachhead.[63]

To counteract the heavy artillery fire that the Germans began using to replace air attacks, Truscott's artillerymen developed a counterbattery fire system controlled by the corps Fire Direction Center. When enemy artillery positions were located, each one would be engaged using the time on target (TOT) method of firing, whereby all guns within range of the target would "so time their fire as to assure all projectiles [would reach] the target simultaneously."[64] The TOT fire was very effective against conventional field artillery but could not silence the German 170mm and 210mm long-range guns and the two 280mm railroad guns. The fire from the railroad guns came to be known as the "Anzio Express" and would plague the beachhead on a daily basis until the breakout.[65] Before Truscott was able to develop effective countermeasures to blunt the effectiveness of the enemy artillery fire, his own villa was struck several times by enemy artillery fire. On one occasion the exploding round destroyed all the windows in his quarters, and on another occasion a round struck the "Chinese latrine in [the] backyard—a 'Chinese Garden Tragedy.'" Fortunately, there were no casualties.[66]

One other "problem" faced by the new corps commander was the depletion of his liquor supplies, forcing Truscott and his "family" to substitute "Anzio Annihilators" for their daily cocktails. Captain Wilson described the Annihilator as "God-awful" but cheap gin produced by an Italian distillery from Navy alcohol and juniper berries from Algeria that was supplied in jeroboams (a wine container holding about four-fifths of a gallon). At about the same time Lucian responded to Sarah's concern that he might be drinking excessively: "I don't think there is much doubt on that score—haven't we all? But I'm trying now to be more careful than ever before—and I've never allowed it to interfere with my work."[67]

While attending to strengthening the beachhead defenses, Truscott had been following the situation along the front line closely. The Germans made repeated limited-objective attacks, mainly in the British sector, whittling away at the

British positions, producing casualties that the British were finding more and more difficult to replace. As a result, both British divisions, but particularly the 56th, were understrength. Truscott kept Clark informed of his "grave concern" about the British units' offensive capabilities and recommended that Clark reinforce the 56th Division with one brigade of the British 5th Division from the southern front, and as quickly as possible send the American 88th Infantry Division or another full-strength American division to replace the 56th Division and the 36th Engineers, thus unifying command of that sector.[68]

Brig. Gen. Frederic B. Butler, Truscott's new American deputy corps commander, arrived on February 25. He had previously served as assistant commander of the 34th Infantry Division and was a welcome addition to corps headquarters.[69] At about the same time Truscott began to suspect that another German attack appeared to be imminent, as intelligence revealed that the enemy was shifting artillery to the east of Campoleone and moving artillery and tanks into the Cisterna area. On the twenty-seventh he informed Clark of his suspicions, telling him that most likely a renewed attack "will come from divergent directions to disperse our artillery effort." He predicted that the attack would begin on February 29 or March 1.

Clark replied that he had informed Alexander of the situation and told Truscott that the British 5th Division had been alerted to move to the beachhead to relieve the 56th Division in place and that the 34th ID was being sent, RCT by RCT, between March 15 and March 20. To Clark's suggestion that he "thin out" the forces on the eastern corps front to reinforce the 56th, Truscott replied that he expected "rather strong diversionary attacks" in that sector, and any further weakening of the 3d Division and 1st SSF sectors "would be hazardous at this time."[70]

Early in the evening of the twenty-eighth Truscott received an intelligence report from Lt. Col. Joseph L. Langevin, his G2, that the Germans would begin their assault the next day. Truscott believed that the main attack would be delivered against the 3d ID west of Cisterna and that the enemy would initiate diversionary actions to convince the Allies that the main effort would be along the Albano Road. Confident that Mackensen would strike the 3d ID front, Truscott ordered General Baehr to plan counterpreparatory fires by every gun in the beachhead one hour before the expected time of the enemy attack, concentrating on enemy "troop assembly areas, reserve positions, artillery locations, and tank concentrations." He also requested that Fifth Army make available maximum aerial reconnaissance beginning at daylight on the twenty-ninth and that all Allied air forces stand by for on-call strikes.[71]

The next morning Truscott awoke to the thunderous roar of artillery, as all guns of the corps began engaging the enemy positions. An hour later, after the firing ceased, all wondered if the Germans would indeed attack that day, or if their expenditure of ammunition, an estimated sixty-six thousand rounds, had been wasted. But soon calls for supporting fires came in, confirming that the attack was on. In the 3d Division sector enemy infantry and tanks struck at a half-dozen points, but only in the 509th Parachute Infantry's sector near Carano did the Germans achieve any appreciable success. Truscott immediately went to the 3d's front, arriving just as roughly one hundred Allied bombers dropped their bomb loads on Cisterna. At the division CP he found O'Daniel to be confident that his lines would hold. To bolster O'Daniel's defenses, Truscott released two battalions of the 30th Infantry, in reserve at Campomorto, to reinforce the 509th's sector. To the east battalion-size enemy forces struck the fronts of the 504th Parachute Infantry and the 1st SSF but made no headway. Heavy fighting continued in the 3d's sector throughout the day. In the afternoon the skies cleared, and Allied bombers, which had largely been grounded in the morning, appeared and pummeled the enemy attackers. Despite heavy losses in his division, O'Daniel launched a counterattack late in the day that regained the few hundred yards of ground that had been lost. Reinforced by the battalions of the 30th Infantry the 509th succeeded in restoring its lines.

Mackensen continued his attacks on March 2 and 3, despite having received Kesselring's March 1 order to halt the attack against the 3d ID and to restrict all future offensive operations within the beachhead to local counterattacks. However, the attacks were noticeably weaker and made no progress. These attacks, the last major German offensive within the beachhead, had ended in failure, at a cost of more than 3,000 casualties and the loss of at least thirty tanks.[72] The four-day battle had cost the Allies 404 killed, 1,982 wounded, and 1,025 captured or missing.[73]

In the southern sector of the Italian front the attack against Cassino and the adjacent mountains began on March 15. However, the attack progressed more slowly than expected because the debris created by the preceding bombings prevented the tanks from passing through the town. On the nineteenth Clark visited Truscott in the beachhead and told him of the situation in the south, pointing out that the attack on Cassino "had just about spent its force." He went on to say that Alexander had decided to shift responsibility for the Cassino front to Eighth Army and move Fifth Army westward to a sector between the coast and the Liri River, where he hoped to launch a major assault about the middle of April. Meanwhile, Truscott's forces were to use the interval to "regroup, reorganize, rest and train troops in preparation for renewing the assault in connection with the major attack on the southern front." Clark also told Truscott that he would send the rest of the 1st AD and possibly the 88th ID to Truscott, supplementing the British 5th Division that had already replaced the 56th Division in the line.[74]

Offsetting that gain, however, were the reassignments of the 504th Parachute Infantry Regiment and the 509th Parachute Infantry Battalion.[75] Because Alexander could not provide sufficient replacements to keep the British 1st and 6th

Divisions up to strength, Truscott concluded that in the coming breakout from the beachhead the American divisions would have to bear most of the burden of the attack. He decided to give that mission to Harmon's 1st Armored and O'Daniel's 3d Infantry Divisions and began reorganizing the front accordingly. The 34th ID would relieve the 3d ID and the 504th Parachute Infantry, and the 3d would withdraw to an area near Nettuno to train for its new mission. The 1st AD would remain in corps reserve and conduct training for the upcoming breakout.[76]

On the thirtieth Truscott was admitted to the 94th Evacuation Hospital ("Doctor Pierce's Promising Hostelry for Harassed Generals") for evaluation of his chronic throat problems. His bed in the hospital was screened from the other beds in the ward by a sheet, and he was supplied with a stove, radio, flowers, and telephone. One duty of his assigned nurses was to see that before each meal and at bedtime Truscott received Doctor Pierce's prescription of two ounces of rye whiskey. By the end of the first day of hospitalization, Truscott had concluded, "Dr. Pierce's hospital is [the] ideal vacation spot."

The next day, however, he decided that "Col. Pierce's palace [was] not so pleasant during [his] physical exam and bronchoscopic operation," both of which revealed "nothing new." He was discharged to duty that day but returned for a follow-up visit on April 15, during which Pierce found a nasal polyp, which he removed two days later. Pierce also told him that his voice and throat problems were most likely due to a maxillary sinus infection and advised him to quit smoking since it could be causing some of the throat problems. On the twenty-first Truscott returned for a maxillary sinus irrigation by Pierce and dental work by Major Pearlman, who found gum recession and "infection [most likely gingivitis]." After the sinus irrigation Truscott noted "marked improvement" in his voice.[77]

On April 27 Truscott and Harmon began a four-day visit to war correspondent Mike Chinigo's "Villa Chinigo" in Naples. During the visit Chinigo introduced Truscott to Crown Prince Umberto, the son of King Vittorio Emanuele. During their stay in Naples, General Alexander appointed both Truscott and Harmon Honorary Companions in the Order of Bath in recognition of their services in Tunisia.[78]

Back in the beachhead, "life . . . was never dull, easy or quiet." While enemy air attacks had diminished to raids by only a few aircraft daily, artillery shelling continued, and no structure and no person within the beachhead were safe. Even hospitals clearly identified by a red cross became targets, resulting in the death and wounding of doctors, nurses, and patients. Shocked by the Germans' targeting of medical facilities, Truscott sent a message to Clark recommending that he bring this violation of the Geneva Convention to the attention of the theater commander. He also directed Baehr to have the corps Fire Direction Center "counterbattery every possible artillery position which could open fire

upon the hospitals." He ordered all hospital commanders to notify him immediately when their hospitals came under fire so that he could order the counterbattery fire.[79]

Living conditions, particularly for the dogfaces, were very primitive. Many of
the infantrymen literally lived in their foxholes, utilizing shelter halves to protect them from the elements. More fortunate souls sought shelter in tents or in
the few surviving buildings within the beachhead. As spring arrived baseball
and softball teams were organized, sometimes playing games as artillery shells
burst within five or six hundred yards of the playing fields. Swimming in the
Tyrrhenian Sea also became popular as the weather warmed.[80]

Frustrated by the failure of the first three attacks to rupture the Gustav line,
Lt. Gen. Sir John Harding, Alexander's new chief of staff, devised a strategy,
code-named DIADEM, to break the line by concentrating Eighth Army for the
assault on Cassino. After breaking through the Gustav line Eighth Army would
advance up the Liri valley along Highway 6 to link up with VI Corps attacking
out of the Anzio beachhead. Fifth Army and General Juin's French Corps, deployed along the Garigliano on the left flank of Eighth Army, were to turn the
southern flank of the German defenses and then move northward south of the
Liri valley. The second blow of Alexander's "one-two punch," a left hook, would
be delivered by Truscott's VI Corps, which was to be prepared to attack out of
the beachhead on twenty-four hours' notice. Alexander presented the DIADEM
plan to his army commanders the first week of April.

Alexander's intended target for his Army Group was Valmontone, not Rome.
With OVERLORD on the horizon, the main strategic objective of DIADEM
was not the capture of Rome but rather the tying down in Italy of as many German divisions as possible. Capture of Valmontone, Alexander believed, would
trap most of Vietinghoff's Tenth Army and force the Germans to move forces
from other fronts, it was hoped from France and the eastern front, into Italy to
compensate for the loss of Tenth Army.[81]

Truscott had already set his staff to work drawing up plans for the breakout
from the beachhead. Four plans emerged, only one of which, Operation BUF-
FALO, complied with Alexander's guidance to capture Valmontone. BUFFA-
LO called for an attack by VI Corps via Cisterna and Cori to cut Highway 6 at
Valmontone. VI Corps staff, however, prepared complete plans for all four attacks and carried out detailed reconnaissance of routes to the lines of departure
so that pre-attack-unit movements to the LODs could be carried out under
cover of darkness. Gun positions were dug under strictest security, ammunition was placed in areas accessible to the gun crews, assembly areas were identified, and orders for movement to the assembly areas and lines of departure
were prepared.[82]

Alexander visited the beachhead on May 5 and, after hearing Truscott's plans,
informed Truscott "very quietly and firmly that there was only one direction in

Plan for Breakout from Anzio, 23 May 1944

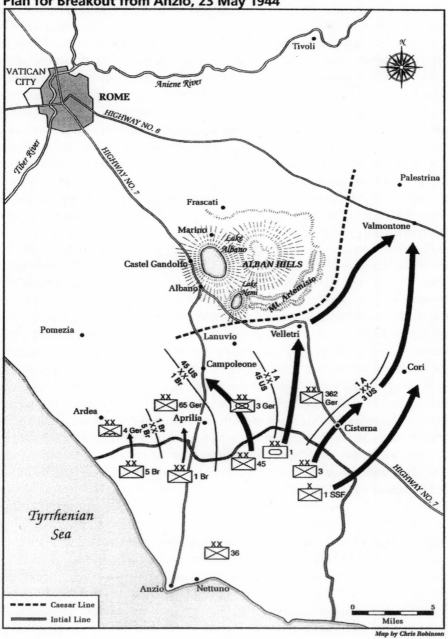

which the attack should or would be launched, and that was from Cisterna to cut Highway 6 in the vicinity of Valmontone in the rear of the German forces. He had . . . reserved to himself the decision as to when he proposed to initiate it." Immediately after Alexander's departure Truscott reported his conversation with Alexander to Clark, pointing out that as a result of the discussion he was giving first priority to preparing for BUFFALO and asked if this met with Clark's approval. Irked by what he believed to be "interference" by Alexander in his chain of command, Clark arrived in the beachhead the next day and told Truscott that "the capture of Rome is the only important objective." Clark was determined that the British would not beat his Fifth Army to the Holy City, and since attacking along the Carroceto-Campoleone axis and then west of the Alban Hills might be the quickest way into Rome, he ordered Truscott to be prepared to attack in that direction as well as toward Cisterna and Valmontone.[83] "Clark's fixation with capturing Rome had by this point turned into an obsession, and it was to color his thinking badly during the planning for the May offensives. . . . Valmontone and Operation Buffalo had absolutely no place in Clark's priorities."[84]

The attack on the Gustav line began at eleven o'clock the night of May 11. There was slow going in the Cassino area for Lt. Gen. Sir Oliver Leese's Eighth Army, Cassino and the Benedictine Monastery not falling until the night of the seventeenth. To the west, II Corps and the French Corps got off to good starts, and the French were soon beginning to outflank the Germans in the Liri valley. With three bridges across the Rapido River the Eighth Army seemed poised to debouch into the Liri valley and push on to the Adolf Hitler line beyond the Sacco River south of Frosinone.

On May 19 Clark directed Truscott to prepare to launch a modified BUFFALO plan two days later, capturing Cisterna and Cori and sending the 1st SSF on toward Artena and Valmontone. After the capture of Cisterna and Cori the remaining forces would regroup and attack northwest from Cisterna. However, Truscott told Clark that the 1st SSF was not strong enough to capture Artena and cut Highway 6 at Valmontone and convinced him to abandon the modified plan. Late in the afternoon of May 21 Truscott received the final word that he would launch his attack on May 23 at 6:30 a.m., based on Clark's May 6 guidance, attacking along the Carroceto-Campoleone axis and then west of the Alban Hills toward Rome, as well as toward Cisterna and Cori.[85]

On the twentieth Truscott briefed his commanders and staff on the final attack plans and then adjourned to his villa for a preattack party. Among the guests were several nurses from nearby Army hospitals. After the party M. Sgt. Louis Barna, Jr., Truscott, and Wilson drove the nurses to their quarters, but on the return journey their vehicle collided with a truck. The sudden stop hurled Wilson from the rear seat onto Truscott, bruising the general severely, and Barna suffered a lacerated chin. Over the next several days Truscott continued to complain of

Clark's Change of Direction toward Rome

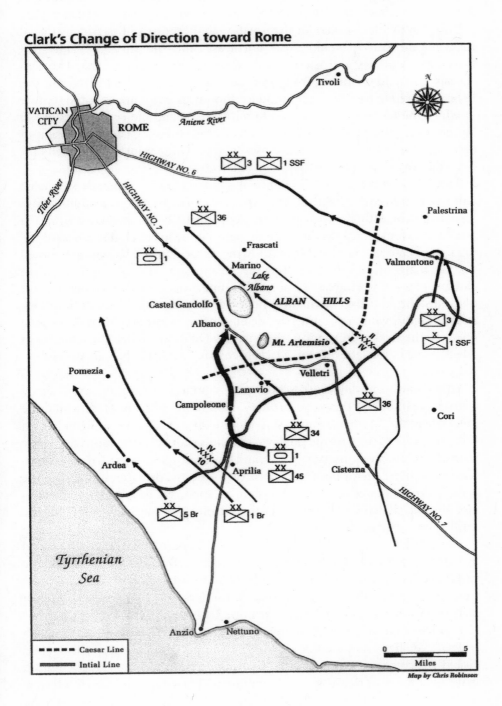

Map by Chris Robinson

173

chest pain, and a visit to the 94th Evacuation Hospital for X-rays revealed that he had several fractured ribs, for which he received appropriate treatment.[86]

The plan of attack called for the isolation and capture of Cisterna by the 3d ID, while the 1st SSF would attack northeast along the Mussolini Canal, cut Highway 7 southeast of Cisterna, and protect the corps' right flank. The 45th ID was to extend the breakthrough west to Carano, and the 36th Division was to be prepared to pass through the 3d for the advance to Cori, after the capture of which the forces would push on to seize Artena and then cut Highway 6 at Valmontone. The 1st AD and the attached 135th Infantry had the mission of breaking through the German defenses west of Feminamorto Creek and cutting Highway 7 between Cisterna and Velletri.[87]

There was a fundamental difference of opinion between Generals Kesselring and Mackensen over what route the expected VI Corps offensive would follow. Kesselring correctly believed that the main thrust of the breakout from the beachhead would be in the direction of Valmontone to cut Highway 6, severing the line of communications to Tenth Army in the South. Mackensen believed that the main attack would be along the Albano Road to Highway 7, and then along Highway 7 northwest to Rome. Therefore, he had positioned his two best divisions, the 3d Panzer Grenadier and the 65th Infantry, to counter the attack in that sector, while relegating the defense of the Cisterna–Mussolini Canal sector to the weaker 362d and 715th Infantry Divisions. When the main corps attack came in the latter sector, Mackensen was unable to shift his strength to the east.[88]

Before dawn on May 23 Truscott, some members of his staff, and General Clark were in one of the corps' artillery observation posts located behind the LOD where the 3d Infantry and 1st Armored Divisions were waiting to launch their attacks. At 5:45 a.m. the predawn darkness suddenly disappeared as more than a thousand guns, mortars, tanks, and tank destroyers began a deadly bombardment of the enemy lines and rear-area positions. Forty minutes later, as the bombardment ceased, bombers and fighters appeared, dropping their bombs and strafing the enemy positions in the vicinity of Cisterna, after which the artillery resumed its firing.

The attack kicked off all along the line from Carano to the Mussolini Canal at 6:00 a.m., as infantry and tanks crossed the LOD. By noon the 1st SSF on the east flank had reached and cut Highway 7 below Cisterna. The 3d Division, after encountering stiff enemy resistance and suffering heavy casualties, reached its first-day objective by nightfall. Harmon's 1st Armored crossed the Cisterna-Campoleone railroad, smashing the enemy main line of resistance.

That evening Brig. Gen. Robert T. Frederick, the commander of the 1st SSF, visited Truscott at his forward CP at Conca, where he found, much to his disgust, that Truscott and Carleton were "celebrating [the] first day's successes [and] were feeling pretty good from drinks." Although Frederick considered Truscott to be "a good combat commander . . . [he] drank heavily . . . [and] at night when he'd get tanked up [he] sometimes would make some rash statements." However, he did not believe that Truscott's "drinking interfered seriously with his intelligent direction of combat operations."[89]

On the second day the advance, aided by fighter-bombers, continued. Although the enemy counterattacked in force, the attacks were all repulsed, with heavy German losses. By nightfall the 3d Division had surrounded Cisterna, and Harmon's forces were probing toward Velletri. Cisterna fell to the 3d Division on the twenty-fifth, netting more than a thousand enemy prisoners. As night fell the 3d Division and 1st SSF units had driven to the base of the Lepini Mountains in front of Cori, and 1st Armored troops had established a position halfway between Velletri and Cori at the entrance to the Velletri Gap, leading to Valmontone.

On May 26 Harmon's force advanced to within two miles of Velletri, and O'Daniel's "reconnaissance units [had] reached the outskirts of Artena, only three miles from the goal of Valmontone and Highway 6." The next day Artena fell, but there the advance halted, in part because Fifth Army attack plans were being "recast" and in part because elements of the Hermann Göring Division, just arrived from northern Italy, were attacking the 3d Division south of Valmontone.

Although the VI Corps attack out of the beachhead had been very successful, costs had been high: more than 4,000 casualties in the first five days. Harmon had lost at least eighty-six tanks and tank destroyers during the first day alone. Enemy casualties had undoubtedly been higher, although no precise figures were available. However, VI Corps forces had taken 4,838 enemy prisoners.[90]

Late in the afternoon of May 25 General Brann, Clark's G3, told Truscott that Clark had directed that he leave the 3d Division and the 1st SSF to capture Valmontone and block Highway 6 and "mount that assault you discussed with him to the northwest as soon as you can." The previous day Truscott had discussed with Clark his belief that continuing the attack toward Valmontone might lead the Germans to concentrate "all available reserves from the Valmontone Gap" there, as well as some forces from the beachhead front to keep Highway 6 open, possibly delaying the cutting of the highway at Valmontone. "*If there was any [enemy] withdrawal from the western part of the beachhead . . . an attack to the northwest might be the best way to cut off the enemy withdrawal north of the Albano Hills.*" He told Clark that VI Corps staff was already preparing plans for such a contingency.

Truscott immediately protested Clark's new order, pointing out that there "*was no evidence of enemy withdrawal from the western part of the beachhead nor of a concentration of enemy troops in the Valmontone area,*" except for reconnaissance elements of the Hermann Göring Division. He recommended instead that there should be a maximum effort to drive through the Valmontone Gap and destroy the retreating German army before Kesselring could reinforce that sector and told Brann that he would not obey the order until he had personally discussed the matter with Clark. When Brann informed him that Clark was not in the beachhead and could not be contacted by radio, Truscott, having no other option, began preparations for the attack to the northwest. In Truscott's words, "Such was the order that turned the main effort of the beachhead forces from the Valmontone Gap and prevented the destruction of the German X Army."[91] At eleven on the night of May 25 Truscott informed O'Daniel and Harmon of Clark's new plan. Both objected vigorously, but Truscott told them that they were to carry out Clark's orders despite their objections.

That same day, as Truscott was planning the redirection of the corps attack, Kesselring, acutely aware of the threat posed by the VI Corps attack toward Valmontone and Highway 6, had ordered Mackensen to hold his present defense positions and to make no further withdrawals. He also began rushing reinforcements into the Velletri and Valmontone Gaps to keep Highway 6 open until Vietinghoff's Tenth Army had cleared Valmontone.

To put Clark's new plan into action, Truscott ordered Harmon to move his division, less his reserve, westward to reinforce the 45th Division, which, along with the 34th Division, was to attack to the northwest from the vicinity of Carano to the line Lanuvio-Campoleone. The 3d Division, with the attached 1st Armored Division reserve, dubbed Task Force Howze, was to continue the attack toward Valmontone and block Highway 6. Joining the 3d Division in the attack would be Frederick's 1st SSF after it moved northward across the Lepini Mountains to the heights above Artena. The 36th ID would relieve the 1st AD and plug the wide gap that would exist between the two attacking forces.[92]

On May 27 the 15th Infantry seized Artena, and by nightfall the 7th Infantry Regiment and the 1st SSF had joined it there. However, the Hermann Göring Division, which regularly poured artillery and tank fire into Artena, retained control of the road leading northward from Artena to Valmontone. To deal with the artillery fire and to drive back the enemy forces guarding the road, O'Daniel ordered the 7th Infantry, the 1st SSF, and a tank battalion to advance to and attack a railway north of Artena and destroy the tanks and 88mm guns there. At the same time a demolition party was to move behind the German lines by infiltration and destroy the overpasses crossing Highway 6 near Valmontone.

The attack began the afternoon of the twenty-eighth but encountered heavy resistance. After a five-hour battle the attackers had captured the railway but could advance no farther along the road to Valmontone. The demolition party found the overpasses heavily guarded and was unable to complete its mission. German reinforcements continued to arrive, denying Highway 6 to O'Daniel's forces and keeping the vital route open for Vietinghoff's retreating Tenth Army. The 1st SSF finally cut Highway 6 at Colleferro, roughly four and one-half miles southeast of Valmontone, on June 2, where it met up with the 3d Algerian Division of the French Expeditionary Corps (FEC) advancing from the south.[93]

Clark's decision to change the axis of the VI Corps attack to the northwest was a flagrant disregard of Alexander's very specific order to "cut Highway 6 in the VALMONTONE area, and thereby prevent the supply and withdrawal of the German Tenth Army opposing the advance of the Eighth and Fifth Armies," and was clearly an act of insubordination. Truscott stated that there had "never been any doubt in [his] mind that had General Clark held loyally to General Alexander's instructions, had he not changed the direction of [his] attack to the northwest on May 26th, the strategic objective of Anzio [that is, to "cut Highway 6 in the VALMONTONE area, and thereby prevent the supply and withdrawal of the German Tenth Army opposing the advance of the Eighth and Fifth Armies"][94] would have been accomplished in full. "To be first in Rome was poor compensation for this lost opportunity."[95]

To carry out the new mission of VI Corps, Truscott ordered the 34th ID to advance from its position below heavily defended Velletri to Lanuvio, while the 45th ID and the 1st AD attacked toward Campoleone Station and Campoleone. The 45th reached Campoleone Station on May 29, the same day the 34th reached the outskirts of Lanuvio. However, further advance was blocked by elements of the I Parachute Corps defending the Caesar line that extended from Ardea just inland from the coast through Lanuvio and Velletri to a position below Valmontone.

On May 30 Truscott decided to have the 34th bypass Lanuvio to the west. At the same time he would replace the 36th ID, occupying the sector south and east of Velletri, with the corps engineers and "move the 36th Infantry Division up behind the 34th Division to climb the Colli Laziali [Alban Hills] and encircle Lanuvio from the east." However, he soon learned from Maj. Gen. Fred L. Walker, the 36th's commander, that division reconnaissance patrols had discovered a gap in the German lines just east of Velletri, where his engineers believed they could construct a road to permit tanks and infantry to reach the crest of the hills back of Velletri. With Truscott's permission the engineers began their work, and by daylight of June 1 Walker's forces had traversed the road and were on the outskirts of Velletri, which fell shortly thereafter. Truscott visited Walker there and ordered him to advance across the Alban Hills on roads to the east of Lakes Nemi and Albano.

Although the attacks on the Campoleone front continued to make little headway, elsewhere in the corps sector the 36th ID was approaching Lake Albano by June 3, a patrol of the 30th Infantry had entered Valmontone on June 2, and II Corps was rapidly advancing north of the Alban Hills. To aid the Campoleone attack Truscott ordered Harmon's tanks back into action in that sector, telling him to attack astride the Anzio road toward its junction with Highway

Breakthrough at Velletri--36th infantry Division, 31 May-2 June 1944

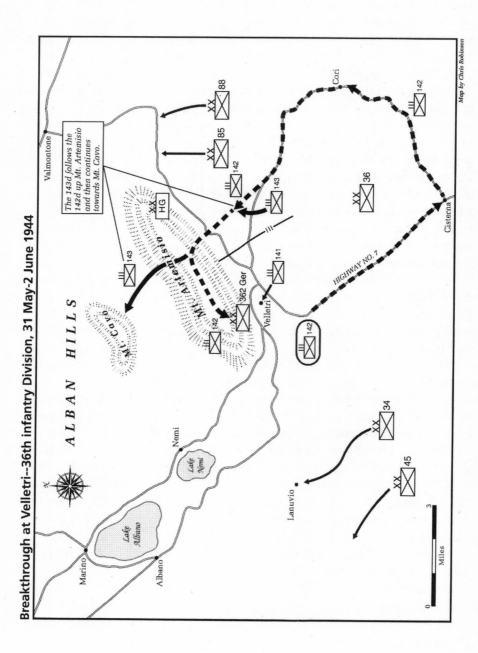

The 143d follows the 142d up Mt. Artemisio and then continues towards Mt. Cavo.

ALBAN HILLS

Map by Chris Robinson

7 at Albano. Truscott then called Eagles and told him that before Harmon's attack his 45th Division was to advance as far as the railroad north of Lanuvio, where the 1st AD would pass through and attack toward Rome along Highway 7 and a parallel road to the south, joining the 36th ID in the final drive to the Eternal City, which on June 3 Kesselring declared an open city.[96]

The night of the third, Mike Chinigo joined Truscott at his CP and told him he had learned that II Corps was planning to enter Rome the next day, June 4, and that Clark would accompany Keyes to make his grand entry. Truscott replied that if he "wanted to be the first correspondent in Rome, he had better stay where he was," and Chinigo elected to do just that. About noon the next day, while driving along Highway 7 toward Rome, Truscott found a long column of Harmon's tanks parked along the road and asked the commander of the armored column what his orders were. The colonel replied that Harmon had ordered him to secure the bridges over the Tiber River. When Truscott asked, "Well Colonel, what are you waiting for?" the colonel saluted, turned, and ordered his tanks to follow him to the river. Truscott then turned to Chinigo, who was in his own jeep, and told him to follow the lead tank to Rome.[97]

By nightfall Harmon's 1st Armored had secured all bridges in its sector and by dawn the next day had pushed on to Rome's western limits. The 36th also entered Rome the night of the fourth. By the morning of June 5 most of Fifth Army had drawn up to the line of the Tiber along a twenty-mile front "from the mouth of the Tiber southwest of Rome to its junction with the Aniene northeast of the city. The British 1st and 5th Divisions were on the left, the U.S. VI Corps and II Corps in the center, and on the right the FEC."[98]

Truscott, meanwhile, had returned to his command post to begin planning for the pursuit of the Germans northward, when he received an order to report to Clark on Capitoline Hill. Neither he nor Bartash, who spoke Italian, had ever been to Rome and had no idea where Capitoline Hill might be, as they set out with Sergeant Barna. Upon entering the city they found the streets filled with people rejoicing in their newfound freedom. Recruiting a young Italian lad who knew where the hill was, they pushed through the crowds, with siren screaming, as the people tossed flowers and offered them wine, food, and embraces. Finally, they reached Capitoline Hill, only to find it virtually empty and the buildings apparently deserted, but learned from one of the Italian officials there that a party of Americans was at the Excelsior Hotel. At the hotel Truscott found the party of Clark, Keyes, Juin, and correspondents trying to force their way through the crowds to Capitoline Hill. After reaching the hill Clark delivered an oration from the balcony where Mussolini had given many speeches. He began by proclaiming, "This is a great day for the Fifth Army." Truscott "reckon[ed that] it was, but [he] was anxious to get out of this posturing and on with the business of war."[99]

Truscott had known for some time that he was to command the assault forces of Seventh Army for the landings in southern France, code-named ANVIL, scheduled to take place as soon as naval assets could be released from Operation OVERLORD. Clark had originally been slated to take command of Seventh Army in mid-March to oversee the ongoing planning for the operation and to lead the assault on southern France. However, since the difficulties his Fifth Army faced in Italy following the Anzio landing made that impossible, General Wilson relieved Clark of any further responsibility for ANVIL and gave command of Seventh Army to Maj. Gen. Alexander M. Patch, who had commanded the Americal Division and the Army XIV Corps on Guadalcanal, and then took command of IV Corps, which he brought from the United States to the Mediterranean theater in 1944.[100]

IV Corps, now commanded by Maj. Gen. Willis D. Crittenberger, was to relieve VI Corps in Italy as soon after the fall of Rome as practicable. Until then VI Corps continued its attack northward, the 45th and the 1st Armored Divisions bearing most of the burden in the corps sector, eventually pushing past Civitavecchia, where they captured the corps' nemesis from Anzio, the "Anzio Express" railway gun. On June 11 Crittenberger and his staff arrived at the VI Corps CP for their briefing, following which Truscott drove up Highway 7 to the point of VI Corps' farthest advance, road marker 136, eighty-five miles north of Rome. There he bade the Italian front "Addio"—or so he thought.[101]

Almost ten years after the Anzio campaign ended, Truscott wrote that he believed he made his greatest contribution to the battle after he became VI Corps commander by "restoring confidence and morale among all elements of the beachhead" by adhering to a fundamental principle of command: the "successful commander must display a spirit of confidence regardless of the dark outlook in any grim situation, and he must be positive and stern in the application of measures which will impress this confidence upon his command."[102]

Chapter 10

SOUTHERN FRANCE

After IV Corps officially relieved VI Corps Truscott enjoyed a few drinks with Colonels Langevin and Harrell before leaving in his sedan for Rome, where he opened VI Corps headquarters in Villa Spiga, 135 Via Trionfale, just ten minutes north of the Vatican. The first order of business after their grueling months of combat in the Anzio beachhead and the exhilarating but frustrating breakout and subsequent drive to Rome was a dinner-dance on June 11, hosted by the general. Among the guests were nurses from a nearby Army hospital. The 3d Infantry Division symphony quartet provided music during the dinner and for the dance that followed.[1]

On the fourteenth Truscott and his aides left for the Vatican, where Truscott had a private audience with Pope Pius XII in his chambers. The next day Truscott told his wife of his papal visit, and in a subsequent letter revealed that he had "found also a spiritual need. The Jefferson Bible [that you sent me] has been very invaluable to me." He then told her that when he returned from overseas they could expect to see changes in one another. But he hastened to assure Sarah that the one thing that would never change was "the spiritual foundation of our lives—in our case our love for each other. . . . [O]ur love and trust must be boundless and I'm afraid mixed with much charity on your part. I have certainly grown to be disagreeable and irritable at times."[2]

The next day their Roman holiday was rudely interrupted by a message from General Patch ordering Truscott and "not more than five key staff officers" to report to his headquarters at the Ecole Normale in Algiers for a briefing on Operation ANVIL. Truscott immediately arranged for a C-47 to fly him and Carleton, Langevin (G2), Harrell (G3), Conway, O'Neill (G4), and his aide, Wilson, to Algiers.

The group arrived at AFHQ the next afternoon, where Truscott's old friends Maj. Gens. David G. Barr, 6th Army Group chief of staff, and Thomas B. Larkin, chief of Services of Supply, NATOUSA, greeted them. They informed Truscott that General Marshall was to arrive in Algiers the next morning, and Barr requested that Truscott join him to greet Marshall on his arrival. Truscott then met General Patch, who drove the party to his villa, where they would be his guests.

Patch and Truscott had not previously met, but Truscott knew that Patch was held in high esteem throughout the Army. Their conversation that evening dwelled on their combat experiences to date. Although Patch had been prominently involved in the Guadalcanal operation, his Americal Division entered the campaign after the amphibious landing, so ANVIL would be the first amphibious operation in which he and his staff would be involved. Truscott's initial and lasting impression of Patch was that he was "a man of outstanding integrity, a courageous and competent leader, and an unselfish comrade-in-arms."[3]

The next day Barr and Truscott met General Marshall at Maison Blanche, where Marshall invited Truscott to join him for the half-hour drive into Algiers, during which they discussed the Anzio operation in some detail. Marshall was particularly interested in hearing Truscott's evaluation of the American "weapons and equipment, and the fighting quality of [the] American soldiers." Marshall then went on to commend Truscott "on a job well done," and informed him that Eisenhower had recently requested that he be assigned to England to command a field army in Operation OVERLORD. However, Marshall had advised Eisenhower that Truscott could not be spared from the Anzio operation.[4]

David P. Colley puts a somewhat different slant on this matter, stating that when Eisenhower made a specific request to Lt. Gen. Jacob L. Devers, commander of NATOUSA and General Wilson's deputy, to release Truscott for field command in the upcoming Normandy invasion, Devers refused to do so, since he had already selected him to command the ANVIL forces. "Eisenhower called Devers 'obstinate' and complained to Marshall that Devers was standing in the way of the Normandy invasion. But . . . Marshall concurred in Devers' decision."[5]

After returning to Algiers Truscott met with Patch for two hours before joining his staff, which was meeting with Force 163, the Algiers planning group for ANVIL. Patch told Truscott that his corps was to make a three-division assault on beaches along the French Riviera east of Toulon, after which the French Expeditionary Corps would land. An additional three or four French divisions would follow the French corps as shipping became available. With VI Corps holding the beachhead and protecting its right flank, the French would move westward to capture Toulon. Truscott's corps would then drive to the west and capture Marseilles and its port, the main objective of the assault.

Truscott updated Patch on "the experience and competence of the divisions, the division commanders and their staffs, and [his] own staff." He particularly stressed the importance of unity of command during the initial phase of the operation and the necessity for the U.S. Army, Air Force, and Navy planners to cooperate from the beginning in developing the detailed operation plans and recommended that he and his staff move VI Corps headquarters to Naples as soon as practicable to coordinate their planning with the naval forces. Truscott also emphasized the importance of "rigorous training" for the troops that would make up the invasion force.

Truscott then joined his staff for the 4:00 p.m. Force 163 briefing, which, surprisingly, Patch did not attend. Truscott and his staff found the briefing "an acute disappointment." Although it covered the landing areas, enemy dispositions in southern France, and the beachhead objectives for the three separate division assaults, the troop list was incomplete, there was no list of allocations of landing craft, and no details of naval and air support were available. Further, the administrative and logistical planning was far behind schedule.[6]

Hoping to learn more about ANVIL, Truscott decided to visit AFHQ, where he found the head of the planning staff to be Brig. Gen. Reuben E. Jenkins, a Command and General Staff School classmate, who had supervised the writing of the original appreciation and outline for ANVIL and had presented the material to the Chiefs of Staff and the Combined Chiefs of Staff in London. Truscott learned that the plan also called for an airborne landing of one regimental combat team to assist VI Corps during its amphibious assault. About D+3 two French corps with about seven divisions would begin landing, with the objective of capturing Toulon and the large port of Marseilles. After that, with the total force built up to some ten divisions, there would be an exploitation northward toward Lyon and Vichy to link up with Eisenhower's forces moving east from their beachheads in Normandy. "Jenkins insisted that an American corps should control the landing and the subsequent operations until the juncture with General Eisenhower's forces, . . . whereupon the US Corps would revert to SHAEF [Supreme Headquarters, Allied Expeditionary Forces]," and the two French corps to the French Army. He also believed that "the French would be insufferable" if given command of VI Corps, and "opinion at AFHQ was unanimous that the French should not, in any case, be entrusted with the assault landings." Indeed, when planning for ANVIL started in January 1944, no French personnel were involved. It was only in March, when Patch assumed command of Seventh Army, that a French staff joined the planning group.

The initial planning for ANVIL envisioned an invasion of southern France in conjunction with the OVERLORD landings in northern France, scheduled for about the first of June. However, in mid-April the combined pressures of OVERLORD and the intensity of the Italian fighting forced a cancellation of ANVIL. But by June 15 General Wilson was convinced that a major amphibious operation would soon be authorized in the Mediterranean theater and ordered that the VI Corps headquarters and the 3d and 45th Divisions be pulled out of the lines by June 17 and the 36th Division by June 27.[7]

On June 20 Patch and Truscott traveled to Salerno to observe a demonstration of some of the support techniques employed during the OVERLORD landings that would be available for the daylight ANVIL landings. At Salerno Truscott met old friends and associates from previous landings, Admirals Hewitt and Lowry, General O'Daniel, and other senior Army and Navy officers, all of whom boarded an LCT for the trip to the beaches. The demonstration included bombardment of the beaches by medium bombers, a battleship, destroyers, and rockets.

Truscott also had time to discuss the coming operation with Admirals Hewitt, Lowry, and Rogers, the latter two slated to command the sub–task forces for landings of the 3d and 45th Divisions. During the discussion Truscott again emphasized his firm belief that unity of command was essential during the assault phase and that it was imperative that Army, Navy, and Air Force commanders and staffs be assembled to produce joint operational plans on which the training of the assault forces could be based. He suggested that Patch and Hewitt move their headquarters to Naples, where he planned to locate his headquarters.

The next day Carleton found a suitable location, and within forty-eight hours the VI Corps planning group was set up and functioning in a former Italian barracks in downtown Naples near the sea front. Nicknamed the "Block House," the barracks was a huge quadrangle with an inner courtyard and contained adequate office space for the Army, Navy, and Air Force planners also. VI Corps headquarters, minus the planning group, was established in Bagnoli, a Naples suburb.[8]

By June 26 Truscott's staff had completed a tentative operation plan, which Truscott sent to Patch. The plan called for the 36th and 45th IDs to land north and south, respectively, of the Argens River, with the 3d Division going in on the Saint Tropez peninsula. It also stated that the "assault units of each division must be mounted on LSTs and not more than one regiment from each division combat loaded [on an] AP [transport ship] ship. *Adm. Lowry informed me this is entirely practicable.* Believe Naval plan loading one entire division on AP ships *will jeopardize the assault in this situation.* Urgently request your concurrence my basic plan so that training here can go on along that line."[9]

The original plan, prepared by Seventh Army and the Western Naval Task Force, had called for putting the 36th ashore on the left, the 45th in the center, and the 3d on the right flank of the beachhead. However, Truscott wanted his most experienced division, the 3d, on the left to form the lead element of a VI Corps attack to the west. The least-experienced division, the 36th, would have a mostly defensive mission after landing farthest to the northeast. Finally, Truscott believed that the original beachhead line should be pulled in on the left, believing that the original line would require him to overextend to the west and compromise his ability to move against Toulon quickly. Both Patch and Hewitt agreed to the suggested changes.[10]

Truscott also learned from Patch's headquarters that the Navy did not plan to have a separate planning staff that would work with the VI Corps staff, allocating planning staffs only at army and division levels. Further, Seventh Army informed him that the 1st SSF, slated to capture the islands of Levant and Port Cros seaward of the Hyères Roadstead, and the airborne force, scheduled to land in the vicinity of Le Muy roughly ten miles inland of the 45th's beaches, would operate directly under Seventh Army control until VI Corps physically linked up with them.

On June 27 Truscott responded directly to Patch regarding the messages. He emphasized his strongly held belief that the planning for the assault and the command of the assault forces should be vested in the assault force commander, namely, Truscott, not the Seventh Army commander, and that any control exercised by the army commander should be channeled through the corps commander. Further, the Army assault force and the Navy assault force commanders should be aboard the same ship during the assault phase. He also strongly emphasized that a naval planning staff should be assigned to work directly with the VI Corps staff to coordinate planning for the assault phase of the operation, since that phase "is largely of Naval concern." In his letter he also objected to landing the 1st SSF on the islands just after dark of D-1, since it would alert the defenders along the entire coast. He agreed to the command arrangements for the airborne operation.

Patch responded the next day, stating that "you have [evidently] not made [a] detailed study of problem," and ordering Truscott, selected corps staff officers, and the corps artillery officer to come to his headquarters "without delay." Truscott and his party arrived in Algiers the next day, where Truscott spent the entire morning with Patch, who eventually accepted all of Truscott's recommendations except for the question of control of the 1st SSF. Truscott next met with Hewitt, where all differences were "ironed out," except for the placing of a naval planning element with the corps staff and the move of the naval headquarters to Naples. He then returned to Patch's villa for cocktails and dinner.[11]

The planned beachhead was approximately forty-five miles in length, extending from the left flank at the eastern shore of Hyères Roadstead northeastward to La Napoule roughly three miles southwest of Cannes. The beachhead line was arc shaped, with its center extending inland to a few miles northwest of Le Muy. The flanks were anchored on high ground, and the depth of the beachhead would protect the forces and supplies within it from long-range German artillery fire, and its size provided adequate maneuver space for the assaulting American and French divisions.

VI Corps had three primary missions to accomplish after securing the landing beaches on D-day, scheduled for 8:00 a.m., August 15: occupy all terrain

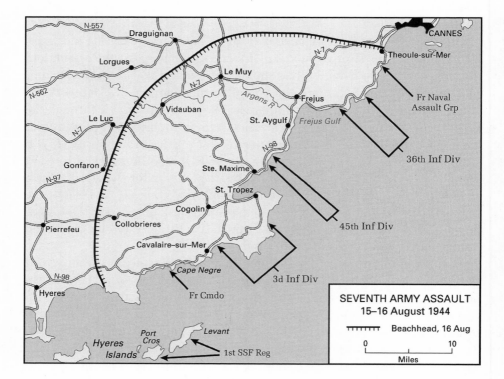

Map labels:

N-557
Draguignan
CANNES
Lorgues
Theoule-sur-Mer
N-7
Le Muy
N-7
N-562
Argens R.
Frejus
Fr Naval Assault Grp
Vidauban
St. Aygulf
Frejus Gulf
Le Luc
N-7
36th Inf Div
N-98
Gonfaron
Ste. Maxime
N-97
St. Tropez
45th Inf Div
Cogolin
Pierrefeu
Collobrieres
Cavalaire–sur–Mer
3d Inf Div
N-98
Cape Negre
Hyeres
Fr Cmdo

Port Cros
Levant
Hyeres Islands
1st SSF Reg

SEVENTH ARMY ASSAULT
15–16 August 1944

Beachhead, 16 Aug

0   10
Miles

within the Corps Beachhead line (Blue line) as quickly as possible, provide right-flank security for Seventh Army, and be prepared to launch attacks to the west and northwest on order. The D-day tasks also included linking up with the airborne forces in the vicinity of Le Muy, capturing the town, and moving out from the flanks of the beachhead to link up with French Commandos who were to land to the east and west of the VI Corps beachhead.

The paratroopers, a division-size force of American and British airborne troops, were to land in the vicinity of Le Muy before daylight on D-day to prevent German forces from moving down the Argens River corridor from Le Muy and Le Luc into the beachhead. The 1st SSF, now under the command of Col. Edwin A. Walker, was to land on the islands Levant and Port Cros about midnight of August 14–15 and neutralize German artillery believed to be emplaced there, which commanded the approach to the westernmost VI Corps landing beaches. The French African Commando Group had the mission of landing on Cape Nègre just after the 1st SSF started ashore, blocking the coastal highway, securing the high ground two miles inland, and preventing any reinforcements from reaching the beachhead from the west. The French Naval Assault Group was to land at Trayas Point at the opposite end of the beachhead and block the coastal highway there.[12]

Opposing the landings was the German Nineteenth Army, consisting of two Panzer divisions, one of which was in transit from Lyon, nine infantry divisions, and a large number of coastal defense units, battle groups, and separate battalions. All beaches were mined and had in place underwater obstacles and beachhead obstructions covered by machine guns, self-propelled guns, and tanks. However, the beach defenses were not organized in depth. Truscott believed that the enemy would initially delay to gain time, and then launch a counterattack against the focal point of the invasion when its location could be determined.[13]

As Truscott studied the map of the beachhead he identified the town of Fréjus as a critical feature because of its port and the fact that the best route inland was along the Argens River, which emptied into the Fréjus Gulf there. Early capture of the town and its port was essential and was assigned to the 36th ID, assisted by the 1st Airborne Task Force moving south from its drop zone. The D-day missions of the 45th Division in the center were to capture Sainte Maxime, seize the high ground south of the Argens River overlooking the beach in front of Fréjus, assist the 36th Division in capturing Fréjus, contact the airborne force, seize the Blue line in zone, and contact the 3d Division on the left. The 3d Division on D-day was to capture Saint Tropez, clear the Saint Tropez peninsula, assist the 45th Division on the right, contact the French Commandos at Cape Nègre, and seize the Blue line in zone. Attached to VI Corps was Combat Command Sudre (CC Sudre) of the French 1st Armored Division, which was to land on corps order, with first priority to the beach in the

Fréjus area, and be prepared to advance to the northwest. The major components of the 1st Airborne Task Force, commanded by the former commander of the 1st SSF, Maj. Gen. Robert T. Frederick, consisted of a British parachute brigade, one American parachute infantry regiment, two American parachute infantry battalions, one American glider infantry battalion, and one glider and two American parachute 75mm howitzer battalions.[14]

On June 19 the 3d ID moved to Pozzuoli, the same training area it had used prior to the Anzio operation. On the twenty-second the 45th arrived at the Invasion Training Center at Salerno, and on July 4 the 36th returned to the Paestum beaches where it had landed during the Salerno fighting. The airborne troops were to conduct their training at Lido de Roma, outside of Rome. Corps and division staffs took up offices in the Block House in Naples and were soon joined by air and naval planners and representatives from Patch's and Hewitt's headquarters.[15]

On July 14 Major General du Touzet du Vigier, commander of the 1st Armored Division (French), invited Truscott to visit Brig. Gen. Aime M. Sudre's combat command near Port aux Poules, Algeria, on the seventeenth. Truscott, accompanied by his staff and representatives of the 3d and 36th Divisions, flew to La Siena, where they met General Sudre and Lt. Gen. Pierre Koenig, commander of the French Forces of the Interior (FFI), guerrillas who were operating in France and who might be employed in German rear areas during the invasion of southern France. The next day Truscott and his group visited Sudre's command and found that it looked "very good indeed." They spent the rest of the morning meeting with Sudre, concentrating particularly on coordinating the actions of his combat command with the 3d and 36th Divisions, with one of which Sudre's force would likely come into contact after landing. The group returned to Naples that afternoon.

Three days later Gen. Jean de Lattre de Tassigny, who commanded the French corps scheduled to land behind VI Corps, invited Truscott to meet him and his staff and division commanders for lunch at his office in Naples. Truscott accepted the invitation and brought Conway along as an interpreter. After a virtually conversationless lunch, de Lattre "launched into a tirade in French directed at [Truscott]," telling him that he "had violated the normal niceties of military and diplomatic protocol by inspecting one of his units without his permission and without his presence. It was a slight to him and to the honor of France." Truscott interrupted de Lattre by informing him that it was "entirely appropriate for inspection of troops that were to serve under [his] command, and that the French commanders concerned had invited him to do so. . . . If that was all he had to discuss, we were wasting our time." De Lattre then asked for a private meeting with Truscott and Conway, where he explained that General de Gaulle and he had consented to "loan" the combat command to the

Americans, but with the understanding that it would be available to de Lattre "when and where he wanted it and in no case later than D plus 3."

Truscott "calmly" described to de Lattre the various missions that he might order the French combat command to carry out and told him that he would be perfectly happy to let him know the orders that he might issue to Sudre during the fighting, "but any idea [that de Lattre] should review and approve or disapprove them was of course entirely unacceptable." Any questions that he might have about such orders would have to be resolved by General Patch. After leaving de Lattre, Truscott reported the matter to Patch, who assured him that he "would be free to employ CC Sudre as the situation warranted" and that the Seventh Army plan contained no provision for returning Sudre's command to de Lattre's command on D+3. Truscott later recommended that an American combat command be substituted for the French unit, but the request was rejected "for political and other reasons."

Truscott was never able to receive assurance from Patch as to how long he would retain control of Sudre's combat command, and Patch's "noncommittal attitude" disturbed him. "Since he was either unable or unwilling to pass judgment in favor of the VI Corps before the invasion, [Truscott] could foresee that once [his corps] was ashore in France, political considerations would dominate any decision with respect to CC Sudre and that they were not likely to be propitious to the smooth operation of the VI Corps. Thus, when we had gotten the command ashore and needed it most, it was more than likely it would be removed from my control regardless of the tactical situation of my command."[16]

Truscott was convinced of his need for armor not only during the establishment of the beachhead but increasingly so as the beachhead expanded and operations beyond the beachhead began, and his discussions with de Lattre and Patch had convinced him that he could not count on having CC Sudre under his command after D+3. He finally concluded that the only solution to the problem was to improvise an armored combat command from elements of VI Corps that would be available if he should lose CC Sudre after the first few days of the operation.[17] To organize and command that provisional force Truscott chose his assistant corps commander, Brig. Gen. Frederic B. Butler, who had previously served as assistant commander of the 34th ID. Truscott told Butler that the most probable mission would be an initial attack to Sisteron on the Durance River, followed by a sweep to the north toward Lyon, after which the task force should be prepared to turn either to the west or to the north.

Realizing that time was short, Butler began tailoring the force immediately. His first step was to select a staff from among the assistants in the various corps staff sections and to prepare a provisional troop list. The major components of the task force were the 117th Cavalry Reconnaissance Squadron, 59th

Armored Field Artillery Battalion, 753d Tank Battalion (less one medium and one light tank company), one infantry battalion, two tank destroyer companies, an engineer regiment, and a medical battalion. Prior to sailing from Naples Truscott confirmed to Butler that he planned to utilize Task Force Butler in a drive to Sisteron, and from there Butler should be prepared to turn north to Grenoble or west to seize the high ground north of Montélimar. Butler accordingly briefed all unit commanders within the task force and all division commanders on the plan.[18]

On August 1 the CCS changed the code name of the operation to DRAGOON, since it was feared the name ANVIL had been compromised. "As an old cavalryman, [Truscott] took this change of name to be a good omen." That same day the Army, Navy, and Air Force elements of DRAGOON received their final orders. The sub–task force's orders would not be distributed until the forces were at sea, since only the senior commanders knew where the operation was to take place.[19]

In overall command of German forces in southern France was Gen. Johannes Blaskowitz, commander of Army Group G. The Nineteenth Army, commanded by Gen. Friedrich Wiese, was responsible for the defense of the Mediterranean coast. By August 15 most of Blaskowitz's best units had been transferred to northern France to blunt the Allied attack there, but Wiese's forces were still reasonably strong. Lt. Gen. Ferdinand Neuling's LXII Corps had responsibility for the coast stretching eastward from Toulon to the Italian border. From Toulon west to Marseilles, Lt. Gen. Baptist Kniess's LXXXV Corps defended the coast. Farther to the west the IV Luftwaffe Field Corps under Lt. Gen. Erich Petersen held the coast from the Rhône delta to the Spanish border.[20]

During the final days before sailing, all of the planners busied themselves with putting the final touches on the assault plans. Patch, his staff, and the naval commanders briefed Generals Wilson and Devers, his deputy, and on August 8 Truscott and his division commanders presented the final briefing on the assault plans to them. Final division reviews followed the briefings.[21]

By August 12 the entire command was aboard ship, and at 9:00 p.m. Truscott was "piped aboard" the USS *Catoctin* (AGC 5), an amphibious force command ship, where Admiral Hewitt warmly greeted him. Learning that Patch and a few members of his staff were aboard, Truscott immediately reported to his commander. As the two discussed the coming operation Patch told Truscott that he was traveling along on the *Catoctin*, but assured him that he was not going to interfere in any way with Truscott's conduct of the battle. Truscott thanked Patch and expressed his desire "to work in the closest possible cooperation" with him and would always welcome his advice. Shortly after lunch the next day the *Catoctin* got under way, part of a naval force totaling some 1,000 ships, all committed to landing some 151,000 troops, including almost 41,000 French forces, and some 21,400 vehicles, including tanks and tank destroyers, successfully on the Riviera beaches. The various convoys converged off the west coast of Corsica on the fourteenth, and then sailed northward that night toward the transport areas, where the troops would disembark and begin their run-ins to the beaches in the landing craft.[22]

On the eve of battle, Truscott wrote to his wife, a practice that he carried out "on the eve of every major undertaking in this war ... so that [she] would know that if anything should happen to [him, she] was in [his] mind and [his] heart." He told her that "within twelve hours we shall be engaged in one of the most difficult operations that any American Army has ever undertaken." He then expressed his hope that she would pray for him "and for these brave lads of mine—that we may do our duty to the full. . . . Yes, we do need prayers because we are fighting a true crusade."[23]

As day broke on the fifteenth, bombers arrived and began hitting their targets on and behind the beaches, followed by a deafening naval bombardment. Soon the assault craft began their runs to shore. The *Catoctin* moved in for Truscott to observe the landings of the 3d Division on its two assigned beaches, Alpha Red, located on the shoreline of Cavalarie Bay, and Alpha Yellow, roughly six miles to the northeast. As he looked toward the beaches Truscott was pleased to see that all appeared to be going well in that sector. To the east, the 45th's landings on Delta Red, Delta Green, Delta Yellow, and Delta Blue also appeared to have been successful.

Near noon the *Catoctin* sailed northeast to the 36th ID's sector, anchoring a few thousand yards off Fréjus. As it turned out, contrary to Truscott's projection, the 36th, now commanded by Maj. Gen. John E. Dahlquist, would face the heaviest opposition mounted by the Germans, who had concentrated most of their defenses in that sector. The 141st Infantry landed over Camel Green beach, turned eastward, and by ten o'clock had secured both Camel Green beach and Camel Blue beach farther east, but had met heavy opposition at Agay Roadstead between the two beaches and did not secure the roadstead's shore until five that afternoon.

The 143d Infantry followed the 141st across Delta Green beach and turned to the west, where it encountered opposition as it drove toward Saint Rafaël. By two o'clock, when the 142d Infantry was scheduled to assault over Camel Red beach in the Fréjus area, the 143d had not yet arrived at Saint Rafaël and could not assist the landing of the 142d. Likewise, to the southwest the 180th Infantry of the 45th, which was also to assist the 142d, had not been able to fight its way to Camel Red. The 142d would now have to secure the port of Fréjus and then drive westward along Route N-7 to assist the airborne force in capturing Le Muy without the expected support from adjacent infantry units.[24]

When Truscott went on deck to observe the landing of the 142d Infantry on Camel Red, he was surprised to see that suddenly "the whole 'flotilla' halted just a few thousand yards from the beach." He was further astounded to see that the flotilla then reversed its course and headed seaward and then began landing on Camel Green beach. Hewitt, Patch, and Truscott were "furious." Just then a message came from Adm. Spencer S. Lewis, the commander of Task Force 87, informing Hewitt that because of the beach obstacles and enemy opposition at Camel Red he had decided to land the 142d over Camel Green, which was the alternate beach that Lewis and Dahlquist had chosen and had already been secured by the 141st Infantry.[25]

Truscott decided to determine for himself why the plan had been changed without consulting him. He immediately set out in an LCVP (landing craft, vehicle, personnel), accompanied by Carleton and Wilson, to find Dahlquist, whom he located on shore. Dahlquist told him that the other landings of his division had gone well and that he expected his division to be on the beachhead Blue line that evening and to have the Fréjus port cleared by the next morning. Truscott believed that the 142d's landing on Camel Green rather than on Camel Red was "the only flaw in an otherwise perfect landing," since it delayed the opening of the Fréjus port by a day, delayed the capture of airfields near Fréjus and the Argens valley, and necessitated a diversion of CC Sudre and tactical air force elements to the 45th Division beaches. The delay in capturing the airfields resulted in the corps' not having tactical air support when it began driving north a few days later. In Truscott's opinion Admiral Lewis's decision "merited reprimand at least."[26]

After returning to the *Catoctin* and reporting to Hewitt and Patch, Truscott and the rest of his command group departed for the Sainte Maxime beaches, where the corps' advance CP had already been established. He visited Eagles at his CP near Sainte Maxime and learned that the 45th ID had taken all of its D-day objectives, was pushing toward the Blue line in its sector, and had made contact with units of the airborne force near Le Muy. Truscott then instructed Eagles to have his 180th Infantry assist in clearing the Camel Red beach.

Back at his CP Truscott and his staff reviewed the day's actions. Except for Fréjus and Camel Red beach, all initial D-day objectives had been achieved, and the 3d and 36th Divisions were advancing to the Blue line. Frederick's 1st Airborne Task Force had begun landing in the Le Muy area at about four thirty in the morning, but the paratroopers were widely scattered throughout the area, since only three of the nine pathfinder teams dropped earlier had landed in their proper drop zones. As a result, only 40 percent of the main force landed in their assigned drop zones, and by six only 60 percent of the paratroopers had been assembled in the Le Muy area. Fortunately, casualties were light, and by the evening of the fifteenth the paratroopers had executed their D-day missions, excepting the capture of Le Muy, and had made first contacts with corps forces. One fortuitous result of the scattered drop was that the landings had isolated the German LXII Corps headquarters at Draguignan, completely dispersed it, and led to the capture of several hundred prisoners, with General Neuling, the corps commander, and his staff narrowly escaping capture. The disruption of the German corps headquarters was to have a very positive impact on VI Corps actions in the coming days.

Truscott calculated that his corps had destroyed the power of two German divisions, had killed and wounded an unknown number of enemy soldiers, and had taken 2,129 prisoners of war. Corps casualties had been much lighter than expected: 183 killed and wounded, with 479 nonbattle casualties. He thought the day's results "a fitting celebration of the twenty-seventh anniversary of my original commission as an officer in the United States Army."[27]

BREAKOUT

As Truscott surveyed the terrain that lay before him he defined the vital area as that lying between the Maritime and High Alps on the east and the Rhône River on the west. If his forces could destroy the bridges crossing the Rhône, the German forces on either side of the river would be incapable of mutual support, and the forces east of the Rhône could withdraw northward only on roads east of the river. Several miles north of Montélimar the Rhône passes through the Cruas Gorge, a narrow gorge that leaves barely enough room for N-7 and the parallel railroad to pass between the east bank of the river and the gorge wall. Control of the high ground north of Montélimar and the terrain north and south of Crest was essential to block German withdrawal northward along N-7.

Truscott believed that when the Allied forces broke out of the beachhead the Germans would most likely shift their forces to block the drive to the west toward Toulon and Marseilles, leaving open the possibility of a northward thrust toward Sisteron and Grenoble to seize the high ground north of Montélimar and block any German withdrawal northward on N-7. No previous Seventh Army plan had considered those possibilities, and Truscott was never able to gain Patch's assurance that CC Sudre would be available to put such a plan into action. However, if the opportunity arose and CC Sudre was not available, he had formed Task Force Butler for just such a maneuver and ordered Butler to prepare for possible employment north of the Durance River.[28]

Truscott's plan was to have the 7th Infantry hold the Carnoulles-Hyères line, while the rest of the 3d ID prepared to strike westward from the Gonfaron–Le Luc area on or about August 20 along the axis of N-7 to Brignoles, twelve miles north of Toulon. The 45th Division was to advance north of the 3d Division along the route from Vidauban through Barjols to the bend in the Durance River at Peyrolles, and CC Sudre would advance between those two routes of attack.

Truscott ordered TF Butler to assemble and reorganize at Le Muy on the seventeenth and begin probing to the northwest the next day. The 36th Division, leaving one regiment to protect the corps' right flank, was to move northwest

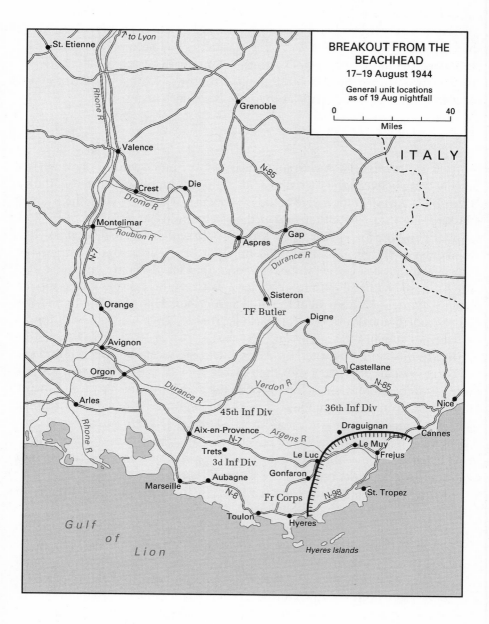

BREAKOUT FROM THE BEACHHEAD
17–19 August 1944

General unit locations
as of 19 Aug nightfall

0   40

Miles

ITALY

St. Etienne

to Lyon

Rhone R

Grenoble

Valence

N-85

Crest   Die

Drome R

Montelimar

Roubion R

Aspres   Gap

Durance R

N-7

Orange

Sisteron

TF Butler   Digne

Avignon

Orgon

Castellane

N-85

Arles

Durance R

Verdon R

Nice

45th Inf Div

36th Inf Div

Aix-en-Provence

Argens R

Draguignan

Cannes

N-7

Le Muy

Trets

Le Luc

Frejus

3d Inf Div

Gonfaron

Marseille

Aubagne

St. Tropez

N-8

Fr Corps

N-98

Toulon

Hyeres

Gulf

of

Lion

Hyeres Islands

194

to relieve the Airborne Task Force in the Le Muy area, and then be prepared to follow TF Butler. General Frederick's Airborne Task Force, after being relieved, was to move to the 36th's former position on the coast, assume responsibility for the corps' right flank, and free the regiment there to rejoin the 36th Division.[29]

On the seventeenth the bulk of the 3d ID began its drive to the west, and by the next day the 15th Infantry was in La Roquebrussanne, ten miles south of Brignoles. To the north the 30th Infantry and CC Sudre, after clearing Le Luc, were also near Brignoles, and after fighting through the night the French and American attackers took Brignoles and the surrounding area. Still farther north the 45th Division advanced out of the Le Luc–Vidauban area on the seventeenth, and by nightfall of the next day was within striking distance of Barjols. To the east the 36th Division had passed through elements of the 1st Airborne Task Force and cleared the Draguignan area on August 18. Other division elements secured the area from Le Muy eastward to the coast, as well as the slopes of the Estérel Massif. The division's reconnaissance troop had meanwhile been conducting long-range patrols twenty-five to thirty miles north and northeast of Le Muy as far as N-85 and found no significant enemy resistance. The patrol findings and ULTRA intercepts confirmed the weakness of German forces along the Seventh Army's right flank and led Truscott to believe that once TF Butler and the 36th ID began their moves to the north and northwest they would face "no significant threat on their right, or northeastern, flank."[30]

Late in the afternoon of the seventeenth Butler joined Truscott at his command post and told him that his task force, with the exception of two units that he expected to arrive that night, had assembled at Le Muy. Truscott ordered Butler to carry out the plan they had drawn up in Naples, namely, the advance of the task force "northwest to the Durance River and then north toward Grenoble or west to seize the high ground north of Montélimar to block a German withdrawal through the Montélimar Gap east of the Rhône." Butler was to begin his advance at 6:00 a.m. the next morning along the Draguignan-Riez-Digne axis, Digne being his first objective.[31]

Although O'Daniel's 3d ID had cut the roads leading to Toulon from the north at Brignoles, General de Lattre, commanding the French II Corps, was not in position to attack Toulon, having delayed his advance from the beachhead until his entire corps was assembled. Truscott was confident that the 3d Division could capture the port within forty-eight hours, but Patch and he realized that to do so would have "grave political repercussions," since the French were to have that honor. The two agreed that the 3d Division would continue its attack westward and isolate both Toulon and Marseilles, leaving them to be captured by de Lattre's corps. Patch, meanwhile, would urge de Lattre to relieve the 3d north of Hyères and begin his attack on Toulon as soon as possible. On the nineteenth Truscott learned that de Lattre was starting the relief of the 7th Infantry north of Hyères.

That same day Gens. Devers, Ira C. Eaker, and Wilton B. Persons joined Truscott on a visit to the front.[32] Finding that the 3d Division was west of Brignoles, Truscott ordered O'Daniel to stay east of Saint Maximin until CC Sudre passed through the city heading south to cut the coastal road west of Toulon. Sudre was then to prepare to join the French II Corps in attacking Toulon. They then went on to Eagles's CP, where Truscott received word from Seventh Army that CC Sudre would be relieved from attachment to VI Corps and would pass to the control of de Lattre's II Corps at 9:00 p.m. that night and was to begin moving east on N-7 immediately to join II Corps at Flassans. Fearing that Sudre's move east against the westward flow of VI Corps traffic along the same highway would cause a monumental traffic jam, Truscott recommended to Patch that CC Sudre pass to de Lattre's control at either Saint Maximin or Aubagne. Patch disapproved Truscott's recommendation, explaining that he had to comply with de Lattre's order for "political reasons." Otherwise, de Lattre "would be increasingly difficult to work with."

Sudre dutifully turned his command east on N-7, across the path of the westward-advancing 3d Division, resulting in "traffic congestion and confusion on that road all through the night and much of the following morning that was almost indescribable." Incredibly, when Sudre reached Flassans, de Lattre turned Sudre's column around and sent it back over "the same road towards the same objective that [Truscott] had proposed to give him," that is, cutting the coastal road west of Toulon and attacking Toulon from the west.[33]

After his conference with Patch, Truscott returned to his CP near Vidauban, where he learned that TF Butler was already at Sisteron, some twenty miles northwest of Digne. During the advance the task force had broken up several German detachments and had captured more than one thousand prisoners, including "one corps headquarters complete with one lieutenant general, his pistol, brandy and staff." The general was Lt. Gen. Ferdinand Neuling, who had earlier narrowly escaped capture at Draguignan. During its advance the task force came into contact with the Maquis, members of the French underground movement, who proved to be a valuable asset, performing such tasks as setting up roadblocks and providing Butler with information about enemy positions, including a large German garrison at Gap and a mobile force in or about Grenoble. At Sisteron, "desperate for instructions" as to whether he should continue his advance toward Grenoble, Butler sent Maj. Kermit R. Hansen, his G3, by plane to Truscott's headquarters early in the morning of the twentieth.

When he had received no word from Hansen by noon, Butler decided to deal with the German force at Gap and sent a strong patrol toward the town to protect the task force's right flank. When the force reached Gap and the German commander refused an offer to surrender, the patrol commander immediately called for artillery fire. After forty rounds of 105mm HE (high explosive) land-ed in the town, a profusion of white flags appeared. When Butler learned that Gap was now in American hands and he had still received no orders from Trus-cott, he ordered the remainder of his task force to prepare to move westward to Aspres, since the only practicable route leading west to the Rhône passed through the town. Butler had also heard a rumor that the 36th ID was begin-ning to move up N-85 behind his task force, so "a move to Aspres seemed the play."[34]

Truscott, learning that TF Butler was at Sisteron, had told Dahlquist to start one RCT of the 36th north the next day to join Butler, while the remainder of the division followed as rapidly as possible. He also dispatched Lt. Col. Conway, his new G3, to tell Butler to turn his task force west, move "with all possible speed to Montélimar," and "block enemy routes of withdrawal up the Rhône valley in that vicinity."[35] Early on the twenty-first Conway arrived at Butler's CP in Gap with Truscott's order for him to be on the heights above Montéli-mar, some ninety miles from Aspres, before nightfall. He also told Butler that Truscott had ordered Dahlquist to support TF Butler with one RCT and one 155mm field artillery battalion and then send the rest of the division toward Montélimar as rapidly as possible. In addition, he had ordered two battalions of corps artillery Long Toms to support the task force. When Dahlquist arrived in the forward area he was to take command of TF Butler. Butler recommended to Conway that the 36th relieve him in the Gap area and take over the outposts to the north, permitting him to start toward Montélimar at daylight with the bulk of his task force, the outpost forces following after their relief by the 36th Division. By daybreak of the twenty-first most of Butler's task force had re-grouped at Aspres, and Butler ordered the advance toward the Montélimar area to begin. By late afternoon TF Butler had moved twenty-five miles westward to Crest, some thirteen miles east of the river. "Before it lay the Rhône valley and the setting for the eight-day battle of Montélimar."[36]

On August 17 and 18 Patch had received intelligence reports based on UL-TRA intercepts that indicated the best move for Seventh Army would be an immediate drive westward toward the Rhône to cut the route of withdrawal of the German Nineteenth Army. However, a shortage of trucks and gasoline pre-cluded any immediate major attempt to cut that line of withdrawal at Avignon or farther north in the Rhône valley. To support such an advance it would be necessary to capture and rehabilitate the ports of Toulon and Marseilles, a task assigned to General de Lattre's corps. Therefore, Patch limited the westward advance of VI Corps to Aix-en-Provence.

De Lattre's forces attacked Toulon on the morning of the twentieth, meet-ing fierce resistance. However, by the twenty-sixth the last organized resistance had ended, and the Germans surrendered on the twenty-eighth, a full week earlier than the Allies had expected. De Lattre believed that the force charged

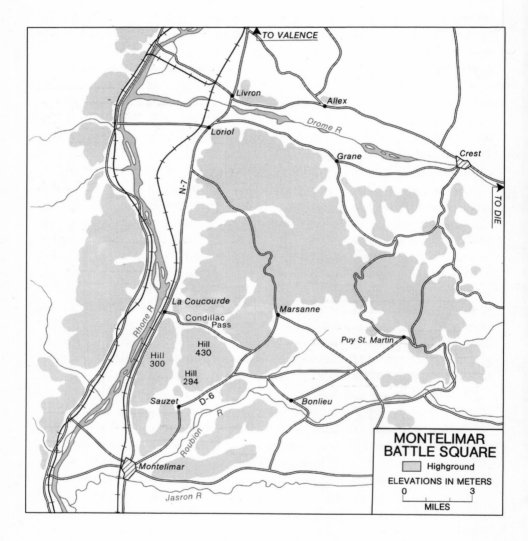

TO VALENCE

Livron

Allex

Drome R

Loriol

Grane

Crest

N-7

TO DIE

Rhone R

La Coucourde

Marsanne

Condillac
Pass

Puy St. Martin

Hill
430

Hill
300

Hill
294

D-6

Sauzet

R

Bonlieu

Roubion

MONTELIMAR
BATTLE SQUARE

Highground

ELEVATIONS IN METERS

Montelimar

0   3

Jasron R

MILES

with the capture of Marseilles was not strong enough for a full-scale battle for the city and ordered the troops to limit their operations to clearing the city's suburbs until reinforcements arrived. The commander on the ground believed a delay might be costly and exempted one of his units from de Lattre's order. On August 23 he ordered that unit into the city where over the next five days it engaged in fierce street-to-street fighting. The city finally capitulated on August 28, the same day Toulon fell.[37]

As the French forces were engaged at Toulon and Marseilles, Truscott had, as Patch had ordered, halted the 3d and 45th Divisions along a north-south line north of Marseilles until the two ports had been captured. The Germans took advantage of the halt to begin the withdrawal of the LXXXV Corps, and by the morning of the twenty-second most of the corps had crossed the Durance River at Orgon to begin the withdrawal along the east bank of the Rhône. The IV Luftwaffe Field Corps was already moving north on the west bank, coming abreast of the LXXXV Corps elements to the east.

That same morning Truscott, satisfied with the progress of the attacks against Toulon and Marseilles, directed that the 3d and 45th Divisions continue their westward advance but to stay south of the Durance River until relieved by French forces. He also ordered Eagles to send one of his regiments north to the 36th Division. Patch's and Truscott's decision that "cautiously limited the 3d Division's movement west . . . may have sacrificed an opportunity to cut off major portions" of the German forces south of the Durance. During the night of August 23–24 the last elements of the LXXXV Corps crossed the Durance and began marching rapidly up the Rhône valley to Montélimar, which was to become the new focus of operations.[38]

THE BATTLE OF MONTÉLIMAR SQUARE

As his task force rested on the high ground overlooking Route N-7 on the east bank of the Rhône River, Butler surveyed the terrain where he would soon begin the battle to cut the line of retreat of the German Nineteenth Army, an engagement that became known as the battle of the Montélimar Square, an area bounded on the north by the Drome River, on the south by the Roubion River, on the west by the Rhône River, and on the east by the foothills of the French Alps. The Square encompassed an area of roughly 250 square miles of terrain composed of "flat, open farmland and rugged, wooded hills, which rose, often steeply, to more than 1,900 feet." In the southwest corner of the Square was the town of Montélimar, through which N-7 passed northward through a narrow gorge at La Coucourde to Loriol just south of the junction of the Drome and Rhône Rivers.[39]

Late in the afternoon of the twenty-first Butler moved the bulk of his task force south from Crest to Puy St. Martin and then westward to Marsanne, with forward elements probing farther west through the Condillac Pass toward La Coucourde and south down Highway D-6 toward Sauzet and Montélimar. The commander of the forward elements, Lt. Col. Joseph G. Felber, quickly realized that Hill 300, flanking N-7 on the east and extending southward from Condillac Pass, was the key terrain feature in the area and established his CP at nearby Chateau Condillac. However, he was "unable to occupy the entire ridgeline of Hill 300 . . . [but] set up outposts, roadblocks, and guard points and posted accompanying FFI soldiers in Sauzet." From his vantage point Felber could see the German forces streaming northward along N-7, and as soon as an artillery battery arrived on the hill he ordered it to begin firing on the withdrawing enemy columns, adding the fire of an additional artillery battery and tanks as they arrived. He also succeeded in getting a small force through Condillac Pass to establish a roadblock across the highway, but the Germans soon drove it back into the pass.[40]

That night Butler sent a message to Truscott to inform him that the task force had reached the objective area but that his forces were thinly spread. However, with the reinforcements that he had been promised—more artillery and a regiment of the 36th Division—he believed that he would be able to hold the area and by the following afternoon would be able to launch a successful attack against Montélimar and the highway.

On the twenty-second the artillery of TF Butler, supplemented by the fire of tanks, tank destroyers, armored cars, and ground-mounted 57mm guns, poured accurate and deadly fire upon Montélimar and the German troops and equipment moving north along the highway. Fire from the 59th Armored Field Artillery Battalion was directed at trains on the rail line east of the river, destroying several trains and blocking the railway, But TF Butler's fires were never able to block completely the highway or railway west of the Rhône.[41]

On that same day the Germans launched an attack northward from Montélimar across the Roubion River and advanced into Puy St. Martin and Marsanne, cutting the American supply route to Crest and Sisteron. The enemy's success was to be short-lived, however, for at just that moment the detachments that Butler had left behind at Gap and the pass north of Gap arrived on the scene. The commander of the group quickly recognized the seriousness of the situation, organized a tank-infantry counterattack, and cleared the enemy from Puy St. Martin. As Butler assessed the situation, he concluded that the attack was most likely only a prelude to a heavier attack that the enemy would probably launch the next day. His task force was now desperately short of ammunition, and the reinforcements from the 36th Division that Truscott had promised him had not yet arrived. Furthermore, although morale remained high, his men were beginning to show the strain of the eight continuous days of combat. That night Butler received word that the 36th's 141st Infantry would arrive the next morning to reinforce his task force.[42]

On August 21 Truscott had told Dahlquist to move the bulk of his force to the Montélimar area to join TF Butler in blocking the route of withdrawal of the Nineteenth Army, with "lesser blocks east of Durance and north of Aspres," and assume command of the task force. He also ordered Eagles to send his 179th Infantry north to Sisteron. At that time Dahlquist's 143d Infantry was ready to push either north to Grenoble or west to Montélimar, and the 142d Infantry was at Gap. Dahlquist gave the mission of reinforcing TF Butler to the 141st Infantry, then in division reserve, and ordered his 143d Infantry to continue its advance northward to Grenoble, which it entered the following afternoon. The regiment was then to swing to the west and south and enter the Square from the north after passing through Valence.[43]

Shortly after eleven on the morning of the twenty-second Truscott, impatient with Dahlquist's delays in getting his forces to the Square, arrived by L-5 at 36th Division headquarters, there to find that Dahlquist was at Gap and that the 141st Infantry had not yet moved out toward Montélimar. Dahlquist's chief of staff told Truscott that Dahlquist had delayed the movement of the 141st westward when he received information, later shown to be inaccurate and exaggerated, that strong enemy forces were advancing south from Grenoble and Gap. Truscott told Col. John W. Harmony to move his 141st Infantry to the Montélimar area at once and told the chief of staff to inform Dahlquist that he was "to proceed to the Montélimar area forthwith with the bulk of his Division" and to tell him that he would have the 179th Infantry attached to his division for employment at Grenoble. After returning to his CP, Truscott wrote a letter to Dahlquist reiterating the orders he had given his chief of staff and re-emphasizing the 36th Division's primary mission of blocking the Rhône valley immediately north of Montélimar. The 45th Division would assume responsibility for the area east of the Sisteron-Grenoble road.[44]

During the morning of August 23, Dahlquist arrived at Butler's headquarters. Although he was to have assumed command of TF Butler, Dahlquist asked Butler to "continue direction of the action until later in the day while he was absorbing the situation and getting organized." Late that afternoon Dahlquist assumed command and ordered that TF Butler be dissolved. However, later that same day Truscott directed that the task force be reconstituted as Dahlquist's reserve.[45]

On the morning of the twenty-fourth Truscott assessed the situation in the Montélimar Square. Aerial reconnaissance reports revealed that enemy columns were still moving northward along both banks of the Rhône, indicating that Butler's blockade had not been as effective as had been hoped. Truscott therefore decided to visit Dahlquist at his headquarters in Marsanne, where he convened a lengthy conference with Generals Dahlquist, Butler, and Robert I. Stack, Dahlquist's assistant division commander. Truscott pointed out that although Butler had succeeded in emplacing artillery in positions to bring fire upon the Germans withdrawing northward, he had failed to hold the most vital terrain, Hill 300, which the Germans now occupied. Furthermore, even though Truscott had not assigned the capture of the town of Montélimar as an objective, two attempts to occupy the town had been attempted and repulsed.

Truscott went on to say that although there had been mistakes, they were "water under the bridge," and the essential task confronting Dahlquist was the occupation of Hill 300. Dahlquist assured Truscott that he had launched an attack to capture the hill that morning and was confident it would succeed. In fact, he was so confident that he would be able to block any further withdrawal of the enemy northward that he asked Truscott if he could order his 143d Infantry, then approaching the Square from the north, to occupy Valence, "in order to avoid trouble in capturing it later." Although he did not completely share Dahlquist's optimism, Truscott authorized him to do so, providing the occupation of Valence did not delay the arrival of the 143d Infantry in the Square. Truscott then flew to Eagles's CP at Aspres, where he learned that the 179th RCT was in Grenoble, the 180th Infantry was in the Gap area, and the 157th Infantry had been relieved north of the Durance River by elements of the 3d Division and was to begin moving north that night. The 179th and 180th had established roadblocks, sent out reconnaissance patrols, and were in contact with scattered enemy forces.

After returning to his CP, Truscott updated Patch on the disposition of his corps' forces and learned that the French, who were still involved in clearing Toulon and Marseilles, had not yet relieved the 3d Division. However, since the 11th Panzer Division had withdrawn north of the Durance, indicating that a general German withdrawal was under way, Patch authorized Truscott to order the 3d Division northward immediately to drive the retreating Germans up N-7 into the roadblock created by Dahlquist's forces. Late that afternoon Dahlquist informed Truscott that the 143d Infantry had bypassed Valence and was in Crest and that his forces had beaten off a German attack northwest of Montélimar.

The morning of the twenty-sixth found Truscott "most unhappy" about the situation in the Square. Despite Dahlquist's repeated assurances about the efficacy of his block, aerial reconnaissance revealed continuing withdrawal of German forces along the banks of the Rhône. In fact, that afternoon the Germans launched an attack eastward from Loriol toward Crest, far north of the area Dahlquist claimed to have blocked; the reconstituted TF Butler repulsed the attack. Truscott set out for Dahlquist's CP south of Crest, determined to relieve him of command. Upon his arrival Truscott told Dahlquist of his intention and gave him five minutes to convince him that he should not do so.

Dahlquist explained that, based on reports that he had received, he believed his troops were on Hill 300, until he visited the area on August 25 and discovered that the troops were not on Hill 300 but on a hill to the east. He had made every effort during the day to seize the correct ridge, but the enemy forces on the hill were too strong. However, he had been able to establish a block at La Coucourde where he had four artillery battalions emplaced. He expressed his belief that he "had done as well as could be expected." Although Truscott did not "fully concur," he decided not to relieve him. Before returning to his CP at Aspres, Truscott visited TF Butler at Condillac, where he found the fighting to be heavy, as it was in the La Coucourde area, where Butler was attempting to reestablish the block on N-7. Heavy fighting continued within the Square for the next two days, particularly northwest of Montélimar, at La Coucourde, and in the Loriol area to the north. By the twenty-seventh the 3d ID had advanced to a point five miles south of Montélimar and finally occupied the town on the twenty-ninth.

Truscott spent many hours in the air on August 27 and 28, visiting the 3d Division and Dahlquist's CP and surveying the damage American artillery and tank fire was inflicting on the withdrawing German forces. The carnage was almost overwhelming, with tanks, other vehicles, and horse-drawn guns and equipment stopped bumper-to-bumper in long, disorganized columns along N-7 between Montélimar and Loriol. Allied fighter-bombers joined in the destruction, inflicting further damage on an already hard-pressed enemy.[46]

On the morning of the twenty-ninth the 141st Infantry drove south toward Montélimar and entered the town, where it joined up with Colonel Harrell's 7th Infantry.[47] The 143d Infantry was also advancing south toward the town through the valley between Hills 300 and 430. The three converging regiments captured more than 1,200 Germans during the fighting of August 28–29, at a cost of 17 killed, 60 wounded, and 15 missing. The 15th Infantry captured 450 Germans, and the 30th Infantry captured several hundred more. On the thirtieth the 3d and 36th Divisions swept the Square area, capturing almost 2,000 more prisoners. In the north TF Butler secured Loriol, and the 142d Infantry cleared Livron on the twenty-ninth. However, neither force was able to push on to the Rhône that day to capture the Germans who were still crossing to the west bank of the river via several remaining fords. The battle finally ended when the 142d Infantry was able to drive to the Rhône and clear the north bank of the Drome River on August 31.[48]

Although the Germans suffered heavy losses of personnel, vehicles, and other equipment, the VI Corps victory at Montélimar Square was somewhat of a disappointment for Truscott, since "most of the 11th Panzer Division and much of the 198th Reserve Division had broken through our block."[49] Overall, the German forces that moved up the east bank of the Rhône River suffered roughly 20 percent losses, most within frontline combat units. About 600 men were killed, 1,500 were wounded, and several thousand were listed as missing; roughly 5,800 men were captured. In addition, much of their artillery and substantial quantities of their vehicles, radios, and crew-served and individual weapons were lost. Along the west bank of the river the IV Luftwaffe Field Corps lost about 270 killed, 580 wounded, and 2,160 missing; about 1,800 were captured. By contrast, the American losses totaled 187 killed, 1,023 wounded, and 365 missing, less than 5 percent of those engaged in the fighting. But despite the relatively heavy German losses, the 11th Panzer Division escaped the trap with relatively few losses, incurring approximately 750 casualties. It arrived at Vienne with roughly 12,500 effectives, 39 of its 42 artillery pieces, more than 30 of its 40-odd heavy tanks, and 75 percent of its other vehicles.[50]

Truscott was particularly disappointed that he had not destroyed Gen. Friedrich Wiese's Nineteenth Army. His inability to concentrate his limited forces rapidly at Montélimar or at some point farther north, such as Loriol or Valence, made it difficult to halt the German withdrawal. In part that failure could be attributed to the unexpectedly rapid success of the landings, forcing Patch and Truscott to move their forces inland before all of their vehicles, ammunition, gasoline, and other supplies and follow-on forces could be landed in an attempt to trap the withdrawing German forces.[51]

According to Truscott, "no Army plan or terrain study had considered the possibility of such an early exploitation . . . northward toward Sisteron and Grenoble, and possibly to block the German withdrawal by seizing the high ground north of Montelimar." Expecting that CC Sudre would not be available for his use, Truscott had ordered General Butler to form a task force for such an exploitation toward either Grenoble or Montélimar. However, Truscott did not give definite orders to Butler to attack westward toward Montélimar rather than northward toward Grenoble until the night of August 20, and he did not order Dahlquist to join TF Butler in the Square until August 21, by which time the German withdrawal up the Rhône valley was well under way.[52] Also, by the time Butler received his orders to move westward, he had already oriented his force toward Grenoble. Reassembling his scattered task force considerably delayed the start of his drive toward Montélimar, and the need to retain a blocking force at Gap and at Croix Haute Pass until the 36th Division could relieve the blocking forces weakened the force entering the Square.[53]

As early as D+1 the rapid progress inland of the three American divisions had created a serious shortage of gasoline, and there was as well a shortage of organic division trucks to transport anything but division troops, ammunition, and supplies. As a result, Patch and Truscott "lacked the wherewithal to assemble TF Butler and the 36th Division quickly at Montélimar and support the force with adequate rations, fuel, and munitions from the beach depots 200 miles to the rear." However, the actions of TF Butler and the 36th Division had considerably weakened Wiese's Nineteenth Army and had necessitated his pressing the 11th Panzer Division, his most mobile force, into action at Montélimar rather than using it as a rear guard for his withdrawing troops. Truscott summarized his conclusions about the battle at Montélimar Square thus: "Even if Montelimar had not been a perfect battle, we could still view the record with some degree of satisfaction."[54]

ADVANCE TO THE NORTH

As the battle in the Montélimar Square came to a close, the remnants of Gen. Friedrich Wiese's Nineteenth Army were in full retreat up the Rhône valley, hoping to forge a linkup in northeastern France with the rest of Gen. Johannes Blaskowitz's Army Group G forces retreating from western France. The two forces then planned to join with Field Marshal Erwin Rommel's Army Group B to form a unified front along the west border of Germany. Seventh Army's plan was to move northward as quickly as possible and link up with Patton's Third Army operating along the right flank of Eisenhower's Allied forces. Supplies, troops, and equipment continued to pour in across the original landing beaches and were speedily moved northward to VI Corps, as French troops cleared and rehabilitated the port cities. French combat units also continued to arrive to join in the push to the north.[55]

On August 25 Patch began issuing plans for future operations of his army. He believed that the city of Lyon, 75 miles north of Montélimar, would be the collecting point for German forces fleeing up the east and west banks of the Rhône and expected the Germans to mount a defense there. With General de Lattre's French Army B still engaged in clearing Toulon and Marseilles, Patch decided to have Truscott's VI Corps attack northward through Valence and Grenoble to Lyon and then continue 110 miles farther north to Dijon. Patch then planned, after gaining Eisenhower's approval, to have VI Corps go on to Strasbourg on the Rhine River some 160 miles to the northeast.

After completing his mission in Toulon and Marseilles, de Lattre was to send elements of his army across the Rhône at Avignon, some to screen Truscott's west flank, others to advance along the west bank of the Rhône to assist in the capture of Lyon. Other elements of French Army B would advance north and northwest to the east of VI Corps into Alsace and pass through the Belfort Gap into the upper Rhine valley. The 1st Airborne Task Force would continue its mission of screening the Franco-Italian border until relieved by French forces.

After receiving and accepting de Lattre's objection that the plan would divide his army into several parts, leaving him with insufficient forces to drive through the Belfort Gap, Patch and de Lattre worked out a compromise: the 1st Airborne Task Force would continue to hold the area along Seventh Army's right flank, a small reconnaissance force assisted by members of the FFI would conduct the reconnoitering west of the Rhône, and de Lattre would send two divisions up the west bank of the Rhône, while other French units would secure

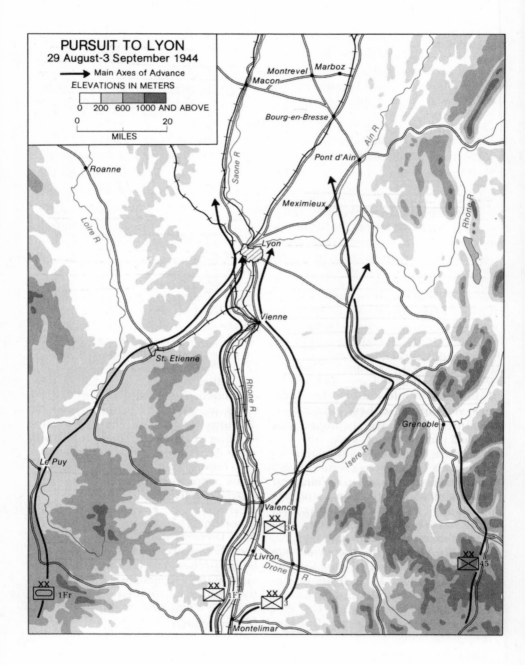

PURSUIT TO LYON
29 August-3 September 1944

Main Axes of Advance
ELEVATIONS IN METERS

0   200   600   1000 AND ABOVE

0 _____ 20
        MILES

Roanne

Saone R

Montrevel   Marboz
Macon

Bourg-en-Bresse

Ain R

Pont d'Ain

Loire R

Meximieux

Rhone R

Lyon

Vienne

St. Etienne

Rhone R

Grenoble

Le Puy

Isere R

Valence

XX
36

XX
45

Livron
Drone   R

XX
1 Fr

XX
1 Fr

XX
3

Montelimar

VI Corps' right flank as it advanced northward from Grenoble. After the fall of Lyon the two divisions west of the Rhône would unite with the eastern French forces for the drive through the Belfort Gap.[56]

Oberbefehlshaber West (OB West), highest ground headquarters of the western front, directed Wiese to continue the withdrawal of Nineteenth Army from Lyon north to Dijon, uniting there with the rest of Army Group G, which was then to extend its northern flank northeast of Dijon toward the withdrawing forces of Rommel's Army Group B, establishing a line from Dijon through Besançon to the Swiss border. The line would secure the approaches to the Belfort Gap and create a salient west of the Vosges Mountains, from which OB West planned to launch an armored counterattack against the southern flank of Patton's advancing Third Army.[57]

On August 28 Truscott received Patch's order confirming Lyon as the next corps objective. Since the first elements of de Lattre's forces were not scheduled to arrive at Grenoble until the thirtieth, Truscott, believing that speed was essential, decided to have his American units begin the drive alone the next day. He therefore told Eagles to capture Bourg-en-Bresse northeast of Lyon as quickly as possible and directed Dahlquist to advance along the east bank of the Rhône through Valence and Vienne to Lyon. The 3d Division was to follow the 45th, but was to be prepared to reinforce either the 45th or the 36th as ordered.[58] By the morning of September 1 the 36th Division had advanced to the eastern outskirts of Lyon, and the 45th Division was south of Bourgen-Bresse, approaching the road leading from Lyon, and was in contact with the 11th Panzer Division. The 3d Division was northwest of Grenoble at Voiron, and the French forces advancing west of the Rhône were nearing Lyon from the southwest.[59]

Despite the growing Allied threat to Lyon, Wiese was confident that by the second he would have most of his Nineteenth Army well north of the city, while the 11th Panzer Division and a regiment of the 338th Division screened to the south and east. On the thirtieth Patch had ordered Truscott to let French forces be the first to enter Lyon, and when they did so on September 3 they found that the Germans had withdrawn northward.[60] On the fourth, elements of the 45th Division captured Bourg-en-Bresse, and the 36th Division had moved into Macon to the west. Patch's original plan had called for VI Corps to continue its drive north in the Saone valley east of the Saone River to Dijon to link up with Patton, while the French forces to the right of VI Corps were to advance northeast to the Belfort Gap and then to the upper Rhine. However, on the second, because of the rapid withdrawal of the Germans to Dijon and the scattered deployment of the French divisions, Truscott dispatched his aide, Captain Wilson, to Patch's headquarters at Brignoles to present an alternate plan.[61]

Since it would take de Lattre at least a week to regroup his divisions for the drive to the Belfort Gap, Truscott suggested that his three divisions take on the mission of securing the gap, "a military objective of the utmost importance." If they moved quickly, no later than September 3, Truscott believed there was a chance to capture the bulk of the withdrawing Nineteenth Army between Dijon and the Vosges Mountains. Wilson arrived at Patch's headquarters about midnight of the second and presented the plan to the general. Patch studied Truscott's plan with his staff, and at 12:50 a.m., September 3, telephoned Truscott and gave him approval to put his plan into operation.[62]

On the fourth VI Corps began its northward drive in the general direction of Besançon, with the 3d Division in the lead, the 36th on the left, and the 45th in the rear. The 3d Algerian Division on the corps' right flank advanced apace, while to the west the French 1st Armored Division advanced toward Dijon. On the morning of the fifth, lead elements of the 3d Division were probing German defenses of Besançon and seeking possible crossing sites on the Doubs River east and west of the city. When he realized that Wiese planned to make a stand at Besançon, Truscott initially considered having the 45th Division and most of the 3d Division bypass the city to the east, but then decided that bypassing the enemy strong point was too risky and ordered the 3d Division to take the city, while Eagles's division advanced on Baume-les-Dames to the northeast and the Algerians launched a strong attack toward Montbeliard, less than ten miles south of Belfort.

O'Daniel's division crossed the Doubs River and occupied the hills around Besançon, effectively surrounding the city, which fell on September 8. The 36th Division crossed the river west of the city on the sixth and routed German defenses near St. Vit, forcing Wiese to order another general withdrawal of his forces. East of Besançon the 180th Infantry crossed the Doubs River south of Baume against no enemy opposition on the seventh, forcing the enemy to evacuate the town the following day. However, German resistance halted the Algerian advance eleven miles south of Montbeliard. It was quite apparent to Truscott that until the French I Corps could bring forward more divisions on his right flank, his VI Corps would have to bear the brunt of the effort to seize the Belfort Gap.[63]

By the evening of the eighth the Nineteenth Army had begun another major withdrawal. In addition, the German high command had decided to move the counterattack assembly area from Dijon to Nancy, farther to the north, from which a counterattack would be launched, not against Seventh Army but against Patton's rapidly advancing Third Army.

On the ninth Truscott ordered his three divisions to change their general axis of attack to the east, assigning the 3d Division the mission of capturing Vesoul, while the 36th Division on the corps' left flank was to execute a wide sweeping movement to the north and then advance east of the Saone River into the foothills of the Vosges Mountains. During its advance toward Vesoul the 3d encountered heavy resistance, but the 36th to the west quickly penetrated the

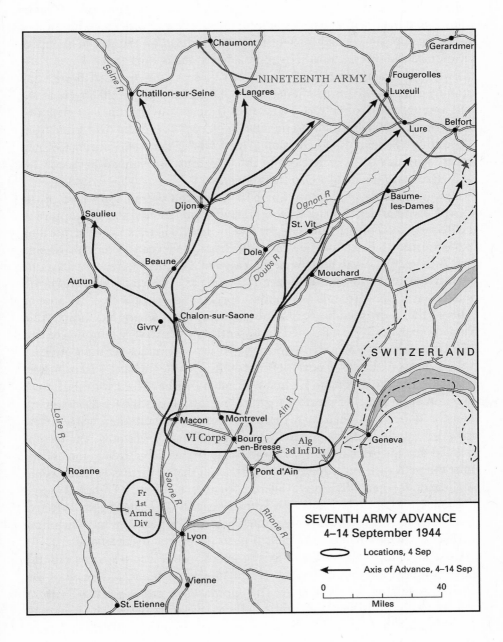

Chaumont

Gerardmer

Seine R

Chatillon-sur-Seine

Langres

NINETEENTH ARMY

Fougerolles

Luxeuil

Belfort

Lure

Ognon R

Saulieu

Dijon

Baume-
les-Dames

St. Vit

Beaune

Dole

Doubs R

Autun

Mouchard

Chalon-sur-Saone

Givry

SWITZERLAND

Loire R

Ain R

Macon

Montrevel

VI Corps

Bourg
-en-Bresse

Alg
3d Inf Div

Geneva

Roanne

Pont d'Ain

Saone R

Fr
1st
Armd
Div

Rhone R

Lyon

SEVENTH ARMY ADVANCE
4–14 September 1944

⬭ Locations, 4 Sep

⬅ Axis of Advance, 4–14 Sep

Vienne

0   40

St. Etienne

Miles

German lines. With the town now almost completely surrounded by the 3d and 36th Divisions, the enemy forces in Vesoul received orders to withdraw, and by three the afternoon of the twelfth elements of both American divisions had secured the town. The fall of Vesoul forced Wiese to order a withdrawal of his forces opposing the advance of the 45th Division on the east to defensive positions defending the northern approaches to the Belfort Gap.

By the fourteenth the three divisions of VI Corps were disposed along a line running through the towns of Fougerolles, Luxeuil, Lure, and Villersexel to the west and northwest of Belfort. The French II Corps was moving into positions north of the 36th Division, and the French I Corps to the east held a line from the southern flank of the 3d Division to the Swiss border. Believing the German forces facing his corps were close to collapse, Truscott planned to launch his final attack into the Belfort Gap that same day.

However, the Seventh Army was now under the overall command of the SHAEF commander, General Eisenhower, who did not consider the capture of the Belfort Gap a priority mission for Patch's army. Therefore, on the morning of the fourteenth Patch sent new orders to Truscott that canceled his mission to seize the gap.[64] VI Corps and the newly assigned XV Corps were to attack along the Luxeuil-Remiremont-Strasbourg-Karlsruhe axis, which lay west and north of the Belfort Gap. Truscott was "both surprised and disappointed" because he believed that it diverted his corps from the mission of seizing a critical terrain feature, the Belfort Gap, relegated the Seventh Army "to a very minor role," and might possibly bog down the army in the Vosges Mountains for the winter.[65]

Truscott spent the entire next morning drafting a letter to Patch that expressed his opinion of the new plan. He first told Patch that he agreed with the latter's assertion at their earlier meeting that the "Belfort Gap is the Gateway to Germany," and then went on to state that it had become obvious the Germans were making "strenuous efforts to strengthen the defense of this area." He recommended that the three American divisions and the available French forces continue their advance toward the gap, pointing out that in three days there would be additional French divisions available, possibly including a French armored division. He went on to assert that French Army B could not begin "effective operations against the Belfort area much before early October, by which time the Boche will have had considerable time to strengthen his defenses."

Truscott believed that the new axis of attack would lead his corps into the Vosges Mountains, with its rugged terrain, limited road net, and excellent defensive capabilities for the enemy. The approaching winter weather, with its rain, snow, and bitter cold, would magnify those difficulties. The net result would be the bottling up of "the three most veteran divisions in the American Army in an operation where they can be contained by a fraction of their strength and where their demonstrated ability to maneuver is so strictly limited." He also told Patch that he believed the Italian campaign was bogged down along the Gothic line and that an attack by VI Corps from Nice toward Genoa might assist in breaking that stalemate, stating that if "French Army B is considered sufficient to break through the Belfort Gap, I believe that this operation for the VI Corps might contribute more to the German defeat than the operation ordered through the Vosges Mountains." He concluded his letter by making the following recommendations for employment of VI Corps: either opening the Belfort Gap, or capturing Genoa, thereby aiding in the destruction of German forces in Italy. He also requested that Patch forward the proposal to higher headquarters, which was now the newly activated 6th Army Group, commanded by General Devers.[66]

That evening Patch called Truscott to express his displeasure with the letter. Truscott assured Patch that he wrote it only to express his beliefs about the planned operation and assured Patch of his wholehearted support if ordered to begin the new operation. He also told Patch that he had already launched an attack toward the east and Belfort Gap as well as northward in compliance with Patch's original order and asked what he should do. Patch told him to keep advancing as he was and said that he would visit him the following day for further discussion.

Patch arrived at Truscott's CP the next day, and the two discussed the Seventh Army plan at length. Patch "was now enthusiastic about the sweep to the north through the Strasbourg Gap" but believed that Truscott should suspend the corps attack until SHAEF had approved the plan, expected within two or three days. During that interval the French relieved the 45th Division south of Lure, freeing that division to assist in the advance northward. Finally, on September 21, VI Corps began crossing the Moselle River, the 36th Division to the north near Remiremont, the 45th Division in the middle near Épinal, and the 3d Division to the south in the Rupt area.[67]

On the sixteenth Truscott learned that both his and Carleton's names had gone forward to the U.S. Senate for confirmation for their promotions to lieutenant general and brigadier general, respectively. Three days later he told his wife that he had been promoted, effective September 2, and that Carleton's promotion had become effective on September 6. Truscott immediately assembled his staff, his Chinese cooks and batman, his driver, and his aides for a "pinning" ceremony. Truscott personally pinned the single star of a brigadier general on Don Carleton, and Carleton and Captains Bartash and Wilson collectively pinned on the additional star signifying Truscott's promotion to lieutenant general. Champagne toasts followed the pinnings. The next afternoon Truscott and his staff assembled for a champagne reception, followed by a cocktail party attended by all corps officers, some eighty strong.[68]

On September 23 Truscott once again met with Patch, who had just returned from a meeting with Eisenhower at Versailles, where he had received "depressing" news: Eisenhower had decided that the British forces in Montgomery's

21st Army Group and most of the American First Army in Bradley's 12th Army Group were to make the SHAEF main effort in the North, namely, to "secure a line far enough to the eastward to cover Antwerp and the roads and railways leading out of it toward the front . . . reduce the German defenses in the areas lying between that city and the sea . . . [and] thrust forward spearheads as far as we could, to include a bridgehead across the Rhine if possible, so as to threaten the Ruhr and facilitate subsequent offensives."[69]

Eisenhower had assigned no specific missions to Devers's Army Group, since from "a theater point of view, a major role in the south seemed pointless, and his forces faced a daunting array of obstacles: the Vosges Mountains, the Rhine River, the West Wall, and finally the Black Forest." Even if 6th Army Group were to thrust through those formidable obstacles and seize Nuremberg and Munich, they "did not seem especially worthwhile objectives." Thus, it appeared that "Eisenhower still expected little from the 6th Army Group, believing that even the most successful advances in the south had little strategic potential." To Truscott it "looked more than ever like a winter in the Vosges."[70]

Colley believes that Eisenhower's decision to assign no specific missions to 6th Army Group, considering that front to be peripheral to the campaigns of Bradley's 12th Army Group and Montgomery's 21st Army Group, "was directly related to a clash of personalities between Ike and Devers. Eisenhower disliked and mistrusted his three-star subordinate, and seemed determined to exclude him from major operations on the western front."[71]

Visiting Truscott at that time was Will Lang, a *Life* magazine war journalist. One morning after his daily meeting with his subordinate commanders, Truscott invited Lang to join him for breakfast. As they were eating, Lang addressed some questions to Truscott about the meeting with his commanders, to which Truscott gave "a few brief answers." As Lang continued his interrogation Truscott barked:

> "Didn't you listen to anything I said in there?" and escorted him into his command trailer. There he went to the map displaying the current tactical deployment of VI Corps, pointed to and moved a pin on the map, and growled, "You saw me move this pin, didn't you? . . . Do you know what that means?" When Lang shook his head, "No," Truscott exclaimed, "It means by noon today 25 of my men will be dead." He then turned and walked out of the trailer and returned to his breakfast. Lang went on to say it was at that moment he learned what a general did in a war, and what war was about.[72]

In this simple act Truscott demonstrated three qualities that all successful combat commanders must possess: a genuine compassion for the men he commands, a recognition that completion of the unit's mission must take precedence over all else and that in completing that mission soldiers often must die, and, having made that decision, to compartmentalize it within his mind and move on to the next task at hand, in this case finishing breakfast.

Devers was not deterred from action by the exclusion of his Army Group from the major offensive action against Germany in the north. On September 27 he and Patch visited Truscott at his CP, where Devers outlined his plan for VI Corps: an advance on Strasbourg through the Vosges Mountains along Saint Dié Pass, while XV Corps attacked eastward to the north of VI Corps along the route from Baccarat and Raon l'Ètape.[73] The weather and terrain that VI Corps encountered during the ensuing weeks before the start of the attack undoubtedly kindled in Truscott's mind memories of the difficulties he and his 3d Division had faced on the Italian boot: almost constant rain, mud, frigid temperatures, rugged mountainous terrain, supply shortages (particularly of ammunition), and almost insurmountable difficulties in moving supplies and replacements forward and casualties rearward. In fact, anticipating a replay of the conditions on the Italian front, Truscott requested that two pack trains be sent from Italy to join his corps. However, the trains did not arrive in the Vosges area until November 23, long after Truscott had relinquished command of VI Corps.[74]

On the fifteenth Truscott had ordered an attack to capture Bruyères, break through the German defenses, and continue the attack in the direction of Saint Dié. The 45th Division, with the attached 442d RCT, which had been guarding the French-Italian border and consisted largely of Japanese Americans, was to attack from the west. The 3d Division was in reserve, prepared to exploit the breakthrough and drive toward Saint Dié. By the seventeenth, as the attack was progressing well, Truscott received orders to report to Patch's CP at Épinal to confer with Patch and General Eisenhower.[75]

On September 25 Eisenhower informed Omar Bradley that he had received a telegram on September 21 from Marshall, stating that "because of our high opinion of Truscott and the fact that he has already been promoted [to lieutenant general], we should look upon him, rather than [Maj. Gen. Leonard T.] Gerow, [commander of V Corps,] as our next Army commander." Eisenhower went on to tell Bradley that in a reply cable to Marshall he had agreed with that recommendation.[76]

General Eisenhower greeted Truscott warmly when he arrived in Épinal, and after a brief discussion of the situation at the front told him that he was going to relieve him from command of VI Corps, stating that because he had been promoted to lieutenant general all of the other corps commanders expected to be promoted to that grade also. He was to organize a new army, the Fifteenth, which would serve as an administrative and training command rather than as an operational field army. Eisenhower told Truscott, "You won't like it, because this Army is not going to be operational. It will be an administrative and training command, and you won't get into the fighting."

Truscott protested the new assignment, pointing out that he would prefer to remain with VI Corps, even if it meant that he would have to revert to the grade of major general. Eisenhower replied that it was not "practicable" for him to remain with VI Corps and that he needed him to organize the Fifteenth Army. Besides, Maj. Gen. Edward H. Brooks, who had commanded the 2d Armored Division, was already on his way to assume command of the corps. However, Truscott would remain with the corps until the present attack was completed and Brooks "had affairs well in hand." After turning the corps over to Brooks, Truscott was to discuss the organization of the new army with Bradley, under whose 12th Army Group the new army would operate, and then report to SHAEF. After a short leave at home Truscott would return to Europe and take up his new command.[77]

Truscott returned to his duties with VI Corps, where he oversaw the capture of Bruyères. When Brooks joined the corps, its three divisions were continuing the attack and progressing well. After briefing Brooks, Truscott, accompanied by Carleton and his aides, visited each of the divisions on the twenty-fourth to say good-bye. The next day Truscott was a guest for an emotional farewell luncheon in the corps' staff mess. Later that day they bade farewell to Patch and his staff and left for 6th Army Group headquarters at Vittel to visit Devers and his staff, where Truscott learned that the headquarters of Fifteenth Army was tentatively set to be located at Rennes.[78]

The group then went on to visit Patton's headquarters at Nancy, Bradley's headquarters in Luxembourg, and Lt. Gen. Courtney Hodges's First Army headquarters in Spa, Belgium. On the thirtieth they arrived at SHAEF headquarters, where Truscott spent a few days in preliminary planning for the organization of Fifteenth Army. He detailed Carleton to remain behind in Europe to confer with the former VI Corps staff officers they were bringing with them to the new assignment and to bring over the elements in England that were to join them in Fifteenth Army. On November 4 Truscott, his aides Bartash and Wilson, and Sergeants Barna and Hong departed for the United States.[79]

Ten years later, while he was writing his memoir, *Command Missions,* Truscott looked back on the operation in southern France. He concluded that the invasion had been as successful as it was because the initial major assault forces were a homogeneous force, composed almost entirely of American troops, and because the corps and division commanders and their staffs had broad experience in planning and conducting amphibious assaults. The homogeneity of the initial assault troops ensured that all were operating under the same tactical doctrines, were using the same command and staff procedures, and had the same weapons and equipment.

Truscott also emphasized "the value of anticipatory planning to exploit enemy weaknesses with speed in execution," as exemplified by his organization of Task Force Butler. If he had not formed that force prior to sailing from Naples,

VI Corps "would not have been able to gain the rear of the German XIX Army at Montélimar. That Army might then have been able to develop an effective withdrawal and our exploitation would then have been far less rapid and extensive." Further, since the assault divisions of VI Corps "had been thoroughly trained in rapid movement," their close pursuit of the withdrawing Germans prevented their setting up new defense lines.

Truscott believed that DRAGOON had proved its worth as a secondary offensive by "clearing the Germans from all of southern and southwestern France south of the advancing flank of General Eisenhower's OVERLORD forces, already extended over a large area and on supply lines of extreme length." In one month the American and French forces in Seventh Army "had almost completely destroyed the XIX Army, captured some 80,000 prisoners." Seventh Army had driven north almost five hundred miles from the French Riviera to the Vosges Mountains, where its troops linked up with Patton's Third Army. "No secondary attack in history ever attained greater results."[80]

However, Churchill considered DRAGOON to have been "a mistake of almost disastrous proportions" because of its diversion of men and supplies from the Italian front. But in 1956 General Marshall firmly stated, "I don't agree with the Prime Minister on ANVIL at all. In fact, I am in almost complete disagreement on every phase of it. He was intent on one thing [the Italian front] and he sways all his arguments to justify that one thing. . . . Almost every thing he said to deter us from that operation down there went exactly the other way with a tremendous success." General Eisenhower also strongly disagreed with the prime minister, pointing out that the distance from the port of Marseilles to the Metz region was less than the distance from Brest and that the rail lines connecting Marseilles and Metz through the Rhône valley were much less tortuous and less subject to enemy interdiction than those from Brest. Further, the presence of a large force in southern France provided protection and support to the right flank of Patton's Third Army during its advance eastward, and the joining of Devers's force with that of Patton trapped all enemy forces west of the point of juncture.[81]

Chapter 11

Army Command

Prior to Truscott's leaving SHAEF Eisenhower had cabled Marshall to inform him of Truscott's impending departure for the continental United States (CONUS), stating that he would initially report to the War Department "to be temporarily available for any kind of information or conferences that you may desire" and that he would then leave for "a short recreational period" before returning to SHAEF. Eisenhower went on to state that he would "personally appreciate anything the War Department can do to add to General TRUSCOTT's convenience." The following day Marshall replied that he would "do anything to make General TRUSCOTT's visit more pleasant." Truscott cabled Marshall that he was "most appreciative of the thoughtfulness of the Chief of Staff" and that he would like his wife to meet him and have Marshall reserve an apartment for the two of them at Fort Myer.[1]

After a long flight, including a stopover in Bermuda, Truscott and his party arrived at Washington National Airport on the afternoon of November 5, where Mrs. Truscott was waiting. After a "big reunion," General and Mrs. Truscott were "whisked out to Fort Myer" and their apartment in the General Officers Quarters. After dropping off the Truscotts' bags in the apartment the entire party enjoyed a late lunch at the Officers' Club. When the gathering broke up, Truscott and his wife adjourned to their quarters for a quiet evening alone, while the aides were "on [the] loose in Washington."[2]

After spending the next day at Marshall's headquarters and with other personnel in the War Department, Truscott was granted nine days of leave after which he returned to Washington for a short period of temporary duty with the Operations Division of the War Department. The evening after his return to Washington some of his former NCOs from Troop E of the 3d Cavalry, now-Major Regeleski and now-Captains Fields, O'Connel, and Powers, joined him for a reunion over drinks at his quarters at Fort Myer.[3]

On the nineteenth Truscott and Wilson departed by air for Stewart Field, New York, to visit Truscott's son Lucian, then in his final year at the United States Military Academy. Following lunch Truscott and Wilson accompanied Lucian to his quarters, where they discussed with him and some of his friends "what to expect as new 2d Lt's in combat." Speaking on behalf of their fathers, Truscott also "gave hell" to Cadets George S. Patton and Hobart R. Gay, Jr., both members of the class of 1946, for their academic shortcomings.[4]

On the twenty-first Truscott returned to the Pentagon for a nine o'clock briefing with Generals Marshall, Henry H. Arnold (U.S. Army Air Forces chief of staff), Thomas T. Handy (assistant chief of staff, Operations Division), John E. Hull (chief, Theater Group, Operations Division), and others. Truscott found the briefing to be "intensely interesting," covering "in detail the military deployment of our military forces in all parts of the world." After the briefing Marshall's staff presented problems to him that required his decision. One of the most pressing was his need to name a successor to General Clark in Italy.[5]

The command structure in Italy had undergone a major revision as a result of the death on November 4 of Field Marshal Sir John Dill, head of the British Joint Staff Mission in Washington. Prime Minister Churchill had recommended to President Roosevelt that Gen. Sir Henry Maitland Wilson, Allied commander in chief of the Mediterranean theater, succeed Dill; Gen. Sir Harold Alexander, commander of 15th Army Group, replace Wilson; and Gen. Mark Clark assume command of 15th Army Group. Roosevelt replied that those proposals were acceptable to him and to the Joint Chiefs of Staff. It fell to Marshall to name Clark's successor.

When asked by his staff whether he wished to name General Keyes, the senior corps commander in Italy, as the new commander of Fifth Army or assign someone else to that command, Marshall turned to Truscott and asked how he would feel about going back to Italy rather than staying with SHAEF as commander of the Fifteenth Army. Taken aback, Truscott replied that he would do his best wherever Marshall decided to send him to serve but admitted that he would prefer to remain in France, serving under Eisenhower. He also pointed out that both of the corps commanders in Italy (Keyes and Crittenberger) were senior to him. At that point, Marshall instructed Hull to obtain Eisenhower's opinion about the matter and adjourned the conference.[6]

That evening Truscott and his party traveled to New York on the first leg of their return trip to Europe. There they enjoyed a sumptuous oyster dinner, during which Truscott devoured two dozen oysters for the absent new VI Corps commander, General Brooks, and one dozen for himself. After spending the night at Fort Totten, the group left La Guardia Field the next afternoon, November 22, for Paris, via Prestwick, Scotland, Truscott not knowing which assignment he would receive—command of Fifteenth Army or command of Fifth Army.[7]

On the twenty-second Marshall explained the situation to Eisenhower in a cable, suggesting that either Lt. Gen. William H. Simpson, then commanding Ninth Army in Bradley's 12th Army Group, or Truscott be named Fifth Army commander. Eisenhower replied that he would be willing to make one of his army commanders available to command Fifth Army but wished to defer a final decision until after he had discussed the matter with Bradley. Later that day Eisenhower cabled Marshall that both Bradley and he believed, "in view of Truscott's familiarity with the Italian theater, and because Simpson, Hodges, Patton and Patch are so intimately engaged in the battle now raging on this front, Truscott should be the man to go to Italy."[8]

Truscott arrived in Paris early in the afternoon of November 24 and following lunch went to SHAEF headquarters to meet with General Eisenhower. In the absence of Eisenhower, who was visiting his forward elements, Beetle Smith told Truscott that he was to take Clark's place as commander of Fifth Army. Two days later he wrote Sarah that he was completely "resigned" to the new assignment, stating that, "at least, I will be fighting . . . and besides, as I see it, there's no use bucking *fate*." Learning that Truscott was "deeply disappointed over the prospect of going to Italy," and believing that there must be "something behind it more than personal preference," Eisenhower invited Truscott to visit him at his forward CP, "Shellburst," at Reims, where, Eisenhower believed, he could "settle the matter without further reference" to Marshall. Truscott dutifully flew to Reims on the twenty-seventh, where he presented his case, but was unable to sway his old friend, who told him that he would assume command of Fifth Army on December 5. Truscott explained to his wife that "Ike could not stomach the alternative—making Jeff [Geoffrey] K[eyes] or [Willis D.] Crit[tenberger] an army commander" and was sure that his new assignment gave Eisenhower assurance that he had someone commanding Fifth Army "in whom he has full confidence." The assignment also gave Truscott the advantage of being on an active front—"killing Boche—which I would not have been here [in France and Germany] for several months at least." The week before leaving for Italy, Truscott accompanied Smith on a trip to both 12th and 6th Army Groups, which gave him an opportunity to say farewell to old friends, including Eisenhower, Bradley, Patton, and Devers, as well as "a lot of others whom I wanted to see before leaving the theater."[9]

Since Eisenhower had authorized Truscott to take with him to Fifth Army the officers whom he had brought from VI Corps as well as other officers of his choosing, he spent the last ten days in France visiting various American headquarters collecting the staff and others whom he wished to accompany him to Italy. His final party included General Carleton (COS) and Cols. John F. Cassidy (assistant COS), Conway (executive and chief of the Planning Syndicate), Harrell (G3), and O'Neill (G4). On the afternoon of December 5 they left Orly Field and arrived in Caserta later the same day, after flying over some of the battlefields in southern France where Truscott's VI Corps had earlier been engaged.[10] As Truscott departed, Eisenhower cabled Marshall that he had sent Truscott to the Mediterranean theater that day and "regretted to have him go because [he had] always had such tremendous confidence in him as a fighting leader and because he so obviously wanted to stay a member of this team. From the over-all picture it looked to me to be the best thing to do."[11]

Maj. Gen. Lowell W. Rooks, deputy chief of staff of AFHQ, met Truscott on his arrival in Caserta late on the fifth and spent two days briefing him. Truscott then spent several days at AFHQ, where he was briefed on the situation confronting Fifth Army, before moving north on the seventh to meet with Clark.[12] Brig. Gen. Donald W. Brann, Clark's G3, met him in Florence and escorted him to the Fifth Army Command Post in Futa Pass, roughly twenty miles north of Florence, where Clark, Maj. Gen. Alfred M. Gruenther, Clark's chief of staff, and other old friends warmly greeted him. When he learned that he would not assume command of Fifth Army until December 16, Truscott decided to spend the ensuing days familiarizing himself with the Fifth Army situation.

The army CP was located near the tiny village of Traversa on Highway 65, the main road between Florence and Bologna, at an altitude of about twenty-seven hundred feet. The staff sections had set up their operations in trailers, tents, and a few prefabricated buildings, including the "Hut," which Clark used for briefings and conferences as well as for a club room. The remaining army headquarters elements were located in the Fifth Army Rear CP in Florence. Clark's "rather luxurious trailer" sat to one side of the Hut, to the rear of which was a tent housing the general's mess. Truscott placed his trailer near Clark's trailer and had tents erected nearby for his personal staff. There "in ice, snow, mud, and fog" the new commander and his staff would spend the remainder of their second Italian winter.[13]

Truscott confided to his wife his impressions of Clark, describing his feelings about the man as "strange—most strange." He admitted that Clark had "plenty of ability, but is one of the most self centered individuals I have ever known. He has always given me 100% support heretofore—and I had almost forgotten my inability to feel complete confidence in him—but it comes back in force. However, it will work out alright I'm sure."[14]

At midnight, December 16, Lieutenant General Truscott, Jr., reached the pinnacle of his Army career, command of Fifth Army.[15] The army front at that time extended westward from the sector held by the British 13 Corps facing Highway 9 between Faenza and Castel San Pietro through the II Corps sector in the center, which extended from Monte Grando overlooking the Po valley to Setta Creek west of Highway 65, and then on to the 6th South African Armored Division sector in the angle between Setta Creek and the Reno River. From there the line ran through Maj. Gen. Willis D. Crittenberger's IV Corps zone, a rather inactive sector extending to the coastal sector north of Leghorn, which was held by the 92d Infantry Division, composed of black enlisted men, commanded and led largely by white officers. Under II Corps command were the 34th, 85th, 88th, and 91st Infantry Divisions and the 1st Armored Division, all preparing to take part in Operation PIANORO, that part of Alexander's planned attack northward along Highway 65. IV Corps controlled only the Brazilian 1st Infantry Division and Task Force 45, composed of former anti-aircraft troops operating as infantry. The inexperienced 92d Infantry Division was under direct Fifth Army control.[16]

Truscott spent the next few days getting the forward CP organized, conferring with his staff on existing plans and preparing plans for possible future operations. He began each day with a staff meeting where each staff section reviewed any problems it was encountering as well as activities in which it was engaged. Weekly the special staff officers from the rear CP in Florence would come to Futa Pass and participate in the staff meetings, thus ensuring that all staff sections were kept completely informed of Fifth Army plans and activities.

On the twenty-second Truscott was visiting the 6th South African Armored Division near Monte Sole when he received a message to meet Clark in Florence. With the Battle of the Bulge raging in Belgium, Luxembourg, and France, Clark was apprehensive that the Germans might attempt a similar counterattack in the Serchio valley north of Leghorn, where intelligence indicated a strong buildup of enemy forces, possibly as many as four additional divisions. The valley had been deemed an inactive front and was held by black troops of the 370th and 366th Infantry Regiments. A strong attack in the Serchio valley sector would place the large Allied supply base at Leghorn in great danger, leading Clark to order that the sector be reinforced.[17] The following day Truscott ordered the attachment of one regiment of the 85th Division to IV Corps and transferred another regiment of the division from II Corps reserve and two brigades of the 8th Indian Division from 13 Corps reserve to positions backing up IV Corps. By Christmas Day the realignments had been completed, and the 92d Division had been placed under IV Corps control.[18]

Although the 370th Infantry Regiment of the 92d had been in Italy since August 1944, attached to the 1st AD, it did not see sustained action until October 1944, when, as the infantry component of Task Force 92 during the drive to capture Massa on the west coast, it failed in its mission to seize Monte Cauala.[19] The remaining two regiments of the division, the 365th and the 371st, arrived in Italy during October.[20] The enlisted ranks of the division were composed entirely of black men, with a mixture of white and black officers. However, there were no black officers commanding companies, battalions, or regiments, and there were no black staff officers at battalion level or above.[21] An unusually high percentage of the enlisted men, 62 percent, had scored in the lowest two categories of the Army General Classification Test, and none had scored in the highest category. Significantly, 13 percent received no score since they were too illiterate to complete the test.[22]

Clark's and Truscott's fears of a German attack in the coastal sector were well founded, since the German Fourteenth Army's commander, General Kurt von Tippelskirch, had made plans to launch on December 26 Operation WINTERGEWITTER (Winter Thunderstorm), a limited-objective attack against the 92d Division to relieve pressure on enemy forces engaged by the Brazilian Expeditionary Force in the Serchio valley. Tippelskirch's objectives were to improve the morale of his troops by giving them a victory over American troops and to afford them an opportunity to gain additional combat experience.

The attack was launched east and west of the Serchio River near Castelnuovo, with the main attack on the east, where the Germans captured Sommocolonia and the high ground at Monte Vano. When Crittenberger learned of the attack he immediately moved the two Indian brigades into positions behind the 92d, and Truscott ordered the 1st AD to move from II Corps westward to the vicinity of Lucca. In addition, one regiment of the 34th ID moved into a position near Viareggio as a reserve. By the afternoon of the twenty-sixth the Germans were threatening to break through the 92d's front east of the Serchio River. At that point, believing that the attack had accomplished its objectives, Tippelskirch ordered a withdrawal, leaving only a screening force in front of IV Corps. By the end of the year the Indian brigades had regained practically all of the ground the Germans had seized during WINTERGEWITTER.

Contrary to Clark's belief, Operation WINTERGEWITTER had no connection with the Battle of the Bulge. However, the offensive had persuaded him to move troops from the II Corps south of Bologna to the threatened Serchio valley, and had so alarmed Truscott and Clark that Clark postponed Operation PIANORO, the plan to attack northward to Bologna, until spring. Other factors had also influenced his decision to postpone PIANORO: a dangerously low ammunition reserve, with no resupply of ammunition expected until the end of January, and the flooding along the Adriatic side of the peninsula that had brought Eighth Army's advance to a standstill. Clark also realized that the snow and ice now blanketing the mountains in front of Fifth Army would make the movement of men, vehicles, and weapons extremely hazardous and difficult.[23]

On December 28 Clark placed Fifth Army on a nine-day alert for resumption of offensive operations in the event the Germans should decide to pull all of their forces out of Italy. Truscott ordered IV Corps to protect the vital supply base at Leghorn "at all costs" and ordered II Corps to hold in its present positions and 13 Corps to continue assisting the adjacent Eighth Army by any means possible. At the end of the year Fifth Army was disposed along a line essentially the same as the one it had occupied on October 26, and over the next two months combat action would consist mainly of "patrol clashes, artillery exchanges, and local attacks by either the Germans or [Allied] troops to improve positions and to test the alertness of the other side."[24]

Shortly after Christmas, Truscott turned to one of the most serious problems confronting him: the state of morale of Fifth Army, particularly within the infantry divisions. During the weeks leading up to Christmas the infantrymen had been busily engaged in preparing for Operation PIANORO and in defending against the German counterattack in the Serchio valley and along the coast. However, with the cessation of those activities and the postponement of any further major offensive actions until spring, the dogfaces who were veterans of the previous winter's campaigns had time to contemplate the prospect of facing "another winter campaign in higher and more rugged mountains under worse conditions of cold, rain, and snow. It was not a pleasing prospect—and was made less palatable because the attention of the world was focused upon the eastern and western fronts in Europe," not the Italian front, the "forgotten front." In some units that had seen long overseas service, many personnel "even held the belief that they had already done their part toward winning the war, and that their places should be taken by others with less overseas service."[25]

The problem was particularly acute in the veteran 34th Infantry Division and had led Keyes to recommend to Truscott that "certain personnel of this division should be withdrawn from combat and returned to the United States if this division is to continue in combat." Truscott personally inspected the 34th Division and concluded that "there was nothing organically wrong, and nothing we could not correct. If the Division was made to feel that only the best was expected of it, as with other divisions, it would not fail us in the test. General Bolté [the division commander] shared these views; his confidence and my own were to be fully justified during the final campaign."[26]

Truscott told Keyes that the problems specific to the 34th Division were due to a lack of discipline and lack of "command responsibility." Other long-serving divisions, such as the 1st, 3d, and 9th Infantry Divisions, had been exposed to similar combat conditions, and the "morale in all these units is excellent to superior." Specifically, he recommended that if there were officers in the division who "had lost their usefulness and their efficiency," General Bolté "should take immediate corrective measures," including referral of such officers to reclassification boards.[27]

Truscott also forwarded Keyes's concerns about the 34th ID to Lt. Gen. Joseph T. McNarney, commanding general of the Mediterranean theater of operations, with a covering letter in which he expressed his belief that there was a need for setting a length of time in combat after which officers and men desiring to do so would be returned to the United States and suggested that the time limit be three years, with the caveat that such a policy would be "determined by the over-all manpower position."[28]

In a lengthy letter dated December 29, McNarney replied to Truscott that based on his familiarity with "the overall personnel situation of the Army and the position of the War Department," he believed "there is little likelihood" that setting a limit of thirty or thirty-six months of overseas service could "possibly be effected." He then went on to point out that the War Department had given each theater a fixed quota of rotations to CONUS, at that time 1,400 rotational places monthly for the Mediterranean theater, of which approximately 450 were for Fifth Army. McNarney assured Truscott that he planned to increase Fifth Army's allotment to 700 or 750, beginning with the February allocation, which Truscott could then suballocate to divisions in any ratio he might determine. He recommended that Truscott address the problem by using the increased rotational quota and his authority to send home on temporary duty "those 34th Division officers and key non-coms whose records are good, but who are causing the most trouble now, and who possibly cannot be re-oriented," but not reassign them to other divisions within Fifth Army. He also encouraged Truscott to utilize officers from the morale services then with Fifth Army to plan "improved orientation programs and publicity for the Fifth Army."[29]

Truscott found the problem of Italy as the "forgotten front" somewhat more difficult to address. He made the situation known to the War Department, hoping that their public relations people would be able to get a more complete picture of the Italian campaign before the public, and enlisted his organic public relations personnel to provide all possible assistance and material to war correspondents assigned to the Mediterranean theater. He also ordered the Fifth Army Public Relations and Historical Section to prepare press releases describing unit actions and identifying within the releases individuals and units when permitted to do so and then mail those releases to newspapers in the hometowns, counties, and states of the involved National Guard units.[30]

Even though the intensity of combat decreased remarkably during the three-month lull, the needs of Fifth Army still had to be addressed. Among the most vital activities was that of supply, not only of the forward combat units but also of those personnel in the rear, for all continued to eat, wear out clothing and equipment, consume fuel and ammunition, and fall victim to disease and injury requiring medical assistance. And even though the troops were defending a currently rather inactive front, there was the need to prepare for the offensive that would resume with the arrival of spring.

Fifth Army supplies from the United States arrived at rear depots by rail and truck from either Naples or Leghorn. From the depots the supplies traveled along Highway 65 some fifty miles to the forward areas of II Corps in the northern Apennines. Once there, jeeps, mules, or the backs of men transported the supplies to the forward elements, since the heavy rains restricted the trucks almost completely to the main roads. Key to keeping the supplies moving were the engineer units, whose men struggled valiantly to keep roads open by constructing bridges, culverts, and revetments to combat the raging rivers and the mud and snow slides brought about by the foul weather. Since the Italian theater had such a low priority for supplies from CONUS, Fifth Army found it necessary to repair and restore to use the damaged and worn-out equipment, particularly trucks. By February the herculean efforts of army personnel had restored supply dumps to desired levels, and repair and salvage activities, supplemented by some resupply from the United States, had eliminated almost completely all shortages of transportation.

As rest centers in Italy grew in size, hundreds of thousands of troops visited them, where they "could sleep in a bed, take baths, visit places of historical interest, and generally indulge in the pleasures and entertainments of civilization, if only for a brief period." At Montecatini an Army-sponsored liquor warehouse grossed an average of three hundred thousand dollars per month.[31]

During the days preceding the Christmas–New Year holiday season the army post offices received and distributed 2,675 pouches and 43,383 sacks of mail. All army units were issued rations of turkey for Christmas and New Year's Day dinners, and even troops living in foxholes and abandoned farm buildings shared in the gastronomic largesse. To enhance even further the Christmas celebrations, the engineers erected atop blustery and snowy Radicosa Pass a forty-foot tree decorated with strings of colored lights and a lighted sign reading "Merry Christmas." On New Year's Day football teams representing Fifth Army and Twelfth Air Force played in the Spaghetti Bowl in the municipal stadium in Florence before a crowd of twenty-five thousand Army and Air Force personnel.

Truscott did not neglect training during the lull. He ordered each major unit of his army out of the line for at least four weeks to receive intensive training in combat tactics and the use of new weapons, as well as refresher training as necessary. Such time away from the front lines also provided an opportunity for the units to assimilate the thousands of replacements that arrived during the lull. Some units were completely reorganized, necessitating extensive training to prepare them for their new duties. As an example, in mid-January personnel from Task Force 45, mainly former antiaircraft personnel and men from other noninfantry units, became the 473d Infantry Regiment, necessitating the implementation of a program to convert those men into infantrymen. To fill the numerous officer vacancies within infantry companies, Fifth Army established local officer candidate schools to commission more infantry officers from the enlisted ranks. That program, and an increase in officer replacements, "allowed the building-up of all understrength units and even the assignment of an overstrength for the next drive."

Fifth Army also received some new units, most notably the 10th Mountain Division, the only division in the U.S. Army organized and trained specifically for mountain and winter warfare, which by January 28 was occupying a position in the rugged but relatively inactive sector of the front previously defended by TF 45. Other reinforcements included field artillery units manning all calibers of guns and howitzers, tank destroyer battalions, the 442d Infantry from the European theater, and the Legnano Group, an Italian unit about two-thirds the size of an American infantry division, one of five Italian units that had been trained and outfitted by the British.[32]

The Eighth Army to the east of Fifth Army had also curtailed its combat activity until spring. By the end of December it had lost one corps headquarters and three divisions, which had been sent to Greece to counter the civil strife raging there. In January the 1st Canadian Corps and its two divisions left Eighth Army to join the other Canadian forces in northwestern Europe. Thus, "there was little the Eighth Army could do but to dig in along the Senio [River] and there await the coming of spring and perhaps better days for the fortunes of Allied arms in Italy."[33]

On January 9, Truscott's fiftieth birthday, he and his staff and aides left the forward CP in the early evening and traveled to his villa in Florence for cocktails and dinner. For the first time since they had been overseas, Truscott and his friends enjoyed a plank steak dinner, following which Truscott opened the presents he had received, the most striking of which was a "beautifully embossed filigreed silver decanter and glasses," a gift from the enlisted personnel of his headquarters.[34]

On February 4 Clark called Truscott and Lt. Gen. Sir R. L. McCreery, Eighth Army commander, to his headquarters, where he informed them that because the Combined Chiefs of Staff had decided to transfer five divisions from Eighth Army to Montgomery's 21st Army Group in northern Europe, Fifth Army would make the main effort in the upcoming spring offensive and that the axis of attack would be west of Highway 65. Eighth Army would relieve Fifth Army on Monte Grando and make as great an effort as possible in the Po valley.

In his reply to Clark on February 7, Truscott indicated his agreement that the initial main effort should be west of Highway 65 to the line Pianoro-Praduro–Monte Mantino, which would form a secure base for further operations. However, since the German defenses west of Highway 64 were much thinner than those west of Highway 65 south of Bologna, Truscott recommended that from the Pianoro line north the main effort should be west of Highway 64 to isolate Bologna from the north and northwest, while a strong holding attack would be made east of the highway. If the operation west of Highway 64 should draw the German defenders to that sector, plans should be sufficiently flexible to permit the main effort to shift to the sector west of Highway 65. Clark replied on the eleventh that he was pleased that Truscott agreed with the general plan that he had outlined but stated forcefully that he could not agree to make the main effort north of the Pianoro line west of Highway 64. However, convinced that his plan offered the greater hope for success, and buoyed by the success of limited-objective attacks in the Monte Belvedere area during late February and early March, Truscott decided to retain that concept in his final plan.[35]

THE DILEMMA OF THE 92D INFANTRY DIVISION

Prior to his assuming command of Fifth Army, Truscott had learned from Devers that Clark had "reported that the [92d] Division was wholly unreliable in combat." Devers, however, believed that the black troops had not yet been given a fair chance to prove themselves and that if given such a chance they would fight well. Truscott agreed with Devers's assessment, basing his belief on his association with the Army's two black cavalry regiments during the inter-war years, when he had come to know "many fine soldiers, . . . men whom I was proud to number among my friends." He was confident that "if this Division was assigned objectives well within its capabilities and was properly instructed it would gain confidence and develop a pride which would insure good results in combat."[36]

Shortly after taking over Fifth Army, Truscott visited the 92d Division and "was favorably impressed with all that [he] saw. Personnel presented a smart appearance. Units were well-equipped, went about their work in a professional manner, and gave every indication of being highly trained." During that visit Truscott discussed with Maj. Gen. Edward M. Almond, the 92d's commander, the employment of his division in a limited-objective attack in the near future, an attack Truscott believed to be well within the capabilities of the division.[37]

To open up Highway 65 and to keep pressure on the enemy, Truscott planned a series of limited-objective attacks in February. The first, code-named FOURTH TERM, was to be carried out by the 92d Division on February 4, with attacks in the mountainous Serchio valley sector and along the coastal plain. The first phase of the operation, a diversionary attack, was a drive up the rugged Serchio valley, followed by the main attack on the coastal sector to secure the Strettoia Hill mass.

On February 4 the first phase began when the 365th Infantry attacked north-ward along a ridge east of the Serchio River, while the attached 366th Infantry advanced west of the river. The attacks initially went well, but as the Italian Fas-cists facing the attackers withdrew, their places were taken by German troops who mounted a counterattack on the night of the seventh, forcing the 365th back almost to its starting point and necessitating the withdrawal of the 366th to safeguard its now-exposed right flank.

On the eighth the main attack began in the coastal sector with the advance of the 370th Infantry toward its objective, the Strettoia Hills. The 371st Infantry was to keep abreast on the right, while on the coastal plain Task Force 1, a tank-infantry team built around a battalion of the 366th Infantry, was to cross the Cinquale Canal about four miles south of Massa. Almost from the beginning the plan began to fall apart, the 371st halting its advance when it encountered an enemy minefield, in the process uncovering the 370th's right flank. However, one battalion of the 370th continued its attack and reached its initial objective, only to meet a German counterattack that drove it back and halted the attack. On the coastal plain TF 1 did succeed in getting some tanks across the canal, but heavy enemy fire, particularly from large-caliber coastal guns located ten miles north at Punta Bianca, halted any advance beyond the canal.[38]

On the ninth Truscott met with assistant division commander Brig. Gen. John E. Wood and his staff to discuss "the problems of employment of Colored troops of the 92 Division and 366th Infantry Regiment." Truscott's observations to date had led him to conclude that the "Colored boys will not stay in position under any sort of fire, nor will their officers get close enough to the front to find out why they won't." He suggested to Wood that he use a "mailed fist" to deal with the problem.[39]

As the attacks faltered, widespread straggling began to plague all engaged units of the division, forcing Almond to call off the operation on the eleventh. From his observations of the performance of the division in those actions as well as in earlier actions in the Serchio valley during Operation WINTERGE-WITTER, Truscott concluded "the troops of the 92d Division could not be utilized in a serious offensive."[40] After the failure of the attacks Truscott reported to Clark that "General Almond's attack was, in my opinion, well planned, well organized, and well supported. The failure is due entirely to the unreliability of infantry units. During the day of the 8th [of February], while I was present, the opposition appeared to be extremely light. There was relatively little artillery, mortar fire was light, and I heard only occasional and light small arms fire." He observed that all other elements of the division had performed their missions satisfactorily: "Artillery support was all that could be asked for. Except for failure to bridge the Cinquale Canal, the Division engineers had performed satisfactorily. Communications had been effective throughout except for some failures in the infantry battalions. All the supply services had functioned smoothly. The Division had been satisfactory in every respect except the one element which justified its existence—the combat infantry."[41]

Hondon B. Hargrove, who served as an artillery officer in the 92d, has raised objections to Truscott's conclusions. He also faults Almond's plan for launching the Serchio valley sector and the coastal attacks simultaneously, "instead of utilizing sufficient forces to first rout the Germans from their mountain defenses, and occupy and hold them. It became evident quickly that as long as the Germans controlled the mountains, it would be *impossible* for our forces to drive them from their coastal positions." Contrary to Truscott's report that the enemy artillery and mortar fire was "relatively light," Hargrove stated that the artillery fire against the attacking forces was very heavy and had a "crushing effect," particularly fire from coastal batteries at Punta Bianca. Hargrove expressed puzzlement that neither Truscott's nor Clark's report mentions such heavy artillery fire.[42]

General Marshall, who was visiting Italy at the time, had also observed the 92d Division's attack and concluded from the division's performance that it was "untrustworthy under fire."[43] Discussing the matter with Clark, Marshall had suggested forming one regiment out of the three existing regiments, forming another from the "AAA [antiaircraft artillery] troops, who had already been converted to infantry," and bringing the 442d Infantry back to Italy as the division's third regiment.[44]

Further reports Truscott received after the 92d's most recent combat led him to conclude that "the fighting capabilities of the Division justified its employment only in a relatively quiet and unimportant defensive sector until more stamina and dependability could be developed. To [his] mind the operation had clearly demonstrated that in spite of excellent and long training, tiptop physical condition, and superior support by artillery and air, the infantry was devoid of the emotional and mental stability necessary for combat. [He] did not believe that further training under the present conditions would make the Division capable of offensive action." He went on to say that "the social and economic system under which [the blacks] had lived and labored had hardly been conducive to the development of pride of race, love of country, the sense of individual responsibility, and qualities of leadership."[45]

On February 17 Truscott met with Generals Clark and Almond to discuss the future plans for the division. They reached a tentative decision to recommend that all the best black personnel of the three regiments, including those who had been decorated, wore the Combat Infantryman Badge, or had won battlefield promotions, be brought together in one regiment, the 370th. The 365th and 371st Regiments would be reassigned to inactive sectors of the front and would be replaced by the 442d Infantry, then with VI Corps, and a new regiment, the 473d, which had just been formed from converted antiaircraft artillery battalions that had made up Task Force 45. The 366th Infantry would be deactivated and the personnel used to form two engineer special service regiments.[46]

Since the 442d was then serving under Eisenhower, Marshall wrote to him to request that he release the regiment for reassignment to Italy, pointing out that even though the 92d had been heavily supported by air and tanks, the infantry "literally dissolved each night abandoning equipment and even clothing in some instances." He went on to say that even though "the artillery, engineers, and other divisional troops appeared excellent, and the command and staff were superior . . . the division itself is not only of little value but weakens the front by necessitating the putting of other divisions in the rear to provide the necessary security against a local German thrust through to Leghorn and supply lines, divisions that should otherwise be disposed in the center of the army."[47]

Eisenhower agreed to release the 442d and ordered the regiment to move to the staging area in Marseilles for shipment to Italy. After its arrival Clark assigned the regiment to Truscott, who attached it to IV Corps under the operational control of the 92d Division.[48] 15th Army Group ordered Almond to prepare his reorganized division for a diversionary limited-objective attack four days before Fifth Army's main attack toward Bologna.[49]

I do not believe that Truscott's comments about the unreliability of the black infantry elements of the 92d ID reflected personal racial bias. As a five- or six-year-old he had developed a close relationship and friendship with a young black man, Will Coleman, who lived in the Truscott home in Chatfield and who served as a driver for Truscott's father, taking him on house calls and running errands in the horse and buggy, often accompanied and assisted by young Lucian. During his service as a cavalryman in the interwar years he had frequent contact with the black cavalrymen of the 9th and 10th Cavalry Regiments, the famed "Buffalo soldiers," many of whom he held in high regard. He went on to say that he had associated closely with black people since childhood and "liked them, believed in them, and sympathized with their problems." In the 92d Division he had found "many brave and competent colored officers," and had "decorated some and commissioned or promoted others who were worthy members of the fraternity of gallant soldiers and who would have been a credit to any organization." He firmly believed that the shortcomings of the black soldiers in combat "were the product of heredity, environment, education, economic and social ills beyond their control—and beyond the sphere of military leaders."[50]

However, the 92d's commander, General Almond, did not share Truscott's attitude toward black soldiers and attributed his division's unsatisfactory performance in combat to "the undependability of the average Negro soldier to operate to his maximum capability, compared to his lassitude toward his performing a task assigned. . . . [T]he general tendency of the Negro soldier is to avoid as much as possible." How could Almond's superiors, in an army that holds preeminent the precept that "a commander is personally responsible for everything that his unit does or fails to do," not hold him responsible for his division's failure, permit him to lay the blame for his division's failure on the shoulders of the men he trained and led, yet retain him as division commander? The failure of Truscott, Clark, and Marshall to hold Almond rather than the men whom he commanded responsible for the division's failure, and allowing him to remain in command of the 92d ID, stands, I believe, as a testimony to "the racial mindset of [Almond's] superiors both in and out of the military."[51] Although Truscott himself was, I believe, devoid of personal racial bias, he had accepted that "racial mindset," and concurred in the decision to retain Almond as the 92d ID commander.

Highway 64 followed roughly the northeastern course of the Reno River to Bologna and for roughly eight miles lay in defilade of an enemy-held ridge to the west that extended northeastward from Monte Belvedere to just southwest of Vergato, which would have to be cleared of the enemy before Highway 64 could be utilized in the advance to Bologna. Clark had ordered two earlier efforts to seize the mountain, but both had failed. That mission would now fall to the 10th Mountain Division. Truscott planned for Maj. Gen. George P. Hays's division to conduct its attack in two phases: In the first phase the division was to capture the mountain complex of Belvedere, Gorgolesco, della Torraccia, and Castello. If successful, and if German resistance was not too great, the 10th, assisted by the Brazilian Expeditionary Force, was then to clear the rest of the ridge as far north as Vergato.[52]

After receiving orders from Truscott to capture the mountains in the south, Hays carried out a careful study of the terrain before him and concluded that previous attempts to seize and hold Monte Belvedere had failed not only because the mountain itself was heavily defended but also because the Germans controlled a higher ridge of mountains to the west and southwest, which came to be known as Riva Ridge. Only by occupying that ridge did Hays believe that his mountaineers could capture and hold Belvedere. Concluding that the Germans would not expect an assault up the nearly perpendicular eastern slope of the ridge, Hays assigned that mission to his 86th Infantry. To further confuse the enemy, Hays ordered his men to make the climb at night without benefit of preparatory artillery fire or aerial bombardment. Over the next weeks 86th Infantry patrols established five routes up the ridge and emplaced climbing ropes along some of them. Members of the regiment also received intensive rock-climbing and marksmanship training. The climb was scheduled for the night of February 18.[53]

As darkness set in that night, teams of climbers assembled at the base of Riva Ridge and began their climb in subzero temperatures. Ascending in almost complete silence they reached the summit, completely surprising the German defenders. By daybreak Riva Ridge was in American hands, without the loss of a single life. With the 86th controlling the ridge, its sister regiments, the 85th and 87th, attacked Belvedere and Monte Gorgolesco to its north. Hays had ordered that again there would be no artillery bombardment prior to the night attack and that the men were not to fire their weapons during the assault, relying only on grenades and bayonets. The operation began just before midnight on the nineteenth, and by daylight a battalion of the 85th Regiment was on the summit of Belvedere.[54]

The attack continued northward against stiff enemy resistance. By the twenty-fifth Belvedere was securely in American hands, as was Monte della Torraccia, and the Brazilians to the right of the 10th Mountain had secured Monte Castello. The ski troopers and the Brazilians continued their attacks and by

March 5 had cleared the area from Monte Grande d'Aiano to Castelnuovo. The attacks had pushed the right flank of IV Corps almost abreast of II Corps's left flank, and since it would be more than a month before the main attack toward Bologna would begin, Truscott decided to halt further advances and ordered consolidation of the line, providing an excellent line of departure for the coming attack.[55]

On January 18 Clark had ordered that 3 Corps be returned to the operational control of Eighth Army, shortening the Fifth Army front to fewer than one hundred miles. The IV Corps sector, extending from the Ligurian Sea to the Reno River, was held by the 92d, 10th Mountain, and 1st Brazilian Divisions; II Corps had the 1st Armored and the 34th and 91st Infantry Divisions, as well as the Legnano Group, holding the sector from the Reno River to Monte Grande. The 88th Infantry Division was in II Corps reserve, and the 6th South African Armored Division (Reinforced) and the 85th Infantry Division constituted army reserve. To the east the British Eighth Army had advanced up the Po valley to the Senio River, roughly twenty miles southeast of Bologna, its line extending northeast along the Adriatic coast to the southern end of Lake Comacchio. Transfer of some of its troops to Greece and to the Netherlands had reduced army strength to seven infantry divisions, one armored division, and three Italian combat groups. Opposing the two armies were twenty-four German divisions and five Italian Fascist divisions. Of those, eight German divisions faced Fifth Army. In addition, two German divisions in reserve south of the Po River could move to the Fifth Army front if ordered to do so.

As they prepared for the final offensive in Italy both Allied armies were rested. The Fifth Army was some seven thousand officers and men overstrength, and "ammunition dumps bulged with huge quantities of explosives. Food, equipment, and supplies of all types were stocked behind the front. After more than five months of relative inactivity Fifth Army was ready for whatever action the spring of 1945 might bring."[56]

Chapter 12

THE FINAL OFFENSIVE

General Clark envisioned a three-phase attack by Fifth and Eighth Armies, which would advance into the Po valley and drive north across the Po River to the Brenner Pass. In phase one Eighth Army was to cross the Santerno River and Fifth Army was to debouch into the Po valley and capture Bologna. In phase two "either or both Armies were to break through German offenses and surround the Germans south of the Po River." In the last phase, both armies were to cross the Po River, advance to the north, capture Verona, and develop the Adige River positions extending northward and southeastward from Verona. Although the plan provided for three distinct phases, Clark hoped that the attack, scheduled to begin in the British sector on April 9, would proceed seamlessly, with no halts between phases. Four days before the kickoff, the reorganized 92d Infantry Division was to carry out a diversionary attack in the coastal sector to seize Massa and the small port of La Spezia to the northwest. Clark and Truscott hoped that the 92d's attack would prevent the enemy from moving any troops from that sector to other areas along the front.[1]

On April 9 the Eighth Army, with the support of the entire Allied Air Forces strength in Italy, was to cross the Senio and Santerno Rivers, attack toward Bastia and Budrio, and then, if conditions permitted, develop toward Ferrara. On the twelfth Fifth Army was to attack into the Po Valley along the axis of Highway 64 and continue on toward Bologna. Prior to the army's main attack the IV Corps, composed of the 10th Mountain, 1st Armored, and 1st Brazilian Divisions, would attack northeast along a ridge west of Highway 64 to the Green line, which would place it abreast of the 6th South African Armored Division on the left flank of II Corps.[2] When IV Corps reached the Green line, II Corps, with its 6th South African Armored and American 88th, 91st, and 34th Infantry Divisions, would join it in the main attack, the two corps advancing abreast

232

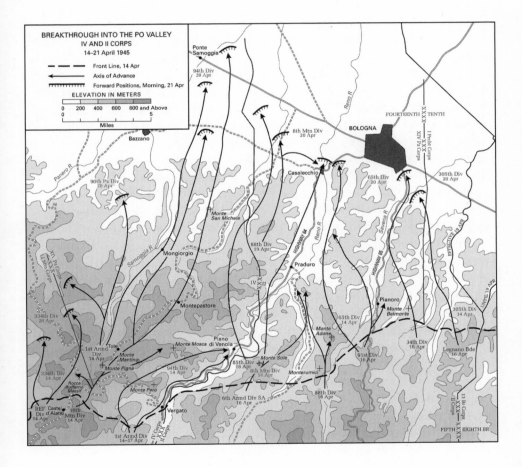

BREAKTHROUGH INTO THE PO VALLEY
IV AND II CORPS
14–21 April 1945

- - - - - Front Line, 14 Apr
◄───── Axis of Advance
⊥⊥⊥⊥⊥⊥ Forward Positions, Morning, 21 Apr

ELEVATION IN METERS

| 0 | 200 | 400 | 600 | 800 and Above |

0   5
Miles

Ponte
Samoggia

94th Div
20 Apr

8th Mtn Div
20 Apr

BOLOGNA

FOURTEENTH   TENTH
I Para Corps
XIV Pz Corps

Reno R.

Bazzano

90th Pz Div
20 Apr

Casalecchio

65th Div
20 Apr

305th Div
20 Apr

Panaro R.

Monte
San Michele

Mongiorgio

88th Div
19 Apr

Samoggia R.

Setta R.

HIGHWAY 64

Reno R.

Praduro

HIGHWAY 65

Pianoro

Monte
Belmonte

305th Div
14 Apr

Montepastore

IV XXII

Monte
Adone

65th Div
14 Apr

334th Div
20 Apr

Piano
Monte Mosca di Venola

Monte Sole

Monte
Manting

Monterumici

91st Div
16 Apr

34th Div
16 Apr

Legnano Bde
16 Apr

1st Armd
Div
18 Apr

Tole

85th Div
18 Apr

8th Mtn Div
14 Apr

334th Div
14 Apr

Monte Pigna

94th Div
14 Apr

Monte Pero

Rocca
Roffeno
Massif

BEF
Div d'Aiano
14 Apr

Castel

88th Div
16 Apr

13 Br Corps
II Corps

10th
Mtn Div
14 Apr

Vergato

6th Armd Div SA
16 Apr

FIFTH   EIGHTH BR

1st Armd Div
14–17 Apr

IV Corps
II Corps

"generally astride of Highway 64, to overrun the line of the Panaro [River] and capture or isolate Bologna." The 85th Infantry Division would serve initially as army reserve but would move on D-day to Vergato to relieve the 1st Armored Division, which, along with the 6th Armored Division, Truscott would employ along any route west of Highway 64 to push into the Po valley to seize the Panaro River line. Clark charged both corps with the mission of capturing that line and then sending out mobile forces to seize crossing sites along the formidable Po River. II Corps had the additional mission of capturing or isolating Bologna and linking up with Eighth Army to the east, while IV Corps protected Fifth Army's left flank.[3]

A vital measure to ensure success of the upcoming attack was implementation of the tactical air support plan that Truscott and Carleton had developed over a two-year period with Brig. Gen. Thomas R. Darcy, commander of XXII Tactical Air Command. The system included a forward air observer, an Air Force pilot, known as "Rover Joe," who was positioned with the forward ground elements and was in radio contact with overhead aircraft and the airfields, and in telephone contact with artillery CPs and the G3 section of the supported command. As supporting aircraft entered an area the lead pilot of the group would contact Rover Joe, who would then assign to the aircraft the appropriate support missions requested by the ground troops.

Truscott and Carleton soon recognized that they could very effectively supplement the forward air controller or provide air support for units without a forward observer by using an overhead observer, "Horsefly," an L-5 reconnaissance aircraft flown by an Air Force pilot who could talk both with a forward observer and with the planes in the area. With him in the plane was a field artillery observer who was able to talk to leading ground elements and to forward artillery observers. Horsefly could direct pilots not only to assigned targets but also to targets of opportunity. The system had proved its worth during the Anzio breakout, and Truscott and Carleton were convinced that it would be a valuable asset during the upcoming attack. General Darcy became a firm supporter of "Rover Joe–Horsefly," and to enhance the rapidity of air support response to maneuver elements he moved his forward CP to Traversa in Futa Pass, adjacent to Truscott's forward CP.[4]

The air support for the attack of the 92d Division was to consist of roughly 160 fighter-bomber sorties on April 5 and 6, with medium bombers concentrating on the coastal batteries in the vicinity of La Spezia. On April 9 and 10 the support would shift to the Eighth Army front as the British attacked across the Senio River. The maximum support would then shift to the Fifth Army sector as its attack got under way. During the first two days IV Corps would have priority of support from tactical fighter-bombers, while heavier bombers concentrated their efforts in front of II Corps.[5]

THE 92D'S DIVERSIONARY ATTACK

The attack in the coastal sector by Almond's 92d Infantry Division was scheduled to begin the morning of April 5. Almond planned to attack with the 442d and 370th Infantry Regiments abreast, the 442d in the mountains overlooking the coastal plain and the 370th on the left in the lower hills along the plain's edge. The attack began promptly that morning, and by nightfall the 442d had taken Monte Fragolito and was nearing the high ground overlooking Massa. The 370th advanced well at first, pushing out about two miles, before withdrawing "in some disorder" in the face of German counterattacks.

The next morning Truscott visited the front, where he found the 442d continuing its advance in very difficult terrain. However, the large number of stragglers in the 370th's sector had reduced the strength of the lead battalion to fewer than one hundred men, preventing the regiment from continuing its attack. He therefore authorized Almond to employ in the coastal sector the 473d, which had been in reserve in the Serchio valley, replacing it in the Serchio valley with the 370th and the 365th Infantry Regiments. By the seventh the 442d had captured the heights above Massa, and the following day the 473d had advanced "through mine fields and pillboxes to the outskirts of Massa," which fell on the tenth. The two regiments continued their advance the next day against stiffening German resistance, capturing Carrara on April 11.[6]

As the major Fifth Army advance began on the fourteenth, the 442d advanced in the direction of Aulla, while the 473d pushed on toward La Spezia, where it soon came under fire from the large coastal guns at Punta Bianca. The enemy fire delayed the advance of the regiment until noon of the twentieth, when the guns suddenly fell silent, allowing the 473d to continue toward La Spezia, which it entered on the twenty-fourth. The newly minted infantrymen soon learned the reason for the cessation of fire: Italian partisan forces had seized the Punta Bianca peninsula from its tip to as far north as Ameglia, where a party of artillery observers from the 473d joined them, set up an observation post overlooking the guns, and directed artillery fire onto the batteries, finally silencing them.[7]

At that point Almond was unsure whether he was to continue on Highway 1 to Genoa or proceed northeast up Highway 63 toward Verona. It so happened that General Brann, Clark's G3, was visiting him at that time, and Almond asked his advice. Brann immediately contacted Clark, who authorized Almond to send the 473d, reorganized into a regimental combat team, toward Genoa. Gruenther, Clark's chief of staff, later called Carleton to inform him of Clark's decision, acknowledging that Clark had not gone through normal command channels in ordering Almond to advance to Genoa. The RCT entered Genoa against disorganized resistance on April 27, took Alessandria the next day, and linked up with French forces on the Franco-Italian border on April 30.[8]

The 442d Infantry, meanwhile, had continued its attack toward Aulla, which controlled the only escape route into the Po valley for Germans withdrawing from the coastal sector. The regiment moved out on the fourteenth and, after advancing over numerous prominent mountain peaks, entered Aulla on April 24, where it was joined by elements of the 370th Infantry, which had been advancing inland of the 442d.[9] Almond then directed the 442d to follow the 473d RCT as quickly as possible toward Genoa, while protecting the division's northeast flank in its zone of advance, and the 370th to attack northward up Highways 62 and 63 to the Cisa and Ceretta passes, the exits from the coastal plain to the Po valley. Truscott later recorded his evaluation of the 92d Division's performance in its advance through the coastal sector: "As a diversionary measure it was wholly successful, the success being due to the courage, endurance, and heroism of these two regiments [the 442d and 473d]. As a test of the fighting ability of colored infantry units, the operation had merely confirmed our previous experience."[10]

THE MAIN ATTACK

In late March the Allies learned from ULTRA that Hitler had ordered the I Parachute Corps, defending Bologna, to dispatch six thousand men to Holland, which amounted to one-quarter of Vietinghoff's infantry units that had been defending the city. Later that month ULTRA revealed that the 29th Panzer Grenadier Division, which had been in position behind Bologna, had been replaced and had moved northward into Tenth Army reserve near the Po River crossing site at Ostiglia. On April 5 additional intercepts disclosed that Vietinghoff had transferred the 90th Panzer Grenadier Division to LI Corps under Fourteenth Army in the west near Modena. "Before the offensive opened on 9 April, all this information was in the hands of Alexander, Clark, McCreery, and Truscott, who could thus begin what was intended to be their final operation in the comfortable certainty that two of the enemy's strongest divisions were far away from the places where he would need them most."[11]

The afternoon of April 9, McCreery's Eighth Army opened the main attack from its positions along the Adriatic coast. The leading elements quickly crossed the Senio River line and drove toward Argenta and Bologna. Although the network of rivers and canals in Eighth Army's sector slowed the advance, by the eleventh it had breached both the Senio and the Santerno River lines and had trapped Bastia within a pincers. Two days later the British crossed the Sillaro.[12]

Truscott's Fifth Army had planned to attack northward at 8:00 a.m. on April 12, but heavy fog grounded all aircraft, forcing Truscott to postpone the attack for twenty-four hours. However, the weather conditions on the thirteenth were identical, necessitating an additional postponement. Early on the morning of April 14, as Truscott, Carleton, Darcy, and Wilson sat in the CP, successive telephone

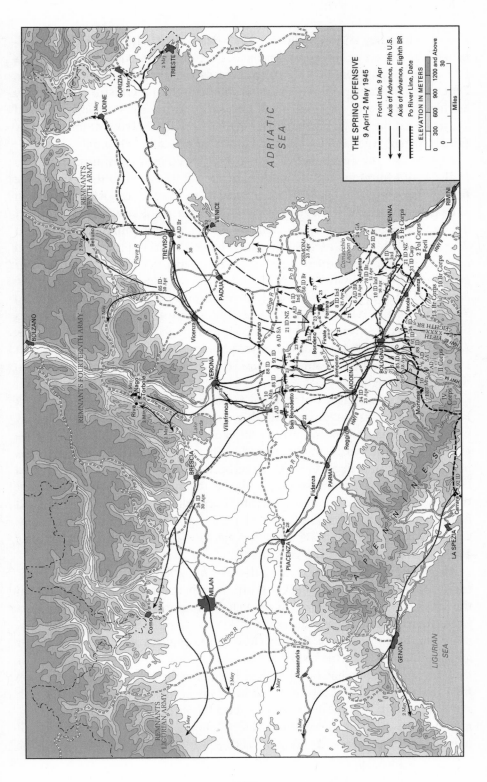

THE SPRING OFFENSIVE
9 April–2 May 1945

Front Line, 9 Apr
Axis of Advance, Fifth U.S.
Axis of Advance, Eighth BR
Po River Line, Date

ELEVATION IN METERS
0   300 600   900 1200 and Above

Miles
0   10   20   30

messages came in, announcing that all air bases were fogged in. Truscott contacted Crittenberger and gave him the bad news but ordered him to hold his IV Corps troops in an alert status to be ready to attack on one hour's notice. Darcy then began periodic checks of weather conditions at his air bases, finally learning that the fog was clearing at Grossetto, and just before 9:00 a.m. told Truscott that the planes had begun taking off from there. Truscott immediately called Crittenberger and told him to launch his attack at 9:00 a.m.[13]

At 8:30 a.m. the bombers from Grossetto passed over the waiting dogfaces of the 10th Mountain and the tankers of the 1st Armored to their right. The field artillery began its deadly fire at 9:10, blasting the enemy positions that had already been battered from above, driving the enemy soldiers deeper into their defensive positions as they awaited the expected armor-infantry assault. At 9:35 the 10th Mountain Division crossed its LOD, two regiments abreast, and attacked along a string of rugged mountains between the Reno and Samoggia Rivers, covered by the overhead tactical aircraft guided to their targets by Rover Joe and Horsefly. Enemy resistance was stubborn, but the men kept up a steady advance despite mounting casualties. By midnight the division was on its initial objective, and by the following night was beyond the Green line. At 4:45 p.m. the 1st AD attacked toward Suzzano, which it captured the next morning. Continuing its attack northward, the division captured Monte Pero the following night.[14]

Later that evening Truscott relayed to Sarah his thoughts about the attack Fifth Army had just begun, stating, "If we can crush this force, the shock may bring the German people to full realization of the hopelessness of further struggle and bring the war to an abrupt end." When the war did end, Truscott told her, he would most likely be assigned to occupation duties in Europe but said that he would prefer to be assigned to the Pacific theater; he doubted, however, that he would get such an assignment. He concluded the letter with the sad news that General Crittenberger's son had been killed in action in Germany. Cpl. Townsend Woodhull Crittenberger, age nineteen, was killed on March 25, 1945, during the Rhine River crossing.[15]

After the 10th Mountain crossed the Green line and the 1st Armored captured Monte Pero, II Corps began its attack early the morning of April 16. On the left the 6th South African Armored Division captured their first-day objectives, the mountains Sole, Caprara, and Abelle, despite stubborn enemy resistance and heavy casualties, thereby clearing the angle between the Reno River and Setta Creek. Truscott visited Keyes and each of his division commanders that day and found that progress had been slow because of the heavy German resistance and that all gains had been small. Reports on the seventeenth showed the 10th Mountain was well beyond the Brown line and the main German defenses and was still moving toward Bologna. II Corps, however, was still meeting heavy resistance. By noon the 10th was attacking its objectives along the

Black line, and the 1st Armored had reached Monte D'Avigo, well beyond the Brown line.

Truscott realized that west of the Samoggia the enemy was resisting stubbornly but that German resistance between the Reno and Samoggia Rivers was disorganized. Because of the limited infantry strength in the 1st Armored, the slow progress of II Corps, and his desire to employ the armor in the Samoggia valley to assist the 10th Mountain, Truscott decided to move the 85th Infantry Division into the line to replace the 1st Armored and ordered one of the division's combat commands to move westward across the rear of the 10th Mountain and advance through the Samoggia valley on the 10th's left flank. The 85th Division, now under IV Corps control, was to advance northward west of the Reno River on the 10th Mountain's right. He also placed Crittenberger in control of all operations west of Highway 64.

The II Corps, however, still advanced very slowly because of the stubborn resistance the Germans were mounting. On the morning of the eighteenth Keyes and his G3 visited Truscott in his CP, where Keyes, noting that IV Corps to his west was making satisfactory progress, proposed moving the 88th Infantry Division, which had just captured Monte Monterumici, to the west and sending it north along the east bank of the Reno River, a proposal that Truscott immediately accepted. Then, accompanied by General McNarney, who had spent the previous night at Truscott's CP, he flew to the IV Corps CP, where they learned that the 10th Mountain and the 85th ID were both making good progress. They next visited the 85th's CP, and then went on to visit General Hays, who informed them that his division was well on its way to Monte Moscoso. On their way back to Crittenberger's CP they encountered Maj. Gen. Vernon E. Prichard, commander of the 1st AD, who told them that his combat command had begun fighting in the Samoggia valley. At the IV Corps CP they learned that aerial reconnaissance reports revealed that enemy forces in front of II Corps were beginning to withdraw as a result of the advances made to the west by IV Corps.

As McNarney prepared to return to Caserta, he asked Truscott when he expected to reach Highway 9 in the Po valley, to which Truscott replied that he expected to have elements across the highway by one o'clock on the twentieth. McNarney proposed a wager of a quart of Scotch that Fifth Army would not meet that timetable. As it turned out, Truscott lost the bet by about an hour and forwarded the whiskey to McNarney, who promptly returned it for Truscott to give to the first soldier who had crossed the highway. Although he did not expect that General Hays would be able to learn the identity of the soldier who had led the way, Truscott sent the bottle on to the division and was surprised to learn that Hays had indeed been able to locate that man and sent a photograph of the "awards ceremony" when he received the bottle of Scotch from Hays.

On April 20, Truscott spent most of the day in the IV Corps sector, monitoring the advances of the corps' units by ground and air reconnaissance, and confirmed that all three of Crittenberger's divisions were out of the Apennines and across Highway 9. He then ordered the 85th Division to move eastward across the sectors of the 88th and South African Divisions to capture Castellichio, a vital road center, hoping to cut the route of withdrawal for Germans in front of II Corps. Early on the morning of the twenty-first Bologna fell, as advancing tanks and infantrymen of the 133d Infantry of the veteran 34th ID and elements of the 91st Division entered the city via Highway 65. Joining in the liberation of the joyous citizens of Bologna were elements of Eighth Army's Polish Corps that were advancing along Highway 9. The rest of the 91st Division moved north beyond Bologna on the heels of the German forces rapidly retreating toward the Po River.[16]

All along the Fifth Army front the enemy was hurrying north in a desperate attempt to escape the onrushing tide of the two Allied armies. On the day Bologna fell the 10th Mountain crossed the Panaro River east of Modena and continued driving toward the Po, as did the 85th, 88th, and 91st Infantry Divisions and the 1st Armored and 6th South African Armored Divisions. The evening of the twenty-second a task force of the 10th reached San Benedetto Po on the Po River, and the next morning crossed the river under heavy German artillery fire, which Allied bombing eventually suppressed. The men of the 10th quickly established a strong beachhead on the northern shore, so swiftly in fact that some six hundred enemy soldiers, including a corps commander, were captured before they could withdraw. The division engineers rapidly threw bridges across the river, and soon guns, tanks, and other vehicles were racing across to continue the advance to the north. The 85th, 88th, and 91st Infantry Divisions and the South African Armored Division reached the river east of the 10th Mountain's crossing site the next day. The American divisions crossed that same day, to be followed the next day by the South Africans.

Meanwhile, the 34th ID, which had been retained in Bologna for mopping-up operations, was assigned to IV Corps and joined elements of the 1st Armored in the attack northwest along the axis of Highway 9. Elements of at least three German divisions and one Italian Fascist division resisted that advance stubbornly until the twenty-fifth, when the 34th crossed the rear of the German forces, cutting the path of retreat for the enemy troops on the Parma-Piacenza line and blocking the escape routes for all enemy forces withdrawing northward toward the Alps in that sector. The 34th then continued its advance to the northwest and captured Piacenza on the twenty-eighth.

Although Milan was near and was a desirable objective, Truscott rejected it as the next objective for the 34th, and instead ordered it to join the main body of the 1st Armored in its northward drive from the Modena area to block the escape routes for the Germans fleeing northward from northwestern Italy. The night of April 25 the 1st Armored crossed the Po, and the next day its leading elements were in Montechiari; by nightfall some of the division units were fighting German SS forces on the outskirts of Brescia.

The Brazilian Expeditionary Force broke out from the mountains into the valley on April 23 and turned to the west, advancing between Highway 9 and the Apennines, blocking German forces attempting to withdraw from the south. Action for the Brazilians ended on the twenty-ninth, when their commander, Maj. Gen. J. B. Mascarhenas de Morales, accepted the surrender of the 148th Panzer Grenadier and the Italian Bersaglieri Divisions. They then pushed on west to the Alessandria area, where they made contact with the 92d Division, which had just liberated Genoa.[17]

To the east the 88th and 85th Infantry Divisions, after crossing the Po, engaged in a heated race northward to Verona, the 88th arriving there in sixteen hours, besting the 85th on its right. From Verona the 88th advanced northeast to Vicenza and then moved northward into the Alps along the Brenta River before swinging westward toward Trento. From Verona the 85th Division attacked northeastward into the Alps toward Belluno. After crossing the Po to the right of the 88th and 85th Divisions, the 91st Infantry Division began a wide sweep to the northeast toward Treviso, where it linked up with the Eighth Army's 6th Armored Division five days later. As Fifth Army units were driving northward beyond the Po, Truscott exulted to his wife, "We took Bologna in seven days—reached the Po the next and now I have three divisions across and will have others tomorrow—and be hard after the fleeing remnants," and concluded that "German power in Italy is broken."[18]

After the 10th Mountain Division reached the northern bank of the Po, Truscott arrived at Hays's CP in an L-5 piloted by General Darcy, who, unfortunately, "cracked up the Cub, landing in a small wheatfield." Fortunately, neither Darcy nor Truscott was injured. They had just completed a P-51 reconnaissance mission over the front, including the San Benedetto crossing site, where Darcy had carried out several strafing attacks against enemy troops. At the CP they met Gen. Henry Arnold, chief of the U.S. Army Air Forces, who was accompanied on his trip to the Italian theater by Truscott's old friend Col. William Darby, who was assigned to the War Department's Operations Division. Truscott learned from Hays that his assistant division commander, Brig. Gen. Robinson Duff, had been badly wounded during the division's advance to the Po, and Hays asked if he could have Darby, who had been seeking another combat command, assigned as Duff's replacement. Truscott agreed to ask Clark and McNarney to request that the War Department release Darby for assignment to the 10th Mountain, to which the War Department agreed.[19]

Hays's orders directed that his division block the Brenner Pass, and as he studied his maps Hays saw that there were two possible routes of attack for his division: up Highway 12 paralleling the Adige River or northward along the east shore of Lake Garda. He chose the lake route, believing that his division could make faster progress along that route.[20] Led by Task Force Darby, the division advanced rapidly but cautiously over the next several days along roads sporadically shelled by enemy artillery and littered with German dead and destroyed enemy vehicles abandoned by the fleeing Germans seeking sanctuary in the Alps. At last the forward elements reached the shores of Lake Garda, where the XIV Panzer Corps, commanded by Generalleutnant Fridolin von Senger und Etterlin, had established its final redoubt. The regional center of Senger und Etterlin's corps lay along the north shore of the lake in the towns of Riva and Torbole, both protected by high mountain walls. Senger und Etterlin had established his headquarters in the home of Count Frederigotti in Pamorolo, some eight miles east of Torbole.

On the twenty-sixth, after the entire division had arrived at the lake, Hays announced his plan for the final attack two days later: the entire division would advance rapidly along the eastern shore of the lake, "one regiment up front marching hard for eight hours while the other two regiments rested. At the end of each shift, a rested regiment would move to the front in transport trucks." Using this shuttle system Hays estimated that the entire division could cover the sixty-mile distance of the shoreline in twenty-four hours.[21]

The road along the eastern shore of the lake was pinched closely by the shoreline of the lake to the west and by a high escarpment to the east. In numerous places the escarpment was so close to the lake that tunnels for the road had been blasted out of the rocky cliffs. As the advancing mountain soldiers approached the first tunnel the Germans blasted the entrance shut, halting the advance. Immediately, enemy 88mm guns mounted on railroad cars on the lake's west shore began blasting away at the rock cliffs above the Americans. The Americans now had three options: wait for the division engineers to arrive to clear the entrance, climb overland across the spine of the escarpment to Torbole, or skirt the blown tunnel in amphibious vehicles. Hays excluded the first option because it would delay the advance considerably and rejected the second option because his men lacked the necessary climbing equipment. Since a convoy of DUKWs that had been used for some of the Po River crossings was close behind the division, Hays chose the third option.[22]

The DUKW convoy came forward to the village of Malcèsine, just south of the tunnel, where the troops boarded. The DUKWs entered the water and headed north, debarking their passengers between tunnels two and three with no casualties. Tunnel three was undamaged, and the troops advanced through the tunnel and reached the mouth of tunnel four by nightfall. Meanwhile, some of the DUKWs continued to ferry additional troops of the division around tunnel one, while others carried troopers to the opposite shore, landing them at Gargnano, the site of Mussolini's villa, where they hoped to capture some high Fascist officials, possibly even Mussolini himself. Finding that all had fled, the mountain soldiers secured the villa and drove north toward Riva. But before leaving the villa the troopers took possession of an ornate sword that Mussolini had received on the tenth anniversary of the founding of the Italian Fascist state. General Hays later presented the sword to Truscott.

As Hays expected, the amphibious outflanking on the eastern shore had forced the Germans to withdraw, but as they did so they continued destroying tunnels, which required further flanking maneuvers. Eventually, the men of the 10th Mountain reached the fifth and last tunnel, where the German resistance strengthened and guns from Riva began firing. One round landed just inside the tunnel exit, killing or wounding fifty-four soldiers and forcing one last amphibious flanking maneuver. On the afternoon of the twenty-eighth the troopers entered Torbole and shortly after linked up with the force that had moved up the west shoreline.

However, for the troops in Torbole the battle had not ended. The Germans drove the Americans out of the town with heavy fire from tanks and self-propelled artillery, not once but twice. Hays, not wanting to incur heavy casualties with the end of the war clearly near, ordered that his men launch no new attacks into the town until he had received assurance from his regimental and battalion commanders that they could hold the town with no appreciable risk to their men.

While holding his men outside the town for the rest of the day, Colonel Darby met with the commander of the 86th Mountain Infantry, Lt. Col. Robert L. Cook, at his CP in a hotel in the north of Torbole to discuss plans for the coming day. After the meeting Darby left the hotel, planning to travel by jeep to visit one of the tunnels. As he was getting into the vehicle, a single artillery round struck the side of the hotel. Shrapnel from the blast instantly killed one enlisted man and mortally wounded Darby, striking him in the heart. Cook and another officer received less serious wounds. The stubborn defense of Torbole and the killing of Darby marked the end of the fighting. By nightfall of the thirtieth all German defenders were fleeing toward Bolzano, Trento, and the Alpine border.[23]

On the Adriatic side of the peninsula the British Eighth Army had also experienced one success after another. Two of McCreery's divisions crossed the Adige River, meeting no resistance, and on the twenty-ninth the 56th Division entered Venice and the 2d New Zealand Division captured Padua. The latter division then moved rapidly onward toward Trieste, linking up with Yugoslav partisans seventeen miles north of the city on May 1. The next day the Kiwis entered the city and accepted the surrender of the German garrison. McCreery also sent the British 6th Armored Division in two columns into the Dolomites, one toward Udine and the other toward Belluno.[24]

On April 30 Truscott met with Clark in Florence, where he learned that the German forces in Italy were to surrender at noon on May 2 but that until then

Fifth Army was to continue its advance. When hostilities ceased at the agreed-upon time, all units would halt in place. Surrender negotiations between Field Marshal Alexander and Lt. Col. Viktor von Schweinitz and Maj. Max Wenner, plenipotentiaries for General von Vietinghoff, who had succeeded Kesselring as commander of Army Group C when the latter was transferred to the western front, and Gen. Karl Wolff, the highest-ranking SS officer in Italy, had begun in Caserta on April 28 and resulted in the signing of the surrender documents the following day at two o'clock.[25]

Clark learned from an intercepted German message on May 2 that all enemy troops had been ordered to lay down their weapons at two o'clock that day, thus ending the war in Italy, and informed Truscott and McCreery that "Allied forces of the 15th Army Group will cease firing forthwith except in event of an overt hostile act by the enemy." In its 601 days of combat since landing at Salerno on September 9, 1943, Fifth Army had suffered 188,746 casualties, including 31,886 dead.[26]

On the last day of combat for his Fifth Army, Truscott remained in his CP south of Verona until the surrender became official, after which he and Wilson flew to the II Corps CP at Bassano. There Truscott told Keyes of the German surrender and, hoping to avoid further bloodshed, gave him orders to hold his corps in place that day "to allow the German command in the area east of Lake Garda and in the Piave and Brenta valleys ample time to get word of the cease-fire to all units" before having his corps move into German-occupied areas. After returning to his CP, Truscott joined his staff and Mike Chinigo, who had arrived that day from Rome, in toasting the victory with "a few magnums of champagne." When the troops and others in the Verona area received the good news, they joined their general in the celebration with "a great deal of noise, fireworks and so on." The net result of the celebrations was a "very late dinner and bed."[27]

The following day, continuing a letter he had started on the second, Truscott told Sarah that "we are all glad of course that the Italian campaign has finally paid off in a big way. Seems quite appropriate since it was for so long the 'forgotten front.'" He went on to point out that his army had "encircled one [German] army completely and almost completely destroyed the other," stating, "With all modesty I can tell you that while the Eighth Army has fought well, the Fifth Army has actually been the spearhead. The divisions have performed brilliantly." He also told Sarah that his Fifth Army headquarters at the moment was scheduled to become the occupation headquarters in Vienna but doubted that it would come to pass, pointing out that his army was going to be "extremely busy administering nearly a million PWs [prisoners of war], engaging in redeployment." Because of those anticipated duties Truscott recommended to McNarney that Fifth Army remain in Italy and that he assign Clark's Fifteenth Army Group, for which there was no further need in Italy, as the occupation headquarters in Vienna, to which McNarney agreed on May 6. The following day a greatly pleased Mark Clark telephoned Truscott to tell him the good news, not knowing that Truscott had played any role in McNarney's decision.[28]

On May 3 the representatives of General von Vietinghoff, including Generalleutnant Ernst Schlemmer, the commander of XIV Panzer Corps, arrived at the American lines north of Lake Garda, where General Hays and a party from the 10th Mountain Division met them and escorted them to Truscott's CP in an olive grove south of Verona. They stayed there overnight before going on to Clark's headquarters in Florence. That afternoon Clark requested that Truscott and Carleton, as well as General McCreery and his chief of staff, join him in Florence to witness the formal surrender ceremony. At the ceremony Truscott soon recognized that Clark's remarks and Schlemmer's reply had been prepared in advance and that the only purpose of the staged meeting "was a photographic record in the best Hollywood tradition."[29]

Truscott's Fifth Army, in accordance with the surrender terms, remained in place, with no immediate assigned responsibilities. On the sixteenth McNarney presented Clark with an Oak-Leaf Cluster to his Distinguished Service Medal, and Clark in turn presented an identical award to Truscott. Days then passed, during which Clark found the Germans "somewhat recalcitrant and increasingly more difficult to deal with. Almost every question had to be referred to a higher headquarters for decision," making progress in implementing occupation policies very slow.

However, an article in the May 18 edition of *Stars and Stripes* brought matters swiftly to a head. The correspondent reported that since the end of fighting armed and "arrogant" German SS troops had been roaming freely through the streets of Bolzano, driving around in automobiles, fraternizing with civilian girls, and eating in restaurants that were off-limits to Italian civilians. SS General Wolff had even forced the 88th Infantry Division to obtain permission to establish a CP and had placed the SS in charge of all billeting arrangements in the city. Truscott immediately ordered Crittenberger and Keyes to "insure that no such conditions as those alleged now exist in areas for which you are responsible, and that all instructions relative to the treatment of surrendered forces are being carried out to the letter."[30]

Clark gave Truscott "responsibility for enforcing the surrender terms and collecting the German forces in PW enclosures—[this] more than two weeks after the surrender." The Germans were to move to the enclosures under supervision of their own officers, who were allowed to retain their sidearms until they were interned and who meticulously followed the instructions provided by Fifth Army, under the oversight of II Corps. "The collection and movement of 250,000 Germans in the Fifth Army area was carried out smoothly, effectively, and without incident." Service units organized from the German PWs replaced American maintenance and service units, engineer troops, and other similar units scheduled for redeployment. Under Truscott's command Fifth Army experienced no difficulty with the German prisoners, who were "well disciplined" and "cooperative and willing workers."[31]

In his letter of May 19 Truscott told Sarah that he would be returning to the United States as a member of one of five groups of senior officers and enlisted men of all grades who would visit several cities during the month of June and that his group was scheduled to arrive in New York on June 12 and go on to San Antonio, Texas, the next day. However, he had requested that Clark give him permission to leave Italy earlier to attend their son Lucian's graduation from West Point on June 5 but had not yet learned if he could do so. He also told her that there was a possibility that he would receive orders to take command of the Fourth Army at Fort Sam Houston, Texas, although he had told Clark's headquarters that he did not want the command, preferring to retain command of Fifth Army until its inactivation. On May 21 Clark telephoned Truscott to tell him that he was refusing his request to leave early to attend Lucian's graduation.[32]

On May 30 Truscott, accompanied by his staff and aides, motored to Anzio, where the general was to deliver the Memorial Day address at the temporary cemetery serving as the resting place for roughly twenty thousand men killed during the fighting in Sicily and south of Rome. After a brief tour of the beachhead area, the party arrived at the cemetery at about eleven thirty. There they found the speaker's platform adorned with bunting, its back toward the seemingly endless rows of white temporary grave markers. Seated in front of the platform on camp chairs were numerous prominent senior officers and civilians, including members of the Senate Armed Services Committee, who were visiting Italy at the time. Behind them were bleachers filled with other visitors.

After the opening ceremonies, General Truscott rose, walked to the podium, did a sharp about-face, and proceeded to address not the guests but the graves holding the bodies of men whom he had so recently commanded. As Bill Mauldin described it, "It was the most moving gesture I ever saw. It came from a hard-boiled old man who was incapable of planned dramatics." In his brief remarks, Truscott apologized to the dead for their presence in the cemetery. He went on to say that "everybody tells leaders it is not their fault that men get killed in war, but that every leader knows in his heart this is not altogether true," asking that any soldier resting there because of a mistake that he made forgive him but acknowledging "that was asking a hell of a lot under the circumstance." He concluded his remarks by stating that "he would not speak about the glorious dead because he didn't see much glory in getting killed in your late teens or early twenties . . . [and] promised that if in the future he ran into anybody, especially old men, who thought death in battle was glorious, he would straighten them out . . . [pointing out that] he thought that was the least he could do."[33]

Chapter 13

THE POSTWAR YEARS

On June 9, accompanied by his aides and Sergeant Hong, Truscott left on his long journey home. They first flew to Paris, where they spent the night at the Villa Coublay. The next morning they met the rest of their group, including Generals Clark and Patch, with whom they would travel to the selected cities. At Orly Field they boarded a C-54 to begin the four-day flight to San Antonio, with stops in the Azores, Newfoundland, Presque Isle, Maine, and New York City.[1] On hand to greet them on their arrival the afternoon of June 13 were the mayor of San Antonio, the entire Chamber of Commerce, Maj. Gen. John P. Lucas, commanding general of Fourth Army, and a host of other dignitaries. After appropriate ruffles and flourishes and a seventeen-gun salute, the party boarded open command cars and began a two-hour parade through San Antonio, ending at the St. Anthony Hotel, where there was another large crowd on hand to greet them.

After checking into their rooms the officers boarded barges that carried them down the San Antonio River to La Vieta, where they attended a cocktail reception, followed by dinner and a Mexican floor show. The festivities did not end until midnight, when the exhausted party returned to the hotel for much-needed sleep. The following morning Truscott flew to Washington, where a captain from the War Department met him and escorted him to Fort Myer. After cocktails and dinner, the general telephoned Sarah before retiring.[2]

The next day Truscott had lunch with Lt. Gen. Thomas T. Handy, Marshall's deputy, during which they discussed Truscott's next assignment. Truscott indicated that he would like to serve in the war against Japan if an opportunity to do so should arise. That afternoon Truscott, accompanied by Generals Patch and Gavin and Major Wilson, drove to the White House for a private meeting with President Harry S. Truman. Col. Harry Vaughn, Truman's longtime friend and military adviser, met them and chatted amiably about baseball before ushering them into the Oval Office. Patch presented a baton to the president that had once belonged to Reichsmarschall Hermann Göring, after which the group adjourned to the White House lawn for photographs. They then returned to the Oval Office, where Truman bade them good-bye.

Anxious to begin an eight-day leave before returning to Italy to await orders for his next assignment, Truscott hurried to Washington National Airport to catch a C-47 waiting there to whisk him to Charlottesville for a reunion with Sarah, newly commissioned 2d Lt. Lucian K. Truscott III, Mary, and Jamie, who were on hand to greet him when the plane landed. They then drove to the house on Jefferson Park Avenue in Charlottesville, which Sarah and he had purchased while he was overseas, where he sat leisurely on the porch, reminiscing with his family before a bath and dinner.[3]

The morning of June 24 Truscott flew back to Washington National Airport and checked into Apartment A at Fort Myer, where Wilson and Hong joined him. That afternoon Truscott met his wartime friend Clare Boothe Luce at the Wardman Park Hotel for cocktails and dinner.[4] The next morning the general went to Capitol Hill, where he met with Speaker of the House Sam Rayburn and other members of the Texas congressional delegation. After the meeting he went to the Pentagon to say farewell to General Handy and to inquire about his requested assignment in the Far East, learning only that General Marshall had not yet made a decision.[5] On the twenty-seventh Truscott and his party left La Guardia Field for Villa Franca, a suburb of Verona, via the Azores, Paris, and Marseilles. After arriving there the evening of the twenty-ninth Truscott flew by L-5 to the airstrip near Lake Garda, where Carleton met him and accompanied him on the boat to his villa on an island in the lake. The following morning Truscott convened a long staff meeting during which his staff brought him up to date on the situation in Fifth Army's sector.[6]

For the next several weeks Truscott busied himself with the multitude of tasks and problems confronting him as overseer of a large sector of northern Italy that included some of the most productive and beautiful land in the new Republic of Italy. One of the first tasks confronting him was to review a report the Mediterranean Theater of Operations, U.S. Army, had submitted to the Army Ground Force Equipment Review Board, including material Fifth Army headquarters had forwarded to the higher headquarters during Truscott's absence in the United States. One of the conclusions reached by MTOUSA was that there was no need in the theater for "horse cavalry except for pack animals." Truscott vigorously disagreed with that conclusion, pointing out that in the campaign in Sicily he had organized provisional mounted units and had utilized the units to outflank enemy positions in mountainous terrain that motorized or tracked vehicles were unable to navigate. He did admit that losses of both men and mounts were high but believed that this was in large part due to the lack of time for proper training of infantrymen in cavalry tactics.

After the Sicilian campaign, anticipating that his 3d Division would be committed in the mountainous terrain of Italy, he intensified the training of his cavalry troop and pack trains and organized a pack artillery battery. In the Italian fighting Truscott used the cavalry troop and the attached pack artillery to outflank enemy delaying positions in the mountain defiles and to provide flank reconnaissance for the division. In a burst of hubris he concluded that if a well-trained regiment of cavalry had been available to him after the Volturno River crossing, "the battle of Cassino would never have taken place, Anzio would have been unnecessary, and the Italian campaign might have terminated many months before it actually did."

However, Truscott did acknowledge, albeit begrudgingly, that "shipping limitations will restrict any wide use of horse cavalry" in future wars fought on foreign soil but said that conditions in those wars might provide limited opportunities to capitalize on the unique capabilities of horse cavalry: mobility to employ firepower in the proper place and at the proper time more rapidly than infantrymen could do so, the capability of dismounted cavalrymen to fight as infantrymen, and the ability of horse cavalry units and attached pack artillery batteries to operate and move rapidly in terrain inaccessible to vehicles of any type then available. His recommendation was that the American Army should "continue to develop horse cavalry for use under conditions where armor and other transport cannot be employed effectively, and for special purposes which [he] had outlined in the preceding paragraphs."[7]

Slightly more than fifty-one years later American soldiers would once again enter combat mounted on horses, when, on October 23, 2001, men of the 5th Special Forces Group accompanied Afghan cavalrymen of the Northern Alliance in a successful cavalry charge against Taliban forces in the Darya Suf River valley of northern Afghanistan. That operation was one of the early engagements that ultimately led to the defeat of the Taliban and al Qaeda forces in Afghanistan following the September 11 attacks on the Twin Towers in New York City and the Pentagon.[8]

Truscott also took exception to a recommendation that all direct support aircraft should be under the command of the major supported unit. His opinion was that "all forces—ground, air, and navy—engaged in a theater of operations should be under a single commander with a combined staff. Direct support command headquarters should be integrated with ground force headquarters on the army or task force level." He also disagreed with the recommendation of the Army Ground Forces Board to set up a "special air force organic within the ground forces," stating that "it would be absurd for the Army Ground Forces to undertake separate research and parallel development in aircraft." He then went on to cite the favorable experience that Fifth Army had enjoyed with the support it received from the U.S. Army Air Forces in Italy, recommending that future efforts should be directed not toward forming a special air force organic to the ground force but "toward improving our equipment and training to in-sure that each element thoroughly appreciates the problems of the other, and to improve our common ground and staff procedures and actual techniques of close ground support."[9]

Beginning on July 19 Truscott took a break from his daily routine and began a three-day trip to Switzerland, where he visited Interlaken, Lucerne, Vevey-Montreux on Lake Geneva (Lac Léman), Château de Chillon, and Brigue. Trus-cott was particularly intrigued by Château de Chillon, located near Montreux on Lake Geneva, having first heard of it in Lord Byron's famous poem "The Prisoner of Chillon." As the guide escorted the general and his party through the chateau Truscott "quote[d] Byron all the way."[10]

On the twenty-ninth Truscott received a cable from Marshall addressing Trus-cott's visit with Handy the previous month, during which he had indicated that he would be interested in a "combat job" in the Far East if it was offered. In the cable Marshall directed Truscott, accompanied by a few key staff officers, to go to China on temporary duty "as a preliminary to such assignment." There he would have an opportunity "to explore the matter fully" with Lt. Gen. Albert C. Wedemeyer, American commander of the China theater and chief of staff for Generalissimo Jiang Jieshi (Chiang Kai-shek), president of China.[11] Following the conferences Marshall would make a decision if Truscott's temporary as-signment there would become permanent.[12] Truscott confided to his wife that he believed that the assignment would indeed become a permanent one, which he knew would disappoint her. However, he could not "conceal [his] own satis-faction at being able to continue an active part in this war—for these occupa-tion duties had already begun to pall upon [him]." Truscott selected Carleton, O'Neill, Harrell, Conway, Bartash, Wilson, and Barna to accompany him on the trip.[13]

On August 8 Truscott's party flew to Villa Franca and then to Campodichino Airport, Naples, where they boarded a C-47 for the flight to Cairo, arriving there that night. The next day they toured Cairo and its environs and visited the pyramids, the Sphinx, the Citadel, the mosques of Mohammed Ali and Has-san, and the Cairo Bazaar. In the evening the group attended a cocktail party at the apartment of a General Ritter, where ladies of the American Red Cross, Women's Army Corps officers, and British officers joined them. After cocktails the group moved to the King's Hunting Lodge on the edge of the desert for dinner and dancing.

The following day they flew to Jerusalem, where they visited the Mount of Olives, the Chapel of the Nations (Basilica of the Agony) in the garden of Geth-semane, the Via Dolorosa, the Wailing Wall, the hill of Calvary, and the Church of the Holy Sepulcher. While at the Jerusalem airport waiting to depart on the next leg of their journey, Truscott heard on the radio the first news of Japan's willingness to surrender. He immediately initiated a Teletype conference with

Marshall's headquarters in Washington and received orders to continue his trip.[14] The group continued on to Calcutta, arriving there on August 13, where Truscott received a message from Wedemeyer requesting that he temporarily halt his journey and await further orders.[15] The following day Wedemeyer notified him that he and his party would not be able to leave Calcutta until August 17, giving them a few days to explore the city, where he found "heat and humidity . . . teeming population . . . docks cluttered with vast quantities of supplies for China only a fraction of which could be delivered."[16]

On the seventeenth the group began the final leg of their long journey, flying over the "Hump" (the Himalayas) to Kunming, and then on to Chungking, landing there in a late-afternoon rainstorm. Truscott immediately went to Wedemeyer's headquarters, where he and Wedemeyer discussed the mission that Wedemeyer envisioned for him, namely, command of a number of Chinese army groups in North China. Lt. Gen. William H. Simpson, who had commanded Ninth Army in Europe, was to hold a similar command in southern China. Those forces would engage the Japanese forces on the Chinese mainland while other Allied forces were assaulting the Japanese home islands.[17]

The following morning Wedemeyer convened a combined staff conference to discuss the surrender terms and occupation plans for China. Following the conference Truscott visited Maj. Gen. Patrick J. Hurley, the American ambassador to China, who presented "the low-down on the Stillwell [sic] affair from both the Army and the Chinese sides," and then went on to discuss the planned reorganization of the Chinese command. Truscott and Carleton next visited Generalissimo Jiang Jieshi, who questioned Truscott at great length on the state of affairs in Italy and invited him to spend the following weekend with him at his country place.[18]

On August 19 they returned to Kunming to visit Brig. Gen. Robert J. McClure at his China Combat Command headquarters, where after dinner the group, including Brig. Gen. Hayden L. Boatner, who had been Stilwell's deputy, had "a long discussion on Chinese politics." Truscott and Carleton then went to Chih Kiang (Yuan Chow) for a two-day stay, during which time a group of Japanese envoys arrived to discuss surrender terms with the Chinese command and representatives of General McClure. Late in the afternoon of the twenty-third Truscott and McClure arrived back in Kunming, where they found a message from Wedemeyer informing Truscott that it would not be necessary for him to return to Chungking and that his planned weekend visit with the generalissimo had been canceled. Undoubtedly disappointed, Truscott began making arrangements to leave China and return to Italy.[19]

Truscott's failure to be named as commander of the Chinese army groups may actually have been a godsend that spared him from the overwhelming frustration which Gen. Joseph W. Stilwell, Wedemeyer's predecessor, had experienced when he attempted to transform Jiang's army into an effective fighting force that could stand up to and defeat the Japanese invaders. However, Stilwell never received Jiang's support in achieving that goal because of Jiang's unwavering commitment to addressing "the demands of his own nation's politics" and his compulsion to "maintain the support of his generals, frustrate the rise of the Communists, husband his military strength for the moment when Nationalist armies must reoccupy Japanese-occupied China, and crush Mao Zedong [Mao Tse-tung]." Meeting, and defeating, the Japanese army on the field of battle was far down on Jiang's list of priorities. Truscott would undoubtedly soon have succumbed to that same exasperation and frustration with Jiang's inertia that Stilwell had experienced.[20]

Truscott left China on August 25 and arrived at Villa Franca the evening of the thirtieth after multiple stops, including Kandy, Ceylon, where he spent a night with his former commander Lord Mountbatten, then serving as the supreme Allied commander in Southeast Asia. He also landed at Caserta, where he learned that Fifth Army was to be inactivated on September 9, the second anniversary of its first battle at Salerno. Remaining personnel were to return to the United States as soon as shipping became available.[21]

After learning of the impending deactivation of Fifth Army, Truscott turned his attention to his postwar future. He believed that he had "accomplished in the Army the purpose I have had all these years," and confided to his wife that he "rather dread[ed] going back to peacetime garrison soldiering," acknowledging that if he stayed in the Army, "the best [I] could hope for [was] a permanent BG [brigadier general] or MG [major general]—and at 64 [the mandatory retirement age for major generals] I'll be just an old fuddy duddy like all the rest and too old to start something to occupy our declining years." He believed that if he could retire within the next year to a farm he might be able to build a profitable nest egg for their retirement years and establish themselves in a community in a home where their children and grandchildren could visit them. "If we stay in the Army, we will never have such a place." He concluded that he did not know what the future held for him but believed that they would have "plenty of time to talk things over when [he] came home."[22]

Less than two weeks after arrival at his headquarters Truscott's preparations for the deactivation and the trip home were rudely interrupted when he was awakened one morning by excruciating pain from a recurrent abscess involving the same tooth that had caused so much difficulty in the past. He immediately went to the 34th Station Hospital, where a dentist removed the offending tooth, "a very painful process." The general then returned to his apartment in Rome where he treated his facial edema with ice packs and the severe pain with "neat whiskey."[23] After a brief recuperation he and Carleton, Bartash, Wilson, and Barna saw remaining Fifth Army personnel off at Leghorn on September 20 for the voyage to Boston aboard the *Hagerstown Victory,* and then left by automobile for

Germany, where Truscott was to meet with Generals Eisenhower and Patton and others before flying to the United States. "At least, so [they] thought."[24]

On May 24 General Clark issued Truscott's final Efficiency Report covering the war years, rating him number one among seventy-one general officers for promotion, and recommended that he be made a permanent general officer. Clark pointed out that Truscott had "a thorough knowledge and quick grasp of military problems, particularly in combat, and makes sound and rapid decisions . . . [and] has a quiet but forceful personality, coupled with obvious personal courage and determination, which inspires confidence and loyalty in all personnel associated with him." He concluded the report by stating, "As Commanding General successively of the 3rd Division, VI Corps and Fifth Army, he has led these major units with conspicuous success in the campaigns in Italy and southern France. The successful battles in which his units have played major parts have included some of the most difficult fighting at Salerno, the Volturno, Anzio and the breakthrough from the Apennines into the Po Valley."[25]

OCCUPATION DUTY

When the Truscott party left on their drive to Germany they had planned to go on to Paris and leave the following week by air for the United States, where they would take part in the Fifth Army deactivation ceremony. In fact, they had placed most of their baggage aboard the *Hagerstown Victory,* carrying with them only sufficient clothes and toiletries for a one-week stay in Germany and France.

Truscott first visited his old friend George Patton in his Third Army headquarters in Bad Tölz on September 22, leaving the next day for Heidelberg to meet with Seventh Army commander Keyes. The next stop was Frankfurt, where Truscott spent the night of the twenty-fourth with Beetle Smith. The following morning Smith escorted Truscott to Eisenhower's headquarters in the I. G. Farben building in Frankfurt. After greeting Truscott warmly, Eisenhower asked him to delay his trip to Paris, explaining that he might find it necessary to relieve Patton of command of his beloved Third Army and name Truscott as his replacement. Patton had "caused a storm of criticism" because of remarks he had made at a recent press conference, when "he justified utilizing Nazis in civil government offices and had likened the German political scene to the struggle between Democrats and Republicans" in the United States. Further, Patton "had also shown a lack of sympathy in caring for Jewish displaced persons whom high level policy had accorded special privileges and accommodations." Eisenhower went on to say that such "ill-considered words and actions could only embarrass the administration and jeopardize the occupation," leading him to believe that he should replace Patton with "someone not as inclined to intemperate outbursts." Truscott replied that he had no desire to replace his old friend as commander of Third Army but would if Eisenhower requested that he do so, explaining that if Patton had to relinquish command he would "probably prefer being replaced by me than by someone who might be less sympathetic." Eisenhower then told him to continue with his visit to Berlin and Paris while he consulted with General Marshall but not to leave for the United States until authorized to do so.

The following day Truscott visited Berlin and then returned to Frankfurt, where he met once again with General Smith, who told him to go on to Paris, there to remain until Eisenhower made his decision about the Patton matter. On his second day in Paris, Truscott received word to return to Frankfurt, where Eisenhower ordered him to replace Patton as commander of Third Army and the Eastern Military District (Bavaria). He specifically instructed Truscott to be "'ruthless' in carrying out denazification and giving preferential treatment to Jewish displaced persons." Among those "preferential" treatments for Jewish displaced persons (DPs) were increased allowances of food, clothing, housing, and other supplies, as well as no restrictions on travel within Bavaria. Undoubtedly, the copy of the Harrison Report that he had recently received from President Truman influenced Eisenhower's comments to Truscott regarding the treatment of Jews.[26]

In June 1945 President Harry S. Truman asked Earl G. Harrison, a prominent attorney and the American representative on the Intergovernmental Committee on Refugees, to undertake a fact-finding trip "to inquire into the conditions and needs of displaced persons in Germany who may be stateless or nonrepatriable, particularly Jews." In his subsequent report to Truman, Harrison recounted in great detail his findings, concluding with a series of recommendations: First, the Jews in Germany and Austria should receive first priority for services from those personnel involved in the rehabilitation and resettling of displaced persons in Germany and Austria. Second, the United States, "under existing immigration laws, [should] permit reasonable numbers" of Jews to immigrate. Third, commanders should make greater efforts to get the Jewish displaced persons out of the camps and into rest homes and tuberculosis sanitariums for those requiring care. The healthier refugees should be placed in permanent buildings, even if it required the requisitioning of German homes and other buildings and forced the displaced Germans to find other accommodations. Fourth, commanders should make greater efforts to have qualified Jewish refugees fill positions within the offices of military government that German civilians were filling. Finally, senior Army headquarters should make more extensive and frequent inspections of the camps and other facilities housing refugees.[27]

Although Truscott was "heartbroken" that he would not be returning home to Sarah, and that he would be relieving his old friend George Patton of command of Third Army, he believed he would "be much happier doing effective work over here than I could ever be in one of those political bushwhacking jobs at home."[28]

In Frankfurt Truscott spent several days discussing with Eisenhower's staff the problems he would face in Bavaria: the role of the Allied Military Government, disposition and handling of prisoners of war and displaced persons, repatriation of Soviet nationals, and prosecution of war criminals. Feeling the need to retain the services of the staff officers with whom he had worked for many years, Truscott contacted Marshall's deputy, Lt. Gen. Thomas Handy, requesting that if possible he make available for assignment to Third Army Cols. E. M. Daniels, Ben Harrell, E. J. O'Neill, and William Clarke and Lt. Col. A. J. Barkin and indicated that he would retain Carleton as his chief of staff.[29]

The night of October 4 Truscott went to Bad Tölz for his final visit with Patton, who, as usual, greeted his fellow cavalryman cordially. During the next two days the two old soldiers discussed occupation procedures and the change of command ceremony, scheduled for Sunday, October 7. As Truscott recalled, "The only sign he ever gave of the blow which he must have felt came when he said, 'Lucian, if you have no objection, I want to have a big formal ceremony and turn over command to you with considerable fanfare and publicity. I don't want Ike or anyone else to get the idea that I am leaving here with my tail between my legs.'" Truscott assured him that he had no objection.

On the seventh the ceremony was, because of bad weather, held in the gymnasium of the former SS *kaserne* (barracks) housing Third Army headquarters. At noon Patton and Truscott joined the four corps commanders and the Third Army staff on the appropriately decorated stage facing the remainder of the personnel of Third Army headquarters and all of the available Army personnel in the Bad Tölz area. After the rendering of ruffles and flourishes Patton made a few farewell comments and handed over the Third Army flag to Truscott, symbolizing the change of command. The ceremony concluded with more ruffles and flourishes and the national anthem. Following the ceremony Patton, Truscott, their staffs, and other senior officers adjourned to the Senior Officers' Mess for cocktails and lunch, following which Truscott accompanied Patton to the railroad station to see him off on the train for Bad Neuheim, the headquarters of Fifteenth Army, where he would oversee the writing of the history of the war in Europe.[30] Truscott then returned to his new headquarters and moved into Patton's former quarters, a villa that had been the residence of the publisher of *Mein Kampf,* quotations from which were molded in relief into the ceiling of the drawing room. The villa was located on the Tegernsee, a beautiful lake a few miles east of Bad Tölz near the Austrian border. Joining him in residence there were Carleton, Bartash, and Wilson.[31]

Truscott's Third Army sector in the American Zone of occupied Germany was divided into four corps sectors: XV Corps in northern Bavaria, XII Corps in eastern Bavaria, XX Corps in southern Bavaria, and XXII Corps in Czechoslovakia. The commanders of the corps and their attached divisions "were responsible for the security of their respective areas, for supervision of displaced persons camps, and for the execution of redeployment plans." Recognizing that a civilian agency would ultimately replace the Military Government, the Americans had decided to separate Military Government administrative functions from the tactical chain of command. To head the Military Government in Bavaria Truscott selected Brig. Gen. Walter Muller, Patton's former G4.[32]

On October 12 Truscott met for the first time with the press, ten correspondents representing both American and international wire services and newspapers. In his introductory remarks he stressed to the correspondents that he considered that "a free press is necessary to a democracy, and, certainly, a free press is essential if we are going to have an informed public opinion." He pointed out that it was their duty "to seek and provide a great deal of the information that goes to make up that informed public opinion." To assist them in carrying out that duty, he assured them that they were "at liberty to go into any part of any area under my Command and to write anything that [they] want to write," as long as they reported only the facts and did not disclose any information that might "later cost the blood of American soldiers." He went on to say that if they discovered any irregularity or any condition needing correction, they were to bring the matter to his attention and promised that he would either correct or improve the condition.[33]

He next turned to the subject of the soldiers who were charged with administering the policies of the military government in Bavaria, acknowledging that the majority of them had little or no combat experience and were for the most part less experienced than the men he had led in combat. He also believed that men who had not seen combat with the Germans and had not witnessed the atrocities committed by some of the enemy would be "much more sympathetic in [their] attitude toward the Germans" than those combat soldiers they were replacing. Truscott assured the correspondents that he intended to "orient every soldier in this Army with a view toward fixing in their minds the German guilt—and, particularly, the Nazi guilt—for loosing upon the world this holocaust of war. It is essential that every soldier who serves in this Occupation Force keep in mind what we have fought for."[34]

Completing his remarks, Truscott opened the floor to questions from the correspondents. To a question concerning the length of time before there would be full civilian control in Bavaria, Truscott responded that he could not answer that question directly, since he had received no directives addressing that issue, but said that it definitely would not take place until denazification had been completed, however long that might take. When asked if his comments that most of the troops in Third Army had not seen combat and witnessed their friends being killed and the atrocities committed by the Germans were "to be taken as an implied criticism of the fraternization bent of the soldiers that are here now," Truscott replied that it was not a criticism of the men but rather an acknowledgment that men who had not been through combat "could not have that intensity of feeling" toward the Germans as did his battle-hardened veterans. Recognizing that, he was planning to institute "an orientation program to set up the war aims and the things we fought for," utilizing an extensive series of lectures and movies "to show the American soldier why he is here and make him believe it." The questioning then turned to the effect he thought the denazification program might have on the economy if carried out in too hurried a fashion. Truscott replied that what he thought about it was unimportant, stating that his "orders are to de-Nazify, and that's exactly what we are going to do . . . and if we disrupt the economic system we will have to do something else about it, but we are going to de-Nazify."[35]

The final questions addressed the issue of SS prisoners, alleging that "SS gentlemen whom you hold at various cages are having a very soft time . . . [and that] the Displaced persons were being fed less than the SS men" being held at Dachau. Truscott replied that in the camps that he had inspected personally he found that all displaced persons' daily rations exceeded twenty-three hundred calories, "and I don't believe that the SS boys are certainly getting more than that." He then went on to say that if the questioner could prove the truth of the charge to him, "somebody will get tried." The day after the press conference Truscott sent a transcript of it to Beetle Smith, who then forwarded it to Eisenhower. In a cover letter he told Smith that he had referred the question concerning the disparity of the quantity of rations going to SS men and to the DPs to his inspector general and would inform the correspondent who had raised the issue of the results of the investigation.[36]

One of the first problems that Truscott addressed was that caused by the massive redeployment of American troops to the United States. Theater orders had specified that all individuals and units awaiting redeployment were exempted from all military drills and training. That policy and the absence of a program to keep the troops informed of redeployment problems, and "a factious editorial policy" followed by the European edition of the *Stars and Stripes,* had contributed to morale and discipline problems among those men awaiting redeployment. Truscott therefore directed his staff to develop recreational, travel, and sports programs similar to those he had instituted within Fifth Army after the cessation of hostilities in Italy. By the end of the year, as the programs took effect and most of the redeployments had been completed, the state of morale and discipline had considerably improved.[37]

The United States, Great Britain, and the Soviet Union had agreed at the Yalta Conference to cooperate in repatriating nationals of various countries whom the Nazi government had displaced to other countries for employment in war industries and those displaced by the war itself. However, the United States had grossly underestimated the enormity of the problem in repatriating many hundreds of thousands of refugees to their home countries, particularly since many of them had previously resided in countries currently under Soviet control, and "hated and feared the Russians even more than they hated the Germans."[38]

In the American Zone alone there were more than a million DPs, many of them in Bavaria. They represented nearly every European and Near Asian nationality, some of whom had come to Germany by personal choice but most of whom had been forcibly displaced either to support the German war effort by their labor or to be imprisoned in the infamous German concentration and elimination camps; many of the latter refugees were Jews. Immediately after the end of the war the Americans, after sorting and classifying them by nationality, had placed the refugees in camps where they could be housed, clothed, fed, and cared for medically while awaiting shipment home or other disposition. The camps, housing from a few hundred to thousands of people, were scattered throughout Bavaria.

Initially, American military personnel operated the camps, obtaining the necessary food and supplies from the local German economy. With that economy in a state of near collapse, however, Eisenhower agreed to accept the assistance of the United Nations Relief and Rehabilitation Administration, and when Truscott assumed command of Eastern Bavaria UNRRA teams were active in some of the camps there. Truscott soon discovered that the teams required extensive support from the American military.

Recognizing that the displaced persons problems would be a major issue for him in his role as military governor, Truscott immediately began a tour of the camps, as well as American troop installations. He found that the hundreds of thousands of DPs were a heterogeneous lot: many were from the Baltic states and had cooperated with the Germans in their invasion of Russia or had voluntarily come to Germany to work in war industries or on German farms; hatred and fear of the Russians united the Baltic refugees. Most of them did not expect or desire to return to their countries of origin, since the Soviets now occupied the Baltic states. Truscott found the Baltic camps to be the cleanest and best administered of the camps he visited.

The DPs of Russian nationality fell into two main groups: those, such as the intensely nationalistic Ukrainians, who had greeted the Germans as liberators and had voluntarily come to Germany to assist the German war effort and those who had fought with the Germans against the Russians and had become prisoners of war. The Ukrainians vowed not to return to their country until it was no longer under control of the Soviets, and the former prisoners of war feared that they would face almost certain death upon their return.

Truscott soon realized, however, that the group posing the most difficult problem facing him was that of Jewish DPs, the disposition of whom had national and international political implications and the vast majority of whom were in Bavaria. Jewish leaders throughout the world, but particularly in the United States, "were determined to exploit the world-wide sympathy for the Jews to obtain the refuge in Palestine which had long been their aim." However, Great Britain, which under the terms of a 1920 League of Nations mandate was made responsible for the territory of Palestine for the "stated purpose of 'establishing in Palestine a national home for the Jewish people,'" did not wish to permit further Jewish immigration for fear of offending the Arabs residing in the mandate territory and possibly jeopardizing access to the oil reserves located there. Complicating matters further was the large number of organizations and individuals who became active in the matter of disposition of the Jewish DPs, chief among them the American Joint Distribution Committee that represented various Jewish congregations and welfare organizations. The high level of priority that Eisenhower assigned to resolving the problem was attested by his having on his staff a special adviser on Jewish affairs, Samuel F. Rifkind, a federal judge from New York.

Truscott's first visits were to the Jewish DP camps at Landsberg, Feldafing, and Wolfratshausen, all located in the Munich area; Patton had been particularly criticized for his administration of the Landsberg and Feldafing camps. Truscott found that a Citizens' Committee, elected by the occupants of the camp, governed each of the camps. The committees wrote the camp rules, appointed the guards, and oversaw all details of camp governance.[39] He was particularly impressed with the Landsberg camp, which was commanded by Maj. Irving Heymont, an American Jew, who was working closely with the UNRRA team there. The camp held approximately sixty-nine hundred occupants, all of whom were Jews. After he assumed command in September 1945, Heymont organized the first democratic elections to select the Citizens' Committee members. In addition, he began publishing a camp newspaper and established schools and workshops. He also helped the members of the camp organize kibbutzim (agricultural collectives) on nearby farms formerly owned by Nazis.[40]

Heymont's accomplishments at Camp Landsberg impressed Truscott, but he was surprised to find that the schools, workshops, and other facilities were only rarely used to their full capacity and noted that many of the occupants spent their days in idleness. Although the accommodations were comparable to those in use by American forces, he noted that those in the camp were not "as clean, sanitary, and well ordered as were the military installations." It soon became evident to him that "there was a concerted plan afoot to obtain publicity which would keep world sympathy stirred up on behalf of these destitute refugees," publicity designed to embarrass military authorities by "alleging military responsibility for crowded and unsatisfactory conditions, for mistreatment of individual displaced persons, for unfavorable treatment in comparison with Germans, and similar unfounded accusations."[41]

One particularly egregious example of such activity occurred in early December, when an American college professor, Dr. Leo Srole, the chief UNRRA welfare officer at Camp Landsberg, "submitted his resignation in a scathing letter denouncing the handling of Jewish DPs by the Army and UNRRA, particularly at Landsberg." Instead of sending the letter through normal command and UNRRA channels, Srole sent it to a Jewish newspaper correspondent in Frankfurt, who, before making the letter public, showed it to General Smith, who immediately called Truscott and read the letter to him. Truscott responded to the accusations by suggesting that Smith make a personal visit to Landsberg and bring with him some news correspondents. The next morning Smith and his party arrived at Landsberg, where Major Heymont met them.

After meeting with the UNRRA team, which included Doctor Srole, and the camp Citizens' Committee, Smith, his party, and Truscott toured the camp. Since Srole's complaints had included in the letter his belief that a typhus outbreak was imminent and that the camp occupants were suffering from malnutrition, Smith had brought with him the theater surgeon and Judge Rifkind. The theater surgeon and the camp doctor concluded that the occupants of the camp were in no greater danger of a typhus outbreak than were people living elsewhere in Germany and that immunization would reduce the threat even further. There was no evidence of malnutrition, and food was adequate. In fact, Smith and some others in his party had lunch in the camp and found the food to be quite acceptable. They did find one cellar apartment where the occupants, newly arrived, had been defecating on the floor, even though adequate toilet facilities were available on the floor above them. Heymont commented that the other camp inmates should not have tolerated such unsanitary practices and that "a good kick in the pants drives home a lesson very fast."

After the inspection Smith said that rather than being "horrified" by what he had seen, he "was very much impressed by the progress that had been made" and that he "admired the energy and drive displayed in the development of the school system and recreational facilities," hoping that similar energy and drive would be used to develop a good camp sanitation program. He promised that he would attempt to improve the variety of rations for the camp and would see that properly slaughtered meat would be provided for those observing kosher dietary laws.[42]

After receiving the Harrison Report, Truman had ordered Eisenhower to establish separate camps for the displaced Jews, and the camps soon became "hotbeds of black market activities." Since Jewish DPs were the only DPs allowed to move freely without restriction from one camp to another, they soon dominated the black market activities and illegal money transactions throughout Bavaria. The Munich and Landsberg camps were among the worst offenders in diverting food and other supplies intended for the camp occupants onto the black market.[43]

Joseph Bendersky defends the Jewish involvement in black market activities, stating, "The black market was quite alluring to Jews who lacked employment, property, money, family, or social networks," and asserts quite correctly that other DPs as well as many American soldiers were also involved in the market. "To Jews, violating German law was 'more of a virtue than a crime.'" Nevertheless, the Jewish dominance of the black market did result in the awakening of latent anti-Semitism among some members of the American armed forces.[44] He goes on to point out that after Truscott assumed responsibility for the DP camps he complied completely with Eisenhower's orders regarding strict implementation of denazification policies, giving preferential treatment to Jewish DPs, setting up separate centers for Jewish refugees, improving their rations and clothing, and dispossessing German nationals to provide houses for the Jews.[45]

Although at Yalta President Roosevelt and Prime Minister Churchill had agreed to Stalin's request to repatriate all displaced persons as rapidly as possible after the German surrender, they probably never considered that many, including a majority of the DPs in Germany, might not wish to return to their countries of origin while they were under Soviet control. To effect the return of such DPs, the Soviets had organized a large Russian Repatriation Commission to repatriate *all* persons, whether they wished to return or not. The Russian commission in the American sector in Germany was located in Frankfurt, and during Truscott's first weeks in command of Third Army he found that commission members were quite actively visiting the DP camps in his area, sometimes causing near riots. He immediately issued orders that any commission members visiting the camps would have to be accompanied by American officers. He also ordered that the commission members were to receive no rosters of the DPs and said that they could conduct interviews of internees only after obtaining their consent, and then only when an American officer was present to prevent any intimidation of the internees and ensure that the internee was aware of American repatriation policies.

However, if the commission wished to ascertain if an internee suspected of committing a punishable offense was in one of the camps, it could send the name of the individual and the suspected offense to Truscott's headquarters, which would institute a search of camp records to attempt to locate the individual. If the suspect was found, the Americans would then evaluate the validity of the charge, and if they found the charge to be true would turn that person over to the commission. From submitted lists of several thousand DPs, the Americans were able to locate about fifteen hundred who had been charged validly and who were placed aboard trains for shipment to the border, where Soviet officials took them into custody. Truscott writes that he was never able to understand why the Soviets were so determined to repatriate DPs who manifested such a clear hatred of them but suspected that they "wished to eliminate a dissident element which would be in opposition to the Soviet regime as long as it remained without the Soviet Union. Possibly another reason was the need for labor to rebuild the devastated country, for needless to say most of those who did return would find themselves in slave labor camps."[46]

One of the major Allied objectives after the cessation of hostilities was the trial of alleged war criminals. Two locations were selected, Nuremberg and Dachau, both within the Third Army zone. The trials to be held in the Palace of Justice in Nuremberg were those of major war criminals accused of "waging aggressive war and other crimes against humanity," while the trials in Dachau were to try those individuals alleged to have committed crimes against American personnel or who were alleged to have committed crimes in "areas allocated to American forces."

A Quadripartite Tribunal made up of representatives of the United States, Great Britain, the Soviet Union, and France conducted the trials in Nuremberg. The chief counsel was Robert H. Jackson, an associate justice of the United States Supreme Court. Theater headquarters was responsible for providing all necessary assistance to Judge Jackson and his Office of Chief Counsel, while Third Army "would merely offer supplies, labor, and give other assistance as specifically directed by Theater Headquarters." The trials in Dachau, which were to be held near the former German concentration camp there, were to be conducted under the provisions of military law before military tribunals.

However, only a week before the Nuremberg trials were to begin on November 14, Eisenhower's headquarters informed Truscott that Third Army was to "be held accountable for the administration and maintenance of the Nürnberg trials," a task that in Truscott's opinion should have been assigned to him in the beginning. To handle the multitude of administrative and maintenance details confronting him Truscott established Nuremberg as a separate area command under Brig. Gen. LeRoy Watson, under whose "able leadership, the support of the Nürnberg trials caused no further trouble."

Truscott visited the courtroom at Nuremberg on many occasions and found that although the room "was one of imposing dignity . . . it was not one to fill me with the pride I have felt in American court rooms." Although he firmly believed that the persons on trial were guilty of major crimes against humanity and should be brought to justice, "when [he] looked down upon the Court Room scene [he] was never able to escape the impression that [he] was witnessing a conquerors' triumph, for it was only the totality of the conqueror's victory that made this impressive spectacle possible." By contrast he believed the trials at Dachau, involving "lesser fry of the Nazi regime," would afford the Americans "an opportunity of giving the Germans an object lesson in the Western method of administering justice." With that in mind he instructed the members of the military tribunal that "fairness, impartiality, and strict application of the laws and rules of procedure were therefore essential."

The prosecution and defense counsels at Dachau were all American officers with legal training, and the presiding judge was Col. James C. Cheever, judge advocate of Third Army. Some German attorneys complemented the American defense counsel staff. At the conclusion of the first trial that involved thirty-eight accused persons, which led to convictions of "all but one or two of the accused," Truscott learned from the lead defense counsel that "prisoner after prisoner told [the American defense counsels] that no German lawyer would ever have made such a fight on their behalf even before a German Court; they felt that their trial had been fair and impartial."[47]

Gen. Joseph T. McNarney, the European theater commander, later commended Truscott for his "highly creditable cooperation in the bringing to justice of major and minor war criminals." Since many of the trials had received worldwide attention, necessitating that the trials be carried out with "dignity, dispatch and justice," McNarney stated that the "unstinting cooperation" of Truscott and his command during all phases of the trials was such as to reflect "great credit upon the Army and upon the United States." He particularly appreciated the "experience, integrity and ability of the personnel" whom Truscott had provided to serve upon the courts and commissions, which ensured "the creditable performance of a most difficult task."[48]

A major question confronting the Allies was how long occupying forces might have to remain in Germany. Many authorities believed that the occupation would continue for years, possibly as long as a generation or more, to eliminate completely Nazism and militarism and to prepare the German people to take their place among the community of democratic nations. Theater headquarters had originally believed that at least a reinforced corps consisting of three or four divisions would be required to carry out the occupation duties within the American Zone. However, with the rapid demobilization of the Army in the immediate postwar years and the aversion of the American people to supporting a large peacetime standing Army, the planners in theater headquarters decided to form a constabulary of roughly thirty thousand officers and men "especially designed for carrying out the occupation tasks, gradually taking over full responsibility as Army divisions were withdrawn." The organization, to be known as the U.S. Constabulary, would consist of a headquarters, selected service units, and two brigades, each composed of a headquarters and two regiments. The organization of the regiments was to be similar to that of mechanized cavalry regiments, "specially designed for police and constabulary work and was to be exceptionally mobile for patrolling the entire zone."

Since the reorganization plans called for the inactivation of Seventh Army and for Third Army to assume command of all Army troops in the American sector, Truscott received orders to form the constabulary and to choose its commander. For that mission he turned to his old friend and fellow cavalryman Maj. Gen. Ernest N. Harmon, who had most recently commanded the XXII

Corps until its inactivation. Harmon set about his task early in 1946, with the goal of having the U.S. Constabulary assume full responsibility for the occupation duties in the American sector by July 1, 1946.[49] The duties of the constabulary were to "exercise broad police powers over civilians and American military personnel." To train the soldiers who were to constitute the constabulary, Harmon established the Constabulary School at Sonthofen. Since the members of the constabulary would have "unusual powers of arrest, search, and seizure," they would undoubtedly be tempted by bribes, leading Harmon to institute a training program that would place special emphasis upon inculcating in the men "good judgment, sensitivity, and honesty." By the target date of July 1 the U.S. Constabulary was prepared to assume its duties.[50]

During the last months of 1945 and the first months of 1946, Truscott continued to busy himself with his duties as the head of the military government in Bavaria. One of his most important and difficult duties was that of denazification, which included removing from governmental positions all those with more than a nominal affiliation with the Nazi Party. For that task, he relied heavily on the Army's Counterintelligence Corps to search out and arrest those individuals. When those persons were identified and located, they were placed in concentration camps, there to await final disposition.[51]

With the coming of 1946 Truscott began to prepare for Third Army to take over control of all American forces in the American Zone after deactivation of Seventh Army on April 1. At that time Third Army headquarters was to relocate to Heidelberg to be closer to theater headquarters in that city. However, in late March his routine was suddenly disrupted when he received word that Sarah had been hospitalized at Walter Reed General Hospital with a perforated duodenal ulcer and was seriously ill. He immediately requested and received emergency leave, and Capt. Lloyd K. Jensen, his new aide, and he left for Washington on March 31, arriving at Washington National Airport at noon the next day. There, to his surprise, Sarah, who had just been discharged from the hospital, and his son James greeted him.[52]

After spending nearly two weeks with his family, Truscott began his return trip to Germany. On the flight to Bermuda, Truscott complained of not feeling well because of a recurrence of a sinus infection and a cough. As the plane continued its flight to Germany, the general's condition steadily worsened and continued to do so after arrival in Heidelberg on the sixteenth. The following day Lieutenant Colonel Ready, the Third Army surgeon, and Captain Kent, a medical officer from the 130th Station Hospital, examined Truscott and advised that he enter the hospital immediately for further evaluation.[53]

On admission he was producing "copious quantities of purulent sputum amounting to as much as approximately one pint a day maximum," and the admitting diagnosis was recurrent bronchial asthma associated with acute and chronic bronchitis. He received seven hundred thousand units of penicillin, which cleared the pulmonary infection in about three days. However, Doctor Kent, aware that "symptoms of asthma sometimes are the precursor of Coronary Disease," initiated serial electrocardiograms. On the twenty-third, two days after he had been discharged to rest at his villa, the electrocardiogram revealed that Truscott had suffered a coronary artery occlusion that produced a myocardial infarct (heart attack).[54]

Col. Alvin B. McKie, the theater chief of professional services, evaluated Truscott and agreed with the diagnosis. He ordered that Truscott remain at complete bed rest for not less than six weeks and arranged for nurses and the necessary medical supplies and equipment to be moved to his villa, fearing that moving him back to the hospital was "too big a danger." Both McKie and Kent agreed that Truscott should be evacuated to the United States for further hospitalization and observation as soon as his medical condition permitted.[55] The following day, Maj. Gen. H. R. Bull, McNarney's chief of staff, visited Truscott. He discussed his condition with the attending physicians and then conveyed that information to McNarney. After much thought McNarney informed Eisenhower, now the Army chief of staff, that he was relieving Truscott of command of Third Army and was arranging for his return to the United States in approximately six weeks. He named General Keyes to succeed Truscott as commander of Third Army.[56]

On April 27 Truscott informed Sarah of his condition, noting that the "electrocardiograph shows spot on heart not normal, but not serious. . . . Feel fine. . . . Should be home by 1st June." Sarah informed Lucian the next day that she was "all right" and would remain in Virginia unless he felt that she should come to Europe.[57] Truscott apparently believed it would be best for her not to make the trip to Germany, since he never requested that she come.

During the next weeks, Truscott's condition steadily improved. He received many visitors during that time, and he continued to host daily cocktail hours. On May 23 Doctor Kent told him that his latest electrocardiogram was "almost normal." To celebrate the good news, Truscott enjoyed "his first cigarette in days, along with a drink." The following morning Captain Lazaroff, a dental officer, his assistant, and Captain Kent arrived to treat a tooth that had been causing Truscott pain since May 2. The dentist decided that he should extract the tooth and received medical clearance from Kent to do so. The extraction was accomplished with no difficulty, and Truscott was "relieved to be rid of [the] tooth." One week later he was able to walk for the first time in six weeks.[58]

On July 2, cleared to return home, Truscott arrived in Naples, where he and his party boarded the *Vulcania* for the voyage to Genoa. After all were aboard, they repaired to the general's stateroom for cocktails. The group sailed from Genoa on the fifth, bound for New York City via Palermo, and arrived in New York on July 16. The cruise was a leisurely one, with good weather and many parties. After enjoying *Oklahoma* and *Three to Make Ready* in New York, Truscott and his party departed by train for Washington on the eighteenth, where they were met by Sarah, their son James, and Truscott's nephew, Lucian. The family immediately left for Sarah's rented apartment in Alexandria.[59]

On July 22 Truscott reported to Walter Reed General Hospital, where he learned that he would begin an extensive medical evaluation that would last until the middle of August. After he completed the evaluation Truscott, accompanied by Sarah and James, drove to Moosehead Lake, Maine, where they spent two weeks fishing and relaxing with Don Carleton and his family. They returned to Washington on September 9, where Truscott once again joined the Walter Reed Detachment of Patients.[60]

On September 28 Truscott received the good news that he would be restored to general service in the Army within the continental United States, with a medical reevaluation in six months. For the next two weeks Truscott spent his time answering a query from the Signal Corps regarding his recommendations pertinent to communications in the field, clearing up accumulated correspondence at the Pentagon, and writing comments about the administration of military justice at the request of the War Department. On October 9 he received orders relieving him from assignment to the Detachment of Patients and reassigning him to the Office, Chief of Staff, U.S. Army, where he would be working for his old friend, General of the Army Dwight D. Eisenhower.[61]

On October 22 he met with Eisenhower and learned that he was to become president of the War Department Screening Board, "one of the agencies prescribed by the Secretary of War to relieve from active duty those officers who do not have the necessary qualifications" for retention. Eisenhower estimated that the board would be meeting for roughly six months, and during that time the Truscott family would reside in General Handy's former quarters at Washington Barracks.[62] The board was formally constituted on October 23 and consisted of Truscott and four other general officers, a recorder and an assistant recorder, and eight alternate representatives from the technical and administrative services who would sit on the board when officers of their respective services were being examined. Upon completion of board action on any case, the complete file, together with the board's recommendation, would be forwarded to the adjutant general for further action.[63]

On October 30, as the Truscotts were moving into their new quarters at Washington Barracks (Fort Lesley J. McNair), Sarah suffered a recurrence of her duodenal peptic ulcer and was admitted once again to Walter Reed General Hospital for treatment, where she remained for several weeks. As the year drew to a close, Sarah had another recurrence of the ulcer, necessitating her readmission to the hospital on December 27, and on February 13 she underwent a partial gastrectomy, which removed the lower half of her stomach. The surgical procedure was apparently successful in curing the ulcer diathesis, since she remained asymptomatic for the rest of her life.[64]

On February 5 the couple's daughter, Mary, had arrived, much to her father's "surprise and pleasure." His aide expected that "with having a woman in the house, the General's life should be considerably less complicated and [should] relieve him of many of these housekeeping duties he has had to perform." On March 2 full normalcy returned to the Truscott household when Sarah returned home from her long stay at Walter Reed.[65]

On March 25 Truscott convened a two-day session of the War Department Screening Board for the purpose of meeting with Maj. Gen. John E. Dahlquist, deputy director of personnel and administration in the War Department. Dahlquist inquired if the board could serve as the nucleus of another board to be formed to screen the records of some three thousand Regular Army officers prior to the submission of their records to a promotion selection board. The board agreed to provide such a nucleus for the new board, to be known as the War Department Personnel Records Board, which met for the first time on April 16.[66]

On Army Day, April 7, Truscott and James were the guests of President Truman in his personal box at the corner of Constitution Avenue and Seventeenth Street, where they reviewed the parade and ceremonies honoring the U.S. Army. That evening he delivered an address at the Mayflower Hotel, which, according to his aide, was "an impressive speech." Five days later Truscott and his aide drove to Arlington National Cemetery to participate in the dedication of Patton Drive, located along the southern boundary of the cemetery.[67]

On April 23 and 24 Truscott reported to Walter Reed General Hospital for reevaluation of his medical condition. Following the examination he received orders to appear before the Disposition Board on May 9. The board found that Truscott had mild generalized arteriosclerosis, "with coronary focalization," and an old myocardial infarct involving the posterolateral wall of the left ventricle that was unchanged from the previous examination. The board concluded that General Truscott "may be incapacitated for active service," although it had no objection to his appearing before the Army Retiring Board for further consideration. On June 19 Truscott appeared before that board, which recommended that he be retired from the Army after taking sixty days of accrued leave to begin on August 1. He received a disability rating of 60 percent, entitling him to monthly disability pay of $550.[68] One of Truscott's last official duties as an Army officer occurred on Memorial Day, when, as a representative of the 3d Infantry Division, he placed a wreath at the Tomb of the Unknown Soldier in Arlington National Cemetery.[69]

Truscott officially retired from the U.S. Army in disabled status on September 30, 1947, in the temporary grade of lieutenant general.[70] However, for practical purposes he began his retirement years on August 2 when he embarked on a sixty-day leave. Before settling into their retirement home they had purchased in Bluemont, Virginia, Lucian, Sarah, and James traveled to southern Colorado for an extended visit with their daughter, Mary, and her husband, Robert Wilbourn, who had served with the 1st Cavalry Division in the Pacific theater during the war and who had also been recently retired from the Army because of a physical disability. At the time of the Truscotts' visit their son-in-law was manager of a ranch on which there were several oil wells.[71]

After their return from Colorado the Truscotts settled into their retirement home, a sixty-nine-acre farm with a main house and a few outbuildings on the outskirts of the village of Bluemont, roughly seventeen miles west of Leesburg. The main house had been built in 1797 and had absolutely no modern conveniences, excepting a single lightbulb suspended from an electrical wire that ran up the wall to the ceiling of the kitchen and was the sole light source in the house. It was Truscott's plan to modernize the house, including complete rewiring, indoor plumbing, and central heating.

The grounds around the house were in weeds, and Lucian and Sarah busied themselves with restoring the grounds while contractors were engaged in putting in the plumbing and heating systems and completing the rewiring. One activity that Truscott thoroughly enjoyed was tending his garden of an acre or so, raising vegetables and some flowers. However, so much work and expense were required to rehabilitate and maintain the property that it became "their entire focus in life." The only breaks from their labors occurred when they would entertain Army friends at dinners and cocktail parties. Otherwise, theirs was a life that centered about physical labor.[72]

On September 1, 1948, the Joint Chiefs of Staff established the Committee for Joint Policies and Procedures and an ad hoc committee consisting of three members, one from each service, "for developing for issue by the Joint Chiefs of Staff, a publication covering basic joint policies and doctrine." The War Department subsequently directed the chief of the Army Field Forces to "establish at an early date three Army Advisory Panels on joint doctrine in the fields of amphibious, airborne, and air defense operations," made up of "the best available authorities in the Army in their respective fields." Each panel was to prepare for approval by the chief of staff "a document which defines the Department of the Army position on basic doctrine, policies, and procedures on joint matters" in its particular field of expertise.[73]

On October 9, 1948, Gen. Jacob L. Devers, chief of Army Field Forces, wrote to Truscott, asking him to serve a period of active duty as chairman of the advisory panel that would "prepare for the Chief of Staff a document which clearly establishes the Army position on basic doctrine, policies, and procedures" in joint amphibious operations. Because of the "importance of the work to be done by these panels, [Devers considered] it highly essential to nominate for membership the best qualified officers" he knew, and that was the reason he was asking Truscott to chair that particular panel.[74] Undoubtedly partly to escape from the rigors of "life on the farm," Truscott eagerly accepted Devers's offer, and just ten days later received orders to report for duty at Devers's headquarters on November 19, to serve as chairman of the Army Advisory Panel on Joint Amphibious Operations.[75]

Devers's choice of Lucian Truscott as the chairman of that panel was an obvious one. No other Army officer had experience to match that of Truscott in planning and executing amphibious operations: Dieppe, TORCH-GOALPOST, HUSKY, SHINGLE, and ANVIL-DRAGOON, as well as the two tactical amphibious operations carried out by his 3d Infantry Division along the northern coast of Sicily during the drive to Messina. In fact, his contemporaries considered Truscott to be the "'best sea-to-land' commander in the U.S. Army," and he was regarded as "one of the U.S. Army's foremost experts on amphibious warfare during the Second World War."[76]

On January 15, 1949, Truscott's panel submitted its recommendations to the Army member of the Committee for Joint Policies and Procedures. First was the establishment of a joint agency "to initiate, supervise the development of, and resolve all matters pertaining to joint amphibious operations," and the establishment of "a joint amphibious center, with the Navy as executive agent, charged with formulating doctrine and procedures, developing and testing equipment, and conducting joint amphibious training of such forces as may be assigned therefor." Second, responsibility for joint amphibious operations should rest in the service, Army or Navy, which has the dominant interest in the operation. Finally, the Army should "recognize and assume full responsibility for the development of invasion doctrines to insure that a limited concept of the amphibious operation will not jeopardize fundamental Army functions."[77]

On February 1 Truscott resumed his status as a retired army officer and returned to his labors at Bluemont. In the final Efficiency Report Truscott received in his long military career, Devers rated him as "Superior" in all categories, and stated that he was "an experienced combat soldier of high ideals, great integrity and character, who can and does deliver in a superior manner on any task assigned."[78]

On Sunday, June 25, 1950, the North Korean Army crossed the Thirty-eighth Parallel and invaded the Republic of Korea, swiftly driving the poorly equipped, outnumbered, and outgunned ROK Army southward. Seoul fell on the twenty-eighth, and by the end of June all of South Korea north of the Han River was in enemy hands. In accordance with a UN resolution to aid the ROK government, President Harry S. Truman ordered Gen. Douglas MacArthur to send American ground troops from Japan to Korea to assist the rapidly retreating ROK Army.

In July Capt. Lucian K. Truscott III received orders to join the 9th Infantry, 2d Infantry Division, as it was preparing to deploy from Fort Lewis to Korea, and visited his parents at Bluemont to bid them farewell. There he talked with his father about what he might expect to face as an infantry officer in combat.

When young Truscott left a few days later, tears were in his father's eyes. Undoubtedly moved by the experience, Truscott submitted through channels a request for his recall to active duty. In early August he received a letter from Gen. J. Lawton Collins, Army chief of staff, thanking him for his "characteristically unselfish offer," but informing him that at present there were no plans to recall retired general officers to active duty. He closed by assuring Truscott that he would "not be overlooked should the need arise."[79]

Chapter 14

Duty with the CIA

In early 1951 Lucian Truscott received a call from his former comrade-in-arms Lt. Gen. Walter Bedell Smith, a call that would lead to a more than eight-year interruption of his retirement. Smith had been serving as the fourth director of central intelligence (DCI) and head of the Central Intelligence Agency since October 7, 1950,[1] and had called to ask Truscott to come to Washington to discuss an important matter with him, one that would afford him another opportunity to serve his country. Truscott quickly agreed and soon was in Smith's office.

Smith explained to Truscott that since becoming head of the CIA he had been reorganizing the agency and its chain of command. One problem that he wished to resolve was that of supervision and coordination of the activities of the overseas Offices of Special Operations (OSO), charged with clandestine collection of intelligence, and the Offices of Policy and Coordination (OPC), which were under the supervision of the Departments of State and Defense rather than the DCI and were charged with conducting all other covert actions. To that end he had devised "a system of Senior Representatives (of the DCI) abroad" to address the problem,[2] and would function as "a local umpire in addition to the station chief" in resolving disputes between the "warring factions of OPC and OSO."[3] They would not be in the chain of command but would function as "local observers for the DCI, reporting directly to him." They "were to be kept fully informed by the field stations under their supervision and could intervene with advice, although not with orders." However, if the offices should disregard their advice, they could submit their recommendations directly to the DCI, who could then issue his own orders to appropriate subordinates.[4]

Smith offered Truscott the position of senior representative in Germany, with headquarters in Frankfurt. He would initially be hired as a consultant, to be compensated at the rate of fifty dollars per day, and would ultimately serve in the grade of GS-18 with the agency, the Civil Service equivalent of a lieutenant general, with an annual salary of fourteen thousand dollars. After conferring with Sarah, Truscott accepted Smith's offer and became the CIA senior representative in Germany, effective February 8, 1951.[5]

Prior to his leaving for Germany, Truscott received from Smith a memorandum outlining his responsibilities as senior representative in Germany: supervise all CIA activities in Germany, review and supervise all CIA budgets and expenditures, coordinate all CIA activities with those of other American intelligence agencies in Germany, maintain access to all CIA communications to and from Germany, and keep "the activities and personnel of OSO and OPC separate from each other [and] separate from the activities and personnel" of all other agency offices in the area. His cover status in Germany was to be that of special consultant to the U.S. high commissioner for Germany (HICOG), John J. McCloy.[6] Shortly thereafter, brief newspaper articles datelined Frankfurt, Germany, May 24, 1951, and Oklahoma City, May 25, 1951, noted that Lt. Gen. Lucian K. Truscott, Jr., had joined High Commissioner McCloy's staff as "co-ordinator and advisor for military security, defense organization and public safety."[7]

After selling their farm in Bluemont the Truscotts traveled to Frankfurt, arriving there in April. Truscott went immediately to his office in the I. G. Farben building in downtown Frankfurt, which at that time was occupied not only by CIA personnel but also by a few elements of the U.S. Army V Corps, then in the process of relocating to Heidelberg, and by High Commissioner of Germany McCloy and his staff and assistants, who would soon move to Bonn, the capital of the German Federal Republic. Truscott moved into an office that he would temporarily share with High Commissioner McCloy's director of intelligence, Benjamin Shute.

The couple's first quarters were in the Victory Guest House some ten miles outside of Frankfurt,[8] but in June they moved into a government-owned and -operated house located in Bad Homburg, just north of Frankfurt. It was a roomy three-story home and came with a household staff made up of a butler, cook, maid, laundress, and gardener, who cared for the spacious grounds, the many fruit and berry trees, and the luxuriant shrubbery.[9]

In June, Jamie, on summer leave from West Point, visited his parents and accompanied them on a whirlwind tour of Germany and Paris, concluding with a visit to the Lido musical cabaret, where General and Mrs. Eisenhower and Maj. John Eisenhower, who had been one of Jamie's instructors at the academy, joined them. General Eisenhower was serving as the first Supreme Allied Commander, Europe, with his headquarters in Paris.[10]

As Truscott settled into his new assignment he found that he was in charge of some fourteen hundred personnel in the agency's German mission, located mainly in Berlin, Frankfurt, and Karlsruhe. In the Farben building there were several CIA elements: the OPC, headed by Michael Burke; the Office of Operations, which conducted overt CIA operations such as contacting businessmen returning from Russia and Eastern Europe and debriefing them; and the small Office of Scientific Intelligence. The OSO office, headed by Gordon Stewart, was located in Karlsruhe, but Truscott soon ordered it to relocate to the Farben building, where all the activities of the German CIA mission would be centralized.[11]

Truscott realized that it would be necessary to coordinate the CIA intelligence activities with those of the U.S. Army in Europe. During the first week of August, when Allen Dulles, Smith's deputy director, was visiting Truscott, the two traveled to Heidelberg, where they discussed with military and CIA personnel issues pertaining to war planning and the setting up of the Supreme Headquarters, Allied Powers Europe (SHAPE), Clandestine Committee that would include CIA representatives and would coordinate clandestine activities of the various intelligence agencies operating in Germany. Dulles emphasized how important Truscott's "help and diplomatic skill" would be in ensuring that the committee would become fully functional and that the CIA would have a voice in the actions of the committee.[12]

After Dulles returned to Washington and briefed DCI Smith on the planning for the SHAPE Clandestine Committee, Smith decided to monitor the progress of Truscott's efforts to form such a committee by having him submit periodic reports to the Intelligence Advisory Committee.[13] Minutes of IAC meetings of May 15 and June 26, 1952, noted discussions of Truscott's reports, and the minutes of July 15 stated that the IAC, apparently satisfied with his progress, advised him "to proceed as appropriate with the intelligence chiefs in Germany."[14]

In the early days of his assignment, Truscott had a very small staff, consisting of a secretary, an administrative officer, a finance officer, and a security officer. He soon found that in order to oversee the activities of the OSO and OPC departments he would need assistants who could provide him "operational assistance" in dealing with them. In June, Stewart assigned Thomas Polgar, who had been the chief of base in Frankfurt, as Truscott's special assistant for OSO activities,[15] and Burke assigned Peter Jessup, who had been working in Frankfurt in a CIA undercover unit known as the Document Disposal Unit, as the special assistant for OPC activities.[16] Stewart became Truscott's deputy, and Burke became Stewart's assistant.[17]

When McCloy moved his headquarters to Bonn, Truscott took over the high commissioner's Directorate of Intelligence functions, including Shute's research analysis division.[18] This provided the Frankfurt CIA mission with a very valuable intelligence asset that it had previously lacked, the capability to analyze the massive amount of raw intelligence coming into Truscott's office, and provided him with the only complete all-source intelligence analytical capability available to the CIA in Germany. In addition to providing intelligence to the

CIA, Truscott analyzed and provided pertinent intelligence to the high commissioner. Another benefit that accrued to Truscott when HICOG moved to Bonn was that he acquired all of the space formally occupied by the Directorate of Intelligence, providing ample room to consolidate all of the CIA activities under his supervision within the Farben building.

When Truscott inherited the functions of the HICOG Directorate of Intelligence he acquired the capability to gain access to all incoming and outgoing cable traffic in Germany. Because the cable traffic was so heavy, Polgar and Jessup, sometimes assisted by the adjutant reports officer, would screen the cable traffic, separating the cables into categories: those that contained information essential for Truscott to know, those that were of interest to him, and those that were of no interest. Thus, each morning Truscott would have to read only a handful of cables containing information of vital interest, holding others for reading at his leisure.[19]

Truscott's actions to consolidate the mission in Frankfurt met with resistance both within Germany and in Washington, as each affected Directorate attempted to retain control of its own turf. One example of the opposition Truscott encountered in Frankfurt occurred shortly after Jessup had been appointed as his special assistant for OPC functions. Learning of a meeting that Burke had called, Jessup arrived at the meeting room, only to be told by Burke's assistant that he could not attend the meeting. Jessup reported this to Truscott, who instructed his administrative assistant, Mrs. C. G. Follich, to get Burke on the phone. However, Burke's secretary informed Mrs. Follich that Burke was "busy" and could not take the phone call. When Mrs. Follich relayed Burke's secretary's response, Truscott ordered Burke to be in his office "in four minutes." When a "flustered" Burke appeared, Truscott dressed him down, pointing out who was "in charge" and saying that Burke should not "forget it." "That was an awakening to Burke [and others] that this guy [Truscott] was here for business."[20]

The opposition from the Washington office was a more serious problem and necessitated Truscott's and Polgar's return to Washington in the early summer of 1952 to discuss the matter with DCI Smith. With Smith's strong and unyielding support, the consolidation of the CIA mission in Germany soon became a fait accompli.[21] On July 15 Smith issued a directive dictating that the two offices cease to exist as separate entities and merge into a single organization, the Clandestine Services, which would be headed by the deputy director for plans. In the same directive, effective August 1, Smith assigned his senior representatives "*command* authority over all CIA activities in their respective areas of responsibility." As a result there would be "only two echelons of command authority: the Director of Central Intelligence in Washington and the Senior Representatives abroad." This action greatly increased the authority and status of the senior representatives, while reducing Smith's span of control, mirroring very closely the military command structure put in place by Army chief of staff Gen. George C. Marshall during World War II.[22]

In the spring of 1952 Truscott eagerly accepted an invitation from the Italian government to give the Memorial Day address at the Sicily-Rome American cemetery. Participating in the ceremony would give him an opportunity to honor many of the men whom he had commanded during the brutal Sicilian campaign and the Italian campaign south of Rome and would also provide him an opportunity to take Sarah to many of the places where he and the men he commanded had fought and defeated the German Army.

They left Frankfurt in a chauffeured auto on May 27, motoring through Munich, Innsbruck, and the Brenner Pass into Italy, stopping first in Riva, on the north shore of Lake Garda. There they saw the highway tunnels on the eastern shore of the lake where the 10th Mountain Division had encountered stubborn German resistance during their northward advance; they also visited the site of the gallant Colonel Darby's death. From there they went to Gardone, where Truscott had established his headquarters in the Hotel Savoy after the war in Europe had ended. After a drink in the Savoy's bar, they continued south across the Po River plain, Truscott pointing out to Sarah places where his troops had fought. Passing through Verona, Parma, and Modena, they arrived in Bologna, where they spent the night.

The next day they began the climb into the Apennines, where Truscott showed Sarah many places where his men had engaged the Germans in bitter fighting. Finally, they arrived at Futa Pass, where Truscott attempted, without success, to locate the spot where he had established his forward CP, but he did find the field where his personal aircraft had landed and taken off so many times. While there Sarah picked up a "pretty gray stone" as a memento of her visit to the site of her husband's command post. They then went on to Florence, enjoying lunch at the Excelsior Hotel where Truscott had stayed during the war. After lunch they continued on to Rome for an overnight stay before going on the next morning to the cemetery.

After an invocation by the American chaplain and a short talk by the Italian minister of defense, the bare-headed Truscott walked to the podium, "his gray hair shining" in the brilliant sunshine. "In a moving, sincere voice [he] spoke of the soldiers lost at Anzio, what the struggle to hold it signified in spirit and sacrifice, and how every man west of the Iron Curtain should realize he is still fighting that fight and [should] honor and respect . . . every man who gave his life." After the ceremony the Truscotts met briefly with Mike Chinigo and visited the villa where Lucian had lived while commanding VI Corps in the beachhead. On their return to Rome they drove through the once-menacing but now beautiful Alban Hills. In Rome they attended a number of formal receptions and dinners, and Lucian was reunited with his former aide Jack Bartash, who was living in Milan and "was absolutely plastered" when he met with Truscott and Sarah. After touring the city and participating in a July 2 celebration commemorating the founding of the Italian Republic, the Truscotts left Rome, visiting Pisa, Milan, Lake Como, and Zurich on their return journey to Frankfurt.[23]

One of the more serious problems facing Truscott was the activities of the Bunddeutsche Jugend (Young German League), a German youth organization formed in 1950 by "a tubby blond ex-Austrian labor organizer who spooked as Henry C. Sutton" and who was operating under U.S. Army cover. Sutton had formed the league to counter the youth organizations the European Communists were then forming. The group, many of whom were not *young* Germans but *old* SS officers, had been set up as a stay-behind group that would develop and carry out plans to oppose the Soviets if they someday overran West Germany. In October 1952 Truscott learned that the league had drawn up a secret list of leftist West German politicians whom they had targeted for assassination on the day of a Soviet attack. Unfortunately, the list included practically all of the leaders of the German Social Democratic Party, including Dr. Georg Zinn, the minister-president of the German state of Hesse, in which Frankfurt is located. Truscott immediately informed the high commissioner of Germany, who directed him to discuss the problem personally with Doctor Zinn, and, since Sutton was operating under U.S. Army cover, relay the information to Gen. Matthew B. Ridgway, then serving as Supreme Allied Commander, Europe. Truscott and Polgar flew to Paris and met with Ridgway, who, after Truscott's briefing, expressed his complete confidence in Truscott's ability to handle the problem. They then went to Wiesbaden to meet with Zinn, Polgar acting as the interpreter. Truscott apologized to Zinn and said that the actions by the youth group were an aberration of which he had had no personal knowledge and that he would quickly shut down the operation. Zinn politely accepted Truscott's apology and explanation, thereby ending the embarrassing episode.

Shortly thereafter Dulles, the deputy director, visited Frankfurt, where Truscott explained to him the potential problems that such activities could cause. Dulles tried to minimize any such problems with his usual "hearty laugh" and rose to leave. Truscott immediately ordered him to "Sit down!" and continued his denunciation of the group and its plans, telling Dulles of the difficulties and personal embarrassment that such actions were producing for him as Smith's senior representative in Germany.[24]

On June 16, 1953, fifty thousand workers began rioting in the streets of East Berlin, attacking the hated East German police and tearing down Communist banners as they marched through the city. The workers had called the strike because of the failure of the East German government to address their complaints about the hardships they were enduring as a result of a policy the Communist government of East Berlin had established in the spring of 1952: a 35 percent increase in productivity for all construction workers and a decrease in pay of up to 35 percent for workers not meeting the production quotas. The workers were also demanding free elections and a united Berlin and called for a general strike of all Berlin workers for the next day.[25]

Although the Soviet leaders had apparently received no intelligence indicating that the East Germans were planning demonstrations and a general strike for the seventeenth, they moved decisively when alerted, deploying two armored divisions and T-34 tanks to Berlin the morning of the seventeenth. At Potsdamerplatz, on the border between the American and Soviet zones, a huge crowd had gathered. Without warning the Soviet tanks began moving into the crowd, firing rounds above the crowd, some of which landed in West Berlin. Since the trouble was confined to East Berlin, the Soviets were confident that the Americans would not respond, allowing them free rein to crush the uprising.

At the CIA's Berlin Base only the deputy chief, German-born Henry Hecksher, believed that a genuine revolution was at hand and recommended that the rioting workers receive American support, which senior CIA officials in Washington refused to grant. Meanwhile, the Soviets continued their savage attacks on the workers, resulting in the deaths of 25 East Berliners and the wounding of 378 others. Having quashed the abortive workers' "revolution," the Soviets reinstalled to power "the puppet leadership that had fled East Berlin for the countryside."[26]

As all of this was transpiring, Truscott and Polgar were returning to Frankfurt from a trip visiting CIA installations in Munich and Nuremberg. They first learned of the East Berlin riots when their train stopped in Würzburg and they heard newspaper vendors shouting the news of the riots. When they arrived in Frankfurt some two hours later, they were told that the East German riots had come as a complete surprise to the CIA station in Germany and appeared to be an intelligence failure of colossal magnitude. However, as Truscott and Polgar and other senior CIA leaders reflected on the issue, they came to the conclusion that "nobody could have gauged . . . the workers' discontent with the Russians" or predicted the ferocity of the Soviet response. Truscott was also convinced that the riots would "not be a signal for East Germany [to rise up against the Soviets] because the Soviets are going to take precautionary measures."

There was, however, one influential American who "was very impressed by the seventeenth of June and what a black eye it gave to the Soviets": Allen Dulles's brother, Secretary of State John Foster Dulles, who believed that "the East German regime is in power by the grace of the Soviet military. And that if the Soviet military weren't there the East German government would be overthrown by the German workers." After attending a foreign ministers' conference in January 1954, Secretary Dulles asked Truscott, Polgar, and Burke to come to Berlin to discuss with him the advisability of having the CIA organize a large public demonstration in front of the Soviet Embassy on Unter den Linden in East Berlin. Truscott's reply in essence was, "You are out of your mind." He went on to say that before the secretary made such a request he should be familiar with the Soviet military posture in East Berlin and went on to describe in detail the "order of battle" of the Soviet armed forces in the German capital. He pointed out to Dulles that before the demonstrators could organize, the Soviet military would respond with overwhelming force and crush the incipient demonstration and would allege that the Americans had had a hand in encouraging the protest. Hearing Truscott's objection and reasons for opposing such a demonstration, Dulles stated, "Okay, I withdraw my request."[27]

One of the first counterintelligence operations in which Truscott became involved was that of constructing a tunnel from the American sector in Berlin into the Soviet sector to gain access to Soviet telecommunications cables.[28] In early 1951 Frank Rowlett, the chief of OSO's Staff D, which was "responsible for clandestine operations against foreign communications abroad," told William K. Harvey, who was to become chief of the CIA's Berlin Base in December 1952, "of his frustration over the loss to American intelligence caused by the Soviet shift from wireless transmissions to land lines," overhead lines, and buried cables in their zones of occupation in Austria and Germany.[29]

CIA officers determined that tapping into the underground cables would be the preferable operation and recommended tunneling from the American sector of Berlin into the Soviet sector to do so. After one of his senior officers briefed him on the tunnel plan in the spring of 1953, Truscott became an enthusiastic supporter of the project. He notified the CIA headquarters in Washington that the cable lines carried valuable Soviet military, KGB (Committee of State Security), and diplomatic telephone and telegraph traffic and recommended approval of the tunnel project. Plans for the tunnel were completed by August 1953 and were forwarded to Allen Dulles, who had succeeded General Smith as director on February 26, 1953.[30] In his cover letter to Dulles, Truscott emphasized that "the success of this project is primarily a matter of maintaining the highest possible degree of security" and indicated his intention to limit knowledge of the project to "only those individuals who can make a specific contribution to the success of this operation."[31] In fact, the only CIA personnel in Germany who had knowledge of the project were Truscott and seven others. Security would be equally tight in Washington.[32]

After lengthy consideration, Dulles approved the project in January 1954. An agent working inside the East Berlin post office had provided information about the locations of the underground cables used by the Soviets, leading the Allies to choose the Altglienicke district within the American Zone of Berlin as the best site for the tunnel. "Using the construction of an Air Force radar site and warehouse as a cover," work on the tunnel began in February 1954 and was completed at the end of February 1955.[33] The completed tunnel ran 1,476 feet from beneath the newly constructed radar site to a point just beyond a heavily traveled highway, Schönefelder Chaussee, where three cables were tapped on

May 11 and 21 and August 2, 1955; monitoring began immediately after each cable was tapped.[34]

However, even before Dulles approved the project the Soviets had learned of the operation. In October 1953 American intelligence officers had briefed an audience of British Secret Intelligence Service (SIS) officers, one of whom, George Blake, was a KGB mole. Blake reported the project to his Soviet case officer, Sergei Kondrashev, at their next meeting in London in December, and by February 1954 a full report of the tunnel project was in the hands of the KGB. By late 1955 a small team from the KGB had located the sites of the cable taps.[35]

When the KGB learned that the tunnel was to be constructed and the cables tapped, the agency decided not to attempt to send disinformation via the tapped cables, fearing that the Allies might have access to other intelligence against which they could compare the accuracy of the intelligence obtained from the tapped cables. If they discovered that the Soviets were sending false or deceptive intelligence, they would quickly conclude that the Soviets were aware of the taps and would instantly start a search for a Soviet mole. The KGB placed a greater value in retaining their mole Blake in the SIS than on allowing the Western allies to intercept the messages traveling along the tapped cables.[36]

However, early in 1956 the Soviets decided to shut the tunnel operation down, and heavy rains in the spring of 1956 provided them with the opportunity to do so without placing Blake at risk. The flooding resulting from the rains had caused some of the cables between Karlshorst and Wünsdorf, including one of the tapped cables, to begin short-circuiting. The Americans in the tunnel soon learned of the short-circuiting problem and informed Truscott on April 20 that the Soviets would most likely dispatch cable-repair teams that might discover the tunnel while digging up the damaged cables. Early in the morning of April 22 the Americans detected a cable-repair team digging above the tunnel just east of the highway. Within an hour the repair team had uncovered the top of the tap chamber, and all American personnel immediately evacuated the tunnel. At about 3:30 a.m. the digging team left, only to return two hours later and resume digging. At 12:30 p.m. the team opened a trapdoor leading from the tap chamber into the tunnel itself, and within two hours they were in the tunnel. At 3:35 a.m. the Soviets cut the cables.[37]

In the eleven months and eleven days that the cable taps were in place approximately forty thousand hours of telephone conversations and six million hours of Teletype traffic were recorded. The CIA concluded, after closely examining the intercepted intelligence in 1961 after the exposure and arrest of Blake, that the intelligence was indeed genuine.[38] American and British officials deemed the information from the intercepted intelligence, code-named RE-GAL, to be "the prime source of early warning concerning Soviet intentions in Europe, if not world-wide." Among the items of intelligence intercepted were the following: Soviet resistance to East German pressure to relinquish control of East Berlin, the Soviet decision to establish an East German Army, Soviet plans to implement the Warsaw Pact, development of improved nuclear delivery capability in the Soviet Air Army in East Germany, the order of battle of Soviet ground forces not previously identified or located by other intelligence sources, and "identification of several hundred Soviet Intelligence personalities in East Germany and Moscow."[39] Truscott's decision to recommend the Berlin tunnel operation to Dulles reaped rich rewards, providing "information that was invaluable in the days before reconnaissance satellites and other, more sophisticated means of collection became operational."[40]

On July 19, 1954, President Eisenhower signed into law a bill naming Lt. Gen. Lucian K. Truscott, Jr., and ten other lieutenant generals for honorary promotion to four-star rank.[41] The elementary school teacher from Oklahoma had reached the apogee of his long military career.

In mid-1952 the CIA had established the War Plans Division that provided "the first controlling head for CIA Unconventional Warfare war planning efforts." Dulles designated Truscott the senior war planner of Europe and formed the European War Plans Group that reported to him to carry out the CIA European war-planning mission. Simultaneously, the Joint Chiefs of Staff established the U.S. European Command, which, in coordination with Truscott's War Plans Group, assumed the responsibility for unconventional warfare planning in the European theater.

A subsequent series of conferences between representatives of Truscott and SHAPE identified 1,120 targets "as military requirements for Unconventional Warfare operations." Truscott's War Plans Group studied those targets and by March 12, 1954, had notified European Command that the group had tentatively accepted 163 targets. Additional conferences took place in the summer of 1954, and the resulting target requirements were forwarded to the Joint Chiefs of Staff in May 1955. The targets finally accepted consisted of subversion (sabotage) targets, guerrilla warfare areas, evasion and escape areas, and one other, the identity of which was redacted in the document released by the CIA.

In May 1955 Truscott thoroughly briefed the deputy commander in chief of Europe on the CIA's assets and capabilities in Europe and "pointed out that the requirements as expressed in the European Command Unconventional Warfare plan were completely unrealistic and beyond CIA's capability to accept." Subsequently, the Joint Chiefs of Staff ordered the chiefs of the three services to review their "requirements for covert operations in preparation for Unconventional Warfare . . . to insure that requirements . . . are current, realistic, and essential to the conduct of Unconventional Warfare in support of plans prepared pursuant to directives of the Joint Chiefs of Staff." As a result Truscott and the commander in chief of Europe were able to develop "a concept of Unconventional Warfare requirements which appeared realistic, flexible and within CIA's capability to accept as objectives for accomplishment."[42]

In the spring of 1955 Premier Zhou Enlai (Chou En-lai) of the People's Republic of China planned to attend a conference of twenty-nine Asian and African nations in Bandung, Indonesia, to promote economic and cultural cooperation and to oppose colonialism. Truscott received information that Asian station officers had planned to assassinate an East Asian leader, later identified as Zhou, by having an indigenous agent place an "undetectable poison" in Zhou's rice bowl at the conference's final banquet that would cause his death some forty-eight hours later, after he had returned to Beijing. Fearing that Zhou's assassination would succeed only in harming America's interests in Asia, Truscott immediately notified Dulles about the plan. "Dulles, who knew, or perhaps believed, that Truscott might pass this information along to [President] Eisenhower, hurriedly acted to terminate the operation."[43]

In the spring of 1955, as Truscott was nearing the end of his tenure as senior representative in Germany, former field marshal Albert Kesselring visited Frankfurt, and at a cocktail reception Truscott and Kesselring met for the first time. A photograph that appeared in the June 4, 1955, issue of the *New York Times* depicted a smiling Sarah Truscott flanked by the two beaming former enemies, her arm entwined with that of Kesselring. There is no record of what the two men discussed.[44]

In November 1954 Truscott's successor, Tracy Barnes, arrived in Frankfurt. Barnes had most recently been deeply involved in the CIA's successful but controversial Operation PBSUCCESS that resulted in the June 1954 overthrow of the Guatemalan president, Jacabo Árbenz Guzmán, from power.[45] Truscott had strongly opposed the appointment of Barnes as his successor, describing "Barnes as a callow Ivy Leaguer who would be likely to undertake risky, insecure operations." Dulles had, however, insisted that Barnes be the next senior representative in Germany.[46] Peter Jessup stated that Dulles "was sympathetic to the 'WASP' [white Anglo-Saxon Protestant] elite that surrounded him. . . . Tracy Barnes was a very attractive guy, with a very attractive wife, very cheerful, good tennis player, and an able fellow. But I think Truscott was right: That isn't what we needed in '55 or '54. You still needed somebody very severe to watch over things, because who could know what would pop up." With Barnes now firmly ensconced in the Frankfurt office, Truscott returned to the Washington base of the Central Intelligence Agency in October 1955.[47]

On September 8, 1956, Truscott received the Distinguished Intelligence Medal, the CIA's second-highest decoration, "for outstanding service and meritorious performance while serving as Coordinator and Special Advisor on Intelligence Matters to the U.S. High Commissioner to Germany during the period of June 1951 to May 1955." He demonstrated "exceptional qualities of leadership, tact, and determination. . . . His personal efforts and skill were in large measure responsible for improved coordination between and more effective activity on the part of the U.S. intelligence community in Germany and elsewhere."[48]

While serving as the senior CIA representative in Germany, Truscott wrote his highly regarded memoir, *Command Missions.* According to Peter Jessup he wrote it in the evenings, never using any government typists or assistants. He worked on the manuscript only at home, never in the office, relying on the records and documents that he had collected during the war. He drew all the maps for the book and typed the entire manuscript on his "beat-up old Smith-Corona portable typewriter."[49] The book was published in 1954 by E. P. Dutton and Company and received rave reviews in such prestigious newspapers and periodicals as the *New York Times,* the *Reporter,* and *Newsweek.*[50]

Lucian and Sarah returned to Washington in October 1955 and moved into a house at 6655 Thirty-second Place N.W. in the Barnaby Woods section of Washington, just west of Rock Creek Park, where they would reside until his retirement from the CIA four years later. He initially served as special assistant to Dulles on the planning and coordination staff and held that position until July 1957. Polgar described the position as "a post that you give to somebody . . . that doesn't want to retire, that needs an office on the seventh floor, and has a car and a driver, and doesn't do any harm." He went on to state that during that period Truscott was essentially "out of circulation" so far as CIA activities were concerned and very frequently complained about his not being consulted about CIA operations that included activities in which he had particular expertise. When asked if this was a deliberate act on the part of Allen Dulles, Polgar replied, "Absolutely, absolutely."[51] It appears that the only assignment Dulles gave Truscott during his term as special assistant was that of serving as liaison officer between the CIA and the Committee on Disarmament, headed by Harold E. Stassen, who was serving as special assistant to President Eisenhower for disarmament matters. Truscott apparently served in that position until July 1, 1957.[52]

In early 1955 President Eisenhower was considering "a possible disarmament agreement between the U.S. and the Soviet Union" and, because of the Soviet opposition to on-site inspections of nuclear weapons facilities and bases, was considering the use of "aerial reconnaissance as the vehicle for inspection and compliance with any proposed disarmament." Eisenhower asked his old friend and comrade-in-arms Lucian Truscott to "apprise him of the pros and cons of a disarmament proposal using aerial reconnaissance." The CIA assigned Dino A. Brugioni, a member of its National Photographic Interpretation Center, to meet with Truscott and show him "the types of information that [they] were holding on Russian plants," including aerial photos and blueprints. After meeting with Brugioni, apparently in the spring or early summer, Truscott asked Brugioni to accompany him to the White House, where they met with Nelson Rockefeller, an Eisenhower aide for foreign affairs. Rockefeller was also impressed "by what could be done with a combination of blueprints and aerial photography" and set about drafting a proposal for Eisenhower to present at a summit conference with the Soviets to be held in Geneva in July. Rockefeller presented the proposal to Secretary of State John Foster Dulles, who promptly rejected it. However, Eisenhower overruled Dulles and presented the proposal to the Soviets at Geneva, only to have Nikita Khrushchev, the Soviet premier, rebuff his offer.[53]

It is ironic that what was possibly the CIA's greatest intelligence coup would lead to one of the greatest disasters of the Cold War, the Hungarian uprising that began in late October 1956. In February 1956 Premier Khrushchev gave a secret speech to the Twentieth Party Congress in Moscow, in which he denounced "Stalin for his criminal cruelty and misgovernment" and hinted that there might soon be a lessening of Communist Party control within Russia and the Soviet satellites in Eastern Europe. Gossip about the speech spread quickly around the world and reached the ears of Allen Dulles, who put out word that he greatly wished to obtain a copy of the speech. Soon he had a copy in hand and, after validating its authenticity through other sources, began discussions about whether to make the speech public. Ray Cline, who subsequently became deputy director of the CIA, was one of the strongest advocates for releasing the speech to the press, and on June 2 Dulles acceded to Cline's wishes. He immediately called his brother, John Foster Dulles, who agreed that the contents of the speech should be made public. After receiving President Eisenhower's concurrence, Dulles ordered his department to send a copy of the speech to the *New York Times*, which published its complete text on June 4.[54] Very quickly Radio Free Europe (RFE) broadcast Khrushchev's speech, and soon thereafter "enthusiasts at Radio Free Europe's Hungarian desk further encouraged anti-Soviet nationalism by hinting at American aid, should there be an uprising." How much influence those urgings had in bringing about the uprising in Budapest is questionable, since East European dissidents later "strongly resented any suggestion that they had been externally manipulated."[55]

On October 23 Hungarian students took to the streets, demanding that Imire Nagy, a Hungarian nationalist, replace the Soviet-installed Stalinist. Workers soon joined the students, and Khrushchev reluctantly agreed to place Nagy in power. However, that was no longer adequate to satisfy the Hungarian demands, and soon the students and workers, encouraged by RFE, CIA-directed groups within Hungary, and John Foster Dulles, "who promised economic assistance to those countries that broke with the Kremlin," were clamoring for complete removal of Soviet troops from Hungary and an end to communism. On October 31 Nagy announced that Hungary would withdraw from the Warsaw Pact, which led a "furious" Khrushchev to order two hundred thousand troops and twenty-five hundred tanks and armored cars to crush the uprising. The ensuing fierce street fighting resulted in the deaths of seven thousand Soviet troops and thirty thousand Hungarians. Despite radio pleas by the embattled freedom fighters and the promises of Dulles, President Eisenhower declined to intervene, making clear to the CIA proponents of American intervention that he would not make any attempt to liberate countries under the heel of the Soviet Union.[56]

Eisenhower did, however, direct that studies begin to determine the role of the CIA in fomenting the Hungarian uprising. One of the individuals to whom he turned was Lucian Truscott, who received the assignment to determine what role RED SOX/RED CAP, a CIA operation that had "involved the training of refugees from Hungary, Poland, Rumania, and Czechoslovakia for covert and paramilitary operations inside their homelands," might have played in the uprising. Eisenhower specifically directed Truscott to ascertain the extent of involvement of RED SOX/RED CAP operatives in urging the Hungarian students and workers to attempt the overthrow of the Soviet-installed government in Budapest and what they had told the insurgents about American promises of support.[57]

In his interviews of Hungarian refugees seeking resettlement in the United States, Truscott uncovered information that he considered "devastating." He found that the RED SOX/RED CAP operatives had told the freedom fighters about the U.S. promises to support them and had sent groups into Budapest to join and help organize them. Truscott believed that "RED SOX/RED CAP was flawed conceptually as well as practically" and that his findings "showed a basic failure on the part of the CIA to distinguish between insurrectional violence, mass uprisings, and revolutionary action in the mid-twentieth century." He concluded that "it could not possibly succeed in any country in which the military and security forces were under the state's control" and that "if the indigenous military and security forces were slow in putting down an uprising or appeared to be having some difficulty, the Soviets were prepared to use all necessary force to preserve their interests." He also learned that despite the debacle in Hungary, the CIA "was pushing ahead to give the Red Sox/Red Cap tactic one more try, this time in Czechoslovakia." Truscott feared that continuing to pursue the objectives of RED SOX/RED CAP increased the prospect of a general war in Europe and recommended to Eisenhower that he order the CIA to terminate the operation. With the concurrence of the Joint Chiefs of Staff, Eisenhower issued that termination order to Allen Dulles.[58]

In part because of the failure of the CIA to provide him with timely intelligence about the Hungarian uprising, Eisenhower believed that Allen Dulles was devoting too much of his time to covert operations, to the detriment of providing the president with intelligence in a timely fashion. Eisenhower concluded that the director was "hesitant to make intelligence summaries or judgments" and preferred to present large amounts of "raw" intelligence, allowing the president to decide what was pertinent while directing his own attention mainly to covert operations. Because Eisenhower did not have the time to read and evaluate the large volume of raw intelligence, he created in January 1956 the President's

Board of Consultants on Foreign Intelligence Activities, composed of retired senior government officials, such as Generals Bradley and Doolittle, "to provide [him] with advice on intelligence matters in general, and to recommend appropriate changes in the CIA."[59]

On December 20 the board made its first report to the president, recommending that Dulles "be provided with a Chief of Staff or Executive Director who would act as his 'Executive Vice-President.'" Dulles was "wholly opposed to the idea of an Executive Director," mainly because it would interrupt the direct chain of command between him and his deputy directors. Instead, he proposed to create the position of deputy director for coordination (DD/C) of intelligence activities and to appoint General Truscott to the post. President Eisenhower approved Dulles's proposal on August 5, 1957, and Truscott became the deputy director for coordination, effective July 1, 1957.[60]

Dulles believed that Truscott was particularly well qualified to assume the role of DD/C, since most of the problems concerning coordination of intelligence activities involved the military services, specifically "the coordination of clandestine intelligence operations of the services where US troops were stationed." Further, while serving as senior representative for the CIA in Germany, Truscott had chaired the Intelligence Coordination Committee for Germany and had gained "firsthand experience with interagency problems."[61] He was to have responsibility for reviewing "all possibilities for increasing integration, reducing duplication, and improving coordination within the intelligence community" and recommending "action by the Director of Central Intelligence to coordinate all elements of the intelligence community."[62]

However, this statement of his duties and responsibility did not empower Truscott with the authority to require the cooperation of the various agencies within the intelligence community, since Eisenhower's memorandum limited his authority to that of *review and recommendation* of actions for coordination of intelligence activities. Further complicating the issue of coordination of the activities of the intelligence community was that Dulles himself had no "direct control over the components of the intelligence community,"[63] that authority resting with the president or the National Security Council.[64]

The members of the president's board, however, were opposed to the creation of a DD/C, believing that it did not achieve the "board's stated objective [, which] had been to move the DCI from the day-to-day running of CIA into the field of interdepartmental coordination. What it got was the appointment of a man [Truscott] to concern himself with the interdepartmental work, which might give the DCI even more time to devote to his responsibilities other than coordination," that is, managing covert activities instead of serving as the president's chief intelligence adviser.[65]

Truscott decided that his staff would be small, consisting mainly of two senior people from the offices of the deputy director of intelligence and the deputy director of plans and, eventually, a representative of the comptroller. "He emphasized that his office would have no management functions and would function primarily to eliminate duplication and initiate economies in government intelligence activities."[66]

However, even with Truscott now ensconced as the DD/C, the president's board persisted in its belief that his appointment "did nothing to provide for better management within CIA." On December 1, 1958, Truscott, learning that the board "was still considering the [Executive Director and] Chief of Staff idea," met with the board's chairman, Gen. John E. Hull, who told him that although the board members thought Truscott's appointment "was a step in the right direction," Dulles was still not "giving high enough priority and personal attention to the problems of intelligence collection, which is the reason for which the Agency was created." In a memorandum to Dulles following his meeting with Hull, Truscott stated, "It is my personal opinion that the Board feels that the cold war activities occupy an undue amount of time, effort and money in the Agency, at the expense of intelligence. They certainly believe that these operations occupy too much of your time." On December 16, 1958, the board met with President Eisenhower and once again unanimously recommended that he have Dulles appoint an executive director–chief of staff for the agency. Eisenhower told the board that he would follow up "personally with the Director of Central Intelligence" but apparently dropped the matter "for the time being."[67]

Truscott spent most of his time as the DD/C "resolving jurisdictional conflicts between the Agency and the military intelligence services," which "had continued their independent clandestine collection operations" after World War II. The services' intelligence activities had "resulted in excessive duplication of the CIA effort and frequently, competition for the same agents." Among the services the Army had been the most active, its manpower greatly outnumbering even that of the CIA, and Truscott found that "the most persistent and troublesome operational problem in intelligence community coordination involved the Army's espionage activities, particularly in Western Europe."

In 1958 he "succeeded in working out an arrangement with the services, which attempted to rationalize clandestine collection activities." As a result of his efforts a National Security Council Intelligence Directive was drawn up that "assigned CIA the primary responsibility for clandestine activities abroad." An accompanying directive gave the field representatives of the director "a modified veto over the [military] services' field activities," by requiring that they refer disagreements to the DCI and the secretary of defense for arbitration. "Although issuing these directives theoretically provided the DCI with authority over espionage activities, in practice the directives only created a means of adjudicating disputes. Military commanders continued to rely on service personnel [rather than CIA personnel] to satisfy their intelligence requirements."[68]

One of Truscott's major contributions as the DD/C was his overseeing the "revision of the principal National Security Directives and related papers" during his final one and a half years of CIA service. "In this most difficult task of coordination, General Truscott's insight and understanding of the wide variety of jurisdictional requirements of all members of the Intelligence Community resulted in effecting a high degree of cooperation and minimizing areas of disagreement."[69]

On June 8, 1958, Truscott received the honorary degree of doctor of laws from Norwich University. In recognition of his "brilliant leadership as a field commander, of your outstanding record as an organizational and administrative officer, and of your inspiring example as a citizen, soldier, and public servant, Norwich University confers upon you the honorary degree of Doctor of Laws with all the rights and privileges pertaining thereto." Conferring the degree was his old friend and fellow cavalryman Maj. Gen. Ernest N. Harmon, U.S.A., Ret., the president of Norwich University.[70]

On May 1, 1959, Truscott notified Dulles that he was requesting retirement "because disabilities increasingly impair physical activities so essential in meeting properly the responsibilities of office."[71] In his reply letter Dulles recognized Truscott's "more than eight years' service in key positions with the Central Intelligence Agency, during a particularly critical and important period in the development of our work" when he had made "a real contribution," and went on to say that he hoped the general "would be available to me and to my associates from time to time for consultation and advice."[72] At the senior staff meeting of June 15, 1959, Dulles announced that General Truscott would be retiring at the end of the month and complimented him on his "distinguished service" while with the agency.[73]

On June 25 Truscott met with a member of Dulles's staff to discuss the terms of his retirement and his acceptance of a new status as a "consultant type independent contractor." According to the final agreed-upon contract, Truscott would be "paid a fee of $50.00 for any day or fraction thereof" and would receive reimbursement for expenses while serving as a consultant. His contract became effective on July 1, 1959, and would continue in force as long as the CIA had need for his services.[74] Although Dulles had suggested to Truscott that he might utilize him as a consultant in the future, he never did. The only CIA operative to do so was James H. Critchfield, who in the 1960s was serving as chief of the Near East and South Asia division. Critchfield was a former cavalry officer who had served in the 36th Infantry Division in Italy and southern France and in 1946 became a member of Truscott's Third Army staff in Germany. After joining the CIA in 1948, Critchfield was posted to Germany, where he had many contacts with Truscott in the 1950s.[75]

Truscott was quite sensitive about Dulles's not utilizing his considerable experience as a senior military officer and veteran CIA senior operative, frequently discussing his feelings with Thomas Polgar whenever they met socially after Truscott's retirement. Polgar stated that immediately after the disastrous Bay of Pigs invasion in April 1961, "Truscott complained to him that he, probably the most experienced amphibious commander in the U.S. military, [had been] kept out of the Bay of Pigs [planning]." When I asked Polgar if that was a deliberate action on the part of Allen Dulles, he responded, "Absolutely, absolutely." Polgar went on to state that if Truscott had been consulted he would have told Dulles, "You can't do it this way" and would have told him exactly what he would need "in terms of air cover, equipment, training, and support, logistics, et cetera."[76]

During Truscott's final tour of duty, Sarah and he maintained a busy social schedule, hosting many dinners and receptions at their home and attending many other similar events at the homes of their friends and associates. They dined frequently with the Polgars, particularly enjoying Mrs. Polgar's "divine Hungarian food." They also attended several White House receptions, Lucian looking "extremely handsome in his full dress." There were several trips to Wild Acres in Charlottesville to visit Sarah's mother and sister, Mary Walker Randolph, and James and "Dudie" (Lucian) and their families occasionally visited the Truscotts in Washington.[77]

However, during those four years Truscott's health continued to deteriorate, as he suffered many bouts of illness related to his pulmonary disease and deteriorating heart function, necessitating several brief hospitalizations at Walter Reed General Hospital, which ultimately led to his request for retirement from the CIA in 1959.[78]

Chapter 15

THE LAST YEARS

When Lucian retired from the CIA he and Sarah were still living in Washington but soon decided to move across the Potomac River to Alexandria. They contracted to build a house there but decided to forgo central air conditioning, which their son James believed was probably a mistake, since in the coming years his father's chronic bronchitis and chronic obstructive pulmonary disease (COPD) continued to worsen. They moved into their new residence at 1111 West Boulevard Drive in January 1960.[1]

Unfortunately, the new year was to be marked by continued worsening of Lucian's COPD, necessitating several hospitalizations and clinic visits at Walter Reed General Hospital for pneumonia and other complications of emphysema. However, the couple continued a fairly active social life, often hosting cocktail parties and dinners for friends and former CIA associates, including Gordon Stewart and his wife, Richard Helms, and James Critchfield. He also heard from men who had served with him overseas, including General O'Daniel, his former assistant division commander. Both James and Dudie and their families continued to visit periodically.

In 1962 Truscott continued to do reasonably well, although he was hospitalized for a few days in August. In 1963 Truscott's pulmonary condition appeared to improve somewhat, but although he was not hospitalized during that year, he continued to make follow-up outpatient visits to Walter Reed for monitoring of his pulmonary and cardiac conditions. His relative good health enabled Sarah and him to pursue a more active social life: in January 1963 the Truscotts attended two "Anzio Parties" to commemorate the landing of his 3d Division at Anzio in 1944; in June they hosted a dinner for old CIA friends, including William Harvey, James Critchfield, Richard Helms, and Peter Karlow and their wives; Dudie and his family visited for two weeks during the summer; and both Dudie and James and their families spent Thanksgiving with their parents. Truscott's health remained fairly stable the following year also, permitting them to host the annual "Anzio Party" in January and to attend a White House reception on May 29, where they met President Lyndon B. Johnson.[2]

During those years Truscott spent many of the spring and summer days pursuing his gardening activities. Often, after finishing his garden chores in the late afternoon, he would shower, throw on his World War II khakis, and invite friends over for drinks on the back porch, where they recalled and relived their times together in the Army or the CIA. The Truscotts' grandson, Lucian K. Truscott IV, often spent part of his summer vacations with his grandparents, and he recalls with pleasure sitting in on those sessions, sometimes being called upon to serve as the bartender. Following the cocktails, Truscott would retire to his room, where he dressed for dinner, always wearing a coat and tie for the evening meal.[3]

During 1965 Truscott's health began to deteriorate rapidly. In September his condition dramatically worsened, necessitating multiple hospitalizations because of his declining pulmonary function, now complicated by congestive heart failure.[4] Because of the repeated hospitalizations, Sarah, in consultation with Dudie, who was stationed at the Pentagon, decided to sell the house in Alexandria and rent a three-bedroom apartment at 2939 Van Ness Street, N.W., which was very close to Walter Reed. As Lucian and Sarah were beginning their move into the apartment, Lucian's condition abruptly worsened, necessitating emergency hospitalization at Walter Reed, where he died at 12:45 p.m., September 12, with Sarah at his side. The causes of death were listed as "pulmonary emphysema, chronic lung disease, pulmonary insufficiency, and myocardial insufficiency."[5] General Truscott's funeral service was held at 3:00 p.m., September 14, in the Fort Myer Chapel, following which a horse-drawn caisson bore his body to its final resting place in Arlington National Cemetery, Section 1, grave 827-B, where members of the 3d Infantry rendered full military honors.[6]

Following her husband's death, Sarah lived for a time with Dudie and his family in Alexandria before moving into an apartment in the Crystal Towers complex in nearby Arlington, where she lived for several years. During that time Sarah, Dudie, and James received an invitation to come to Carlisle Barracks, Pennsylvania, for the dedication of Truscott Hall, erected to honor General Truscott's service to his country. Subsequently, she suffered several falls, and Dudie moved her into a nursing home in Albuquerque, New Mexico, where he was then living. In 1973 Sarah fell once again, fracturing her hip. She died on August 17, 1974, of complications resulting from the fracture and was buried next to her beloved Lucian in Arlington National Cemetery.[7]

AFTERWORD

In the introduction to this book I make numerous references to the high ranking his contemporary superior officers and succeeding military historians have accorded Lucian K. Truscott as a combat *commander*. However, little has been written about his effectiveness as a combat *leader*. As Gen. Eric K. Shinseki, U.S.A., Ret., said in his farewell address in 2003 as he stepped down from his position as chief of staff of the U.S. Army after thirty-eight years of service, there is an "important distinction between command and effective leadership. . . . [C]ommand is about authority, about an appointment to position—a set of orders granting title." Shinseki went on to point out that "those, who are privileged to be selected for command, [should] approach their duties with a sense of reverence, trust, and the willingness to sacrifice all, if necessary, for those they lead. You must love those you lead before you can be an effective leader. You can certainly command without that sense of commitment, but you cannot lead without it; and without leadership, command is a hollow experience—a vacuum often filled with mistrust and arrogance."[1]

One of the first tasks Truscott accomplished after assuming command of his regimental combat team, division, corps, or field army was to visit as many of his frontline units as possible, wearing a lacquered helmet bearing the shining emblems of his rank and his trademark silk scarf, faded russet leather jacket, jodhpurs, and well-worn cavalry boots, often arriving in his jeep that sported his command's guidon mounted on the hood, with a siren on one fender and a flashing red light on the other.[2] By so doing he was able not only to gain a better understanding of the tactical situation facing that subordinate commander but also to display to his officers and men that he was willing to share the risks that they faced. His forward command posts were always located near the front lines, often in buildings exposed to enemy fire, rather than in wine cellars or sheltered locations far from the scene of fighting.

That Truscott loved those whom he led into combat, particularly the infantrymen who served as the tip of his spear, is attested by the terms of endearment that he used in describing their accomplishments to Sarah in his wartime letters, referring often to his men as "my lads," "my brave lads," "my lads, the best there are," and "these brave lads of mine." His love for the "dogfaces" was graphically demonstrated when, just before the assault at Anzio, he ordered the leaders of the 3d Infantry Division Band to set the catchy tune "Dogface Soldier" to march tempo to honor the men of his division.[3] It remains the official march of the 3d Infantry Division to this day.

However, probably the most moving example of his love and affection for the men he commanded and led into combat occurred at the dedication ceremony for the Sicily-Rome American cemetery on Memorial Day, 1945. There, instead of addressing the dignitaries and other attendees, he turned to the thousands of graves stretching before him and addressed the corpses in those graves, apologizing for any personal mistakes he had made as their leader that had consigned them to their premature deaths and asking them for their forgiveness, realizing "that was asking a hell of a lot under the circumstances."[4]

Generals Marshall, Eisenhower, Bradley, and Patton held Lucian Truscott in high esteem, which undoubtedly played a great role in his meteoric rise to high command in 1943 and 1944. As early as October 1943, Patton, who had been told by Eisenhower's chief of staff, Maj. Gen. Walter B. Smith, that he would command a field army in the Normandy invasion, stated that he would like to have Truscott as a corps commander in that army.[5]

On June 29, 1943, Eisenhower, then commander of Allied Forces Headquarters in North Africa, visited Truscott's 3d Infantry Division in Tunisia and later cabled Marshall that "from every indication it is the best unit we have brought over here.... Truscott is the quiet, forceful, enthusiastic type that subordinates instinctively follow. If his command does not give a splendid account of itself, then all signs by which I know how to judge an organization are completely false."[6] Eisenhower closely followed the Sicily and southern Italy campaigns and the early days of the Anzio operation and was so impressed with Truscott's performance as division commander in combat that he informed Marshall he rated Truscott as the number-one choice for corps command,[7] either in the Mediterranean theater or in the Normandy campaign, although he would prefer to have him as commander of one of the two American corps that would lead the assault on Normandy. He subsequently cabled Lt. Gen. Jacob L. Devers, commander of North African Theater of Operations, U.S. Army, and told him that since he and Truscott "have been together a long time ... [he] would particularly desire him as an assault corps commander.... He is exceptionally well-experienced in planning and executing an amphibious assault." However, when Truscott was named to replace Lucas as VI Corps commander, "Eisenhower lost his last chance to have him under his command."[8]

Eisenhower continued to be impressed by Truscott's performance as VI Corps commander during the breakout from the Anzio beachhead and the drive to Rome. His handling of ANVIL-DRAGOON and the advance northward through the Rhône valley confirmed his opinion that Truscott should become the next field army commander. After discussing the matter with Bradley, he had forwarded that recommendation to General Marshall in September 1944. In December Truscott returned to Italy to assume command of Fifth Army.[9]

In February 1945 Eisenhower compiled a list of thirty-eight U.S. Army and Army Air Forces general officers serving in the European and Mediterranean theaters of operations, ranking them numerically based on his "conclusions as to value of services each officer has rendered in this war." Eisenhower ranked Truscott fifth overall, and second only to Patton as an army commander.[10] On December 1, 1944, Eisenhower had asked Bradley to rank twenty-four commanders; on Bradley's list Truscott also ranked fifth, one place ahead of Patton.[11]

Although consigned to a secondary front, the Mediterranean theater of operations, Truscott and the forces he commanded contributed significantly to the defeat of Germany. In Italy the Allies, fighting in some of the most hostile terrain on earth and under the most appalling of weather conditions, tied down some thirty German divisions that might have been used decisively in Normandy or on the eastern front. The three Allied amphibious operations, HUSKY, AVALANCHE, and SHINGLE, in two of which Truscott played a key role, induced the Germans to divert reserves badly need elsewhere to guard against a possible fourth such operation on another flank.[12] Operation ANVIL-DRAGOON and the advance of Truscott's VI Corps up the Rhône River valley probably cost the German Nineteenth Army more than half of its 250,000 troops, denying their use farther north to oppose Patton's rapidly advancing Third Army. "From the beginning it was Truscott's relentless pursuit that set the tenor of the Franco-American effort," reducing the German effort "almost entirely to reacting to Allied moves,"[13] leading noted military historian Russell F. Weigley to conclude, "No American commander drove harder than Truscott, and none clung more steadfastly to the principle that destroying the enemy army was the goal."[14]

The end of World War II and Truscott's retirement from the Army did not bring to an end his contributions to America's security, for he became significantly involved in the Cold War when he accepted Beetle Smith's invitation to join the Central Intelligence Agency.[15] Assigned as Smith's senior representative in Germany, Truscott soon recognized that optimizing the collection of Soviet intelligence would require the integration of CIA intelligence activities with those of the U.S. Army in Europe. His efforts resulted in the establishment of the Supreme Headquarters, Allied Powers Europe, Clandestine Committee to coordinate the clandestine activities of the various Allied intelligence agencies operating in Europe. When the high commissioner for Germany moved his headquarters to Bonn, Truscott took over the commissioner's Directorate of Intelligence, the research analysis division of which provided the CIA with the only complete all-source intelligence analytical capability in Europe, giving the agency access to all incoming and outgoing cable traffic in Germany. The Berlin tunnel, completed under the direction of Truscott, further enhanced the capability of the Allies to intercept Soviet cable traffic by tapping into underground cables.

After returning to CIA headquarters in Washington, Truscott made a major contribution to the American effort in the Cold War when, at the request of President Eisenhower, he investigated the extent of CIA involvement in fomenting the Hungarian uprising in October 1956, which the Soviets quickly and brutally put down, with heavy loss of life. His findings revealed that indeed the agency had been involved in organizing the uprising and led Truscott to conclude that the CIA's concept of encouraging, organizing, and supporting such operations was flawed and had seriously underestimated the ferocity of the Soviet response. Learning that the agency, despite the failure of the uprising in Budapest, was planning to carry out such operations in other Eastern European countries, and fearing that such actions greatly increased the risk of a general war, Truscott recommended to Eisenhower that he shut down all such CIA activities, which the president ordered the CIA director to do. Truscott's actions materially reduced the prospect of a confrontation with the Soviet Union that might well have resulted in hostilities.

Unfortunately, Truscott had little opportunity during his final years with the CIA in Washington to utilize the leadership skills honed over a lifetime in the Army. According to Thomas Polgar, Truscott complained "very frequently" to him that CIA director Allen Dulles failed to give him any significant responsibilities and sequestered him in an office on the seventh floor of the CIA headquarters, where he would not "do any harm." Truscott was particularly perturbed when Dulles failed to consult him during the planning for the Bay of Pigs amphibious operation, the very type of operation in which Truscott had particular expertise.[16]

Truscott was not a man in the mold of a Patton or a Clark, who were masters of the art of public relations and actively sought recognition of their accomplishments. Rather, he pursued his career in a quiet, workmanlike fashion, always obedient to the chain of command and faithful to his superiors and, more important, to the men who served under him. He never lost sight of his obligation to his soldiers, and he made every effort to share the hardships and dangers his beloved "dogfaces" encountered daily in the mountains, heat, rain, snow, and mud of Sicily, Italy, and France, always keeping uppermost in his mind that their very lives lay in his hands and their fate would be determined by the decisions he made. As a result, he never hesitated to question orders from his superiors that he believed would result in unnecessary loss of life, as he did with Patton on the north coast of Sicily, when he asked Patton to delay the amphibious operation at Brolo for one day, and with Clark at the Rapido River, when he pointed out to Clark that the enemy artillery on the heights above the river would prevent reinforcement of the assault force on the opposite bank. When Patton refused to reconsider his decision, Truscott faithfully carried out the order, incurring the heavy losses that he had predicted. However, his protest to Clark led to his canceling the crossing of the Rapido by the 3d Infantry Division.[17]

Lucian K. Truscott's career as a faithful and consummate soldier, commander and leader of men, victorious general, and warrior of the Cold War deserves greater recognition, and it is my hope that this volume will serve that purpose.

Glossary and Abbreviations

AAF	Army Air Forces
Abwehr	German intelligence service
AD	Armored Division
AFHQ	Allied Force Headquarters
AGF	Army Ground Forces
AR	Army Regulations
AWOL	Absent without leave
BCT	Battalion combat team
Bigot	Special security classification for future operations
BLT	Battalion landing team
Bn.	Battalion
CARL	Combined Arms Research Library
CCO	Commander, Combined Operations
CCS	Combined Chiefs of Staff
CG	Commanding general
CGAFG	Commanding general, Army Ground Forces
CG USAFBI	Commanding general, U.S. Army Forces, British Isles
COHQ	Combined Operations Headquarters
COMINT	Communications intelligence
CONUS	Continental United States
COS	Chief(s) of Staff
CP	Command Post
CREST	CIA Research Search Tool
DCI	Director of Central Intelligence
DD/C	Deputy director for coordination
DIA	Defense Intelligence Agency
Div.	Division
DOD	Department of Defense
DUKW	Two-and-a-half-ton amphibious truck
FEC	French Expeditionary Corps

FFI	French Forces of the Interior
FO	Field Order
G1	Personnel section of divisional or higher staff
G2	Intelligence section of divisional or higher staff
G3	Operations and training section of divisional or higher staff
G4	Logistics section of divisional or higher staff
GHQ	General Headquarters
GI	Government issue. Originally a term applied to any standardized item issued by the U.S. Army. During World War II the term came to be used to refer to any member of the Army, especially an enlisted man.
GO	General Order
GSC	General Staff Corps
HQ	Headquarters
HQAGF	Headquarters, Army Ground Forces
HQ USAFBI	Headquarters, U.S. Army Forces, British Isles
IAC	Intelligence Advisory Committee
ID	Infantry Division
LCI	Landing craft, infantry
LCM	Landing craft, mechanized
LCT	Landing craft, tank
LCVP	Landing craft, vehicle, personnel
LOD	Line of departure
LST	Landing ship, tank
Maquis	Members of the French underground movement
MTOUSA	Mediterranean Theater of Operations, U.S. Army
NACP	National Archives, College Park, Maryland
NATOUSA	North African Theater of Operations, United States Army
NCO	Noncommissioned officer
NPRC	National Personnel Records Center
OB West	Oberbefehlshaber West (highest ground headquarters of the western front)
OMPF	Official Military Personnel File
OPC	Office of Policy Coordination
OPD	Operations Division, War Department General Staff
ORC	Officers' Reserve Corps
OSO	Office of Special Operations
OTC	Officers' Training Camps
POE	Port of embarkation
RCT	Regimental combat team
Regt.	Regiment
RG	Record Group

S1	Personnel section of regimental or battalion staff
S2	Intelligence section of regimental or battalion staff
S3	Operations and training section of regimental or battalion staff
S4	Logistics section of regimental or battalion staff
SHAEF	Supreme Headquarters, Allied Expeditionary Forces
SHAPE	Supreme Headquarters, Allied Powers, Europe
SO	Special Order
SS	Schutzstaffel (elite guard)
TF	Task Force
TO&E	Table of Organization and Equipment
USACGS	U.S. Army Command and General Staff School
USAMHI	United States Army Military History Institute
USANIF	U.S. Army Northern Ireland Forces
USAT	U.S. Army Transport
USCIB	U.S. Communications Intelligence Board
USMA	United States Military Academy
WD	War Department
Wehrmacht	German Armed Forces
XO	Executive officer

Code Names

ANVIL Early plan for invasion of southern France

ARCADIA The first Anglo-American conference to consider war strategy, December 24, 1941–January 14, 1942, Washington, D.C.

AVALANCHE Invasion of Italy at Salerno

BOLERO Buildup of U.S. forces and supplies in United Kingdom for cross-Channel attack

COPYBOOK Rehearsal for 3d ID landing in Sicily, June 20–26, 1943

DIADEM Full-scale ground offensive launched by the Allied command in Italy, May 12, 1944

DRAGOON Final code name for invasion of southern France

ENCORE IV Corps limited-objective attacks against Monte Belvedere, February 1945

Enigma A German cipher machine used to encrypt and decrypt secret messages

ENSA The force of which the 3d Infantry Division was a part for the invasion of Sicily; later code-named JOSS Force

FOURTH TERM IV Corps limited objective operation in Serchio valley, February 1945

GOALPOST Sub–task force formed for capture of Port Lyautey, French Morocco, November 1942

GYMNAST 1941 plan for Allied invasion of Northwest Africa

HUSKY Allied invasion of Sicily, July 1943

JOSS Assault beaches in the Licata area of Sicily

JUBILEE Dieppe, France, raid by Canadian, British, and U.S. forces, August 1942

MINCEMEAT Deception plan for the invasion of Sicily

MULBERRIES Artificial harbors for OVERLOAD

OVERLORD Allied cross-Channel invasion of Northwest Europe, June 1944

RED SOX/RED CAP	CIA program for training refugees from Hungary, Poland, Romania, and Czechoslovakia for covert and paramilitary operations inside their homelands
REGAL	Intelligence obtained from the Berlin spy-tunnel cable taps
ROUNDUP	Plan for major U.S.-British cross-Channel operation in 1943
RUTTER	Initial plan for Dieppe, France, raid, July 1942
SATIN	Allied attack toward Sfax, planned for January 1943; not executed
SHINGLE	Amphibious operation at Anzio, Italy
SLEDGEHAMMER	Plan for limited cross-Channel attack in 1942
STOPWATCH/GOLD	The Berlin spy-tunnel operation
TORCH	Allied invasion of Northwest Africa
ULTRA	Intelligence derived from Enigma decrypts
WEBFOOT	Rehearsal for SHINGLE
WINTERGEWITTER	German limited-objective counterattack against the U.S. IV Corps, December 26, 1944

NOTES

PREFACE

1. There is one extant biography of Truscott (H. Paul Jeffers, *Command of Honor: General Lucian Truscott's Path to Victory in World War II*), but this account of Truscott's long career is quite abbreviated and relies almost entirely on secondary sources.

2. Martin Blumenson, "America's World War II Leaders in Europe: Some Thoughts," 10–11; Carlo D'Este, *Eisenhower: A Soldier's Life*, 269; Cole C. Kingseed, *Old Glory Stories: American Combat Leadership in World War*, 325n3; Roger J. Spiller, "World War II General."

3. Truscott makes no mention of his service with the CIA in any of his personal materials at the Marshall Library, and none of the numerous biographical sketches of Truscott note his service with the agency. Jeffers's recounting of Truscott's CIA years in *Command of Honor* betrays an absence of serious research into that phase of Truscott's life and career.

INTRODUCTION

1. Blumenson, "America's World War II Leaders," 10; D'Este, *Eisenhower: A Soldier's Life*, 269; Kingseed, *Old Glory Stories*, 325n3; Spiller, "World War II General"; Mark Perry, *Partners in Command: George Marshall and Dwight Eisenhower in War and Peace*, 293, 413; Matthew B. Ridgway, *Soldier: The Memoirs of Matthew B. Ridgway*, 96; John S. D. Eisenhower, *They Fought at Anzio*, 36–37; Dominick Graham and Shelford Bidwell, *Tug of War: The Battle for Italy, 1943–45*, 329; Lloyd Clark, *Anzio: Italy and the Battle for Rome*, 199–200.

2. Spiller, "World War II General."

3. Eric Larrabee, *Commander in Chief: Franklin Delano Roosevelt, His Lieutenants, and Their War*, 487.

4. The U.S. Army traditionally uses Arabic numbers to designate battalions, regiments, divisions, and Army groups; roman numbers to designate corps; and ordinal numbers to designate field armies.

5. Kingseed, *Old Glory Stories*, 127–30.

6. Anne Roth and Helen Demarest, eds., *Current Biography: Who's News and Why*, s.v. "Truscott, Lucian K(ing, Jr.)."

7. Alfred D. Chandler Jr., ed., *Papers of Dwight David Eisenhower: The War Years*, vol. 4, Document (hereafter "Doc.") 1998, September 23, 1944, 2192; Doc. 2271, February 1, 1945, 2466–67.

8. Trevor N. Dupuy, Curt Johnson, and David L. Bongard, *Harper Encyclopedia of Military Biography*, s.v. "Truscott, Lucian King, Jr.," by Ken Stringer and David L. Bon-

gard; Carlo D'Este, *Fatal Decision: Anzio and the Battle for Rome*, 272–73; Graham and Bidwell, *Tug of War*, 329; Donald G. Taggart, ed., *The History of the Third Infantry Division in World War II*, 373; Lucian K. Truscott, Jr., *Command Missions: A Personal Story*, 178.

9. Kingseed, *Old Glory Stories*, 131; (quote) Truscott, *Command Missions*, 447–48.

10. Rick Atkinson, *The Day of Battle: The War in Sicily and Italy, 1943–1944*, 84, referring to a comment by Brig. Gen. Robert T. Frederick in an interview by Sidney Mathews that Truscott "drank heavily."

11. Ibid., 487; James Wilson interview; Thomas Polgar interview; James J. Truscott interview; Maj. Gen. Robert T. Frederick interview, 17. Frederick, though "disgusted" with Truscott's heavy drinking during the breakout from the Anzio beachhead, "didn't think his drinking interfered seriously with his intelligent direction of combat operations." Truscott was without question a heavy drinker. However, on the basis of the information available to me I am unable to state unequivocally that his drinking habits meet the diagnostic criteria for alcohol dependence ("alcoholism") as defined in the American Psychiatric Association's *Diagnostic and Statistical Manual of Mental Disorders*, 4th ed.

12. Biographical Sketch, Paul M. Robinett Papers. I am indebted to Jörg Muth, a doctoral candidate in the Department of History, University of Utah, for supplying me with copies of the Robinett material. Andrew Roberts has described Robinett "as an established high-flier," pointing out that at the first Anglo-American conference to consider war strategy, code-named ARCADIA, December 24, 1941–January 14, 1942, Robinett served as the senior U.S. Army member of the Joint Secretariat of the Combined Chiefs of Staff (*Masters and Commanders: How Four Titans Won the War in the West, 1941–1945*, 73).

13. Paul M. Robinett, "The Tender Threads of Fate," box 18, folder 4, Loose Leaf Notebook no. 6, Short Short Stories, Robinett Papers.

14. See note 1 for specific citations.

15. Carlo D'Este, *Patton: A Genius for War*, 801; Lucian K. Truscott Jr., *The Twilight of the U.S. Cavalry: Life in the Old Army, 1917–1942*, xiv.

16. Lucian K. Truscott Jr. to Sarah Randolph Truscott, November 10, 1943, box 1, folder 7; November 7, 1942, box 1, folder 4; December 26, 1943, box 1, folder 7; November 7, 1942, box 1, folder 4, Lucian Truscott Papers; Truscott, *Twilight of the U.S. Cavalry*, xvi.

17. Donald P. Steury, "V: Berlin Tunnel," 330.

18. "Unconventional Warfare Planning in Europe," CIA-RDP88-00374R000100290-003-6, Lucian K. Truscott Jr. Files, CIA Research Search Tool (CREST).

19. RED SOX/RED CAP was a CIA program for training refugees from Hungary, Poland, Romania, and Czechoslovakia for covert and paramilitary operations inside their homelands.

20. Stephen E. Ambrose, *Ike's Spies: Eisenhower and the Espionage Establishment*, 239; William R. Corson, *The Armies of Ignorance: The Rise of the American Intelligence Empire*, 370–71 (quotes).

21. "Portrait of General Truscott Takes Honored Place at USMA." The portrait was a copy by Gregory Stapko of a portrait by Boleslaw Jan Czedekowski commissioned by Truscott in 1945 while he was serving as commander of Fifth Army. The portrait no longer hangs in Grant Hall and is now part of the West Point Art Museum Collection, Museum no. 12017 (Gary Hood, curator, West Point Museum Art Collection, e-mail message to author, May 5, 2009).

22. Taggart, *Third Infantry Division*, 479; Dedication Ceremony, Truscott Hall, box 21, folder 9, and box 22, folder 12 (photograph of Truscott family at the ceremony), Truscott Papers.

23. S. L. A. Marshall, "Labors of Command"; Charles Poore, "Books of the *Times*," *New York Times*, February 13, 1954, CIA-RDP-75-00001R00000040040017-1, CREST; Hanson W. Baldwin, "A Fighting General Speaks Out," *New York Times*, February 7, 1954, BR3.

24. Edward M. Coffman, foreword to *Twilight of the U.S. Cavalry*, by Truscott, x; Leonard L. Lewane, review of *Twilight of the U.S. Cavalry*; Clarence E. Wunderlin Jr., review of *Twilight of the U.S. Cavalry*.

CHAPTER 1: THE EARLY YEARS

1. Truscott family tree appended to biographical sketch of early years of Lucian K. Truscott Jr., box 21, folder 6, Truscott Papers; Joseph B. Thoburn, "Thomas I. Truscott," in *A Standard History of Oklahoma: An Authentic Narrative of Its Development*, 1884–85. Ms. Jean McCracken, Cleveland County Genealogical Society, Norman, Oklahoma, kindly provided a transcribed copy of the pertinent pages from this volume.

2. Truscott family tree, box 21, folder 6, Truscott Papers; Thoburn, *Standard History of Oklahoma*, 1884. Thoburn writes that James Truscott's wife was "Eliza" Kirkland, and on page 586 of *Between the Wichitas* his wife is identified as "Eliza Jane Dickason, of Illinois." I have elected to accept the family tree listing as the most authoritative source, since a member of the Truscott family undoubtedly prepared it. There is some question regarding exactly where and in what year Doctor Truscott was born: *Between the Wichitas*, Litchfield, Illinois, in 1862 (587); director of [medical] licensing for the State of Oklahoma: Kane, Greene County, Illinois, on October 5, 1864 (Robyn Hall, e-mail message to author, March 7, 2002); Hickory Grove Cemetery, near Haywood, Oklahoma, where Lucian Truscott and his wife are buried ("Pittsburg County, Hickory Grove [Okla.] Cemetery," 5, and the Truscott family tree, 3): 1861; Lucian Jr.: Carlinsville, Illinois, on October 5, 1861 (Personal History Statement, February 14, 1951, Official Central Intelligence File, Lucian K. Truscott Jr. [hereafter cited as Truscott CIA File]). Since Doctor Truscott presumably personally supplied his birth information to the Oklahoma medical licensing agency, I have accepted that information as being the most reliable.

3. *Between the Wichitas*, 585; Paul G. Anderson, associate professor and archivist, Washington University School of Medicine, St. Louis, e-mail message to author, April 10, 2002. There is no record of Truscott's having attended college prior to his enrolling in medical school. Missouri Medical College merged into the Washington University Medical Department in 1899 ("Origins and History of the Washington University School of Medicine: Institutional Roots, 1840–1908," 1).

4. The marriage certificate of Lucian Truscott and Maria Tully indicates that Benjamin, Texas, was the residence of the groom at the time of the marriage. This certificate is located in the Special Collections, McCracken County Public Library, Paducah, Kentucky. Lori Robbins kindly supplied me with a copy of that certificate.

5. Biographical sketch of the early years of Lucian K. Truscott Jr., box 21, folder 6, 1, Truscott Papers. No author's name appears on the document, but I suspect that Sarah Randolph Truscott may have written it.

6. Marriage certificate of Lucian K. Truscott and Maria T. Tully, box 21, folder 6, Truscott Papers; Truscott family tree, 3, Truscott Papers; "Paducah City Directory," 1890–1891, Special Collections, McCracken County Public Library, Paducah, Kentucky. Lori Robbins kindly supplied me with a copy of the directory.

7. "Chatfield, TX"; Truscott family tree, box 21, folder 6, 3, Truscott Papers; Social Security Death Index, courtesy of Jean McCracken, Cleveland County, Oklahoma, Genealogical Society, e-mail message to author, March 12, 2002; "Dr. Lucian K. Truscott," School Census of District no. 1, Cleveland County, Oklahoma, June 30, 1912, kindly supplied by Dorinda Harvey, county clerk.

8. Judge Robert N. Jones Jr., e-mail message to author, March 10, 2002.

9. "Well Known Corsicana Negro Veterinarian Was Employed in Truscott Home Near Chatfield," *Corsicana (Tex.) Daily Sun,* October 6, 1945, box 22, folder 3, Truscott Papers.

10. Biographical sketch of early life of Lucian King Truscott Jr., 1; Luther B. Hill, *A History of the State of Oklahoma,* biographical sketch of "Dr. L. K. Truscott," 504–5. The author of the biographical sketch of Truscott's early life had originally typed the date of "fall of 1898," but crossed out that date and wrote in "winter of 1900–1."

11. Jean McCracken, e-mail message to author, March 3, 2002.

12. Jean McCracken has informed me that Summer Normals provided a means for rural teachers in the Oklahoma Territory to complete their work for certification as teachers while continuing to teach during the regular school term (ibid.).

13. Biographical sketch of early life of Lucian King Truscott Jr., 1.

14. Ibid., 2; Service Record, Official Military Personnel File, Lucian K. Truscott Jr. (hereafter cited as Truscott OMPF). I have not been able to learn where Dr. Truscott practiced subsequent to his stay in Onapa. However, he died of pneumonia in Haywood, Oklahoma, in June 1922. Truscott's mother died on August 7, 1938, of an "intestinal disorder" in the station hospital at Fort Leavenworth, Kansas, where she was living with her son and his family (Personal History Statement, February 14, 1951, MORI DocID: 1423217, Truscott CIA File; *Leavenworth [Kans.] Times;* "Pittsburg County, Hickory Grove Cemetery," 5).

15. Biographical sketch of early life of Lucian King Truscott Jr., 2–3.

16. Thoburn, *History of Oklahoma,* 1884–85; Will Lang, "Lucian King Truscott Jr.: A Tough U.S. General, Once an Oklahoma School Master, Wants to Be Provost Marshal of Berlin," 105.

17. Bryan Farwell, *Over There: The United States in the Great War, 1917–1918,* 35. For a concise summary of the events leading Wilson to ask for a declaration of war against Germany, see ibid., 11–34.

18. Ibid., 27, 38, 39, 50.

19. Ibid., 26.

20. John Garry Clifford, *The Citizen Soldiers: The Plattsburg Training Camp Movement, 1913–1920,* 228–29, 230. The camps were located at the following sites: two each at Plattsburg; Fort Benjamin Harrison, Indiana; and Fort Sheridan, Illinois; and one each at Fort Niagara, New York; Madison Barracks, New York; Fort Myer, Virginia; Fort McPherson, Georgia; Fort Oglethorpe, Georgia; Fort Logan H. Roots, Arkansas; Fort Riley, Kansas; Fort Snelling, Minnesota; Leon Springs, Texas; and the Presidio at San Francisco (ibid., 235).

21. *Order of Battle of the United States Land Forces in the World War,* vol. 3, part 2, 80.

22. Clifford, *Citizen Soldiers,* 234–35.

23. Certificate of Examining Officer and accompanying affidavit, Truscott OMPF. I can find nothing that indicates why Truscott was ordered to Fort Logan H. Roots rather than Leon Springs. Since the fort was closer to Truscott's home in Eufaula, the Army may have made the decision on the basis of proximity.

24. Service Record, Truscott OMPF.

25. Edward M. Coffman, *The War to End All Wars: The American Military Experience in World War I,* 55.

26. Rating Card, Truscott OMPF.

27. Efficiency Report, August 1, 1917, Truscott OMPF. "Excellent" was the highest rating an officer candidate could receive. If the service of those officers holding provisional commissions proved satisfactory during a period of two years, their commissions would become permanent (Truscott, *Twilight of the U.S. Cavalry,* 4).

28. Fort Logan H. Roots Post Returns, folder "Citizens Training Camp, 1917, Fort Logan H. Roots," World War I Strength Returns, Fort Logan H. Roots, Fort Logan, Colorado, Los Angeles, Calif.

29. Truscott, *Twilight of the U.S. Cavalry*, 4.

30. Ibid., 2. "Forward" was the motto of the 17th Cavalry Regiment (Mary Lee Stubbs and Stanley Russell Connor, *Armor-Cavalry: Part I, Regular Army and Army Reserve*, 255).

31. Folder "17th Cavalry Regiment, 1917–1918, Off's Ret. and Rosters, Return of 17th Regiment of Cavalry, August and September 1917, in 16th and 17th Cavalry Regiments, World War I Strength Returns, Cavalry (hereafter cited as "Return of 17th Cav. Regt., [date]").

32. Truscott, *Twilight of the U.S. Cavalry*, 5–6.

33. Ibid., 6.

34. Ibid., 7, 17.

35. "The Seventeenth Cavalry, Regimental History," 2.

36. Truscott, *Twilight of the U.S. Cavalry*, 22.

37. Proceedings of a Board of Officers convened at Douglas, Arizona, June 12, 1918, 2, Truscott OMPF.

38. Ibid., 17–18, 46; Adjutant General's Office, Finding of an Efficiency Board in the case of 1st Lieutenant Lucian K. Truscott, August 2, 1918, Truscott OMPF.

39. First Lieutenant Commission, Lucian K. Truscott, March 8, 1919, Truscott OMPF.

40. Return of 17th Cav. Regt., June 1918; James J. Truscott, e-mail message to author, August 23, 2005. As a toddler Truscott had swallowed some carbolic acid, leaving him with a "rock-crusher voice" (Lang, "Tough U.S. General," 98). James Truscott states that this accident rendered his father sensitive to dust in the air for the rest of his life and "may have contributed to the illness for which Doctor Randolph was treating him" (telephone conversation with James J. Truscott, August 11, 2005).

41. Copies of telegrams, June 23 and 24, from Major Wilde to Mrs. L. K. Truscott, Truscott OMPF; Return of 17th Cav. Regt., July 1918, and an untitled form in the Truscott OMPF that I have arbitrarily labeled "Station and Duty Status Report," which covers the years 1918–1919.

42. Robert Isham Randolph, *The Randolphs of Virginia: A Compilation of the Descendants of William Randolph of Turkey Island and His Wife Mary Isham of Bermuda Hundred*, 71–72. The Albemarle-Charlottesville Historical Society in Charlottesville kindly supplied me with an excerpt from this publication.

43. "Dr. Wm. Randolph Dies at Home Here," *Charlottesville Daily Progress*, January 26, 1944, courtesy of the Albemarle-Charlottesville Historical Society in Charlottesville.

44. James J. Truscott, e-mail message to author, August 23, 2005 (quotes); Randolph, *Randolphs of Virginia*, 72; Residence and Dependency Report, September 7, 1951, Truscott CIA File. In Truscott's Personal History Statement, February 14, 1951, Truscott CIA File, Truscott states that the marriage took place at Warren, Arizona, which is a suburb of present-day Bisbee.

45. Truscott, *Twilight of the U.S. Cavalry*, xvi (quote); James G. Johnson, *Graduates, Charlottesville, Virginia, High School: Containing a List of the Persons Who Graduated from This School during the Years 1894–1936*, 9, courtesy of the Albemarle-Charlottesville Historical Society in Charlottesville.

46. Truscott, *Twilight of the U.S. Cavalry*, xvi (emphasis in original).

47. Ibid., 23–24.

48. Ibid., 25–26.

49. Ibid., 27–28.

50. Ibid., 30–31.

51. Ibid., 34–35.

52. Ibid., 36–37; Return of 17th Cav. Regt., 1919.

53. "17th Cavalry, Regimental History," 1919; Truscott, *Twilight of the U.S. Cavalry,* 39–40.

54. Proceedings of a Board of Officers Convened under Provisions of Special Order (SO) 133, July 14, 1919, Truscott OMPF; SO 251-A, War Department, October 27, 1919, Truscott OMPF.

55. "17th Cavalry, Regimental History," 1920; Truscott, *Twilight of the U.S. Cavalry,* 38; "17th Cavalry, Regimental History," 1920.

56. Randolph, *Randolphs of Virginia,* 72; James J. Truscott, e-mail message to author, August 10, 2005.

57. Cablegram 919, para. 3, Adjutant General to Morton, Honolulu, April 5, 1921, Truscott OMPF; Edward M. Coffman, e-mail message to author, April 24, 2006; Truscott, *Twilight of the U.S. Cavalry,* xi; Adjutant General to Capt. Lucian K. Truscott Jr., Cavalry, "Subject: Promotion," August 20, 1935, Truscott OMPF.

58. Truscott, *Twilight of the U.S. Cavalry,* 45–46; Memorandum for the Adjutant General of the Army, July 29, 1921, Folder, "Organizations—17th Cavalry Regiment, Central Decimal Files, Project Files, 1917–1925, Organizations 13th Cavalry Regiment to 24th Cavalry Regiment," Records of the Adjutant General's Office, Record Group (RG) 407, National Archives, College Park, Maryland (hereafter cited as "NACP").

59. Truscott, *Twilight of the U.S. Cavalry,* 45–46; "17th Cavalry, Regimental History," 1921.

60. Station and Duty Status Report, April 13, 1919–July 27, 1934, Truscott OMPF; James J. Truscott, e-mail message to author, August 10, 2005; Randolph, *Randolphs of Virginia,* 72. Most likely, Sarah's mother also accompanied the family on the voyage to San Francisco.

61. This information was extracted from the Station and Duty Status Report, from a biographical sketch of Truscott's military career through June 12, 1944, and from "Orders and Assignments" and War Department, SO 283-0, December 7, 1921, all in Truscott OMPF. There is no record of his specific duties during his time in San Francisco.

62. Truscott, *Twilight of the U.S. Cavalry,* xiv, xv. D'Este describes Truscott as "an expert polo player with a four-goal handicap" (*Fatal Decision,* 271). For a lucid explanation of polo-player handicaps, see *Encyclopaedia Britannica,* s.v. "Polo."

CHAPTER 2: ON THE ROAD TO HIGH COMMAND

1. Truscott, *Twilight of the U.S. Cavalry,* 53, 61.

2. Ibid., 60–61.

3. Ibid., 75–76 (quotes); Randolph to Harris, typed letter, signed, August 10, 1920, Truscott OMPF; Harris to Randolph, typed letter, August 13, 1920, Truscott OMPF; Capt. L. K. Truscott Jr., Camp Marfa, Texas, to Commanding Officer, 1st Cav., Camp Marfa, Texas, January 5, 1925; Index Sheet, Application and recommendations officers to attend Troop Officers Class, Cav. Sch., April 22, 1924 [*sic*], Truscott OMPF (the date on the latter form is apparently a typographical error); War Department (WD) SO 79, para. 4, April 4, 1925, Truscott OMPF.

4. Capt. L. K. Truscott Jr., Camp Marfa, Texas, to Commanding General (CG), First Cav. Div., Fort Bliss, Texas, May 12, 1925, with four indorsements (the U.S. Army uses *indorsement* rather than *endorsement* in official documents), Truscott OMPF.

5. Truscott, *Twilight of the U.S. Cavalry,* 74.

6. Capt. L. K. Truscott Jr., Fort Bliss, Texas, to CG, 1st Cav. Div., Fort Bliss, Texas, August 17, 1925, Truscott OMPF; Orders and Assignments, 1920–1930, Truscott OMPF.

7. *The United States Polo Association Year Book, 1926*, 41–43.

8. Truscott, *Twilight of the U.S. Cavalry*, 76–78.

9. Ibid., 81–82, 84.

10. Allotment of Hours—Troop Officers' Course—1924–1925. Since I was unable to find a list of the courses for the 1925–1926 academic year, I have used this source, assuming that there would have been only minimal if any changes in the curriculum.

11. Truscott, *Twilight of the U.S. Cavalry*, 85–86.

12. Ibid., 97.

13. Annual Report of the Commandant, the Cavalry School, 1926, 220.63 Cav. School (12-17-29) to 352.07 Cav. School (6-16-39); Truscott, *Twilight of the U.S. Cavalry*, 90–92.

14. Orders and Assignments, 1920–1926, Truscott OMPF; Special Efficiency Report, Capt. Lucian K. Truscott, June 30, 1926, Truscott OMPF; Truscott, *Twilight of the U.S. Cavalry*, 80 (quote).

15. WD SO 72, para. 33, March 28, 1927, Truscott OMPF; Special Efficiency Report, Capt. Lucian K. Truscott, June 10, 1927, Truscott OMPF.

16. Troop Officers' Class, Academic Year, 1927–1928, 220.63 Cav School (12-17-29) to 352.07 Cav. School (6-6-39); Truscott, *Twilight of the U.S. Cavalry*, 86.

17. James J. Truscott, telephone communication, San Antonio, Texas, August 23, 2005.

18. WD SO 60, para. 54, March 13, 1931, Truscott OMPF; Truscott, *Twilight of the U.S. Cavalry*, 109; "Arlington National Cemetery"; "History of Fort Myer."

19. Stubbs and Connor, *Armor-Cavalry*, 119–21; "Blood and Steel! The History, Customs, and Traditions of the 3d Armored Cavalry Regiment," 2.

20. Truscott, *Twilight of the U.S. Cavalry*, 109–10.

21. Ibid., 105,110, 117–18.

22. Ibid., 113–14.

23. Ibid., 120; Forrest C. Pogue, *George C. Marshall: Education of a General, 1880–1939*, 271, 284.

24. Truscott, *Twilight of the U.S. Cavalry*, 120.

25. "World War Adjusted Compensation Act, May 19, 1924, during the Coolidge Administration"; Paul Dickson and Thomas B. Allen, *The Bonus Army: An American Epic*, 18, 26, 56–60, 63. One of the veterans who applied for compensation under the provisions of that act was Captain Truscott, who completed his application on November 5, 1927, and forwarded it to the War Department ("Application for Adjusted Compensation," Truscott OMPF).

26. Dickson and Allen, *Bonus Army*, 73–75.

27. Truscott, *Twilight of the U.S. Cavalry*, 122; Dickson and Allen, *Bonus Army*, 110, 123–24 (quote), 152, 159–60.

28. Truscott, *Twilight of the U.S. Cavalry*, 127.

29. D. Clayton James, *The Years of MacArthur*, 397–98.

30. Ibid., 398–99.

31. Truscott, *Twilight of the U.S. Cavalry*, 127–29.

32. Kendall D. Gott, *Confrontation at Anacostia Flats: The Bonus Army of 1932*, 15. Nineteen years later, in April 1951, MacArthur, then in Tokyo, Japan, would once again "ignore" an order from an American president, Harry S. Truman. However, Truman was made of sterner stuff and had a far different view of insubordination than did Herbert Hoover, and he promptly relieved MacArthur of all commands, including supreme commander of the Allied Powers; commander in chief, Far East; and commander of the UN forces fighting in Korea.

33. Truscott, *Twilight of the U.S. Cavalry*, 129. Truscott states that "no one knew who set off the first fires," but Dickson and Allen cite the accounts of several eyewitnesses who reported that the infantrymen ignited the blazes (*Bonus Army*, 180–81). Major

Eisenhower, in a report he prepared for General MacArthur to forward to the War Department, concluded, on the basis of his personal observations, that "responsibility for firing the main camp lay definitely with the Bonus Marchers" (Daniel D. Holt and James W. Leyerzapf, eds., *Eisenhower: The Prewar Diaries and Selected Papers, 1905–1941,* 241).

34. "Summary of Events, 2d Squadron, 3d Cavalry, and Attached Troops, July 28–29, 1932," July 30, 1932, in "Military District of Washington, III Corps Area: Report of Operation against Bonus Marchers," Army Commands, RG 394, NACP.

35. Truscott, *Twilight of the U.S. Cavalry,* 130. In his account Truscott claims that the operation was accomplished "without bloodshed."

36. "An International Polo Match: The U.S. Army vs. the Mexican Army," 305, 313, 315, 317–18. Truscott apparently made a complete recovery from the injury.

37. WD SO 88, para. 6, April 13, 1934, Truscott OMPF; Efficiency Reports for the periods June 10, 1931–June 30, 1932; July 1, 1932–June 30, 1933; July 1, 1933–March 9, 1934; and May 1–June 30, 1934, all in Truscott OMPF.

38. Harry P. Ball, *Of Responsible Command: A History of the U.S. Army War College,* 183, 210, 497. Although Timothy K. Nenninger states that the two-year course began in 1929, he goes on to state that the first students attending that course graduated in 1930 ("Creating Officers: The Leavenworth Experience, 1920–1940," 60).

39. Station and Duty Status Report, August 27, 1934–February 24, 1941, Truscott OMPF. I do not know the exact number who began the two-year course of study, but on March 27, 1936, the class members totaled 121 (Command and General Staff School, 1935–1936, Second-Year Class, 27 March 1936).

40. Designation of Beneficiary, 1935, Truscott OMPF.

41. Nenninger, "Creating Officers," 64.

42. *Annual Report of the Command and General Staff School, Fort Leavenworth, Kansas, 1935–1936,* 3–5; Robert H. Berlin, "United States Army World War II Corps Commanders: A Composite Biography," 157. During his second year at the CGSS, Truscott, after fifteen years in the grade of captain, was promoted to major (WD SO 224, para. 1, September 22, 1935, Truscott OMPF).

43. Wilson A. Heefner, *Twentieth Century Warrior: The Life and Service of Major General Edwin D. Patrick,* 163 (Capt. Doyle O. Hickey, 3d Armored Division); 165 (Maj. Albert C. Smith, 14th Armored Division; 165 (Maj. Lucian K. Truscott Jr., 3d Infantry Division); 171 (Capt. Paul W. Kendall, 88th Infantry Division); 173 (Capt. Robert B. McClure, Americal Division); Berlin, "World War II Corps Commanders," 157, 164–65.

44. Efficiency Reports, June 30, 1935, and June 19, 1936, Truscott OMPF; Special School Report, June 20, 1936, Truscott OMPF.

45. Index Sheet, December 10, 1935, Truscott OMPF; WD SO 34, para. 22, February 10, 1936, Truscott OMPF. In 1936 the War Department, recognizing the need for more trained general staff officers, reduced the course of instruction to one year (Nenninger, "Creating Officers," 60).

46. Assignment of Instructors, 1937–1938 and 1938–1939; chart 1, School Organization and Duties, in *Instruction Circular No. 1, 1938–1939: The Command and General Staff School, Fort Leavenworth, Kansas, 1 July 1938,* facing p. 10.

47. Truscott, *Twilight of the U.S. Cavalry,* xvi.

48. WD SO 78, para. 47, April 2, 1940, Truscott OMPF; WD SO 113, para. 1, May 13, 1940, Orders and Assignments, Truscott OMPF.

49. Efficiency Reports, July 1, 1936–March 22, 1937; March 23–June 30, 1937; July 1, 1937–June 30, 1938; July 1–September 15, 1938; September 16, 1938–June 30, 1939; July 7–August 14, 1939; September 5, 1939–June 28, 1940, Truscott OMPF.

50. Truscott, *Twilight of the U.S. Cavalry,* 154–55.

51. Ball, *Of Responsible Command,* 257, 236.

52. WD SO 149, para. 19, June 25, 1940, Truscott OMPF.

53. Station and Duty Status Report, Truscott OMPF.

54. James J. Truscott, e-mail message to author, May 27, 2007; Truscott, *Twilight of the U.S. Cavalry*, xvii, 155.

55. WD SO 196, para. 6, Aug. 20, 1940, Truscott OMPF. When Sarah Truscott's parents moved back to Charlottesville from Texas in 1928, Doctor Randolph purchased a property known as "Wild Acres," just north of Charlottesville. Lucian K. Truscott IV told me that the house into which the Randolphs moved was located on thirty acres of wooded land, and during Prohibition had been a "roadhouse," with a "gambling joint" on the first floor and a brothel on the second floor (Lucian K. Truscott IV interview).

56. Truscott, *Twilight of the U.S. Cavalry*, 160; Edward M. Coffman, *The Regulars: The American Army, 1898–1941*, 387.

Chapter 3: Prelude to War

1. Stubbs and Connor, *Armor-Cavalry*, 58.

2. WD SO 204, para. 7, August 29, 1940, Truscott OMPF. Assigning a lieutenant colonel as a battalion executive officer is very unusual, since he would hold the same grade as the battalion commander; the authorized grade of a battalion XO is major. I can only conclude that such an unusual assignment was made because Truscott had not been assigned to a troop unit in more than six years, thus depriving him of the opportunity of serving in one or more battalion staff positions, as a line officer would usually have done after he had successfully served as a company or troop commander. By occupying the position of XO and battalion chief of staff, Truscott would have an opportunity to interdigitate with the battalion staff and put into practice what he had learned and taught at the CGSS, thus preparing him for possible assignment as a battalion commander.

3. Truscott, *Twilight of the U.S. Cavalry*, 159–60; James J. Truscott, e-mail message to author, May 28, 2007.

4. First-echelon maintenance was the vehicle maintenance performed, usually on at least a daily basis, by the vehicle's driver and crew.

5. Truscott, *Twilight of the U.S. Cavalry*, 160, 161–62.

6. Report of Change, November 7, 1940, Truscott OMPF.

7. WD SO 32, para. 4, February 8, 1941, Truscott OMPF.

8. Efficiency Report, November 7, 1940–February 15, 1941, Truscott OMPF.

9. Truscott, *Command Missions*, 15.

10. Truscott, *Twilight of the U.S. Cavalry*, 169; D'Este, *Eisenhower: A Soldier's Life*, 269.

11. Military History of Lucian King Truscott, Junior, Truscott OMPF; Truscott, *Command Missions*, 15; Efficiency Report, July 12, 1941, Truscott OMPF; Truscott, *Twilight of the U.S. Cavalry*, 171 (quotes).

12. "A table which describes the normal mission, organizational structure, and personnel and equipment authorization for a military unit" (*Dictionary of United States Army Terms*, s.v. "table of organization and equipment").

13. Truscott, *Twilight of the U.S. Cavalry*, 171–72. The new triangular divisions contained three regiments, whereas the square divisions were composed of two brigades of two regiments each.

14. *IX Corps Unit History, 1940–1963*, 2; Truscott, *Twilight of the U.S. Cavalry*, 172–73.

15. D'Este, *Eisenhower: A Soldier's Life*, 271–72.

16. Holt and Leyerzapf, *Eisenhower*, 532–33.

17. Truscott to wife, May 25, June 4, 17, 20, 1941, box 1, folder 1, Truscott Papers.

18. Truscott, *Twilight of the U.S. Cavalry*, 175; John B. Wilson, comp., *Armies, Corps, Divisions, and Separate Brigades*, 56; Shelby L. Stanton, *Order of Battle: U.S. Army, World War II*, 79, 87, 124, 126.

19. Truscott, *Twilight of the U.S. Cavalry,* 175–76. Truscott mistakenly places the August Fourth Army maneuvers chronologically *after* the September Second–Third Army maneuvers.

20. Ibid., 175.

21. Lt. Gen. Lesley J. McNair to CG, Fourth Army, September 28, 1931, Truscott OMPF.

22. D'Este, *Eisenhower: A Soldier's Life,* 277, 279–80.

23. First Indorsement, McNair to CG, Fourth Army, October 6, 1941, Truscott OMPF.

24. WD SO 251, para. 8, October 27, 1941, cited in Report of Change, November 22, 1941, Truscott OMPF; HQ 1st Cav. Div. General Order (GO) 41, para. 2, November 24, 1941, Truscott OMPF.

25. Efficiency Reports, July 19, 1941, and November 28, 1941, Truscott OMPF.

26. Maj. Gen. Kenyon A. Joyce to Adjutant General, Washington, D.C., July 29, 1941, Truscott OMPF.

27. James J. Truscott, e-mail message to author, May 27, 2007; HQ 1st Cav. Div., GO 41, para. 2, November 24, 1941, Truscott OMPF; Truscott, *Twilight of the U.S. Cavalry,* 178–81.

28. Truscott, *Twilight of the U.S. Cavalry,* 181–82.

29. Ibid., 182–83.

30. Ibid., 184.

31. WD SO 304, para. 2, December 31, 1941, Truscott OMPF.

32. Truscott, *Command Missions,* 17.

33. Ibid.; Index Sheet, April 23, 1942, Truscott OMPF.

34. James J. Truscott, e-mail message to author, May 27, 2007.

35. Ibid.; "Lucian King Truscott III," in *Register of Graduates and Former Cadets of the United States Military Academy,* 526.

36. Truscott, *Command Missions,* 17; Efficiency Report, April 27, 1942, Truscott OMPF.

CHAPTER 4: BIRTH OF THE RANGERS

1. Truscott, *Command Missions,* 18. Unless otherwise indicated, the following material is based on this source, 18–40. I have also referenced the sources of all quotations. Throughout *Command Missions* there are minor errors and many misspellings, corrected in an "errata" located in the front matter of the book. I have omitted the misspelled words and the other errors and substituted the spellings and corrections indicated in the "errata."

2. WD Orders [no order number], April 25, 1942, Truscott OMPF.

3. Truscott, *Command Missions,* 20.

4. Ibid., 22.

5. Ibid., 23.

6. Letter of Instructions from Maj. Gen. Dwight D. Eisenhower to Col. L. K. Truscott Jr., May 5, 1942, box 9, folder 1, Truscott Papers.

7. HQ USAFBI Orders, SO 74, para. 4, May 25, 1942, Truscott OMPF.

8. HQ USAFBI Order [no order number], May 18, 1942, Truscott OMPF.

9. Truscott, *Command Missions,* 27.

10. Ibid., 29; Truscott to wife, June 2, 1942, box 1, folder 3, Truscott Papers.

11. Truscott, *Command Missions,* 34.

12. WD SO 140, para. 1, May 28, 1942, Truscott OMPF; Truscott to wife, May 26, 1942, box 1, folder 3, Truscott Papers; HQ USAFBI, SO 80, para. 5, May 31, 1942, Truscott OMPF; Truscott, *Command Missions,* 37.

13. Truscott, *Command Missions,* 37–38; Memorandum, Truscott to Bolte, "American Commando," May 26, 1942, box 10, folder 3, Truscott Papers; Gen. T. J. Conway interview, 7.

14. Truscott, *Command Missions*, 38–39.

15. Commando Organization, HQ USNAIF and V Army Corps (Reinf), June 7, 1942, box 10, folder 4, Truscott Papers.

16. Although William O. Darby states that General Marshall chose the name "Rangers," the name that Maj. Robert Rogers had adopted for his band that operated in the French and Indian War (Darby and William H. Baumer, *Darby's Rangers: We Led the Way*, 25), Conway, in his interview by Ensslin, clearly states that Truscott chose the name "Rangers" (7). Truscott himself states, "I selected 'Rangers' because few words have a more glorious connotation in American military history" (*Command Missions*, 40).

17. Truscott, *Command Missions*, 39.

18. Robert W. Black, *Rangers in World War II*, 13.

19. Response to WD directive, untitled, undated, and unsigned, May 27, 1942, box 10, folder 4, Truscott Papers.

20. Darby and Baumer, *Darby's Rangers*, 27.

21. Black, *Rangers in World War II*, 18; 1st Ranger Battalion Diary, June 19 and 25, 1942.

22. James Ladd, *Commandos and Rangers of World War II*, 168.

23. Black, *Rangers in World War II*, 22–23 (quote on 22); Darby and Baumer, *Darby's Rangers*, 31.

24. Black, *Rangers in World War II*, 24; "U.S. Army Rangers: History—World War II Battalions," 1; Truscott to wife, July 31, 1942, box 1, folder 3, Truscott Papers.

25. 1st Ranger Battalion Diary, September 3, 24, October 17, 18–19, 26, 1942; Darby and Baumer, *Darby's Rangers*, 49–50. Those desiring greater detail about the training of the Rangers at Achnacarry, Dorlin House, and Dundee should consult Darby and Baumer's *Darby's Rangers*, 27–40, 46–50, and Lt. Col. L. E. Vaughn's report to HQ, Special Service Brigade, describing the results of the Rangers' training at Achnacarry, including his detailed comments about the attributes and shortcomings of the officers and enlisted men who completed the course of instruction ("Report on 1st Bn. U.S. Rangers," August 2, 1942, box 10, folder 4, Truscott Papers).

26. P. Antill, "Operation 'Rutter': The Planned Attack on Dieppe, 7 July 1942," 1; P. Antill, "Operation Jubilee: The Disaster at Dieppe—Part 1, 19 August 1942," 4; "The Raid on Dieppe: August 19, 1942," 1; Truscott, *Command Missions*, 64. E-boats were German torpedo boats.

27. Antill, "Operation 'Rutter,'" 1–2; 1st Ranger Battalion Diary, June 19, 1942.

28. Truscott, *Command Missions*, 54.

29. Antill, "Operation 'Rutter,'" 2–3; Antill, "Operation Jubilee," 3–4.

30. Truscott, *Command Missions*, 63.

31. HQ, 1st Ranger Bn., SO 13, para. 16, August 1, 1942, Folder "History—Darby's Rangers," RG 94, NACP. Capt. Roy A. Murray, who participated in the raid, states in his report to Major Darby that four officers and thirty-six enlisted men participated in the attack (Report on 1st Ranger Battalion Detachment Assigned to 3 Commando, August 26, 1942, 1). However, the 1st Ranger Battalion Diary entry for August 19 indicates that "six officers and forty-four enlisted men participated in raid on Dieppe." Terence Robertson (*Dieppe: The Shame and the Glory*, 43) states that Truscott selected six officers and forty-four men to accompany the attack force but appears to rely on Truscott for that figure (*Command Missions*, 57). I have chosen SO 13 and Captain Murray's report as the most definitive and reliable sources. There are also conflicting statements about the distribution of the Rangers among the units making up the attacking force: Murray states that all of the Rangers were attached to No. 3 Commando (Report on 1st Ranger Battalion Detachment, 1), while Robertson (*Dieppe*, 197) and Pvt. Frank Koons ("Dieppe"), who participated in the raid with No. 4 Commando, state that the Rangers were distributed among the two Commandos and the Canadian forces that landed in the Dieppe area.

32. Antill, "Operation Jubilee," 5–6.

33. Ibid., 6–8.

34. Truscott, *Command Missions,* 63.

35. Ibid., 67; "Raid on Dieppe," 1–3 (quote on 3); Report on 1st Ranger Battalion Detachment, 2.

36. Truscott, *Command Missions,* 69.

37. "Operation Jubilee: The Disaster at Dieppe—Part 2, 19 August 1942," 1–5; "Raid on Dieppe," 1–3; Truscott, *Command Missions,* 71–72.

38. Robin Neillands, *The Dieppe Raid: The Story of the Disastrous 1942 Expedition,* 247–61; Truscott, *Command Missions,* 64, 70. Truscott mistakenly refers to Brigadier Mann as the chief of staff of the 1st rather than the 2d Canadian Division (*Command Missions,* 64).

39. Truscott, *Command Missions,* 70.

40. Ibid., 70–71.

41. Ibid.

42. "Raid on Dieppe," 3.

43. Darby to the Adjutant General. Capt. Roy A. Murray, in Report on 1st Ranger Battalion Detachment, states that four men were wounded and one officer and three men were missing. I have relied on the figures in Darby's report, since it lists the missing and wounded by name, rank, and service number.

44. Ladd, *Commandos and Rangers,* 85.

45. Robertson, *Dieppe,* 43; "Stephen's Study Room: British Military and Criminal History in the Period 1900 to 1999," 2.

46. Truscott to wife, August 20, 1942, box 1, folder 3, Truscott Papers; Truscott, *Command Missions,* 533–34; Gordon A. Harrison, *Cross-Channel Attack,* 55–56; Leonard Mosley, *Backs to the Wall: London under Fire, 1940–45,* 288. Professor Lindemann, a professor of experimental philosophy (physics) at Oxford University, was a close adviser of Churchill. In 1941 he was elevated to the peerage as Lord Cherwell (Henry Pelling, *Winston Churchill,* 338, 480).

47. Truscott, *Command Missions,* 72.

CHAPTER 5: OPERATION TORCH

1. Forrest C. Pogue, *The Supreme Command,* 99.

2. Ibid.

3. Chandler, *Papers of Eisenhower,* vol. 1, Doc. 162, February 28, 1942, 149–52. In this memorandum Eisenhower also discussed in detail his concept of the operations to be conducted in the Pacific theater of operations (152–55).

4. Forrest C. Pogue, *George C. Marshall: Ordeal and Hope, 1939–1942,* 314–15.

5. Ibid., 306, 314–18.

6. Pogue, *Supreme Command,* 100–101 (quotes); Pogue, *Ordeal and Hope,* 326 (reference to Molotov's meeting with Roosevelt).

7. Truscott, *Command Missions,* 48–49.

8. Pogue, *Supreme Command,* 101; Rick Atkinson, *An Army at Dawn: The War in North Africa, 1942–1943,* 16.

9. Truscott, *Command Missions,* 53. The French still harbored considerable animosity toward the British, dating from the fall of France, when the British destroyed French ships in North African ports to prevent their capture by the Germans, in the process killing many French sailors. The Combined Chiefs believed that "the French command in Africa would not cooperate with a British invasion force" (Charles R. Anderson, *Algeria–French Morocco,* 5–6).

10. Truscott, *Command Missions,* 56–59.

11. Ibid., 59.

12. An RCT is a task force organization consisting of an infantry regiment, a supporting 105mm field artillery battalion, reconnaissance units, and a company of combat engineers. The RCT operates under the command of the regimental commander.

13. Ibid., 59, 61–62.

14. Ibid., 72–78.

15. Lord Mountbatten to Lucian K. Truscott Jr., September 18, 1942, box 1, folder 4, Truscott Papers.

16. Truscott, *Command Missions*, 533.

17. The coast artillery antiaircraft batteries were equipped with halftracks mounting a 37mm automatic cannon and two .50-caliber machine guns that could be utilized as both antiaircraft and antitank weapons (M-15 Multiple Gun Motor Carriage [GMC]).

18. Truscott, *Command Missions*, 79–81; George F. Howe, *Northwest Africa: Seizing the Initiative in the West*, 150; Anderson, *Algeria–French Morocco*, 10.

19. Truscott, *Command Missions*, 81–83; Aide's Diaries, October 10, 1942, box 18, folder 1, Truscott Papers.

20. Truscott, *Command Missions*, 83–84.

21. Martin Blumenson, ed., *The Patton Papers, 1940–1945*, 89.

22. Truscott, *Command Missions*, 84.

23. Ibid., 94–95; Operations Order 1, Sub–Task Force GOALPOST, October 1942, box 10, folder 13, Truscott Papers.

24. Aide's Diaries, October 18, 1942, box 18, folder 1, Truscott Papers; Truscott, *Command Missions*, 86–87. Blumenson states that the relationship between Patton's staff and Hewitt's staff "was often quite stormy." The relationship between the two grew so bad that "at one point the Navy considered asking the army to replace Patton with someone easier to work with" (*Patton Papers*, 88).

25. Truscott, *Command Missions*, 87–88.

26. These two incidents are striking examples of one of Truscott's leadership qualities, that of unhesitatingly bringing to the attention of superior officers what he considered to be serious defects or deficiencies in their plans, defects or deficiencies that might endanger the lives of the men under his command or adversely affect the outcome of the operation. Truscott would continue this practice throughout the war.

27. Truscott, *Command Missions*, 87–88; Aide's Diaries, October 18, 20, 1942, box 18, folder 1, Truscott Papers.

28. Truscott, *Command Missions*, 88; Truscott to wife, October 22, 1942, box 1, folder 4, Truscott Papers.

29. Aide's Diaries, October 23, 1942, box 18, folder 1, Truscott Papers; Truscott, *Command Missions*, 89.

30. Aide's Diaries, October 24, 1942, box 18, folder 1, Truscott Papers.

31. Ibid., October 30, 1942; Truscott, *Command Missions*, 90–92.

32. Truscott to wife, November 7, 1942, box 1, folder 4, Truscott Papers.

33. Truscott, *Command Missions*, 93, 96.

34. Operations Order 1, October 1942, box 10, folder 13, Truscott Papers; Anderson, *Algeria–French Morocco*, 10–11.

35. Truscott, *Command Missions*, 95, 108–23; Anderson, *Algeria–French Morocco*, 11–13.

36. Atkinson, *An Army at Dawn*, 147.

37. Anderson, *Algeria–French Morocco*, 8–10.

38. Ibid., 13–21, 28; Howe, *Northwest Africa*, 121.

39. Anderson, *Algeria–French Morocco*, 6, 21–28.

40. Ralph Bennett, *Ultra and Mediterranean Strategy*, 15–17, 187. Enigma was the name given to a decoding machine resembling an oversized typewriter that had been

patented in 1919 by a German firm as a means to safeguard commercial secrets. Hugh Sebag-Montefiore covers in detail the history of the breaking of the code in *Enigma: The Battle for the Code.*

41. Bennett, *Ultra and Mediterranean Strategy,* 184–86.

42. Anderson, *Algeria–French Morocco,* 28, 31. For a concise analysis of the problems encountered during TORCH, consult ibid., 28–31.

43. Truscott to wife, November 25, 1942, box 1, folder 4, Truscott Papers.

44. Aide's Diaries, November 26, 1942, box 18, folder 1, Truscott Papers. Lee was a soldier of Chinese descent whom Truscott had encountered on D-day, when the former was looking for his engineer unit. He informed Truscott that he was a cook in that unit, a fact that Truscott remembered "after the battle ended, when I needed a cook" (Truscott, *Command Missions,* 114). Truscott was apparently successful in having Lee assigned to his headquarters.

45. Aide's Diaries, December 15, 19, 1942, box 18, folder 1, Truscott Papers; promotion certificate, November 21, 1942, Truscott OMPF. Dental problems were to plague Truscott throughout the remainder of the war.

46. Aide's Diaries, December 22, 23, 26 (quote), 1942, box 18, folder 1, Truscott Papers; Truscott, *Command Missions,* 124; Allied Force Headquarters, APO 512, GO 28, para. 4, December 15, 1942, Truscott OMPF.

47. Efficiency Report, September 11–December 31, 1942, Truscott OMPF; Blumenson, *Patton Papers,* 89, citing Patton's entry in his journal that he was "just a little worried about ability of Truscott."

48. Truscott, *Command Missions,* 534–36.

CHAPTER 6: DUTY WITH IKE

1. Charles R. Anderson, *Tunisia,* 7–8; Bennett, *Ultra and Mediterranean Strategy,* 190–91 (quote).

2. Anderson, *Tunisia,* 6–11; Bennett, *Ultra and Mediterranean Strategy,* 195–96; Truscott, *Command Missions,* 126–27.

3. Truscott, *Command Missions,* 124–27 (quotes); Aide's Diaries, December 29, 1942, box 18, folder 1, Truscott Papers.

4. Howe, *Northwest Africa,* 374; Truscott, *Command Missions,* 128–30; Aide's Diaries, January 17, 1943, box 18, folder 2, Truscott Papers.

5. Truscott, *Command Missions,* 131–32.

6. Anderson, *Tunisia,* 15; Truscott, *Command Missions,* 133.

7. Aide's Diaries, January 18, 1943, box 18, folder 2, Truscott Papers; Truscott, *Command Missions,* 133–34 (quotes).

8. Truscott, *Command Missions,* 135–38. Gen. Maurice Mathenet, the officer who had surrendered Point Lyautey to Truscott a little more than two months earlier, commanded the French forces.

9. Ibid., 139–40.

10. Ibid., 140–41. Whereas the Americans use roman numerals to designate the various corps, the British use Arabic numerals for their corps designations.

11. Truscott to Eisenhower, January 24, 1943, Truscott, Lucian K., box 116, Principal File, Dwight D. Eisenhower Pre-presidential Papers, 1916–1952.

12. Truscott, *Command Missions,* 142–43.

13. Ibid., 147–49; Howe, *Northwest Africa,* 388–93; Aide's Diaries, January 31, 1943, box 18, folder 2, Truscott Papers.

14. Howe, *Northwest Africa,* 393, 395–96; Martin Blumenson, *Kasserine Pass: Rommel's Bloody, Climactic Battle for Tunisia,* 102–4.

15. Howe, *Northwest Africa,* 395–98.

16. Anderson, *Tunisia,* 16(quote); Chandler, *Papers of Eisenhower,* vol. 2, Doc. 805, February 3, 1943, 934–36 (emphasis added).

17. Truscott, *Command Missions,* 150–51.

18. Ibid., 152.

19. Blumenson, *Kasserine Pass,* 117 (first quote); Truscott, *Command Missions,* 152–53.

20. Blumenson, *Kasserine Pass,* 120–23.

21. Bennett, *Ultra and Mediterranean Strategy,* 204.

22. D'Este, *Eisenhower: A Soldier's Life,* 389–90; Aide's Diaries, February 12, 1943, box 18, folder 2, Truscott Papers.

23. Truscott, *Command Missions,* 153–58.

24. Chandler, *Papers of Eisenhower,* vol. 2, Doc. 820, February 16, 1943, 957–58 (emphasis in original); Truscott, *Command Missions,* 158–59.

25. Ibid., 159–63.

26. Anderson, *Tunisia,* 17.

27. Truscott, *Command Missions,* 163, 165, 164.

28. Ibid., 169, 170.

29. Howe, *Northwest Africa,* 439–40.

30. Blumenson, *Kasserine Pass,* 221.

31. Howe, *Northwest Africa,* 442–43.

32. Blumenson, *Kasserine Pass,* 238–57.

33. Ibid., 261–83.

34. Albert Kesselring, *The Memoirs of Field-Marshal Kesselring,* 151–52; Blumenson, *Kasserine Pass,* 284–85. The first two quotations are from Kesselring's book, the third from Blumenson's book.

35. Truscott, *Command Missions,* 170.

36. Ibid., 172.

37. Anderson, *Tunisia,* 17; Atkinson, *An Army at Dawn,* 389; Howe, *Northwest Africa,* 477n45.

38. Truscott, *Command Missions,* 172–73; Truscott to wife, March 2, 1943, box 1, folder 4, Truscott Papers.

39. Truscott, *Command Missions,* 173. As early as February 1943 Truscott had suggested to Eisenhower that he "bring Patton over here" to II Corps, "since II Corps is predominantly armored" (Truscott to Eisenhower, February 19, 1943, box 116, Eisenhower Pre-presidential Papers).

40. Truscott to wife, March 5, 1943, box 1, folder 5, Truscott Papers.

41. Truscott, *Command Missions,* 537–38.

Chapter 7: Operation HUSKY

1. HQ North African Theater of Operations, United States Army, SO 27, paras. 2–4, March 4, 1943, Truscott OMPF. After participating in the Casablanca operation the division was assigned to garrison French Morocco and western Algeria. In late February approximately thirty-four hundred of the division members, mostly infantry volunteers, left for Tunisia as replacements for the heavy casualties sustained in the fighting there. Most of those men later returned to the division (Taggart, *Third Infantry Division,* 37–38, 41–42, map on 47).

2. Truscott, *Command Missions,* 175, 177–78. Interestingly, the Aide's Diary entry for the eighth states that Truscott "was not impressed with either [regimental commander] but will give them benefit of doubt" (Aide's Diaries, March 8, 1943, box 18, folder 2, Truscott Papers). Sherman proved to be one of the best regimental and assistant division

commanders Truscott was to know in combat. The 3d's assistant division commander, division artillery commander, and two of the three regimental commanders had been senior to Truscott before his wartime promotions.

3. Truscott, *Command Missions,* 178–79.

4. Ibid., 178. Truscott's first cook became Patton's chief cook when Truscott departed for duty with Eisenhower (ibid., 114).

5. William Randolph Hearst Jr., "A Day of Action in France with Lt. Gen. Truscott," Hearst Newspapers, October 22, 1944, box 22, folder 1, Truscott Papers. The photocopy of the newspaper article does not identify the specific newspaper containing the article.

6. Truscott to wife, March 15, 1943, box 1, folder 5, Truscott Papers.

7. Taggart, *Third Infantry Division,* 42; Truscott, *Command Missions,* 182.

8. Aide's Diaries, March 15, 1943, box 18, folder 2, Truscott Papers; Truscott, *Command Missions,* 182.

9. Jim DeFelice, *Rangers at Dieppe: The First Combat Action of U.S. Army Rangers in World War II,* 45–46.

10. Truscott, *Command Missions,* 180.

11. Taggart, *Third Infantry Division,* 42.

12. Truscott, *Command Missions,* 179–80, 185.

13. A rolling artillery barrage is "a barrage in which the fire of units or subunits progresses by leapfrogging" (*Dictionary of United States Army Terms,* s.v. "rolling barrage").

14. The origin of the nickname "dogfaces" for American soldiers is uncertain. James Tobias of the U.S. Army Center of Military History believes that it first came into use during the Civil War, when soldiers began comparing their lives to that of a dog and began referring to each other as "dogfaces" (e-mail message to author, July 26, 2007).

15. For a comprehensive description and discussion of the capabilities of the various types of Allied landing craft and landing ships, see Al Adcock, *WW II U.S. Landing Craft in Action.*

16. Taggart, *Third Infantry Division,* 42–43; Section I—Operations (Training Phase), 1. The first two quotations are from Taggart, and the third is from the second citation. There is no explanation for the 30th Infantry's not making a night landing.

17. Truscott, *Command Missions,* 187.

18. On March 5 Patton had assumed temporary command of the II Corps vice Fredendall but still retained command of the 1st Armored Corps, headquartered in Rabat. He placed Keyes in temporary command of the latter corps to oversee the ongoing planning for the invasion of Sicily that Patton would command. On April 14 Patton relinquished command of II Corps to Maj. Gen. Omar N. Bradley, who had been serving as his deputy, and returned to I Armored Corps (Blumenson, *Patton Papers,* 180, 182, 220).

19. Truscott, *Command Missions,* 174–75, 183.

20. Ibid., 183.

21. Ibid., 180–81.

22. I have been unable to pinpoint the location of Pont du Cheliff. However, the Cheliff River, after passing through the Tell Atlas mountains, empties into the Mediterranean Sea at the city of Mostaganem on the eastern shore of the Gulf of Arzew. Thus, the mountain warfare training location was most likely located south of the gulf in the Tell Atlas mountains.

23. Section I—Operations (Training Phase), 1–2.

24. Truscott, *Command Missions,* 187.

25. Ibid., 187–91.

26. Ibid., 191–92; Taggart, *Third Infantry Division*, 46; Aide's Diaries, May 12, 1943, box 18, folder 2, Truscott Papers (quotes). For a comprehensive discussion of "lessons learned," see *Lessons from the Tunisian Campaign, 15 October 1943*.

27. Anderson, *Tunisia*, 30.

28. Albert N. Garland and Howard McGaw Smyth, *Sicily and the Surrender of Italy*, 100; Truscott, *Command Missions*, 192–93. A shore-to-shore operation utilizes special ships and landing craft that can lift "men, weapons, and transport from one shore and disembark them on the hostile shore prepared to fight without the necessity of assembling craft from other vessels to assist in the disembarkation" (Truscott, *Command Missions*, 196).

29. The major components of Force JOSS were 3d Infantry Division; CCA, 2d Armored Division; 3d Ranger Battalion; and 4th Moroccan Tabor (Taggart, *Third Infantry Division*, 51; Garland and Smyth, *Sicily and the Surrender of Italy*, 98). A tabor was a battalion-size unit composed of Moroccan soldiers, known as *goumiers* or *goums*, who served under French officers and noncommissioned officers (Garland and Smyth, *Sicily and the Surrender of Italy*, 96).

30. Truscott, *Command Missions*, 196.

31. Ibid., 198.

32. Ibid., 200–201.

33. Taggart, *Third Infantry Division*, 46–47; Section I—Operations (Training Phase), 2.

34. Truscott, *Command Missions*, 202.

35. Julian William Cummings with Gwendolyn Kay Cummings, *Grasshopper Pilot: A Memoir*, 29–33.

36. Truscott, *Command Missions*, 202–3.

37. Taggart, *Third Infantry Division*, 44–45.

38. Truscott, *Command Missions*, 204–5.

39. Ibid., 206–7.

40. Taggart, *Third Infantry Division*, 47.

41. Chandler, *Papers of Eisenhower*, vol. 2, Doc. 1092, July 1, 1943, 1233–34.

42. Efficiency Report, January 1–June 30, 1943, Truscott OMPF.

43. Taggert, *Third Infantry Division*, 47–48.

44. Andrew J. Birtle, *Sicily, 9 July–17 August 1943*, 3–6; Garland and Smyth, *Sicily and the Surrender of Italy*, 53.

45. At the end of the Tunisian campaign Alexander's 18th Army Group headquarters had been deactivated and merged into Force 141, the headquarters charged with planning HUSKY. On the day of the Sicily invasion that headquarters became 15th Army Group, commanded by General Alexander (Garland and Smyth, *Sicily and the Surrender of Italy*, 56).

46. Garland and Smyth, *Sicily and the Surrender of Italy*, 55, 57, 33, 35–36; Kesselring, *Memoirs*, 157.

47. Birtle, *Sicily*, 8 (quote); Frido von Senger und Etterlin, *Neither Fear nor Hope: The Wartime Career of General Frido von Senger und Etterlin, Defender of Cassino*, 129–30.

48. Carlos D'Este, *Bitter Victory: The Battle for Sicily, 1943*, 192–94.

49. Garland and Smyth, *Sicily and the Surrender of Italy*, 82.

50. Senger und Etterlin, *Neither Fear nor Hope*, 128, 131. Senger und Etterlin suggests that Kesselring's decision to place the Hermann Göring Division in the East may have been due to the division's namesake's personal intervention or because Kesselring, a Luftwaffe officer, "felt that he should comply with the wishes of his superior officer in the Luftwaffe" (133).

51. Garland and Smyth, *Sicily and the Surrender of Italy*, 89–92; Birtle, *Sicily*, 7. The first two quotations are from Garland and Smyth; the latter two are from Birtle.

52. Garland and Smyth, *Sicily and the Surrender of Italy*, 92–98; Birtle, *Sicily*, 6–8; Ladd, *Commandos and Rangers of World War II*, 129–30.

53. Truscott, *Command Missions*, 210.

54. Ibid., 208.

55. Ibid., 209; Taggart, *Third Infantry Division*, 53–54; Birtle, *Sicily*, 9.

56. Birtle, *Sicily*, 9–10.

57. Truscott, *Command Missions*, 213; Cummings with Cummings, *Grasshopper Pilot: A Memoir*, 35, 38.

58. Truscott, *Command Missions*, 213–14.

59. Birtle, *Sicily*, 10–11, 14.

60. Truscott, *Command Missions*, 214; Section I—Operations (Operation Phase), 11.

61. Truscott, *Command Missions*, 214–15.

62. Ibid., 217.

63. Birtle, *Sicily*, 15.

64. Ibid., 15–17; Garland and Smyth, *Sicily and the Surrender of Italy*, 209–11.

65. Truscott, *Command Missions*, 217–19 (quotes); Garland and Smyth, *Sicily and the Surrender of Italy*, 224.

66. Taggart, *Third Infantry Division*, 57.

67. Blumenson, *Patton Papers*, 289–90; General Albert C. Wedemeyer, *Wedemeyer Reports!* 225.

68. Patton had decided to give Bradley's II Corps, composed of the 1st and 45th Infantry Divisions, the mission of protecting the Eighth Army's rear by securing the Enna–Caltanissetta–San Caterina area, "advancing within its zone to the North and Northeast, cut Highways 121, 120, and 113, and be prepared to attack Palermo from the East" (Truscott, *Command Missions*, 222).

69. Ibid., 222–24; Birtle, *Sicily*, 17.

70. Ibid., 224–27.

71. Aide's Diaries, July 24, 1943, box 18, folder 5, Truscott Papers.

72. Garland and Smyth, *Sicily and the Surrender of Italy*, 255, 300.

73. Birtle, *Sicily*, map, 18–19.

74. Garland and Smyth, *Sicily and the Surrender of Italy*, 303–4; Birtle, *Sicily*, 17, 20.

75. Garland and Smyth, *Sicily and the Surrender of Italy*, 304–5.

76. Truscott, *Command Missions*, 228–29.

77. Ibid., 229–30.

78. Ibid., 230–34.

79. Truscott refers to the river as the "Zoppulo" River (ibid., 234), whereas Taggart spells it as I have indicated in the text (*Third Infantry Division*, 71).

80. Truscott, *Command Missions*, 234–35.

81. Ibid., 235–36.

82. Taggart, *Third Infantry Division*, 71; Truscott, *Command Missions*, 236–40 (quotes).

83. "Outline of Operation of Third Infantry Division, August 1–17, 1943," 3–4, box 11, folder 12, Truscott Papers; Ernie Pyle, *Brave Men*, 73 (quote).

84. "Outline of Operation of Third Infantry Division, August 1–17, 1943," 3, box 11, folder 12, Truscott Papers.

85. Truscott, *Command Missions*, 243.

86. Aide's Diaries, August 18, 1943, box 18, folder 3, Truscott Papers.

87. Hanson W. Baldwin, *Battles Lost and Won: Great Campaigns of World War II*, 225–27; Birtle, *Sicily*, 27; Atkinson, *Day of Battle*, 173 (quote).

88. D'Este, *Bitter Victory*, 558–59.

89. Folder 0100/5, 0A01/3, Lessons of Campaign of Sicily.

90. Taggart, *Third Infantry Division*, 76.

91. Truscott to wife, August 25, 28, 1943, box 1, folder 6, Truscott Papers.

92. Truscott to Eisenhower, August 25, 1943, box 116, Eisenhower Pre-presidential Papers; Truscott to CG, NATOUSA, "Re-assignment of Colonel Charles R. Johnson," September 1, 1943, box 11, folder 12, Truscott Papers.

CHAPTER 8: FIGHTING ON THE "BOOT"

1. Truscott, *Command Missions,* 245.

2. Ibid., 246–48; Harold A. Winters et al., *Battling the Elements: Weather and Terrain in the Conduct of War,* 197 (quote). I am puzzled by the absence of Truscott's G3, Lt. Col. Bert Connor, from the meeting.

3. On August 14 the QUADRANT Conference opened in Québec City, attended by President Roosevelt, Prime Minister Churchill, and the Combined Chiefs of Staff. On the eighteenth the CCS directed Eisenhower to open "unconditional surrender" negotiations with the Badoglio government in Lisbon, Portugal. Eisenhower dispatched as his representatives Maj. Gen. Walter B. Smith and Brigadier Kenneth W. D. Strong, AFHQ G2, to negotiate the unconditional surrender of Italy. After prolonged negotiations Italy finally accepted the terms of unconditional surrender on September 3, but Eisenhower withheld public announcement of the surrender until the night of the eighth, when the Allied invasion fleet lay off Salerno and Paestum (Mary H. Williams, comp., *Chronology, 1941–1945,* 127, 128, 131; D'Este, *Eisenhower: A Soldier's Life,* 445–46).

4. Truscott, *Command Missions,* 247.

5. Aide's Diaries, September 7, 1943, box 18, folder 3, Truscott Papers. The Packard sedan was government issue. Division commanders were entitled to Packard sedans; corps and army commanders were issued Cadillacs (Wilson interview).

6. Truscott, *Command Missions,* 247.

7. This recounting of the battles in the Salerno beachhead is a distillation of material in the following sources: Martin Blumenson, *Salerno to Cassino,* 73–132; William Breuer, *They Jumped at Midnight: The "Crash" Parachute Missions That Turned the Tide at Salerno,* 71–85; Mark W. Clark, *Calculated Risk,* 188–208; D'Este, *Eisenhower: A Soldier's Life,* 452–53; Vincent J. Esposito, ed., *The West Point Atlas of American Wars,* maps 95 and 96 with accompanying text; Ladd, *Commandos and Rangers of World War II,* 139; Charles B. MacDonald, *The Mighty Endeavor: American Armed Forces in the European Theater in World War II,* 178–86; and Winfried Heinemann, "Salerno: A Defender's View," 12, 17. The first quotation is from Heinemann, "Salerno: A Defender's View," 12, and the second is from MacDonald, *Mighty Endeavor,* 184–85.

8. M. Clark, *Calculated Risk,* 208. Clark does not cite a specific reason in his memoir for relieving Dawley, but Blumenson states that Clark was "dissatisfied with Dawley's exercise of control" and his "seeming indifference to the threat to the corps left flank" (*Salerno to Cassino,* 149). For a balanced critique of Dawley's performance during the Salerno fighting, see ibid., 148–52.

9. Truscott, *Command Missions,* 249–54 (quotes); Taggart, *Third Infantry Division,* 80; Report of Operations, September 19–22.

10. Kesselring, *Memoirs,* 186–87 (quote); Blumenson, *Salerno to Cassino,* 207–8.

11. Blumenson, *Salerno to Cassino,* 157; Truscott, *Command Missions,* 254.

12. Blumenson, *Salerno to Cassino,* 158; Forrest C. Pogue, *George C. Marshall: Organizer of Victory, 1943–1945,* 331–32; S. Stanton, *Order of Battle,* 79; John P. Lucas Diary, June 12, 1943; Chandler, *Papers of Eisenhower,* vol. 3, Doc. 1267, Eisenhower to Marshall, September 19, 1943, 1436.

13. Truscott, *Command Missions,* 258–62 (quote); Report of Operations, September 19–22, 23–30, 1943.

14. Truscott, *Command Missions,* 262–65; Report of Operations, October 1–12, 1943 (quote). For an exhaustive analysis of the effects of mud on military operations, consult C. E. Wood, *Mud: A Military History.*

15. Truscott, *Command Missions,* 266.

16. Aide's Diaries, October 10, 1943, box 18, folder 3, Truscott Papers. Charles IV, one of the Bourbon kings, built the palace in 1768 to rival his ancestors' palaces at Versailles and Escorial ("Caserta: The Extravagant Whimsy of the Bourbons"). Later in October General Clark established Fifth Army headquarters at the palace.

17. Blumenson, *Salerno to Cassino,* 204, 196.

18. Ibid., 196–97; Taggart, *Third Infantry Division,* 88.

19. Report of Operations, October 13–19, 1943; Truscott to wife, October 14, 1943, box 1, folder 7, Truscott Papers.

20. Blumenson, *Salerno to Cassino,* 199; Truscott, *Command Missions,* 273, 274, 276.

21. Report of Operations, October 13–19, 1943.

22. Blumenson, *Salerno to Cassino,* 203–5.

23. Truscott, *Command Missions,* 274.

24. Report of Operations, October 13–19, 1943.

25. Blumenson, *Salerno to Cassino,* 210; Lucas Diary, October 19, 1943.

26. Blumenson, *Salerno to Cassino,* 217.

27. Ibid., 204–5, 214–15.

28. Bennett, *Ultra and Mediterranean Strategy,* 250–53.

29. Truscott, *Command Missions,* 280; Blumenson, *Salerno to Cassino,* 219.

30. Unless indicated otherwise, this account of the operation in the Mignano Gap area is from Truscott, *Command Missions,* 282, 284, 285; Taggart, *Third Infantry Division,* 98–99; and Report of Operations, November 1–18, 1943.

31. Blumenson, *Salerno to Cassino,* 219. The 3d ID received its sobriquet "Rock of the Marne" for its stand on the south bank of the Marne River east of Château Thierry on July 15, 1918, when it fought off two German divisions advancing on Paris, contributing in great measure to Gen. Erich Ludendorff's decision to call off the drive toward Paris (John S. D. Eisenhower, *Yanks: The Epic Story of the American Army in World War I,* 152–61).

32. Lucas Diary, November 9, 1943. This account of the move of the 30th Infantry east to Rocca Pipirozzi is based on Truscott's account in his memoir, *Command Missions,* 284, and on Blumenson's account in *Salerno to Cassino,* 229–30, which cites Truscott's memoir and a personal communication from Truscott in 1964 (230n30). In his diary entry of November 6 Lucas wrote that he was unable to contact Truscott to order the 30th's move, and he personally ordered the regiment to move to Rocca Pipirozzi, an action that made Truscott "furious." I am at a loss to explain the striking difference in the two men's recounting of the episode.

33. Report of Operations, November 7–10 and November 11–18, 1943; Truscott, *Command Missions,* 285.

34. Truscott, *Command Missions,* 282–84; M. Clark, *Calculated Risk,* 231–32. I have found no record of any reply by Gruenther to Truscott's inquiry.

35. Taggart, *Third Infantry Division,* 102. In a note Taggart states, "It is estimated that these figures [for the enemy] reflect not more than five per cent of the casualties inflicted on the enemy by the 3rd Division and its attached units."

36. Division Commander's Address to Division Officers, November 22, 1943, box 12, folder 3, Truscott Papers.

37. Truscott to Eisenhower, November 24, 1943, box 11, folder 11, Truscott Papers; Eisenhower to Truscott, December 16, 1943, box 116, Eisenhower Pre-presidential Papers.

38. Truscott to Walter B. "Beetle" Smith, December 1, 1943, box 11, folder 11, Truscott Papers.

CHAPTER 9: ANZIO AND THE ROAD TO ROME

1. Truscott, *Command Missions*, 286–88.

2. M. Clark, *Calculated Risk*, 239–40.

3. Truscott, *Command Missions*, 289.

4. Ibid., 290; James A. Wood, *We Move Only Forward: Canada, the United States, and the First Special Service Force, 1942–1944*, 82–86; M. Clark, *Calculated Risk*, 240–42.

5. Truscott, *Command Missions*, 291–92 (emphasis added).

6. Ibid., 292–96.

7. Aide's Diaries, December 13, 1943, January 13, 1944, box 18, folders 3 and 4, respectively, Truscott Papers; Truscott, *Command Missions*, 295–96. "Dogface Soldier" was composed in 1942 by Cpl. Bert Gold and Lt. Ken Hart, both of Long Island, New York. The song became quite popular among soldiers during World War II and was introduced to the public in 1955 in Audie Murphy's autobiographical movie, *To Hell and Back*. Murphy was a member of Company B, 15th Infantry ("Dogface Soldier").

8. Truscott, *Command Missions*, 298.

9. D'Este points out that Wilson did not invite either General Clark or General Lucas to the meeting. Thus, Anzio "was planned with its commanding general largely filling the role of spectator while others sealed his fate" (*Warlord: A Life of Winston Churchill at War, 1874–1945*, 652).

10. Truscott, *Command Missions*, 298–302.

11. Bennett, *Ultra and Mediterranean Strategy*, 262–63.

12. D'Este, *Fatal Decision*, 111, 112 (emphasis added).

13. John Bowditch III, *Anzio Beachhead, 22 January–25 May 1944*, 5–6 (quote); Taggart, *Third Infantry Division*, 107–8; Truscott, *Command Missions*, 301.

14. Lucas Diary, January 15, 1944.

15. Truscott, *Command Missions*, 303. "DUKW is an acronym based on D indicating the model year (1942); U referring to the body style, utility (amphibious); K for all-wheel drive; and W for dual rear axles" ("DUKW").

16. Lucas Diary, January 19, 1944; Truscott, *Command Missions*, 304 (second quote).

17. Truscott, *Command Missions*, 304.

18. Kesselring, *Memoirs*, 192–93 (quotes); Senger und Etterlin, *Neither Fear nor Hope*, 192.

19. Lang, "Tough U.S. General," 98.

20. Blumenson, *Salerno to Cassino*, 357–58.

21. Lucas Diary, January 24, 1944.

22. Truscott, *Command Missions*, 309; Taggart, *Third Infantry Division*, 108–9. Taggart refers to the Provisional Mounted Troop as the 3d Provisional Reconnaissance Troop.

23. Blumenson, *Salerno to Cassino*, 358–59.

24. Truscott, *Command Missions*, 310.

25. Kesselring, *Memoirs*, 194; Blumenson, *Salerno to Cassino*, 361.

26. Truscott, *Command Missions*, 310–11. For a comprehensive discussion of Lucas's decision not to advance to the Alban Hills immediately after landing his forces virtually unopposed, see Martin Blumenson, "The Trouble with Anzio."

27. Aide's Diaries, January 24, 1943, box 18, folder 4, Truscott Papers. Major Renne is not further identified but may have been one of Lucas's aides.

28. Truscott, *Command Missions*, 313; J. Eisenhower, *They Fought at Anzio*, 133–34. Eisenhower mistakenly identifies the highway as "Route 6."

29. J. Eisenhower, *They Fought at Anzio*, 134.

30. Truscott, *Command Missions*, 313.

31. Bowditch, *Anzio Beachhead*, 28–33; Truscott, *Command Missions*, 313–15; J. Eisenhower, *They Fought at Anzio*, 134–41; Darby and Baumer, *Darby's Rangers*, 158–70. Ladd

states that there were eighteen survivors of the 1st and 3d Rangers who escaped capture (*Commandos and Rangers,* 265), differing from the figure of six recorded by Darby and Baumer (*Darby's Rangers,* 170), which I have chosen to accept since Darby was a participant.

32. Blumenson, *Salerno to Cassino,* 391.

33. Truscott, *Command Missions,* 314; Robert W. Black, *Rangers in World War II,* 174.

34. Truscott, *Command Missions,* 315 (emphasis added); Bennett, *Ultra and Mediterranean Strategy,* 267.

35. Bowditch, *Anzio Beachhead,* 44.

36. Blumenson, *Salerno to Cassino,* 395–96.

37. Truscott, *Command Missions,* 317(quote); Lucas Diary, February 6, 14, 1944. Truscott later learned that Eagles had used only one infantry battalion and two tank companies in the counterattacks against the Factory, a task that Truscott estimated required a regiment to ensure success (*Command Missions,* 317).

38. Aide's Diaries, February 7, 1944, box 18, folder 4, Truscott Papers; NATOUSA GO 9, para. 1, February 8, 1944, Truscott OMPF.

39. Kesselring, *Memoirs,* 195–96. Kesselring has confused Aprilia with Apulia, which is located far to the south in the "heel" of Italy.

40. Bennett, *Ultra and Mediterranean Strategy,* 268.

41. Truscott, *Command Missions,* 317–18. The 1st SSF had arrived in the beachhead on February 1 (J. Wood, *We Move Only Forward,* 111).

42. Truscott, *Command Missions,* 318–19.

43. Lucas Diary, February 15, 1944.

44. Aide's Diaries, February 16, 1944, box 18, folder 4, Truscott Papers.

45. Truscott, *Command Missions,* 319–20.

46. Aide's Diaries, February 17, 1944, box 18, folder 4, Truscott Papers; Truscott, *Command Missions,* 320.

47. Francesco Rossi and Silvano Casaldi, *Those Days at Nettuno,* 218–19. It is interesting that Lucas, a highly regarded artilleryman, chose the "Tavern of the Artilleryman" as the entrance to his underground CP.

48. Truscott, *Command Missions,* 321–22 (quote); Wilson interview, 20. Wilson went on to say that throughout the period when Truscott was serving as deputy corps commander he was in ill health, suffering from a severe cold brought on by his visit to Harmon and Eagles in the bitter, rainy weather, compounded by his recurring dental problems. A wadi is "a stream or watercourse that is dry except during periods of rainfall" (*The Random House College Dictionary,* s.v., "Wadi.")

49. Truscott, *Command Missions,* 322–23.

50. Ibid., 323.

51. Ibid., 324–26. Major Kerwin rose to the grade of general and served as Army vice chief of staff, 1974–1978 ("General Walter T. Kerwin, Jr. Remembered," 33).

52. Truscott, *Command Missions,* 326; Bennett, *Ultra and Mediterranean Strategy,* 268–69.

53. Truscott, *Command Missions,* 327–28; Aide's Diaries, February 22, 1944, Truscott Papers. The diaries record several visits by Truscott to medical treatment facilities for treatment of a chronic throat condition. The exact nature of the malady is not mentioned, but it quite possibly was related to his swallowing carbolic acid as a child and to his longtime addiction to cigarettes. James Wilson, his aide, described Truscott as a "chain smoker" (Wilson interview, 19).

54. Efficiency Report, February 22, 1944, OMPF; Form for a Special Rating of General Officers, February 27, 1944, OMPF (quotes).

55. Aide's Diaries, February 22, 1944, box 18, folder 4, Truscott Papers.

56. Truscott, *Command Missions,* 328–31.

57. Ibid., 331–32.

58. Ibid., 333–34 (emphasis in original).

59. VI Corps, GO 8, para. 1, February 26, 1944, box 13, folder 2, Truscott Papers.

60. Truscott, *Command Missions,* 333.

61. Bill Mauldin was an enlisted man in the 45th Infantry Division whose cartoons depicting his characters Willie and Joe as dogface soldiers bearing up under the abominable discomforts of combat in Italy and southern Europe made him one of the most famous cartoonists of World War II.

62. Truscott, *Command Missions,* 333.

63. Ibid., 334–36.

64. *Dictionary of United States Army Terms,* s.v. "time on target (artillery)."

65. Truscott, *Command Missions,* 337.

66. Aide's Diaries, February 26, March 19, 1944, box 18, folder 4, Truscott Papers.

67. Ibid., March 9, 1944; Wilson interview, 16; Truscott to wife, March 1, 1945, box 1, folder 3, Truscott Papers.

68. Truscott, *Command Missions,* 341–43.

69. Aide's Diaries, February 25, 1944, box 18, folder 4, Truscott Papers; *Register of Graduates,* 344.

70. Truscott, *Command Missions,* 343–44.

71. Ibid., 344–45.

72. Ibid., 345–47; Bowditch, *Anzio Beachhead,* 96–104; Blumenson, *Salerno to Cassino,* 429–31.

73. M. Clark, *Calculated Risk,* 310.

74. Truscott, *Command Missions,* 350–52.

75. The 504th Parachute Infantry Regiment was redeployed to England where it rejoined the 82d Airborne Division in training for the Normandy invasion, and the 509th Parachute Infantry Battalion was redeployed to train for the invasion of southern France as part of the 1st Airborne Task Force (Gerard M. Devlin, *Paratrooper! The Saga of U.S. Army and Marine Parachute and Glider Combat Troops during World War II,* 351–52).

76. Truscott, *Command Missions,* 352.

77. Aide's Diaries, March 30, 31, April 7, 13, 15, 17, 19, 21, 1944, box 18, folder 4, Truscott Papers. Doctor (Colonel) Pierce was an eye, ear, nose, and throat specialist and was the commander of the hospital.

78. Aide's Diaries, April 27, 28, 1944, box 18, folder 4, Truscott Papers; Truscott, *Command Missions,* 368.

79. Truscott, *Command Missions,* 361, 357–58.

80. Ibid., 361–62.

81. Ernest F. Fisher Jr., *Cassino to the Alps,* 26–27; D'Este, *Fatal Decision,* 333–35; Truscott, *Command Missions,* 366.

82. Truscott, *Command Missions,* 366–67.

83. Ibid., 368–69. In *Calculated Risk,* Mark W. Clark does not mention his visit to Truscott or the substance of his remarks to him. He states only that he called Alexander to express his surprise at Truscott's message indicating that "Alexander had issued instructions contrary to mine" and that Truscott had called Clark for clarification. Clark then went on to ask Alexander "to please issue orders through me instead of dealing directly with my subordinates. He understood and assured me that he had no intention of interfering" (ibid., 342).

84. D'Este, *Fatal Decision,* 337.

85. Truscott, *Command Missions,* 370–71.

86. Aide's Diaries, May 20, 30, 1944, box 18, folder 4, Truscott Papers.

87. Truscott, *Command Missions,* 372.

88. Fisher, *Cassino to the Alps*, 107; Bowditch, *Anzio Beachhead*, 119.

89. Frederick interview, 17.

90. Truscott, *Command Missions*, 371–74; Bowditch, *Anzio Beachhead*, 119–20 (quotes).

91. Truscott, *Command Missions*, 374–75 (emphasis added).

92. D'Este, *Fatal Decision*, 369, 373, 377–78; Bowditch, *Anzio Beachhead*, 120; Truscott, *Command Missions*, 375.

93. D'Este, *Fatal Decision*, 379–80; J. Wood, *We Move Only Forward*, 146.

94. Truscott, *Command Missions*, 550.

95. Ibid. An exhaustive discussion of Clark's decision to shift the axis of attack of VI Corps from Valmontone to the drive on Rome can be found in Sidney T. Mathews's "General Clark's Decision to Drive on Rome."

96. Truscott, *Command Missions*, 375–78; Bowditch, *Anzio Beachhead*, 120–22; Fisher, *Cassino to the Alps*, 200–202, 206.

97. Truscott, *Command Missions*, 378–79. The first Allied element to enter Rome was a patrol composed of Americans and Canadians of the 1st Special Service Force, which entered at 6:00 a.m., June 4, 1944 (Robert W. Jones Jr., "The Race to Rome," 8).

98. Fisher, *Cassino to the Alps*, 220–21.

99. Truscott, *Command Missions*, 379–80.

100. Ibid., 380; Jeffrey J. Clarke and Robert Ross Smith, *Riviera to the Rhine*, 30–32.

101. Truscott, *Command Missions*, 380.

102. Ibid., 546.

CHAPTER 10: SOUTHERN FRANCE

1. Aide's Diaries, June 11, 1944, box 18, folder 4, Truscott Papers.

2. Ibid., June 14, 1944; Truscott to wife, June 15, 25, 1944, box 1, folder 9, Truscott Papers. The Jefferson Bible, formally titled *The Life and Morals of Jesus of Nazareth*, was Thomas Jefferson's version of the Bible in which he removed all mention of Jesus's miracles and all claims to Jesus's being divine or his mother a virgin ("Jefferson Bible").

3. Truscott, *Command Missions*, 382–83.

4. Ibid., 383; Aide's Diaries, June 17, 1944, box 18, folder 4, Truscott Papers. In an "eyes only" April 30, 1944, message to Marshall, Eisenhower informed him that he was prepared to "relieve [Patton] from command [of Third Army] and send him home" unless Patton could "produce additional mitigating evidence" regarding statements that he had made at the opening of a service club for American servicemen in Knutsford, England. In that message Eisenhower expressed his regret at not having requested at the time of his assignment to England in November 1943 Truscott's assignment to the OVERLORD command as a potential senior ground commander, pointing out that "he would make an ideal commander of the Third Army" (Chandler, *Papers of Eisenhower*, vol. 3, Doc. 1660, Eisenhower to Marshall, April 30, 1944, 1840–41). D'Este describes in detail the incident at Knutsford in *Patton*, 585–92.

5. David P. Colley, *Decision at Strasbourg: Ike's Strategic Mistake to Halt the Sixth Army Group at the Rhine in 1944*, 86.

6. Truscott, *Command Missions*, 384–85; Aide's Diaries, June 17, 1944, box 18, folder 4, Truscott Papers. Truscott clearly states in his memoir that VI Corps was to capture Marseilles. Clarke and Smith, however, indicate that the French were to have that mission (*Riviera to the Rhine*, 80). The first two quotations are from Truscott, the latter from the Aide's Diary entry.

7. Truscott, *Command Missions*, 385–87 (quotes); Clarke and Smith, *Riviera to the Rhine*, 36.

8. Truscott, *Command Missions*, 387–88.

9. Message, HQ VI Corps to CG, Seventh Army, June 26, 1944, box 12, folder 7, Truscott Papers. Truscott inserted the italicized sentence and phrase manually in the typed message before he sent it. The phrase replaced the scratched-out words "tactically impractical." In the referenced document, X's were substituted for periods, as is the standard practice in preparing military messages. I have replaced the X's with periods for easier comprehension.

10. Clarke and Smith, *Riviera to the Rhine*, 78; Truscott, *Command Missions*, 384, where he states, "My Corps was to hold the beachhead and to protect the right flank while the French Corps captured Toulon," which agrees with VI Corps Field Order 1, the operation order for ANVIL (FO 1, VI Corps, July 30, 1944, box 13, folder 9, Truscott Papers). Clarke and Smith mistakenly state the 3d ID was to spearhead the assault on Toulon.

11. Truscott, *Command Missions*, 388–91.

12. Clarke and Smith, *Riviera to the Rhine*, 76–77; FO 1, VI Corps, July 30, 1944, box 13, folder 9, Truscott Papers.

13. Truscott, *Command Missions*, 394.

14. VI Corps Combat Troop List, Operation ANVIL, August 1, 1944; Truscott, *Command Missions*, 397–400; FO 1, VI Corps, July 30, 1944, box 13, folder 9, Truscott Papers. The French combat command bore the name of its commander, Brig. Gen. Aime M. Sudre.

15. Truscott, *Command Missions*, 397.

16. Ibid., 402–5.

17. Ibid., 407.

18. Brig. Gen. Frederic B. Butler, "Southern France Exploits of Task Force Butler," 12–13.

19. Truscott, *Command Missions*, 408.

20. Clarke and Smith, *Riviera to the Rhine*, 57, 65–66.

21. Truscott, *Command Missions*, 408.

22. Ibid., 408–10; Clarke and Smith, *Riviera to the Rhine*, 92.

23. Truscott to wife, August 14, 1944, box 1, folder 9, Truscott Papers.

24. Truscott, *Command Missions*, 412–13; Clarke and Smith, *Riviera to the Rhine*, 112–15.

25. Truscott, *Command Missions*, 413.

26. Ibid., 413–14. The official Army historians state that they feel Truscott's adverse criticism of the decision to land the 142d over Camel Green appears to be "unjustified." They go on to point out that although the 36th "did not secure the St. Raphael–Fréjus area until mid-afternoon on 16 August, . . . the task of clearing offshore and beach obstacles proved to be so great that Army engineers and Navy demolition experts were unable to open Camel Red for discharge operations until 1900 [7:00 p.m.] on 17 August, D plus 2." Even if the 142d had secured Camel Red the afternoon of the fifteenth, "the beach would not have been ready to receive CC Sudre or any other unit until late on the 16th at the earliest." Further, since CC Sudre landed successfully over the 45th Division beaches the night of August 15–16, it was available earlier than if it had been landed over Camel Red beach as originally planned (Clarke and Smith, *Riviera to the Rhine*, 123).

27. Truscott, *Command Missions*, 414–15, 419–20; Clarke and Smith, *Riviera to the Rhine*, 101–4.

28. Truscott, *Command Missions*, 415–18; Clarke and Smith, *Riviera to the Rhine*, map 7, 127.

29. Truscott, *Command Missions*, 418–19; Clarke and Smith, *Riviera to the Rhine*, 126.

30. Clarke and Smith, *Riviera to the Rhine*, 129; Bennett, *Ultra and Mediterranean Strategy*, 296–97. ULTRA revealed that "on the morning of 17 August, Hitler had ordered the main body of Army Group G to retire up the Rhône valley with all speed," while its two easternmost divisions withdrew across the Franco-Italian border. That information reassured the Americans that the right flank of Seventh Army was in no danger but also provided, albeit retrospectively, proof that DRAGOON had not drawn German forces *away from the front in northern France,* one of the major objectives of the operation. Rather than ordering reinforcements south, *Hitler ordered evacuation from the southern front.* Bennett discusses the withdrawal of Army Group G in greater detail in his earlier book, *Ultra in the West: The Normandy Campaign, 1944–45,* 158–61.

31. Truscott, *Command Missions,* 420.

32. Lt. Gen. Ira C. Eaker was commander in chief, Mediterranean Allied Air Forces, and commanding general, U.S. Army Air Forces, NATOUSA. Maj. Gen. Wilton B. Persons was a member of General Marshall's staff.

33. Ibid., 421–23.

34. Butler, "Southern France Exploits," 14–15, 32–33.

35. Truscott, *Command Missions,* 423–25.

36. Butler, "Southern France Exploits," 33–34; Clarke and Smith, *Riviera to the Rhine,* 144–47 (quote).

37. Clarke and Smith, *Riviera to the Rhine,* 137–40.

38. Ibid., 142–43.

39. Ibid., 147–48 (quote); Butler, "Southern France Exploits," 34–35.

40. Clarke and Smith, *Riviera to the Rhine,* 149 (quote); Butler, "Southern France Exploits," 36.

41. Butler, "Southern France Exploits," 36.

42. Clarke and Smith, *Riviera to the Rhine,* 149–50; Butler, "Southern France Exploits," 37.

43. Truscott, *Command Missions,* 425 (quote); Clarke and Smith, *Riviera to the Rhine,* 151.

44. Truscott, *Command Missions,* 426–27. Truscott states that his visit to Dahlquist's CP took place on the twenty-fourth, but careful reading of the text reveals that the visit was actually on the twenty-second.

45. Butler, "Southern France Exploits," 37.

46. Truscott, *Command Missions,* 429–32 (quotes); Aide's Diaries, August 24, 1944, box 18, folder 5, Truscott Papers.

47. On August 27, at O'Daniel's request, Truscott assigned his G3, Colonel Harrell, to the 3d Division to command the 7th Infantry. Lt. Col. Theodore J. Conway replaced Harrell as VI Corps G3 (HQ VI Corps, GO 26, August 27, 1944, NACP).

48. Clarke and Smith, *Riviera to the Rhine,* 166–67.

49. Truscott, *Command Missions,* 432.

50. Clarke and Smith, *Riviera to the Rhine,* 167–68.

51. Ibid., 169.

52. Truscott, *Command Missions,* 417–18, 420, 425.

53. Clarke and Smith, *Riviera to the Rhine,* 147.

54. Ibid., 169–70; Truscott, *Command Missions,* 433.

55. Clarke and Smith, *Riviera to the Rhine,* 171.

56. Ibid., 171–73; Truscott, *Command Missions,* 433.

57. Clarke and Smith, *Riviera to the Rhine,* 173–74.

58. Ibid., 175.

59. Truscott, *Command Missions,* 434.

60. Clarke and Smith, *Riviera to the Rhine,* 177–78; Truscott, *Command Missions,* 434.

61. Clarke and Smith, *Riviera to the Rhine*, 181; Truscott, *Command Missions*, 434. In my interview of James Wilson he went into considerable detail about his two-hundred–mile journey from Grenoble to Brignoles. During the trip he and his driver sought shelter from the drenching rain in a French Army mobile brothel, where the French commander provided them with a cup of coffee. Wilson stated that Patch's CP was at Saint Tropez, while Truscott indicates Brignoles as its location. I have chosen to accept Truscott's statement.

62. Truscott, *Command Missions*, 434–37.

63. Clarke and Smith, *Riviera to the Rhine*, 186–90.

64. Ibid., 190–93.

65. Aide's Diaries, September 14, 1944, box 18, folder 5, Truscott Papers.

66. Truscott, *Command Missions*, 441–43. Truscott and Devers were old friends, having met on the polo fields during the interwar years. Truscott described him as a "prince" and "the most loyal person to subordinates who do their stuff I have ever seen except Ike maybe. The two of them are tops in my opinion" (Truscott to wife, October 11, 1944, box 1, folder 10, Truscott Papers).

67. Truscott, *Command Missions*, 443–45.

68. Truscott to wife, September 16, 19, 1944, box 1, folder 10, Truscott Papers; Aide's Diaries, September 18, 19, 1944, box 18, folder 5, Truscott Papers.

69. Truscott, *Command Missions*, 445; Dwight D. Eisenhower, *Crusade in Europe*, 304 (quote).

70. Clarke and Smith, *Riviera to the Rhine*, 229–30; Truscott, *Command Missions*, 445.

71. Colley, *Decision at Strasbourg*, 85.

72. Lucian K. Truscott IV, e-mail message to author, October 30, 2008, describing a discussion he had with Lang in 1967.

73. Unless otherwise indicated I have extracted the account of Truscott's final weeks with VI Corps from his *Command Missions*, 445–46.

74. Clarke and Smith, *Riviera to the Rhine*, 292.

75. Truscott, *Command Missions*, 445.

76. Chandler, *Papers of Eisenhower*, vol. 4, Doc. 1998, Eisenhower to Bradley, September 25, 1944, 2192. In an earlier cable to Marshall, Eisenhower had expressed his opinion that if Gerow's performance "continues at the present high standard between now and October 1 [the date Gerow was to leave V Corps to return to Washington to appear before the Pearl Harbor Board] we will probably make him an army commander designate at that time and place another officer in command of V Corps" (ibid., Doc. 1902, Eisenhower to Marshall, August 19, 1944, 2079–80).

77. Truscott, *Command Missions*, 445–46; S. Stanton, *Order of Battle*, 49. Eisenhower had decided that after the surrender of Germany he would need an additional army headquarters that would be responsible for "anticipated administrative and occupational tasks" (Chandler, *Papers of Eisenhower*, vol. 4, Doc. 2134, Eisenhower to Marshall, November 22, 1944, 2315). In July 1944 Eisenhower and Marshall had discussed the desirability of activating a new Army headquarters, the Fifteenth Army, for assignment to SHAEF later that year. Eisenhower expressed his desire that the headquarters, to be activated in CONUS, come to Europe without a commander, allowing him to choose the commander, either Truscott, McNair, or Gerow (ibid., vol. 3, Doc. 1847, Eisenhower to Marshall, July 22, 1944, 2022–23). General McNair was killed in Normandy on July 25 by Eighth Air Force bombs that fell within American lines at the beginning of Operation COBRA (Dupuy, Johnson, and Bongard, *Harper Encyclopedia of Military Biography*, s.v. "McNair, Lesley James").

78. Aide's Diaries, October 25, 26, 1944, box 18, folder 5, Truscott Papers.

79. Truscott, *Command Missions*, 446.

80. Ibid., 551–52.

81. Pogue, *Organizer of Victory,* 415; D. Eisenhower, *Crusade in Europe,* 282. The pre–D-day planners had predicted that until the Allies had captured and opened the port of Antwerp the limited availability of port capacity through Normandy and Brittany would limit the forces that could be maintained. Although the port of Antwerp fell to the British on September 4, the Schelde estuary leading from the English Channel to the port remained under German control until November 8, and the first Allied ships did not reach Antwerp until November 28. (Charles B. MacDonald, *The Siegfried Line Campaign,* 207, 229). During the more than three-month interval from the capture of Antwerp to the opening of its port the harbors of Marseilles and Toulon played a major role in supporting the advance of Eisenhower's forces.

CHAPTER 11: ARMY COMMAND

1. Eisenhower to Marshall, Ref. no. S-64796, October 31, 1944; AG WD to SHAEF MAIN, Ref. no. W-55343, November 1, 1944; SHAEF MAIN to AG WD, Ref. no. S-64932, November 1, 1944, Folder 201—Truscott, Lucien [*sic*] K. (General).

2. Aide's Diaries, November 5, 1944, box 18, folder 5, Truscott Papers.

3. Memorandum for Secretary, General Staff, November 7, 1944, Folder OPD 201, Truscott, L. K. (O); Aide's Diaries, November 17, 1944, box 18, folder 5, Truscott Papers.

4. Aide's Diaries, November 19, 1944, box 18, folder 5, Truscott Papers. When they graduated in June 1946 Patton stood 812th and Gay stood 735th in a class of 874 (*Register of Graduates,* 546, 548). Cadet Gay's father was serving as Patton's chief of staff.

5. Truscott, *Command Missions,* 447.

6. Ibid., 447–48; Aide's Diaries, November 21, 22, 1944, box 18, folder 5, Truscott Papers; Winston S. Churchill, *The Second World War: Triumph and Tragedy,* 262–64; Truscott, *Command Missions,* 447–48.

7. Aide's Diaries, November 21, 1944, box 18, folder 5, Truscott Papers; OPD to Air Transport Command, November 22, 1944, Folder OPD 201, Truscott, L. K. (O); Truscott to wife, November 26, 1944, box 1, folder 11, Truscott Papers.

8. Chandler, *Papers of Eisenhower,* vol. 4, Doc. 2134, Eisenhower to Marshall, November 22, 1944, 2315; Doc. 2135, Eisenhower to Marshall, November 22, 1944, 2315–16.

9. Truscott to wife, November 26, 1944, box 1, folder 11, Truscott Papers; Chandler, *Papers of Eisenhower,* vol. 4, Doc. 2143, Eisenhower to Marshall, November 27, 1944, 2320–21; Aide's Diaries, November 27, 1944, box 18, folder 5, Truscott Papers; Truscott to wife, December 4, 1944, box 1, folder 11, Truscott Papers.

10. Truscott to wife, December 4, 1944, box 1, folder 11, Truscott Papers; Truscott, *Command Missions,* 448, 454; Truscott to wife, December 11, 1944, box 1, folder 11, Truscott Papers; Orders, European theater of operations, December 4, 1944, para. 1, Truscott OMPF.

11. Chandler, *Papers of Eisenhower,* vol. 4, Doc. 2154, Eisenhower to Marshall, December 5, 1944, 2336.

12. Truscott to wife, December 11, 1944, box 1, folder 11, Truscott Papers.

13. Truscott, *Command Missions,* 448–49.

14. Truscott to wife, December 11, 1944, box 1, folder 11, Truscott Papers.

15. Fifth Army, GO 183, December 16, 1944, Truscott OMPF.

16. Truscott, *Command Missions,* 452; S. Stanton, *Order of Battle,* 166.

17. Truscott, *Command Missions,* 454.

18. Fisher, *Cassino to the Alps,* 406–8; S. Stanton, *Order of Battle,* 166.

19. Paul Goodman, *A Fragment of Victory in Italy: The 92nd Infantry Division in World War II,* 38–40; Stanton, *Order of Battle,* 167.

20. S. Stanton, *Order of Battle*, 167.

21. Hondon B. Hargrove, *Buffalo Soldiers in Italy: Black Americans in World War II*, 9.

22. Fisher, *Cassino to the Alps*, 407.

23. Ibid., 408–10; Truscott, *Command Missions*, 456.

24. Chester G. Starr, *From Salerno to the Alps: A History of the Fifth Army, 1943–1945*, 371.

25. Truscott, *Command Missions*, 459–60.

26. Ibid., 461–64.

27. Ibid., 462.

28. Ibid.

29. HQ Mediterranean Theater of Operations, McNarney to Truscott, December 29, 1944, box 15, folder 3, Truscott Papers.

30. Truscott, *Command Missions*, 464.

31. According to the Federal Reserve Bank of Minneapolis online calculator, $300,000 in 1944 dollars equaled $3,731,893 in 2009 dollars.

32. Starr, *From Salerno to the Alps*, 371–77.

33. Fisher, *Cassino to the Alps*, 411.

34. Aide's Diaries, January 9, 1945, box 19, folder 1, Truscott Papers. A "plank steak" is prepared on a wooden plank.

35. Truscott, *Command Missions*, 477–78.

36. Ibid., 468–69.

37. Ibid., 469–70.

38. Starr, *From Salerno to the Alps*, 383; Fisher, *Cassino to the Alps*, 421–24.

39. Aide's Diaries, February 9, 1945, box 19, folder 1, Truscott Papers.

40. Fisher, *Cassino to the Alps*, 421 (quote); Starr, *From Salerno to the Alps*, 383.

41. Truscott, *Command Missions*, 473.

42. Hargrove, *Buffalo Soldiers in Italy*, 98 (emphasis in original). Both Fisher (*Cassino to the Alps*, 424) and Goodman (*Fragment of Victory*, 99) mention the fire from the coastal batteries at Punta Bianca in their accounts of the operation. Truscott does state in his report to Clark that he personally observed the operation only during the first day, February 8, a point confirmed by Fisher (*Cassino to the Alps*, 422), and thereafter followed the operation "by reports from the Commanding General IV Corps" (471). Therefore, if the coastal guns did not by chance fire during the first day's action, Truscott might have been unaware of their presence and of their contribution to the defeat of TF 1.

43. Pogue, *Organizer of Victory*, 538.

44. Ulysses Lee, *The Employment of Negro Troops*, 573.

45. Truscott, *Command Missions*, 474.

46. Aide's Diaries, February 17, 1945, box 19, folder 1, Truscott Papers; Lee, *Employment of Negro Troops*, 573; Stanton, *Order of Battle*, 252.

47. Pogue, *Organizer of Victory*, 538. Pogue points out the great disappointment that Marshall felt after witnessing the performance of the division, since he had been "a strong advocate of protection of rights of black troops from his days as senior instructor of the 33d Division in Illinois and as the head of the Infantry School" and "had pressed hard for equitable treatment for Negroes as Chief of Staff of the Army" (538–39).

48. Orville C. Shirey, *Americans: The Story of the 442d Combat Team*, 77–78.

49. Goodman, *Fragment of Victory*, 110; Lee, *Employment of Negro Troops*, 579; HQ 15th Army Group to CG, Fifth Army, "Fifth Army's Operations in Coastal Sector," February 22, 1945, box 15, folder 3, Truscott Papers.

50. Truscott, *Command Missions*, 469, 474.

51. Dale E. Wilson, "Recipe for Failure: Major General Edward M. Almond and Preparation of the U.S. 92d Infantry Division for Combat in World War II," 474. For

a comprehensive discussion of racial segregation in the Army and the combat performance of the two black infantry divisions, the 92d and the 93d, in World War II, see
Morris J. MacGregor, *Integration of the Armed Forces, 1940–1965,* 130–43.

52. Truscott, *Command Missions,* 466–67.

53. Peter Shelton, *Climb to Conquer: The Untold Story of World War II's 10th Mountain Division Ski Troops,* 125–29.

54. Thomas R. Brooks, *The War North of Rome, June 1944–May 1945,* 354–55.

55. Ibid., 356–59.

56. Truscott, *Command Missions,* 479–80; Starr, *From Salerno to the Alps,* 383–85
(quote). Truscott states that the Eighth Army consisted of ten infantry divisions, one
armored division, five armored and several separate brigades and detachments, and
three Italian groups. I have accepted Starr's figures since his book is a condensation of
the nine-volume official *Fifth Army History,* "which was prepared in full accordance
with the principles of historical scholarship" (*From Salerno to the Alps,* xii).

CHAPTER 12: THE FINAL OFFENSIVE

1. Truscott, *Command Missions,* 480 (quote); Starr, *From Salerno to the Alps,* 387–88.

2. Truscott had established three phase lines for his main attack, from south to north,
Green, Brown, and Black (Starr, *From Salerno to the Alps,* 391).

3. Truscott, *Command Missions,* 481–82 (quote); Starr, *From Salerno to the Alps,*
391–92.

4. Memorandum for General Truscott from Chief of Staff, Fifth Army, March 29,
1945, box 1, Don E. Carleton Papers.

5. Truscott, *Command Missions,* 483.

6. Ibid., 484–85.

7. Goodman, *Fragment of Victory,* 138–44.

8. Gruenther to Carleton, telephone call, 3:50 p.m., April 24, 1945, Po Valley Tele-
phone Calls, box 2, Carleton Papers; S. Stanton, *Order of Battle,* 167. According to
Shelby Stanton, the 92d Division was under Fifth Army control at that time (*Order of
Battle,* 166).

9. Hargrove, *Buffalo Soldiers in Italy,* 165–68.

10. Goodman, *Fragment of Victory,* 152–53; Truscott, *Command Missions,* 485.

11. Bennett, *Ultra and Mediterranean Strategy,* 316–20.

12. M. Clark, *Calculated Risk,* 429–30.

13. Truscott, *Command Missions,* 486.

14. *19 Days from the Apennines to the Alps: The Story of the Po Valley Campaign,*
38–39; Truscott, *Command Missions,* 487–88.

15. Truscott to wife, April 15, 1945, box 1, folder 11, Truscott Papers; "Willis D. Crittenberger"; James J. Truscott, e-mail message to author, November 18, 2007.

16. Truscott, *Command Missions,* 488–91; *19 Days,* 51.

17. *19 Days,* 52–56; Truscott, *Command Missions,* 494–95; McKay Jenkins, *The Last
Ridge: The Epic Story of the U.S. Army's 10th Mountain Division and the Assault on
Hitler's Europe,* 232–34.

18. Brooks, *War North of Rome,* 384; Truscott to wife, April 23, 1945, box 1, folder 11,
Truscott Papers.

19. Truscott, *Command Missions,* 492–93.

20. Brooks, *War North of Rome,* 386.

21. Jenkins, *Last Ridge,* 237–38; Senger und Etterlin, *Neither Fear nor Hope,* 302.

22. Shelton, *Climb to Conquer,* 200–202. Hays had wisely recognized that the Germans might well block the east shore road by destroying the tunnels and had arranged

for several companies of DUKWs to be brought forward to the division rear (Fisher, *Cassino to the Alps,* 507).

23. Fisher, *Cassino to the Alps,* 507–11; Darby and Baumer, *Darby's Rangers,* 178–79. Fisher records that Darby and Cook were standing on a promenade when they were struck by shrapnel from the aerial explosion of an artillery round (*Cassino to the Alps,* 511). The accounts of Darby's death by Brooks (*War North of Rome,* 387) and Jenkins (*Last Ridge,* 243) mirror the account that I have cited from *Darby's Rangers.* The account of the recovery of the sword is from a memorandum, Truscott to Lt. Gen. Thomas T. Handy, July 24, 1945, in which Truscott explains that the Mussolini sword that Mrs. Truscott had just sent to his office was a gift from Fifth Army to General Marshall (box 15, folder 4, Truscott Papers).

24. Fisher, *Cassino to the Alps,* 511–12.

25. Truscott, *Command Missions,* 495; Fisher, *Cassino to the Alps,* 520–24; M. Clark, *Calculated Risk,* 437.

26. M. Clark, *Calculated Risk,* 437–38. Those readers desiring an encyclopedic account of the top-secret negotiations leading to the German surrender in Italy should consult Allen Dulles, *The Secret Surrender.*

27. Aide's Diaries, May 2, 1945, box 19, folder 1, Truscott Papers; Fisher, *Cassino to the Alps,* 531 (quotes). This account of the happenings at Truscott's CP after the surrender differs considerably from Truscott's description of the events in a letter to his wife: "All in all, our soldiers took the news with quiet satisfaction. There has been no outburst of enthusiasm or celebration such as marked the end of World War I even in the trenches" (May 2, 3, 1945, box 1, folder 11, Truscott Papers).

28. Truscott to wife, May 2, 3, 1945, box 1, folder 11, Truscott Papers; Truscott, *Command Missions,* 504.

29. Truscott, *Command Missions,* 500–501.

30. Ibid., 501.

31. Ibid., 501–2.

32. Truscott to wife, May 19, 1945, box 1, folder 11, Truscott Papers; Aide's Diaries, May 18, 21, 1945, box 19, folder 1, Truscott Papers.

33. Aide's Diaries, May 30, 1945, box 19, folder 1, Truscott Papers; Bill Mauldin, *The Brass Ring: A Sort of a Memoir,* 272.

CHAPTER 13: THE POSTWAR YEARS

1. Aide's Diaries, June 9, 10, 11, 13, 1945, box 19, folder 1, Truscott Papers.

2. Ibid., June 13, 14, 1945. I have been unable to learn exactly what "La Vieta" was. Most likely, it was a large, fashionable restaurant.

3. Ibid., June 15, 1945; James J. Truscott, e-mail message to author, February 3, 2008. Truscott's original orders directing him to return to the United States authorized him a leave that would not exceed fifteen days (HQ European Theater of Operations, Order, June 9, 1945, paras. 1 and 2, Truscott OMPF). James Truscott informed me that in the summer of 1944 his mother and he moved out of Wild Acres after Sarah and her mother had "a falling-out." Sarah eventually purchased the house on Jefferson Park Avenue.

4. Aide's Diaries, June 24, 1945, box 19, folder 1, Truscott Papers. Truscott had met Mrs. Luce when, as a member of Congress, she had visited the Italian front.

5. Ibid., June 25, 1945.

6. Ibid., June 29, 30, 1945.

7. "Army Ground Force Equipment Review Board Preliminary Study—Fifth Army and MTOUSA Reports Thereon," July 14, 1945, box 15, folder 3, Truscott Papers.

8. Doug Stanton, *Horse Soldiers: The Extraordinary Story of a Band of U.S. Soldiers Who Rode to Victory in Afghanistan,* 164–68.

9. "Army Ground Force Equipment Review Board Preliminary Study—Fifth Army and MTOUSA Reports Thereon."

10. Aide's Diaries, July 21, 1945, box 19, folder 2, Truscott Papers (quote); "Castle of Chillon."

11. I have used the pinyin romanization system for Chinese names, with the Wade-Giles spelling enclosed in parentheses.

12. Cable, Marshall to Truscott, July 29, 1945, box 15, folder 3, Truscott Papers; Dupuy, Johnson, and Bongard, *Harper Encyclopedia of Military Biography,* s.v. "Wedemeyer, Albert C." and "Chiang Kai-shek." Marshall had notified Wedemeyer that he would make available to him for assignment in China Generals Patton, Simpson, and Truscott (Wedemeyer, *Wedemeyer Reports!* 331).

13. Truscott to wife, July 31, 1945, box 1, folder 11, Truscott Papers; letter order 547, HQ Fifth Army, August 5, 1945, para. 1, Truscott OMPF. In his memoir Truscott states that Sergeant Hong accompanied him on the trip to China (*Command Missions,* 504). However, Hong's name does not appear in the Fifth Army letter order.

14. Aide's Diaries, August 8, 9, 10, 1945, box 19, folder 2, Truscott Papers. In his memoir Truscott states that he heard the radio report of Japan's willingness to surrender in Cairo and does not mention a stop in Jerusalem (*Command Missions,* 504). I have accepted the account in the Aide's Diaries because they are a contemporary record of Truscott's daily activities.

15. Aide's Diaries, August 13, 1945, box 19, folder 2, Truscott Papers; Truscott, *Command Missions,* 504–5; message, Wedemeyer to Truscott, August 12, 1945, box 15, folder 3, Truscott Papers. I have found no reason for Wedemeyer's request that Truscott stop temporarily in Calcutta.

16. Truscott, *Command Missions,* 505.

17. Aide's Diaries, August 17, 1945, box 19, folder 2, Truscott Papers; Truscott, *Command Missions,* 505.

18. Aide's Diaries, August 18, 1945, box 19, folder 2, Truscott Papers. For a comprehensive discussion of the Stilwell–Jiang Jieshi controversy, see Barbara A. Tuchman, *Stilwell and the American Experience in China, 1911–45,* 571–636.

19. Aide's Diaries, August 23, 1945, box 19, folder 2, Truscott Papers; Truscott, *Command Missions,* 505. In his memoir Truscott gives no reason for the abrupt termination of his China trip, simply stating, "Having seen what we could of China, there was nothing further to hold us" (*Command Missions,* 505). Wedemeyer also gives no explanation for Truscott's sudden decision to leave China, stating that Truscott, after receiving notice of the Japanese surrender, returned immediately to "the States," and "consequently did not have the opportunity of visiting the Generalissimo and the capital, Chungking" (*Wedemeyer Reports!* 332). The reason for such a gross misstatement by Wedemeyer that Truscott never met with Jiang is unclear to the author.

20. Max Hastings, *Retribution: The Battle for Japan, 1944–45,* 216.

21. Aide's Diaries, August 30, 1945, box 19, folder 2, Truscott Papers.

22. Truscott to wife, August 26, 1945, box 1, folder 12, Truscott Papers.

23. Aide's Diaries, September 12, 1945, box 19, folder 2, Truscott Papers.

24. Truscott, *Command Missions,* 506.

25. HQ 15th Army Group, "Special Rating of General Officer," May 24, 1945, Truscott OMPF.

26. Truscott, *Command Missions,* 507–8 (quotes); Aide's Diaries, September 25, 27, 1945, box 19, folder 2, Truscott Papers; Joseph W. Bendersky, *The "Jewish Threat": Anti-Semitic Policies of the U.S. Army,* 358. Those readers desiring more detailed accounts of the events leading to Patton's relief should consult Ladislas Farago, *The Last Days*

of Patton; D'Este, *Patton,* 760–82; and Blumenson, *Patton Papers,* 761–94. Bendersky, "Jewish Threat," 352–58, covers Patton's views of and attitudes toward Jewish displaced persons.

27. "Letter from President Truman to Gen. Eisenhower enclosing the Harrison Report on the treatment of displaced Jews in the U.S. Zone," 1, 7–13.

28. Truscott to wife, September 29, 1945, box 1, folder 12, Truscott Papers.

29. Truscott to Handy, September 30, 1945, Folder OPD 201, Truscott, L. K. (O).

30. Truscott, *Command Missions,* 508–9 (quote); Aide's Diaries, October 7, 1945, box 19, folder 2, Truscott Papers; D'Este, *Patton,* 776–77.

31. Truscott, *Command Missions,* 509–10.

32. Ibid., 510–13.

33. Press Conference, Folder 201, Truscott, Lucien [*sic*] K. (General), 1–2.

34. Ibid., 3–5.

35. Ibid., 9, 10–11, 13.

36. Ibid., 16–17, cover letter.

37. Truscott, *Command Missions,* 513–14.

38. Ibid., 514–15.

39. Ibid., 515–18; "British Mandate Overview" (quotes describing terms of British Mandate).

40. "The Future Began at the DP–Camp Landsberg." Landsberg was the town where Adolf Hitler was imprisoned after his attempted putsch in Munich in 1923 and where he wrote *Mein Kampf.*

41. Truscott, *Command Missions,* 519.

42. Irving Heymont, *After the Deluge: The Landsberg Jewish DP Camp, 1945,* 187–90. A copy of this book is in the library of the U.S. Army Military History Institute, Carlisle Barracks, Pennsylvania.

43. Truscott, *Command Missions,* 520. In his memoir Truscott makes no mention of any measures he took to combat the black-market activities within Bavaria.

44. Bendersky, "Jewish Threat," 354. Bendersky singles out Patton as being one of the most vocal opponents of policies granting special privileges to Jews, policies that he believed were "inspired by American Jews." Bendersky states that Patton confided to his diary in September 1945 that "Harrison and his ilk believe that the displaced person is a human being, which he is not, and this applies particularly to the Jews, who are lower than animals" (356–57).

45. Ibid., 358.

46. Truscott, *Command Missions,* 520–22.

47. Ibid., 523–26.

48. McNarney to Truscott, March 25, 1946, Folder 201, Truscott, Lucien [*sic*] K. (General).

49. Truscott, *Command Missions,* 527–29.

50. E. N. Harmon, Major General, with Milton MacKaye and William Ross MacKaye, *Combat Commander: Autobiography of a Soldier,* 280–84.

51. Truscott, *Command Missions,* 529.

52. Ibid., 530–31; Orders, U.S. Forces, European Theater, March 29, 1946, para. 1, Truscott OMPF; Cable, McNarney to Adjutant General, April 3, 1946, Folder 201, Truscott, Lucien [*sic*] K. (General); Aide's Diaries, April 1, 1946, box 19, folder 3, Truscott Papers; James J. Truscott, e-mail message to author, December 18, 2007.

53. Aide's Diaries, April 17, 1946, box 19, folder 3, Truscott Papers.

54. Truscott, *Command Missions,* 531; Colonel Waligora to Major General Bull, April 24, 1946, Folder 201, Truscott, Lucien [*sic*] K. (General), 1; Truscott to wife, April 24, 1946, box 1, folder 13, Truscott Papers. In his letter to his wife Truscott included a sketch of his heart and coronary arteries that Doctor Kent had drawn, showing the

locations of the coronary artery occlusion and the infarct. As pictured, the occlusion lies in the left circumflex coronary artery, and the infarct appears to involve the posterolateral wall of the left ventricle.

55. Colonel McKie to theater surgeon, April 24, 1946, Folder 201, Truscott, Lucien [*sic*] K. (General).

56. Cable, McNarney to Eisenhower, April 25, 1946, ibid.

57. Cable, Truscott to wife, April 27, 1946, Folder OPD 201, Truscott L. K. (O); Cable, Hull to Truscott, April 28, 1946, ibid.

58. Aide's Diaries, April 22–May 23, 24, 30, 1946, box 19, folder 3, Truscott Papers.

59. Ibid., July 2, 6–18, 1946. In the summer of 1945 Sarah sold the house in Charlottesville, and Jamie and she moved to Alexandria, Virginia, eventually occupying an apartment in the Parkfairfax complex in that city (James J. Truscott, e-mail message to author, February 3, 2008).

60. Aide's Diaries, August 13, September 9, 1946, box 19, folder 4, Truscott Papers.

61. Ibid., September 28, 30, October 1–5, 1946; SO 218, para. 1, War Department, October 9, 1946, Truscott OMPF.

62. Aide's Diaries, October 22, 1946, box 19, folder 4, Truscott Papers. In 1948 Washington Barracks was renamed Fort Lesley J. McNair to honor General McNair, who was killed in Normandy by friendly fire on July 25, 1944, during Operation COBRA ("Fort Lesley J. McNair," 1).

63. Adjutant General to President, War Department Screening Board, October 23, 1946, Truscott OMPF.

64. Aide's Diaries, October 30, December 27, 1946, February 13, 1947, box 19, folder 4, Truscott Papers; James J. Truscott, e-mail message to author, December 18, 2007.

65. Aide's Diaries, February 5, March 2, 1947, box 19, folder 5, Truscott Papers.

66. Ibid., March 25, April 16, 1947; Adjutant General to President, War Department Personnel Records Board, April 11, 1947, Truscott OMPF. I have located no records describing actions taken by either of the two boards.

67. Aide's Diaries, April 7, 12, 1947, box 19, folder 5, Truscott Papers.

68. Surgeon General's Office to Personnel Actions Branch, Regular Army Subsection, AGO, May 20, 1947, Truscott OMPF; Proceedings of Army Retiring Board, July 7, 1947, Truscott OMPF; Information for Processing Former Physically Disabled Members of the Army, March 13, 1950, Truscott OMPF. Truscott's 1947 monthly retirement pay would be equivalent to $5,338 in 2009 dollars ("Inflation Calculator").

69. Aide's Diaries, May 30, 1947, box 19, folder 5, Truscott Papers.

70. WD SO 3, para. 1, September 22, 1947, Truscott OMPF.

71. Adjutant General to Truscott, "Leave of absence prior to retirement," July 22, 1947, Truscott OMPF; Military Record and Report of Separation, Certificate of Service, WD AGO Form 53–98, Truscott OMPF; James J. Truscott, e-mail message to author, February 14, 2006. James Truscott could not recall any specific activities in which his father participated while at the ranch but is certain that it included extensive horseback riding.

72. J. Truscott interview.

73. WD to Chief, Army Field Forces, Establishment of Army Advisory Panels in the Fields of Amphibious, Airborne, and Air Defense Operations, box 20, folder 1, Truscott Papers.

74. Devers to Truscott, October 9, 1948, box 20, folder 1, Truscott Papers.

75. Report of the Army Advisory Panel on Joint Amphibious Operations, January 15, 1949, box 20, folder 2, Truscott Papers.

76. Leo J. Daugherty III, "The Forgotten Amphibians: Major General Charles D. Barrett, USMC, and Lieutenant General Lucian A. [*sic*] Truscott, U.S. Army, and World War II."

77. Report of the Army Advisory Panel on Joint Amphibious Operations, January 15, 1949, box 20, folder 2, Truscott Papers.

78. Efficiency Report, January 12, 1949, Truscott OMPF.

79. Wilson A. Heefner, *Patton's Bulldog: The Life and Service of General Walton H. Walker*, 166–71; Truscott, *Twilight of the U.S. Cavalry*, xiv; *Register of Graduates*, 526; Collins to Truscott, August 2, 1950, Truscott OMPF.

CHAPTER 14: DUTY WITH THE CIA

1. Douglas F. Garthoff, *Directors of Central Intelligence as Leaders of the U.S. Intelligence Community, 1946–2005*, 2.

2. Ludwell Lee Montague, *General Walter Bedell Smith as Director of Central Intelligence, October 1950–February 1953*, 77, 219.

3. Ray S. Cline, *Secrets, Spies, and Scholars: Blueprint of the Essential CIA*, 123–24.

4. Montague, *General Walter Bedell Smith*, 219.

5. Personal service contract, MORI DocID: 1423288; CIA to Truscott, undated, MORI DocID: 1423218; Appointment Affidavits, MORI DocID: 1423216, all in Truscott CIA File. At that time Smith also appointed Brig. Gen. Thomas Betts as his senior representative in London (Cline, *Secrets, Spies, and Scholars*, 124), and in February 1952 Smith appointed an Admiral Overesch as his senior representative in Austria (minutes of meeting of Intelligence Advisory Committee, February 7, 1952, CIA-RDP 85S00326R000200030004-2, CREST). Truscott became a member of the CIA staff with the grade of GS-18 on September 1, 1951 (Statement of Prior Federal and Military Service, April 10, 1953, MORI DocID: 1423236, Truscott CIA File). His $50 daily fee and his annual salary of $14,000 would be equivalent to $420 and $117,728, respectively, in 2009 dollars ("Inflation Calculator").

6. Memorandum, Smith to Truscott, March 9, 1951, Truscott CIA File. Montague postulates that Smith desired "to maintain a clear distinction between clandestine intelligence collection and covert action operations by preserving an organizational distinction between the OSO and OPC" within the agency and within all of its overseas stations (*General Walter Bedell Smith*, 219). Coordination of the two offices would be the responsibility of the deputy director of central intelligence in the agency headquarters and of senior representatives at overseas stations.

7. Copies of two newspaper articles, CIA-RDP57-00384R000500050002-2, CREST.

8. Polgar interview; Sarah R. Truscott Trip Narratives, Germany, 1951–1952, May 9, 1951, box 3, folder 1, Truscott Papers.

9. Jessup interview; Sarah Truscott Trip Narratives, June 30, August 15, 1951, box 3, folder 1, Truscott Papers.

10. Sarah Truscott Trip Narratives, June 30, 1951, box 3, folder 1, Truscott Papers.

11. Polgar interview; Evan Thomas, *The Very Best Men—Four Who Dared: The Early Years of the CIA*, 65.

12. Dulles to Truscott, August 7, 1951, Case #F-1985-00856, Truscott CIA File.

13. The IAC was the successor to the Intelligence Advisory Board that President Truman had established in 1946, and included representatives of the Departments of State, War, and Navy and other persons as dictated by the National Intelligence Agency and was to serve as an advisory body for the newly appointed DCI (Garthoff, *Directors of Central Intelligence*, 13, 17–18; Montague, *General Walter Bedell Smith*, 25–26).

14. IAC Minutes, May 15 (CIA-RDP85S00362R000200030017-8, CREST); IAC Minutes, June 26 (CIA-RDP85S00362R000200030023-1, CREST); IAC Progress Report (CIA-RDP85S00362R000200140023-9, CREST).

15. Polgar interview; Thomas Polgar, "CIA German Station in 1951: Arrival of General Lucian K. Truscott, Jr.," August 9, 2004. In his interview Polgar commented that

Truscott would readily accept him, a Hungarian, as his special assistant, since Sergeant Barna, his driver during the war, was Hungarian.

16. Jessup interview.

17. Polgar interview.

18. During World War II Benjamin Shute, working with Undersecretary of War John J. McCloy, had organized an "all-source [intelligence] analytical office in the office of the Secretary of War," and had brought all of those experienced intelligence analysts into his HICOG intelligence office (Polgar interview).

19. Ibid.

20. Jessup interview.

21. Polgar interview.

22. Montague, *General Walter Bedell Smith,* 227 (emphasis in original). According to Polgar (e-mail to author, March 22, 2008), Truscott and he attended the meetings in Washington during which Smith prepared and issued his directive. He states that after reviewing Truscott's reorganization of the German CIA mission, Smith decided to merge the OSO and OPC. During World War II Marshall, while retaining overall authority and responsibility for the U.S. Army's actions in World War II, delegated command authority to his major theater commanders, Eisenhower, MacArthur, and Stilwell.

23. Sarah Truscott Trip Narratives, Italy, box 3, folder 2, Truscott Papers.

24. Polgar interview; Burton Hersh, *The Old Boys: The American Elite and the Origins of the CIA,* 336–37; Thomas, *Very Best Men,* 65–66. The first quotation is from Hersh and the latter two are from Thomas. According to Polgar, Dulles never forgave Truscott for his impertinence in ordering him, the deputy director of central intelligence, to "sit down," and after Truscott returned to Washington, DCI Dulles never assigned Truscott to "an important job" (Polgar interview).

25. David E. Murphy, Sergei A. Kondrashev, and George Bailey, *Battleground Berlin: CIA vs. the KGB in the Cold War,* 164–65; Joseph J. Trento, *The Secret History of the CIA,* 101.

26. Trento, *Secret History of the CIA,* 102–4.

27. Polgar interview.

28. For comprehensive accounts of the Berlin tunnel operation, see David Stafford, *Spies beneath Berlin;* "Clandestine Services History: The Berlin Tunnel Operation, 1952–1956"; and Steury, "V: The Berlin Tunnel" and "V-1: Field Project Outline."

29. Stafford, *Spies beneath Berlin,* 53; Murphy, Kondrashev, and Bailey, *Battleground Berlin,* 208–9 (quotes).

30. Steury, "V: Berlin Tunnel," 328; Stafford, *Spies beneath Berlin,* 57.

31. Steury, "V-1: Field Project Outline," 332.

32. Stafford, *Spies beneath Berlin,* 78.

33. Steury, "V: Berlin Tunnel," 329.

34. "Clandestine Services History," fig. 16 and p. 21; Murphy, Kondrashev, and Bailey, *Battleground Berlin,* 234.

35. Steury, "V: Berlin Tunnel," 329.

36. Stafford, *Spies beneath Berlin,* 180.

37. Ibid., 146–53; Murphy, Kondrashev, and Bailey, *Battleground Berlin,* 229–31.

38. Steury, "V: Berlin Tunnel," 330.

39. "Clandestine Services History," appx. B.

40. Steury, "V: Berlin Tunnel," 330.

41. MORI DocID: 1423284 and 424021, Truscott CIA File.

42. "Unconventional Warfare Planning in Europe," CIA-RDP88-00374R000100290-003-6, CREST.

43. Corson, *Armies of Ignorance,* 360, 365–66.

44. Bernard Burton, "An Open Letter to General Truscott: At Anzio All of Us Knew Kesselring," CIA-RDP75-00001R000400410013-5, CREST. In his open letter, Burton, a former member of Truscott's 3d Infantry Division and a veteran of the Anzio fighting, castigates Truscott for "laughing and sipping cocktails with Field Marshall [sic] Kesselring," pointing out that Kesselring was convicted of war crimes committed in Italy and was sentenced to death by the military tribunal in Nuremberg, a sentence that two months later was commuted to life imprisonment. He was freed from prison in 1952.

45. For detailed descriptions and analysis of the operation, see Ambrose, *Ike's Spies*, 215–34; Thomas, *Very Best Men*, 111–26; William Blum, *Killing Hope: U.S. Military and CIA Interventions since World War II*, 72–83; and Mary Ann Heiss, "The CIA in the World in the 1950s," 8–15, 17–21. From review of heavily redacted material the author obtained from the CIA under the Freedom of Information Act, it appears that Truscott was involved to some extent in the planning for PBSUCCESS (CIA FOIA–Para-Military Appraisal of PBSUCCESS and CIA FOIA–Project PBSUCCESS [Deleted] Daily Notes Re Arms Shipments to Guatemala, April 7, 1954, CIA Archives). However, I have found absolutely no evidence in the CIA records that I obtained under the provisions of FOIA or in the CREST files at the National Archives that Truscott was involved to the extent that Jeffers claims in his book (*Command of Honor*, 294–98) for either the CIA's Guatemala operation or the earlier CIA operation that overthrew Premier Mohammad Mossadeq in Iran. Jeffers provides no documentation to substantiate his allegations of Truscott's involvement in the operations. Further, Thomas Polgar stated, "I do not recall any discussion with General Truscott re Guatemala or Iran prior to the overthrow of the respective governments" (e-mail message to author, June 23, 2008).

46. Thomas, *Very Best Men*, 127.

47. Jessup interview; MORI DocID: 424021, Truscott CIA File.

48. MORI Doc ID: 1423291, Truscott CIA File; "CIA Medals."

49. Jessup interview; J. Truscott interview.

50. CIA-RDP75-00001R000400410017-1, CIA-RDP75-00001R000400410012-6, and CIA-RDP75-00001R000400410018-0, CREST.

51. J. Truscott interview; MORI DocID: 424021, Truscott CIA File; Polgar interview. I have been unable to determine exactly when Truscott returned to Washington. The cited CIA document indicates that he was assigned as Dulles's special assistant in October 1955, while Dino A. Brugioni indicates that he met with Truscott in Washington in the spring or early summer of 1955 (*Eyeball to Eyeball: The Inside Story of the Cuban Missile Crisis*, 25–26).

52. Deputies' Meeting, January 30, 1956, CIA-RDP80B01676R002300190030-6; Memorandum for DCI, April 26, 1956, CIA-RDP80B01676R00420015004-6, CREST; MORI DocID: 424021, Truscott CIA File.

53. Brugioni, *Eyeball to Eyeball*, 25–26 (quotes); Ambrose, *Ike's Spies*, 270–71.

54. Ambrose, *Ike's Spies*, 236–38; Cline, *Secrets, Spies, and Scholars*, 162–64 (quote).

55. Rhodri Jeffreys-Jones, *The CIA and American Democracy*, 94.

56. Ambrose, *Ike's Spies*, 238–39.

57. Ibid., 237, 239.

58. Corson, *Armies of Ignorance*, 370–71.

59. Ambrose, *Ike's Spies*, 242.

60. Wayne G. Jackson, "Allen Welsh Dulles as Director of Central Intelligence, 26 February 1953–29 November 1961," 4:63–68.

61. Ibid., 67–68.

62. Eisenhower to Statutory Members of the National Security Council and the Directors of Central Intelligence, August 5, 1957, MORI DocID: 1423297, Truscott CIA File.

63. *Final Report of the Select Committee to Study Governmental Operations with Respect to Intelligence Activities, United States Senate*, 63.

64. Jackson, "Allen Welsh Dulles," 2:170.

65. Ibid., 4:70 (quote); Ambrose, *Ike's Spies*, 242–43.

66. Senior Staff Meeting, June 3, 1957, CIA-RDP80B01676R002400010058-4, CREST.

67. Jackson, "Allen Welsh Dulles," 4:71–78.

68. *Final Report of the Select Committee*, 61–62.

69. Allen Dulles, "Fitness Report on General Lucian K. Truscott, Jr.," February 4, 1959, MORI DocID: 1423299, Truscott CIA File.

70. MORI DocID: 1423214, Truscott CIA File.

71. Truscott to Dulles, May 1, 1959, MORI DocID: 1423275, Truscott CIA File. The disabilities that Truscott refers to were most likely secondary to his chronic bronchitis and chronic obstructive pulmonary disease.

72. Dulles to Truscott, May 31, 1959, CIA-RDP80B01676R003200200006-1, CREST.

73. Senior Staff Meting of June 15, 1959, CIA-RDP80B01676R002400010085-4, CREST.

74. Memorandum for the Record, undated, MORI DocID: 1423274, Truscott CIA File.

75. Office Memorandum re General Truscott, Independent Contractor, June 25, 1962, MORI DocID: 1423303, Truscott CIA File; Memorandum re General Lucian K. Truscott, Consultant, June 11, 1963, CIA-RDP84-00780R000300040014-2, CREST; James H. Critchfield, *Partners at the Creation: The Men behind Postwar Germany's Defense and Intelligence Establishments*, 49–50, 79, 88–91. Mrs. Lois Critchfield informed me that her husband was a close friend and great admirer of Truscott.

76. Polgar interview. The Bay of Pigs invasion was part of a CIA-planned and -directed operation to overthrow the Fidel Castro regime in Cuba. See "JFK in History: The Bay of Pigs" and Peter Wyden, *Bay of Pigs: The Untold Story.*

77. Sarah R. Truscott, Diaries, 1956, 1957, and 1959, box 3, folder 5, Truscott Papers.

78. Ibid.

CHAPTER 15: THE LAST YEARS

1. J. Truscott interview.

2. Sarah Truscott Diaries, 1961–1964, box 3, folder 5, Truscott Papers.

3. L. Truscott interview.

4. Sarah Truscott Diaries, September, October, December 1965, box 3, folder 5, Truscott Papers.

5. J. Truscott interview; Report of Casualty, September 14, 1965, Truscott OMPF.

6. "General Truscott, 70, Dies; Commanded Two Armies," *Washington, D.C., Evening Star*, September 13, 1945, B5, Truscott OMPF; "Nationwide Gravesite Locator, Arlington National Cemetery."

7. J. Truscott interview; James J. Truscott, e-mail message to author, August 23, 2005; undated photograph of the Truscott family in front of Truscott Hall. Unfortunately, Truscott Hall no longer stands. The building was demolished in 2007, after the director of public works at Carlisle Barracks determined that there was no longer a need for on-post bachelor officer or additional senior noncommissioned officer quarters and that it was not economically feasible to convert it to administrative use (Richard J. Sommers, U.S. Army Military History Institute, e-mail message to author, May 11, 2009).

AFTERWORD

1. "General Eric K. Shinseki, 34th Chief of Staff of the Army, Retirement Ceremony, June 11, 2003," 3.

2. William Randolph Hearst Jr., "Truscott's Life on Battle Front," Hearst Newspapers, October 23, 1944, box 22, folder 1, Truscott Papers.

3. Truscott, *Command Missions*, 295–96.

4. Mauldin, *Brass Ring*, 272.

5. Blumenson, *Patton Papers*, 366, 368.

6. Chandler, *Papers of Eisenhower*, vol. 2, Doc. 1092, Eisenhower to Marshall, July 1, 1943, 1233.

7. Ibid., vol. 3, Doc. 1440, Eisenhower to Marshall, December 27, 1943, 1623; Doc. 1553, Eisenhower to Marshall, February 16, 1944, 1731. Eisenhower had concluded prior to his leaving the Mediterranean theater that three division commanders were "best fitted to take over a corps—one, Truscott, two, Eagles [45th Infantry Division], three, Harmon [1st Armored Division]. The gap between one and two is very great" (ibid., Doc. 1553, Eisenhower to Marshall, February 16, 1944, 1731).

8. Ibid., Doc. 1486, Eisenhower to Marshall, January 18, 1944, 1665; Doc. 1482, Eisenhower to Devers, January 16, 1944, 1660; Doc. 1520, Eisenhower to Marshall, January 29, 1944, 1696n9.

9. Ibid., vol. 4, Doc. 1998, Eisenhower to Bradley, September 25, 1944, 2192.

10. Ibid., Doc. 2271, Memo, February 1, 1945, 2466–69.

11. Russell F. Weigley, *Eisenhower's Lieutenants: The Campaigns of France and Germany, 1944–45*, 2:1098–99.

12. Fisher, *Cassino to the Alps*, 535, 539.

13. Jeffrey J. Clarke, *Southern France, 15 August–14 September 1944*, 30.

14. Weigley, *Eisenhower's Lieutenants*, 1:346.

15. The following conclusions are based on material in Chapter 14 of this book.

16. Polgar interview.

17. Truscott, *Command Missions*, 234–40, 294–95. A few weeks later Clark ordered the 36th Infantry Division to make that crossing, which was "a costly failure."

BIBLIOGRAPHY

PRIMARY SOURCES

COLLECTIONS

Carleton, Don E. Papers. Hoover Institution Archives, Stanford, Calif.
Eisenhower, Dwight D. Pre-presidential Papers, 1916–1952. Eisenhower Library, Abilene, Kans.
Robinett, Paul M. Papers. George C. Marshall Research Library, Lexington, Va.
Special Collections. McCracken County Public Library, Paducah, Ky.
Truscott, Lucian K., Jr. Files. CIA Research Search Tool (CREST). National Archives, College Park, Md.
———. Official Central Intelligence File. Central Intelligence Agency Archives, Washington, D.C.
———. Official Military Personnel File (OMPF). National Personnel Records Center, St. Louis.
———. Papers. George C. Marshall Research Library, Lexington, Va.

INTERVIEWS

Blumenson, Martin. Discussion with author. September 1992. Paestum, Italy.
Conway, Gen. T. J. Interview by Col. Robert F. Ensslin, September 29, 1977. Box "Recollections and Reflections: Transcript of the Debriefing of General Conway." Archives, United States Army Military History Institute, Carlisle Barracks, Pa.
Frederick, Maj. Gen. Robert T. Interview by Sidney Mathews, January 7, 1949. Mathews Box 3, Office of the Chief of Military History Collection, United States Army Military History Institute, Carlisle Barracks, Pa.
Jessup, Peter. Interview by author. Tape recording. September 16, 2004. Chevy Chase, Md.
Koons, Frank. 1st Ranger Battalion. "Dieppe." Interview by Pat O'Donnell. June 1998. http://www.thedropzone.org/europe/Raids/Koons.html.

Polgar, Thomas. Interview by author. Tape recording. April 21, 2004. Maitland, Fla.

Truscott, James J. Interview by author. Tape recording. March 26, 2008. San Antonio, Texas.

Truscott, Lucian K., IV. Interview by author. Tape recording. April 7, 2005. Pasadena, Calif.

Wilson, James M., Jr. Interview by author. Tape recording. September 20, 2004. Chevy Chase, Md.

Published Sources

Annual Report of the Command and General Staff School, Fort Leavenworth, Kansas, 1935–1936. Fort Leavenworth, Kans.: Command and General Staff School Press, 1936.

Butler, Brig. Gen. Frederic B. "Southern France Exploits of Task Force Butler." Pts. 1 and 2. *Armored Cavalry Journal* (January–February): 12–18; (March–April 1948): 30–38.

Chandler, Alfred D., Jr., ed. *The Papers of Dwight David Eisenhower: The War Years.* Vols. 1–4. Baltimore: Johns Hopkins University Press, 1970.

Churchill, Winston S. *The Second World War: Triumph and Tragedy.* Boston: Houghton Mifflin, 1953.

Clark, Mark W. *Calculated Risk.* New York: Harper and Brothers, 1950.

Cummings, Julian William, with Gwendolyn Kay Cummings. *Grasshopper Pilot: A Memoir.* Kent, Ohio: Kent State University Press, 2005.

Darby, William O., and William H. Baumer. *Darby's Rangers: We Led the Way.* San Rafael, Calif.: Presidio Press, 1980.

Dulles, Allen. *The Secret Surrender.* New York: Harper and Row, 1966.

Eisenhower, Dwight D. *Crusade in Europe.* 1948. Reprint, New York: Da Capo Press, 1977.

Harmon, E. N., Major General, with Milton MacKaye and William Ross MacKaye. *Combat Commander: Autobiography of a Soldier.* Englewood Cliffs, N.J.: Prentice-Hall, 1970.

Heymont, Irving. *After the Deluge: The Landsberg Jewish DP Camp, 1945.* McLean, Va.: General Research Corporation, 1981.

Holt, Daniel D., and James W. Leyerzapf, eds. *Eisenhower: The Prewar Diaries and Selected Papers, 1905–1941.* Baltimore: Johns Hopkins University Press, 1998.

Instruction Circular No. 1, 1938–1939: The Command and General Staff School, Fort Leavenworth, Kansas, 1 July 1938. Fort Leavenworth, Kans.: Command and General Staff School Press, 1938.

Kesselring, Albert. *The Memoirs of Field-Marshal Kesselring.* Translated by William Kimber Limited. St. Paul: MBI Publishing, 2007.

Mauldin, Bill. *The Brass Ring: A Sort of a Memoir.* New York: W. W. Norton, 1971.

Register of Graduates and Former Cadets of the United States Military Academy. West Point, N.Y.: Association of Graduates, USMA, 1974.

Senger und Etterlin, Frido von. *Neither Fear nor Hope: The Wartime Career of General Frido von Senger und Etterlin, Defender of Cassino.* Translated by George Malcolm. 1963. Reprint, Novato, Calif.: Presidio Press, 1989.

Truscott, Lucian K., Jr. *Command Missions: A Personal Story.* 1954. Reprint, New York: Arno Press, 1979.

———. *The Twilight of the U.S. Cavalry: Life in the Old Army, 1917–1942.* Lawrence: University Press of Kansas, 1989.

UNPUBLISHED SOURCES

Aide's Diaries. Box 18, folders 1–5. Box 19, folders 1–5. Lucian Truscott Papers. George C. Marshall Research Library, Lexington, Va.

Allotment of Hours—Troop Officers' Course—1924–1925. Annual Report of the Commandant, the Cavalry School, Fort Riley, Kansas, 1925. Folder "The Cavalry School, Fort Riley, Kansas (AG 319.12 to 354.1)," Central Decimal Files, Project Files, 1917–1925, Army Schools, Cavalry School, Fort Riley, Kansas, to Chemical Warfare School, Edgewood Arsenal, Maryland. Records of the Adjutant General's Office. RG 407. National Archives, College Park, Md.

Annual Report of the Commandant, the Cavalry School, 1926, 220.63 Cav. School (12–17–29) to 352.07 Cav. School (6–16–39). Office of the Adjutant Central Files, 1926–39. RG 407. National Archives, College Park, Md.

"Army Ground Force Equipment Review Board Preliminary Study—Fifth Army and MTOUSA Reports Thereon." July 14, 1945. Lucian Truscott Papers. Box 15, folder 3. George C. Marshall Research Library, Lexington, Va.

Assignment of Instructors, 1937–1938 and 1938–1939. Roster of Instructors, 1939–1940. Combined Arms Research Library, U.S. Army Command and Staff School, Fort Leavenworth, Kans.

Command and General Staff School, 1935–1936, Second-Year Class, 27 March 1936. Combined Arms Research Library, U.S. Army Command and General Staff School, Fort Leavenworth, Kans.

Darby to the Adjutant General. Report of Action against Dieppe, January 11, 1942. Folder "History—Darby's Rangers—1st, 3d, 4th Ranger Bns, 1942–48." Infantry. RG 94. National Archives, College Park, Md.

1st Ranger Battalion Diary. Folder "History—Darby's Rangers—1st, 3d, 4th Ranger Bns, 1942–1944." World War II Operations Reports, 1940–48,

Infantry. RG 94. National Archives, College Park, Md.

Folder "Military District of Washington, III Corps Area: Report of Operations against Bonus Marchers." "Summary of Events, 2d Squadron 3d Cavalry and Attached Troops, July 28–29, 1932." Army Commands. RG 394. National Archives, College Park, Md.

Folder OPD 201, Truscott, L. K. (O). Office of the Director of Plans and Operations, General Records—Correspondence, Security Classified, General Correspondence, 1942–45. Records of the War Department General and Special Staffs. RG 165. National Archives, College Park, Md.

Folder "17th Cavalry Regiment, 1917–1918, Off's Ret. and Rosters, Return of 17th Regiment of Cavalry, August and September 1917, in 16th and 17th Cavalry Regiments, World War I Strength Returns, Cavalry." Records of the Adjutant General's Office. RG 407. National Archives, College Park, Md.

Folder 0100/5, 0A01/3: Lessons of Campaign of Sicily. Vol. 1, "Aug.–Oct. 43" (130320A), Serial 165, Allied Force Headquarters Command Group, Office of the Chief Administrative Officer, Executive Section, Numeric File 1942–46, 0100/5/165 through 0100/5/168. Records of Allied Operational and Occupation Headquarters, World War II. RG 331. National Archives, College Park, Md.

Folder 201, Truscott, Lucien [sic] K. (General). Records of the Secretary, General Staff, General Correspondence Relating to Individuals ("201"). Records of the European Theater of Operations, U.S. Army. RG 332. National Archives, College Park, Md.

"General Eric K. Shinseki, 34th Chief of Staff of the Army, Retirement Ceremony, June 11, 2003." http://www.army.mil/features/shinsekifarewell.farewellremarks.htm.

HQ VI Corps, GO no. 6, February 23, 1944, and no. 26, August 27, 1944. Folder "VI Corps G.O.'s 1944, VI Corps, Adjutant Section, General Orders, General Court-Martial Orders, 1940–1946." U.S. Army Commands. RG 338. National Archives, College Park, Md.

Lucas, John P. Diary. Box 4. Archives, U.S. Army Military History Institute, Carlisle Barracks, Pa.

Memorandum for the Adjutant General of the Army, July 29, 1921, Folder "Organizations—17th Cavalry Regiment, Central Decimal Files, Project Files, 1917–1925, Organizations 13th Cavalry Regiment to 24th Cavalry Regiment." Records of the Adjutant General's Office. RG 407. National Archives, College Park, Md.

Polgar, Thomas. "CIA German Station in 1951: Arrival of General Lucian K. Truscott, Jr." In author's file.

Report of Operations. Folder "Report of Opns, Italian Campaign, 3rd Infantry Div, 18 Sep.–18 Nov. 43." World War II Operations Reports, 1940–1948,

3rd Infantry Division. RG 94. National Archives, College Park, Md.

Report on 1st Ranger Battalion Detachment Assigned to 3 Commando, August 26, 1942. Folder "History—Darby's Rangers—1st, 3d, 4th Ranger Bns, 1942–1944." World War II Operations Reports, 1940–48, Infantry. RG 94. National Archives, College Park, Md.

Section I—Operations (Operation Phase). Folder "The 3rd Infantry Division in the Sicilian Campaign, 10–18 July 1943." World War II Operations Reports, 1940–1948, 3rd Infantry Division. RG 94. National Archives, College Park, Md.

Section I—Operations (Training Phase). Folder "The 3rd Infantry Division in the Sicilian Campaign, 10–18 July 1943." World War II Operations Reports, 1940–1948, 3rd Infantry Division. RG 94. National Archives, College Park, Md.

"The Seventeenth Cavalry, Regimental History." Folder "History, 17th Cav., War College and War Plans Division, Subordinate Offices—Army War College Historical Section, Cavalry Regiments, 16th and 17th Cav. Regts., Miscellaneous Historical Records." Records of the War Department General and Special Staffs. RG 165. National Archives, College Park, Md.

VI Corps Combat Troop List, Operation "ANVIL," Aug. 1, 1944. Folder HQ VI Corps—Plans and Operations—"Bigot-Anvil." Vol. 1, 8 July–7 Aug. 1944. WW II Operations Reports, 1940–48, VI Corps. RG 94. National Archives, College Park, Md.

Troop Officers' Class, Academic Year, 1927–1928, 220.63 Cav. School (12-17-29) to 352.07 Cav. School (6-16-39). Office of the Adjutant General Central Files, 1926–39. RG 407. National Archives, College Park, Md.

Truman, President, to General Eisenhower enclosing the Harrison Report on the treatment of displaced Jews in the U.S. Zone. http://www.jewish-virtuallibrary.org/jsource/Holocaust/truman_on_harrison.html.

Truscott, Lucian K., Jr. Letters to Sarah R. Truscott. Lucian Truscott Papers. Box 1. George C. Marshall Research Library, Lexington, Va.

Truscott, Sarah R. Diaries, 1956, 1957, 1959, and 1961–1965. Lucian Truscott Papers. Box 3, folder 5. George C. Marshall Research Library, Lexington, Va.

———. Trip Narratives, Germany, 1951–1952. Lucian Truscott Papers. Box 3. George C. Marshall Research Library, Lexington, Va.

220.63 Cav. School (12-17-29) to 352.07 Cav. School (6-16-39). Office of the Adjutant General Central Files, 1926–39. RG 407. National Archives, College Park, Md.

World War I Strength Returns, Cavalry, 16th and 17th Cavalry Regiments. Records of the Adjutant General's Office. RG 407. National Archives, College Park, Md.

World War I Strength Returns, Fort Logan H. Roots, Fort Logan, Colorado, Los Angeles, Calif. Records of the Adjutant General's Office. RG 407. National Archives, College Park, Md.

SECONDARY SOURCES

PUBLISHED SOURCES

Adcock, Al. *WW II U.S. Landing Craft in Action.* Carrolton, Texas: Squadron/ Signal Publications, 2003.

Ambrose, Stephen E. *Ike's Spies: Eisenhower and the Espionage Establishment.* 1981. Reprint, Jackson: University Press of Mississippi, 1999.

Anderson, Charles R. *Algeria–French Morocco.* The U.S. Army Campaigns of World War II. Washington, D.C.: Center of Military History, United States Army, 1972.

———. *Tunisia.* Washington, D.C.: Center of Military History, United States Army, 1972.

Atkinson, Rick. *An Army at Dawn: The War in North Africa, 1942–1943.* New York: Henry Holt, 2002.

———. *The Day of Battle: The War in Sicily and Italy, 1943–1944.* New York: Henry Holt, 2007.

Baldwin, Hanson W. *Battles Lost and Won: Great Campaigns of World War II.* New York: Harper and Row, 1966.

Ball, Harry P. *Of Responsible Command: A History of the U.S. Army War College.* Carlisle Barracks, Pa.: Alumni Association of the United States Army War College, 1983.

Bendersky, Joseph W. *The "Jewish Threat": Anti-Semitic Policies of the U.S. Army.* New York: Basic Books, 2000.

Bennett, Ralph. *Ultra and Mediterranean Strategy.* New York: William Morrow, 1989.

———. *Ultra in the West: The Normandy Campaign, 1944–45.* New York: Charles Scribner's Sons, 1979.

Berlin, Robert H. "United States Army World War II Corps Commanders: A Composite Biography." *Journal of Military History* 53 (April 1989): 147–67.

Between the Wichitas. Truscott, Texas: Truscott Historical Preservation Association, 1985.

Birtle, Andrew J. *Sicily, 9 July–17 August 1943.* The U.S. Army Campaigns of World War II. Washington, D.C.: Center of Military History, United States Army, 1972.

Black, Robert W. *Rangers in World War II.* New York: Ivy Books, 1992.

Blum, William. *Killing Hope: U.S. Military and CIA Interventions since World War II*. Monroe, Maine: Common Courage Press, 1995.

Blumenson, Martin. "America's World War II Leaders in Europe: Some Thoughts." *Parameters* 19 (December 1989): 10–11.

———. *Kasserine Pass: Rommel's Bloody, Climactic Battle for Tunisia*. 1966. Reprint, New York: Cooper Square Press, 2000.

———. *Salerno to Cassino*. United States Army in World War II: The Mediterranean Theater of Operations. Washington, D.C.: Center of Military History, United States Army, 1988.

———. "The Trouble with Anzio." *Army* (January 1994): 40–46.

———, ed. *The Patton Papers, 1940–1945*. Boston: Houghton Mifflin, 1974.

Bowditch, John, III. *Anzio Beachhead, 22 January–25 May 1944*. 1948. Reprint, Washington, D.C.: Center of Military History, United States Army, 1990.

Breuer, William. *They Jumped at Midnight: The "Crash" Parachute Missions That Turned the Tide at Salerno*. St. Louis: Zeus Publishers, 1983.

Brooks, Thomas R. *The War North of Rome, June 1944–May 1945*. 1996. Reprint, Edison, N.J.: Castle Books, 2001.

Brugioni, Dino A. *Eyeball to Eyeball: The Inside Story of the Cuban Missile Crisis*. New York: Random House, 1991.

Clark, Lloyd. *Anzio: Italy and the Battle for Rome*. New York: Atlantic Monthly Press, 2006.

Clarke, Jeffrey J. *Southern France, 15 August–14 September 1944*. The U.S. Army Campaigns of World War II. Washington, D.C.: Center of Military History, United States Army, 1972.

Clarke, Jeffrey J., and Robert Ross Smith. *Riviera to the Rhine*. United States Army in World War II: The European Theater of Operations. Washington, D.C.: Center of Military History, United States Army, 1993.

Clifford, John Garry. *The Citizen Soldiers: The Plattsburg Training Camp Movement, 1913–1920*. Lexington: University Press of Kentucky, 1972.

Cline, Ray S. *Secrets, Spies, and Scholars: Blueprint of the Essential CIA*. Washington, D.C.: Acropolis Books, 1976.

Coffman, Edward M. Foreword to *Twilight of the U.S. Cavalry: Life in the Old Army, 1917–1942*, by Lucian K. Truscott, Jr. Lawrence: University Press of Kansas, 1989.

———. *The Regulars: The American Army, 1898–1941*. Cambridge: Belknap Press of Harvard University Press, 2004.

———. *The War to End All Wars: The American Military Experience in World War I*. Lexington: University Press of Kentucky, 1998.

Colley, David P. *Decision at Strasbourg: Ike's Strategic Mistake to Halt the Sixth Army Group at the Rhine in 1944*. Annapolis, Md.: Naval Institute Press, 2008.

Corson, William R. *The Armies of Ignorance: The Rise of the American Intelligence Empire.* New York: Dial Press/James Wade Books, 1977.

Critchfield, James H. *Partners at the Creation: The Men behind Postwar Germany's Defense and Intelligence Establishments.* Annapolis, Md.: Naval Institute Press, 2003.

DeFelice, Jim. *Rangers at Dieppe: The First Combat Action of U.S. Army Rangers in World War II.* New York: Berkley Caliber, 2008.

D'Este, Carlo. *Bitter Victory: The Battle for Sicily, 1943.* New York: E. P. Dutton, 1988.

———. *Eisenhower: A Soldier's Life.* New York: Henry Holt, 2002.

———. *Fatal Decision: Anzio and the Battle for Rome.* New York: HarperCollins, 1991.

———. *Patton: A Genius for War.* New York: HarperCollins, 1995.

———. *Warlord: A Life of Winston Churchill at War.* New York: Harper, 2008.

Devlin, Gerard M. *Paratrooper! The Saga of U.S. Army and Marine Parachute and Glider Combat Troops during World War II.* New York: St. Martin's Press, 1979.

Dickson, Paul, and Thomas B. Allen. *The Bonus Army: An American Epic.* New York: Walker and Company, 2004.

Dictionary of United States Army Terms. Washington, D.C.: Headquarters, Department of the Army, AR 320–5, February 1963.

Dupuy, Trevor N., Curt Johnson, and David L. Bongard. *The Harper Encyclopedia of Military Biography.* Edison, N.J.: Castle Books, 1995.

Dusenberry, Harris. *The North Apennines and Beyond with the 10th Mountain Division.* Portland, Ore.: Binford and Mort, 1998.

Eisenhower, John S. D. *They Fought at Anzio.* Columbia: University of Missouri Press, 2007.

———. *Yanks: The Epic Story of the American Army in World War I.* New York: Free Press, 2001.

Esposito, Vincent J., ed. *The West Point Atlas of American Wars.* Vol. 2. 1959. Reprint, New York: Praeger.

Farago, Ladislas. *The Last Days of Patton.* New York: McGraw-Hill, 1981.

Farwell, Byron. *Over There: The United States in the Great War, 1917–1918.* New York: W. W. Norton, 1999.

Final Report of the Select Committee to Study Governmental Operations with Respect to Intelligence Activities, United States Senate. Book 4. Washington, D.C.: U.S. Government Printing Office, 1976.

Fisher, Ernest F., Jr. *Cassino to the Alps.* United States Army in World War II: The Mediterranean Theater of Operations. Washington, D.C.: Center of Military History, United States Army, 1989.

Garland, Albert N., and Howard McGaw Smyth. *Sicily and the Surrender of Italy.* United States Army in World War II: The Mediterranean Theater of Operations. Washington, D.C.: Center of Military History, United States Army, 1986.

Garthoff, Douglas F. *Directors of Central Intelligence as Leaders of the U.S. Intelligence Community, 1946–2005.* Washington, D.C.: Center for the Study of Intelligence, Central Intelligence Agency, 2005.

"General Walter T. Kerwin, Jr. Remembered." *On Point: The Journal of Army History* 14, no. 1 (Summer 2008).

Goodman, Paul. *A Fragment of Victory in Italy: The 92nd Infantry Division in World War II.* Nashville: Battery Press, 1993.

Gott, Kendall D. *Confrontation at Anacostia Flats: The Bonus Army of 1932.* Arlington, Va.: Institute of Land Warfare, Association of the United States Army, 2007.

Graham, Dominick, and Shelford Bidwell. *Tug of War: The Battle for Italy, 1943–45.* New York: St. Martin's Press, 1986.

Hargrove, Hondon B. *Buffalo Soldiers in Italy: Black Americans in World War II.* 1985. Reprint, Jefferson, N.C.: McFarland, n.d.

Harrison, Gordon A. *Cross-Channel Attack.* United States Army in World War II: The European Theater of Operations. Washington, D.C.: Office of the Chief of Military History, United States Army, 1951.

Hastings, Max. *Retribution: The Battle for Japan, 1944–45.* New York: Alfred A. Knopf, 2008.

Heefner, Wilson A. *Patton's Bulldog: The Life and Service of General Walton H. Walker.* Shippensburg, Pa.: White Mane, 2001.

———. *Twentieth Century Warrior: The Life and Service of Major General Edwin D. Patrick.* Shippensburg, Pa: White Mane, 1995.

Heinemann, Winfried. "Salerno: A Defender's View." *Army History* (Spring 2008): 6–18.

Hersh, Burton. *The Old Boys: The American Elite and the Origins of the CIA.* St. Petersburg, Fla.: Tree Farm Books, 2002.

Hill, Luther B. *A History of the State of Oklahoma.* Vol. 1. Chicago: Lewis Publishing, 1908.

Holt, Daniel D., and James W. Leyerzapf, eds. *Eisenhower: The Prewar Diaries and Selected Papers, 1905–1941.* Baltimore: Johns Hopkins University Press, 1998.

Howe, George F. *Northwest Africa: Seizing the Initiative in the West.* United States Army in World War II: The Mediterranean Theater of Operations. Washington, D.C.: Center of Military History, United States Army, 1991.

"An International Polo Match: The U.S. Army vs. the Mexican Army." *Field Artillery Journal* 24 (July–August 1934): 305–18.

James, D. Clayton. *The Years of MacArthur.* Vol. 1, *1880–1941.* Boston: Houghton Mifflin, 1970.

Jeffers, H. Paul. *Command of Honor: General Lucian Truscott's Path to Victory in World War II*. New York: NAL Caliber, 2008.

Jeffreys-Jones, Rhodri. *The CIA and American Democracy*. 2d ed. New Haven, Conn.: Yale University Press, 1989.

Jenkins, McKay. *The Last Ridge: The Epic Story of the U.S. Army's 10th Mountain Division and the Assault on Hitler's Europe*. New York: Random House, 2003.

Johnson, James G. *Graduates, Charlottesville, Virginia, High School: Containing a List of the Persons Who Graduated from This School during the Years 1894–1936*. N.p., n.d.

Jones, Robert W., Jr. "The Race to Rome." *Veritas: Journal of Army Special Operations History* 2, no. 3 (2006): 3–11.

Kingseed, Cole C. *Old Glory Stories: American Combat Leadership in World War II*. Annapolis, Md.: Naval Institute Press, 2006.

Ladd, James. *Commandos and Rangers of World War II*. New York: St. Martin's Press, 1978.

Lang, Will. "Lucian King Truscott Jr.: A Tough U.S. General, Once an Oklahoma School Master, Wants to Be Provost Marshal of Berlin." *Life*, October 2, 1944, 96–111.

Larrabee, Eric. *Commander in Chief: Franklin Delano Roosevelt, His Lieutenants, and Their War*. Touchstone Edition. New York: Simon and Schuster, 1988.

Lee, Ulysses. *The Employment of Negro Troops*. United States Army in World War II: Special Studies. Washington, D.C.: Center of Military History, United States Army, 1986.

Lessons from the Tunisian Campaign, 15 October 1943. Washington, 1943. Reprint, West Chester, Ohio: Nafziger Collection, 2000.

Lewane, Leonard L. Review of *The Twilight of the U.S. Cavalry: Life in the Old Army, 1917–1942*, by Lucian K. Truscott, Jr. *Journal of Military History* 53 (October 1989): 445–46.

MacDonald, Charles B. *The Mighty Endeavor: American Armed Forces in the European Theater in World War II*. New York: Oxford University Press, 1969.

———. *The Siegfried Line Campaign*. United States Army in World War II: The European Theater of Operations. Washington, D.C.: Center of Military History, United States Army, 1984.

MacGregor, Morris J. *Integration of the Armed Forces, 1940–1965*. Defense Studies Series. Washington, D.C.: Center of Military History, United States Army, 2001.

Marshall, S. L. A. "Labors of Command." *Saturday Review*, April 17, 1954, 14.

Mathews, Sidney T. "General Clark's Decision to Drive on Rome." In *Command Decisions*, ed. Kent Robert Greenfield, 351–63. Washington, D.C.: Center of Military History, United States Army, 1984.

Montague, Ludwell Lee. *General Walter Bedell Smith as Director of Central Intelligence, October 1950–February 1953.* University Park: Pennsylvania State University Press, 1992.

Mosley, Leonard. *Backs to the Wall: London under Fire, 1940–45.* London: Weidenfeld and Nicolson, 1971.

Murphy, David E., Sergei A. Kondrashev, and George Bailey. *Battleground Berlin: CIA vs. KGB in the Cold War.* New Haven, Conn.: Yale University Press, 1997.

Neillands, Robin. *The Dieppe Raid: The Story of the Disastrous 1942 Expedition.* Bloomington: Indiana University Press, 2005.

Nenninger, Timothy K. "Creating Officers: The Leavenworth Experience, 1920–1940." *Military Review* 69 (November 1989): 58–68.

19 Days from the Apennines to the Alps: The Story of the Po Valley Campaign. Nashville: Battery Press, 1987.

IX Corps Unit History, 1940–1963. N.p., n.d.

Order of Battle of the United States Land Forces in the World War. Vol. 3, pt. 1, *Zone of the Interior: Organization and Activities of the War Department.* Washington, D.C.: Center of Military History, United States Army, 1988.

Pelling, Henry. *Winston Churchill.* 2d ed. London: Macmillan, 1989.

Perry, Mark. *Partners in Command: George Marshall and Dwight Eisenhower in War and Peace.* New York: Penguin Press, 2007.

Pogue, Forrest C. *George C. Marshall: Education of a General, 1880–1939.* New York: Viking Press, 1963.

———. *George C. Marshall: Ordeal and Hope, 1939–1942.* New York: Viking Press, 1966.

———. *George C. Marshall: Organizer of Victory, 1943–1945.* New York: Viking Press, 1973.

———. *The Supreme Command.* United States Army in World War II: The European Theater of Operations. Washington, D.C.: Center of Military History, United States Army, 1989.

Popa, Thomas A. *Po Valley, 5 April–8 May 1945.* The U.S. Army Campaigns of World War II. Washington, D.C.: Center of Military History, United States Army, 1972.

"Portrait of General Truscott Takes Honored Place at USMA." *Voice of the First U.S. Army* 9, no. 9 (November 1, 1961): 1, 7. Lucian Truscott Papers. Box 21, folder 6. George C. Marshall Research Library, Lexington, Va.

Pyle, Ernie. *Brave Men.* Bison Books Edition. Lincoln: University of Nebraska Press, 2001.

Randolph, Robert Isham. *The Randolphs of Virginia: A Compilation of the Descendants of William Randolph of Turkey Island and Mary Isham of Bermuda Hundred.* N.p., n.d.

Ridgway, Matthew B. *Soldier: The Memoirs of Matthew B. Ridgway*. New York: Harper and Brothers, 1956.

Roberts, Andrew. *Masters and Commanders: How Four Titans Won the War in the West, 1941–1945*. New York: Harper, 2009.

Robertson, Terence. *Dieppe: The Shame and the Glory*. Boston: Little, Brown, 1962.

Rossi, Francesco, and Silvano Casaldi. *Those Days at Nettuno*. Nettuno, Italy: Edizioni Abete, 1989.

Roth, Anne, and Helen Demarest, eds. *Current Biography: Who's News and Why*. New York: H. W. Wilson, 1945.

Sebag-Montefiore, Hugh. *Enigma: The Battle for the Code*. New York: John Wiley and Sons, 2000.

Shelton, Peter. *Climb to Conquer: The Untold Story of World War II's 10th Mountain Division Ski Troops*. New York: Scribner, 2003.

Shirey, Orville C. *Americans: The Story of the 442d Combat Team*. 1946. Reprint, Nashville: Battery Press, 1998.

Spiller, Roger J. "Overrated, Underrated." *American Heritage* 53 (October 2002): 52.

Stafford, David. *Spies beneath Berlin*. Woodstock, N.Y.: Overlook Press, 2003.

Stanton, Doug. *Horse Soldiers: The Extraordinary Story of a Band of U.S. Soldiers Who Rode to Victory in Afghanistan*. New York: Scribner, 2009.

Stanton, Shelby L. *Order of Battle: U.S. Army, World War II*. Novato, Calif.: Presidio Press, 1984.

Starr, Chester G. *From Salerno to the Alps: A History of the Fifth Army, 1943–1945*. 1948. Reprint, Nashville: Battery Press, 1979.

Steury, Donald P. "V: The Berlin Tunnel." In *On the Front Lines of the Cold War: Documents on the Intelligence War in Berlin, 1946 to 1961*, ed. Donald P. Steury. Washington, D.C.: CIA History Staff, Center for the Study of Intelligence, 1999.

————. "V-1: Field Project Outline." In *On the Front Lines of the Cold War: Documents on the Intelligence War in Berlin, 1946 to 1961*, ed. Donald P. Steury. Washington, D.C.: CIA History Staff, Center for the Study of Intelligence, 1999.

Stubbs, Mary Lee, and Stanley Russell Connor. *Armor-Cavalry: Part I, Regular Army and Reserve*. Army Lineage Series. Washington, D.C.: Office of the Chief of Military History, United States Army, 1969.

Taggart, Donald G., ed. *The History of the Third Infantry Division in World War II*. Nashville: Battery Press, 1987.

Thoburn, Joseph B. *A Standard History of Oklahoma: An Authentic Narrative of Its Development*. Vol. 3. Chicago and New York: American Historical Society, 1916.

Thomas, Evan. *The Very Best Men—Four Who Dared: The Early Years of the CIA*. New York: Simon and Schuster, 1995.

Trento, Joseph J. *The Secret History of the CIA*. Roseville, Calif.: Prima Publishing, 2001.

Tuchman, Barbara A. *Stilwell and the American Experience in China, 1911–45*. New York: Macmillan, 1970, 1971.

The United States Polo Association Year Book, 1926. N.p., 1926.

Wade, Gary. "World War II Division Commanders." CSI Report no. 7. Fort Leavenworth, Kans.: Combat Studies Institute, 1983.

Wedemeyer, General Albert C. *Wedemeyer Reports!* New York: Henry Holt, 1958.

Weigley, Russell F. *Eisenhower's Lieutenants: The Campaigns of France and Germany, 1944–1945*, Vols. 1–2. Bloomington: Indiana University Press, 1981.

Williams, Mary H., comp. *Chronology, 1941–1945*. United States Army in World War II: Special Studies. Washington, D.C.: Center of Military History, United States Army, 1989.

Wilson, Dale E. "Recipe for Failure: Major General Edward M. Almond and Preparation of the U.S. 92d Infantry Division for Combat in World War II." *Journal of Military History* 56 (July 1992): 473–88.

Wilson, John B., comp. *Armies, Corps, Divisions, and Separate Brigades*. Army Lineage Series. Washington, D.C.: Center of Military History, United States Army, 1987.

Winters, Harold A., with Gerald E. Galloway, William J. Reynolds, and David W. Rhyne. *Battling the Elements: Weather and Terrain in the Conduct of War*. Baltimore: Johns Hopkins University Press, 1998.

Wood, C. E. *Mud: A Military History*. Washington, D.C.: Potomac Books, 2006.

Wood, James A. *We Move Only Forward: Canada, the United States, and the First Special Service Force, 1942–1944*. St. Catherines, Ont.: Vanwell Publishing, 2006.

Wunderlin, Clarence E., Jr. Review of *The Twilight of the U.S. Cavalry: Life in the Old Army, 1917–1942*, by Lucian K. Truscott, Jr. *Journal of American History* 77 (June 1990): 337.

Wyden, Peter. *Bay of Pigs: The Untold Story*. New York: Simon and Schuster, 1979.

UNPUBLISHED SOURCES

Antill, P. "Operation Jubilee: The Disaster at Dieppe—Part 1, 19 August 1942." April 6, 2001. http://www.historyofwar.org/articles/battles_dieppe1.html, 3–4.

———. "Operation 'Rutter': The Planned Attack on Dieppe, 7 July 1942."

February 1, 2004. http://www.historyofwar.org/articles/battles_rutter. html.

"Arlington Cemetery." http://www.arlingtoncemetery.net/ftmyer.htm.

"Blood and Steel! The History, Customs, and Traditions of the 3d Armored Cavalry Regiment." http://www.hood.army.mil/3d_acr/docs/part_1.pdf.

"British Mandate Overview." http://www.palestinefacts.org/pf_mandate_overview.php.

"Caserta: The Extravagant Whimsy of the Bourbons." http://www.initaly.com/regions/campania/caserta.htm.

"Castle of Chillon." http://europeforvisitors.com/switzaustria/vaud/montreux/castle-of-chillon.htm.

"Chatfield, TX." *The Handbook of Texas Online.* http://www.tsha.utexas.edu/handbook/online/articles/view/CC/hnc49.html.

"CIA Medals." In *1997 Factbook on Intelligence.* http://www.fas.org/irp/cia/product/fact97/medals.htm.

"Clandestine Services History: The Berlin Tunnel Operation, 1952–1956." 1968. http://www.fas.org/irp/cia/product/tunnel-200702.pdf.

Daugherty, Leo J., III. "The Forgotten Amphibians: Major General Charles D. Barrett, USMC, and Lieutenant General Lucian A. [*sic*] Truscott, U.S. Army, and World War II." Copy of unpublished manuscript in the author's file.

"Dogface Soldier." http://www.dogfacesoldiers.org/info/dogface.htm.

"DUKW." http://www.britannica.com/dday/article-9344575.

Federal Reserve Bank of Minneapolis online calculator. http://www.minneapolisfed.org/Research/data/us/calc.

"Fort Lesley J. McNair." http://www.globalsecurity.org/military/facility/fort-mcnair.htm.

"The Future Began at the DP–Camp Landsberg." http://www.buergervereinigung-landsberg.org/english/dpcamp/dp_camp.shtml.

Heiss, Mary Ann. Department of History, Kent State University, Kent, Ohio. "The CIA in the World in the 1950s." 2004. Author's file.

"History of Fort Myer." http://www.fmmc.army.mil/sites/about/history-myer. asp.

"Inflation Calculator." http://www.dollartimes.com/calculators/inflation.htm.

Jackson, Wayne G. "Allen Welsh Dulles as Director of Central Intelligence, 26 February 1953–29 November 1961." Vol. 2, *Coordination of Intelligence.* Vol. 4, *Congressional Oversight and Internal Administration.* HRP 91-2/1, Central Intelligence Agency. RG 263. National Archives, College Park, Md.

"Jefferson Bible." http://www.arthistoryclub.com/art_history/Jefferson_Bible.

"JFK in History: The Bay of Pigs." http://www.jfklibrary.org Historical+Resources/JFK+in+history/JFK+and+the+Bay+of+Pigs.htm.

M-15 Multiple Gun Motor Carriage (GMC). http://www.olive-drab.com/idphoto/id_photos_m15_multiple_gmc.php.

"Nationwide Gravesite Locator, Arlington National Cemetery." http://grave-locator.cem.va.gov/j2ee/servlet/NGL_v1.

"Operation Jubilee: The Disaster at Dieppe—Part 1, 19 August 1942." http://www.ricard.karoo.net/articles/battles_dieppe2.html.

"Operation Jubilee: The Disaster at Dieppe—Part 2, 19 August 1942." http://www.ricard.karoo.net/articles/battles_dieppe2.html.

"Origins and History of the Washington University School of Medicine: Institutional Roots, 1840–1908." http://beckerexhibits.wustl.edu/wusm-hist/roots/index.htm.

"Pittsburg County, Hickory Grove [Okla.] Cemetery." http://www.rootsweb.com/~okpitts2/hickorygrovecem.html.

"The Raid on Dieppe: August 19, 1942." http://usersskynet.be/advocaat.depickere/Text/dieppe.html.

"Stephen's Study Room: British Military and Criminal History in the Period 1900 to 1999." UK Medals. http://www.stephen-stratford.co.uk/gallantry.htm.

"Unconventional Warfare Planning in Europe." CIA-RDP88-00374R000100290003-6. CREST. National Archives, College Park, Md.

"U.S. Army Rangers: History—World War II Battalions." http://www.ranger.org/rangerHistoryWorldWarIIBattalions.html.

"Willis D. Crittenberger." http://www.arlingtoncemetery.net/wdcritte.htm.

"World War Adjusted Compensation Act, May 19, 1924, during the Coolidge Administration." http://www.u-s-history.com/pages/h1399.html.

INDEX